What Women Want

What Women Want

An Agenda for the Women's Movement

DEBORAH L. RHODE

OXFORD
UNIVERSITY PRESS

OXFORD

UNIVERSITY PRESS

Oxford University Press is a department of the University of Oxford.
It furthers the University's objective of excellence in research, scholarship,
and education by publishing worldwide.

Oxford New York

Auckland Cape Town Dar es Salaam Hong Kong Karachi
Kuala Lumpur Madrid Melbourne Mexico City Nairobi
New Delhi Shanghai Taipei Toronto

With offices in
Argentina Austria Brazil Chile Czech Republic France Greece
Guatemala Hungary Italy Japan Poland Portugal Singapore
South Korea Switzerland Thailand Turkey Ukraine Vietnam

Oxford is a registered trade mark of Oxford University Press
in the UK and certain other countries.

Published in the United States of America by
Oxford University Press
198 Madison Avenue, New York, NY 10016

Library of Congress Cataloging-in-Publication Data
Rhode, Deborah L.
What women want / Deborah L. Rhode.
p. cm.
ISBN 978–0–19–934827–5 (hardback : alk. paper) 1. Feminism—History—21st century. 2. Women—
Social conditions. 3. Women—Employment. 4. Women—Family relationships. I. Title.
HQ1155.R46 2014
305.42009'05—dc23   2013049615

1   3   5   7   9   8   6   4   2

Printed in the United States of America on acid-free paper

For Ralph

CONTENTS

ACKNOWLEDGMENTS

This book owes many debts. I am deeply grateful to David McBride at Oxford University Press, who supported this project from the outset and shepherded it through publication. I am also indebted to Richard Banks, Vicki Shabo, Reva Siegel, and Joan Williams for their insightful comments, and to Christina Black, Rachel Dempsey, Katherine Lin, and Laurel Schroeder for their excellent research. The staff of the Stanford Law library provided invaluable reference assistance: Paul Lomio, Sonia Moss, Rich Porter, Rachael Samberg, Sergio Stone, George Vizvary, Erika Wayne, and George Wilson. Finally, I owe my greatest debt to my husband, Ralph Cavanagh, whose unflagging support and editorial guidance made this book possible.

Introduction

Women writing about women's issues inevitably confront questions. Why are you writing about *that*? Is there a chip on your shoulder, and if so, how did it get there?

What started me down the path to this book was an unusually gendered college experience. I arrived at Yale in 1970, the second year that the university began admitting women undergraduates. The transition was still bumpy. Administrators reassured unhappy alumni that they would not reduce the number of men to accommodate coeds, so my class was described as "a thousand male leaders and 250 women." Our arrival unsettled a campus with a two-hundred-year tradition of all-male clubs and classrooms. An alumni reunion preceding my arrival captured the flavor of the times. As William Buckley later recalled, the Provost was present while two "striptease artists . . . put their hearts into their work." After they finished, someone asked, "What is the official Yale position toward this?" The Provost cast a stern look in their direction and replied, "Yale's position is that the Second One is better than the First."[1]

The University's position on coeducation was more complicated. The reasons are recounted in a 1971 book, *Women at Yale: The Liberation of a College Campus*. When I arrived, most of the men gave little evidence of having been liberated. Some greeted the female invasion with obvious distaste. Yale's responsibility was to produce leaders, which by definition excluded women. As one professor noted, it was "not an accident of history" that virtually all world leaders were men.[2] Another common view, expressed with uncommon candor by a disgruntled alumnus, was that male undergraduates who wanted to concentrate on important matters like "the basic principles of thermodynamics" would be diverted by the "idiotic trivia that all women try to impose on men."[3] The type of female student who might want to focus on topics like thermodynamics was equally unappealing. Women who were assertive in the classroom or too "intellectual" outside it were "unfeminine."[4] In some courses, it was clear that coeds were meant to be seen but not heard; our comments were dismissed, devalued, or simply ignored. Women were captive to the perennial double standard and double bind: We were at risk of appearing too feminine or not feminine enough, and what was assertive for a man was abrasive for a woman.

There were petty indignities as well. At a party following the Harvard-Yale football game for team members and their "guests," everyone referred to me as "Greg's date." No one even pretended that the women were important enough to have first names.

Although the university's leaders saw coeducation as the wave of the future, they appeared unprepared for the transformations that it implied. Ironically enough, for two centuries, women had been excluded from institutions like Yale on the assumption that they were different. But once they were admitted, the official assumption was that they were the same, and that only modest adjustments would be necessary to accommodate their presence. So my freshman dormitory got renovated bathrooms with extra mirrors, along with a security guard whose function was unclear. Was he there to protect morals or just to give the appearance of doing so? In the face of ambiguity, he steered a prudent middle course. Male visitors were not barred at indiscreet hours but they were greeted with reproachful glares, reminiscent of a vigilant junior prom chaperone.

Athletics were a source of particular friction. Women's arrival on campus created turf battles literally and figuratively. Many athletes and coaches were reluctant to share space and resources with women, some of whom were products of undemanding physical education programs including rhythmic ring toss and pep club rallies.[5] My roommate's field hockey team requested practice space; it ended up in a vacant parking lot. My women's varsity tennis team insisted on court time but gave up on bathrooms, and settled for coaching by a local physical education teacher. Her role was to bring iced tea and cookies to matches and to murmur "good shot" at appropriate intervals. For years, the women's crew team politely and ineffectually pleaded for shower facilities at the boathouse. The women sat, cold and wet, in a bus after practice while their male classmates showered and changed. The situation changed only after some resourceful women crew members discovered a new law, Title IX of the Civil Rights Act, prohibiting sex discrimination by institutions receiving federal funds. Female rowers arranged a meeting with the Director of Athletics and showed up with "Title IX" printed in block letters on their bare backs. They removed their shirts in the presence of invited guests, including a *New York Times* photographer. A picture ran the following day; the showers followed soon after.[6]

Similar skirmishes involving traditionally all-male enclaves occurred in every corner of the campus, as well as its outposts in other cities. Sacred terrain was gradually, but not always gracefully, surrendered. The New York Yale

Club was a site of long-standing struggle. Uppity women kept escalating their demands: first to use the main entrance, then the second floor lounge, and ultimately the swimming pool.[7]

The curriculum for years remained a largely male preserve, with almost no courses by or about women. But occasionally the subject surfaced in classes like my introduction to sociology course, where I had a female graduate student teaching assistant. When I asked for help on a final paper topic related to poverty, she suggested instead that I might want do some research on the women's movement.

> "I'm not really interested in that," I responded.
>
> "Why?" she wanted to know.
>
> "Well, I don't really see women as an oppressed group." The ones I had seen while growing up in an affluent Chicago suburb seemed like a pretty privileged bunch.
>
> "What about women who are poor?" the teaching assistant asked.
>
> "That's why I want to write about poverty." I hoped she would then get with the program and suggest a topic on economic injustice.

Instead she asked what I knew about the women's movement. "Bra burners" were all that came to mind, and I was observant enough not to bring that up. She wasn't wearing a brassiere (a fact widely noted by the male students in the class) and it suddenly occurred to me that she might have been one of the burners. So I admitted to ignorance, which gave her the opportunity to suggest that before I dismissed the topic out of hand, perhaps I should at least learn something about it. We agreed that I would read one book on the woman's movement, and that if I still wasn't interested, she'd suggest a topic on poverty.

The book was Simone de Beauvoir's *The Second Sex*. I recall reading it, sitting in the Sterling Memorial Library and suddenly seeing the world in a different way. My parents' unequal relationship, Yale students' sexist comments, and the absence of women from the university faculty and curricula all began to seem like part of a pattern. My history class on American Progressive movements relegated an entire century's struggle for suffrage to a single run-on sentence. The professor said something like, "Just after World War I, women's activism increased, and in gratitude for their war service, they received a constitutional amendment granting them the vote." My experience was not unusual. A survey of history texts at the time revealed a biological oddity: a nation with only founding fathers. Material on women constituted less than one percent of the total. In one leading text, the development of the six-shooter received more coverage than the women's suffrage movement.[8] Many students graduated from the best universities unaware that there *was* a significant movement.

My first foray into empirical research confirmed the extent of historical am-
nesia. As a student representative of the University's Committee on Women,
I was surprised to discover that the Committee doubted the need for more
curricular coverage of issues concerning women. To convince committee
members of the need, I conducted a random sample of Yale undergraduates
to determine how many could name two leaders in women's rights. The result
was about 10 percent, and even that required giving the benefit of the doubt
to answers like Joan of Arc and Catherine the Great. The standard curriculum at Yale and elsewhere remained hostage to "great man" historical frameworks. The texts were as Jane Austen once described them: "The quarrels of
popes and kings in every page; the men all so good for nothing and hardly any
women at all."[9]

As I became more interested in women's issues, I developed a senior thesis
in political science on the campaign for an Equal Rights Amendment [ERA]
to the United States Constitution. I looked at the beginnings of the struggle in
Illinois, where ERA opponent Phyllis Schlafly got her start, and the campaign
for state ratification of the amendment began to founder. I interviewed participants in the struggle and unearthed local newspaper accounts chronicling
the efforts of groups like Winsome Wives and Homemakers, and Women
Who Want to Be Women. Their members were full-time mothers who felt that
feminists had demeaned their status and devalued their choices. All too often,
feminists responded in ways that confirmed those views and reinforced media
caricatures. For example, to combat anti-ERA claims that supporters of the
amendment were rabid sexless man haters, a Chicago women's rights group
organized a press conference featuring a Playboy bunny. The event proved
comically counterproductive. When a reporter inquired whether the bunny
ever discussed equal rights with her customers, she responded, "No, they are
a perfect example of pigism." The Chicago papers had a field day. "A bunny
hops on rights issue," ran the headline of an article trivializing the serious
issues at stake.[10]

That research changed my life. It sparked an interest that I returned to later
as a legal scholar. And it propelled me toward a legal career. Although I briefly
considered graduate school in political science, the only encouragement I received came with sexual strings attached. We didn't have the term "sex harassment" in those years, much less any formal complaint channels. We talked
about having a "problem" with a professor. And the problem was always ours,
never his. In my case, I blamed myself for having accepted dinner invitations
from a professor. How could I have been so foolish as to think that those invitations came because he was seriously interested in my views on political theory?
When he tried to kiss me, I was shocked. The man was married and old enough
to be my father. It was only later that I learned that he had a habit of hitting on

female students. And the absence of any complaint procedures made his conduct costless, at least from his standpoint.

After that incident, law seemed more welcoming to women than graduate school. Perhaps it was, but it was a relatively low bar. Only a small percentage of my class at Yale was female, I never had a course taught by or about women, there were no women's organizations, and gender was again notable for its absence in the curriculum. Things could have been worse, however. Other law schools, including Harvard, were notorious for "ladies days." Professors didn't call on women except on those days, when the subject matter was specially adapted for their benefit: rape cases with embarrassing facts, or hypothetical problems involving knitting and cooking. What is striking to me now is how little of this was striking to me then. It was just how law and life were. Sex discrimination was everywhere except in the curricula.

In seeking a clerkship position to follow graduation from law school, I learned that the judge I most hoped to work for had not seriously considered me because he had already hired a woman. Having two would be unseemly. For decades, of course, he had hired two men and no eyebrows were raised, at least among his colleagues, who were, needless to say, all male. But I managed to land another clerkship, and then one with Supreme Court Justice Thurgood Marshall, who didn't mind having two women among his four clerks. He was also supportive of my idea of becoming a law school professor and teaching a course on gender. But he couldn't resist baiting me about whether students "really needed a class on sex discrimination." "In most of the country," he noted, "it seems to come naturally."

After the clerkship, I entered law teaching at Stanford. It was 1979, and I was for many years the second woman on a faculty of about 36 men. Initially, I indicated that gender and law was a subject I'd like to teach. The Dean was horrified. I would, as he put it, be "typed as a woman." "Well," I responded with faint irony, "it probably wouldn't come as a surprise to most of my colleagues. And what, after all, are my alternatives?" But he thought I had missed his point. It was about academic credibility, and to establish that, I needed a "real subject." He suggested negotiable instruments. We compromised on contracts, a field where I languished for seven years until the law school got a new dean and I got tenure.

In the interim, I was unprepared for the solitary confinement that my status entailed. I didn't fit easily into any of the school's social networks. The perfunctory "welcome to Stanford" lunch and dinner invitations dried up fairly quickly. In my first summer on campus, I was sure I could die in my office and only when the stench became overwhelming would anyone notice.

There were a few collegial activities open to everyone, which I tried hard to enjoy. One was a Friday law professors' lunch at the Faculty Club. Preferred conversation topics were sports (men's), and gossip about academics (also men) whom I didn't know. The apparent objective was to earn an A in small talk through some obscure nugget of knowledge or witty aside. I sat silently through these exchanges, managing an occasional smile to suggest that I was appreciative, or at least awake. Although my colleagues were generally well meaning and unfailingly polite, they were essentially clueless about what it was like to feel the pressure and isolation of being one of two women on the faculty. Some couldn't manage to keep the two of our names straight, although we bore no physical resemblance. I was short and blonde; the other female professor was tall and brunette, and I was never sure whether to correct the colleagues who occasionally called me Barbara. These experiences might not have been so hurtful if I had known at the time that they were typical byproducts of tokenism. Even the most prominent women can experience the problem. In the late 1990s, lawyers appearing before the Supreme Court mixed up the names of Justices Sandra Day O'Connor and Ruth Bader Ginsburg so often that the Women Judges' Association once presented them with T-shirts reading "I'm Ruth, not Sandra" and "I'm Sandra, not Ruth."[11]

My attempts to remedy the faculty's gender imbalance by speaking up for female candidates during the faculty appointments process was a largely futile gesture. "Of course Deborah is for her," was the unspoken but obvious reaction. On the infrequent occasions when I did not push for a woman, it did little to bolster my credibility. The apparent assumption was that the candidate was so unqualified that not even *I* could muster support.

On most issues of gender, the school had an obvious blind spot. My most vivid memory from those years was the Dean's retirement dinner. The alumni threw a party at the local country club and hired a stripper to come and simulate her routine. None of the women present could quite believe it was happening. But the Dean appreciated the thought behind the invitation and, well-fortified by bourbon, warmly embraced the invited guest. It was at that moment I decided "to hell with contracts." The law school needed a course on gender.

Now, some three decades later, the legal landscape has been transformed. Women are moving up and barriers are coming down. About half of law students and 30 percent of full professors are female, and examples of blatant discrimination are rare. I teach a course on gender that raises no administrative eyebrows.

Yet at the same time, this progress has created its own difficulties. A central problem for women is the lack of consensus that there still *is* a serious problem, or one that they have any capacity or responsibility to address. This "no problem" problem is one theme of the chapters that follow. Their central premise is that major challenges of gender inequality remain unsolved. Over the past half century, we have made major strides in identifying the barriers to equal opportunity. But we have done far less well in developing solutions. On virtually every major dimension of social status, financial well-being, and physical safety, women still fare worse than men. Sexual violence remains common, and reproductive rights are by no means secure. Women assume disproportionate burdens in the home and pay a price in the world outside it. Yet these issues are not cultural priorities. Why that is, why it matters, and how best to respond are the questions that prompt this book.

Chapter 1 begins the analysis with an overview of the women's movement. It explores why so many women are reluctant to identify as feminists and why it matters. The discussion is informed by interviews with heads of leading women's organizations on key questions. Is the movement stalled? What are the major obstacles it confronts? What are its key priorities and what strategies might advance them?

Chapter 2 surveys employment issues. It reviews the unconscious biases and workplace practices that help explain the gender gap in pay and leadership positions. The analysis also addresses the limits of legal strategies in addressing those inequalities. Despite four decades of enforcement of equal employment legislation, women's employment status remains far from equal. Discussion focuses on what can be done at the individual, organizational, and political level to respond more effectively.

Chapter 3 explores work/family issues. It surveys the inflexible workplace structures and gendered division of domestic responsibilities that encourage women to opt out or to limit their workforce participation, as well as the pressures on men that discourage equal sharing of household tasks. The United States has the least family-friendly policies in the developed world. The analysis focuses on the initiatives that are necessary to level the playing field for workers with caretaking responsibilities, including paid family and sick leave, greater flexibility in work arrangements, and more affordable quality childcare.

Chapter 4 focuses on sex and marriage. Its discussion centers on controversies surrounding recent practices such as sexting, hookups, cohabitation, divorce, and same-sex marriage. These controversies shed light on deeper contested questions about what women want in intimate relationships, what stands in the way, and what social policies might better serve women's interests.

Chapter 5 addresses issues of reproductive and economic autonomy. Both are essential to gender equality and human flourishing, and both are at risk under current policies. Over 85 percent of counties have no abortion provider, and a third to a fifth of poor women cannot obtain abortions that they desire. America has the developed world's highest rate of adolescent pregnancy, and

the reasons have much to do with inadequate access to birth control information and services. As to economic security, one in seven women, and almost
a third of households headed by single women, are in poverty. Yet only about
a quarter of the poor are receiving welfare, and benefits are 50 percent below
the poverty line. The human costs are substantial. Millions of families suffer
from shortages in food and housing, and the inadequate safety net keeps many
women trapped in violent relationships.

Chapter 6 explores sexual harassment, rape, domestic violence, and trafficking. An estimated quarter of all women experience sexual or physical violence
by an intimate partner; a fifth experience rape or attempted rape. The United
States has the world's second highest rate of reported rape. Few of these crimes
result in convictions, and recent reform efforts have done nothing to increase
the chances of a successful prosecution. What accounts for the persistence and
pervasiveness of sexual abuse, and what can be done about it, are the focus of
analysis.

Chapter 7 focuses on appearance. Although this is not among the most
critical issues facing women, it is the one on which the women's movement
has made the least progress. In some respects, the problem has grown worse.
Almost half of American women are dissatisfied with their bodies, which is
higher than a quarter century ago. After money, appearance is women's greatest source of dissatisfaction. How to reduce the discrimination, guilt, and economic costs associated with appearance is the focus of discussion.

Chapter 8 centers on politics and strategies for change. What accounts for
women's underrepresentation in public office? What difference does it make?
What can be done to increase the number of women in leadership positions
and to mobilize more women around women's issues?

The stakes in this book's agenda are substantial. At issue are fundamental
issues of social equality, physical safety, and economic livelihood. What can
convince women to identify and to act on what they want is the subject of the
chapters to follow.

1

The Women's Movement

In a *New Yorker* cartoon, a woman frostily informs her obviously skeptical husband, "Yes, Harold, I do speak for all women." This is not a claim that any contemporary feminist will readily make. Women do not speak with one voice on women's issues. But to build a powerful political movement, we must be prepared to generalize about the interests of women as a group. We need to say something about what social theorists label "enlightened preferences."[1] What would most women want if they were fully informed and free to choose? What should women want if the goal is true equality between the sexes? This book aims to jump-start a conversation about that agenda.

This chapter begins with a historical overview of the challenges facing the women's movement. It concludes with findings from interviews of heads of leading women's organizations concerning their key priorities and the obstacles standing in the way. One major problem is the failure of women to recognize that there *is* a problem, and one that they need to address. "I'm not a feminist, but" is an overused cliché that captures a partial truth. The vast majority of Americans agree with the basic principles of the feminist movement and recognize its value, but refuse to identify as members. What that means and why it matters are questions of considerable social importance. What keeps most women from mobilizing as women sheds light on the future of public policies that shape the quality of life for all Americans.

I'm Not a Feminist but . . . : The Demonization of Feminism

For decades, the media has run periodic stories claiming that the women's movement is dead, dying, or seriously stalled. Press headlines have painted the movement as a "passing fancy" and "a lost cause," and have often held feminists responsible.[2] A representative article from the *Los Angeles Times* came straight to the point: "Feminists Have Killed Feminism."[3] Pronouncements that "feminism has fizzled" are typically followed by some galvanizing event that arouses women, and the movement will appear at least temporarily revived.[4] The widespread coverage of Sheryl Sandberg's book *Lean In* is the latest illustration.

The demonization of feminism has extended roots. A *Harper's Magazine* article is typical.

> "Feminism" has become a term of opprobrium to the modern young woman. For the word suggests either the old school of fighting feminists who wore flat heels and had very little feminine charm, or the current species who antagonize men with their constant clamor about maiden names, equal rights, [and] women's place in the world. . . .[5]

The year was 1927. For much of the last quarter century, commentators on feminism have been posing a common question. As *Time* put it to Gloria Steinem, "Since most women today embrace the goals of the women's movement, why are so many of them reluctant to embrace the feminist label?" Steinem responded: "Women have two problems with the label. The first is that people don't know what it means. . . . The second is that people do know what it means."[6] She has a point. One problem in mobilizing around women's issues is the negative association that many women have with the term "feminism." The term has been demonized by the right and caricatured by the press. A second problem is that feminism implies activism, and that makes many women uncomfortable.

Public opinion polls over the last two decades underscore the problem. Taken together, they reveal a striking ambivalence. On the one hand, the women's movement and its underlying principles have commanded widespread support. For example, over 75 percent of American women report that the women's movement has made life better, and has been helpful to them; four-fifths of women and men approve of the movement to strengthen women's rights.[7] When asked if the United States continues to need a strong women's movement to push for changes that benefit women, between 48 and 58 percent of Americans say yes.[8] And when polls give the dictionary definition of feminism as someone who supports political, economic, and social equality for women, most polls find 65–77 percent of women and 58–70 percent of men consider themselves feminist; in one 2013 survey, 82 percent of Americans agreed with the statement.[9] On the other hand, the most recent polls offering no definition find that only about a quarter to a half of women identify as feminist.[10] In one survey, less than half of women believed that feminism is relevant to most women, and only about a quarter (28 percent) felt that it is relevant to them personally.[11] Negative perceptions persist, even among those who believe that gender bias is a problem. In a survey of registered voters, a majority thought that women are not treated equally in the workplace (63 percent), in politics, (63 percent), in the armed forces (55 percent), and in the press (54 percent). But only 14 percent considered themselves a feminist and only 17 percent would want their daughter to be one.[12]

Multiple studies have focused on why women who support feminist goals fail to identify as feminists and whether it matters.[13] The consensus is that identification is significant because it correlates with activism.[14] The disconnect between the substance and image of feminism has been a long-standing barrier to mobilizing Americans around gender issues. Those negative associations are partly as a result of how the media framed early activism. Press caricatures often perpetuated the image problem they claimed only to describe. If, as *Time* magazine once argued, "[h]airy legs haunt the feminist movement, as do images of being strident and lesbian," one reason is that mainstream publications continually featured such descriptions.[15] Disproportionate early coverage of the movement centered on sensational tactics by fringe groups, such as the SCUM (Society to Cut Up Men), and WITCH (the Women's International Feminist Conspiracy from Hell), which made headlines by hexing First Lady Pat Nixon.[16] Shulamith Firestone told CBS News that "pregnancy is barbaric," and Ti-Grace Atkinson likened marriage to cancer.[17] When protestors at the 1968 Miss America pageant deposited lingerie and cosmetics in a trash can, the media took poetic license. Although no bras were in fact burned, the label stuck. Media coverage of the 1977 International Women's Year conference in Houston centered not on mainstream women's issues, such as passage of the Equal Rights Amendment, but on radical conference planks and placards such as one reading "Mother Nature is a Lesbian."[18]

Although radical tactics declined after the 1970s, the image of militancy stuck. In 2012, Yahoo CEO Marissa Mayer told documentary filmmakers that she didn't consider herself a feminist because although she "certainly believe[d] in equal rights" she didn't have the "militant drive and the sort of . . . chip on the shoulder" that she associated with the label.[19] That association has been repeatedly reinforced by a broad range of religious and social conservatives, men's rights activists, and media commentators. Groups like the Independent Women's Forum and Concerned Women for America provide a platform for female critics, and right-wing talk shows feature anti-feminist men. Some research finds that these conservative women's groups receive more mainstream media coverage than organizations like NOW and the Feminist Majority Foundation.[20]

From the conservative vantage, the women's movement is responsible for an assortment of social ills. Suzanne Venker and Phyllis Schlafly, in *The Flipside of Feminism,* round up the usual suspects: "STDs, abortion, and the

heartache associated with casual sex; failed marriages, the neglect of children, men's demotion. . . ."[21] The Vatican recently added to the list when it
denounced the Leadership Conference of Women Religious nuns as "radical
feminists" for failing to promote Catholic teachings on abortion and homosexuality.[22] Branding activists on women's issues as "feminazis" is a time-honored
tradition among right-wing talk show hosts.[23] When Rush Limbaugh labeled
Georgetown Law student Sandra Fluke a "slut" and "prostitute" for testifying
before the Senate on behalf of health insurance coverage for contraception, his
choice of language was simply an extreme form of sentiments common among
Far Right commentators.[24]

I was given a personal window on this dynamic after delivering an address
on gender inequality at the all-male Wabash College. The student paper ran
an article under the title: "Rhode Unleashes Vicious Hissy Fit on Traditional
Masculinity." It began by denouncing my statistical profile of the gender gap
in pay and leadership as a "typical femi-nazi rant." It then continued: "[Rhode
believes that] despite total equality under the law, women are being permanently oppressed by an evil patriarchal society and a culture that refuses to
alter its gender roles. . . . Deborah Rhode is an unhappy person. She is unhappy
with gender roles, unhappy with society, unhappy with biology's truths, and
unhappy with men in general." Who knew.

Men's rights activists are among the most vocal opponents of what they see
as rampant feminism in legal, political, and cultural arenas. As one overview
noted, "they see everything through the lens of zero-sum gender war. Everywhere, men get a raw deal at the hands of women. Anywhere women have
made advances, it's at the expense of men."[25] In his study, *Angry White Men*,
sociologist Michael Kimmel labels this stance "aggrieved entitlement."[26] From
this vantage, America is a "malicious matriarchy," with laws and policies that
"idealize women and treat men as social pariahs."[27] Common complaints include biased family courts, vindictive ex-wives, false accusations of rape and
sexual violence, the feminization of education, and male bashing in women's
studies programs. "Feminism's insistence on continuing to portray women
as the victims is all about feminists maintaining their own power, which
they routinely abuse. . . . Women now out-privilege men in every area of well
being, health, lifestyle and longevity, and will soon do so in regard to wealth
as well."[28] A report by the Southern Poverty Law Center notes that "[t]here are
literally hundreds of websites, blogs and forums devoted to attacking virtually
all women. . . ."[29]

In several well-publicized incidents, men's rights activists have turned to
violence to express their beliefs. One case featured a man who drew attention to his protest by committing suicide. He lit himself on fire on the steps
of a courthouse in New Hampshire after a long custody battle and pending

imprisonment for failure to pay child support.[30] In another case, George Sodini walked into a Pennsylvania fitness gym and opened fire on women in an aerobics class. He killed five and injured 12 before killing himself. What is most chilling is the support that he received on some men's rights blogs. Many saw him as a "hero" for taking a "last stand" against feminism and the "frigid harpies" at the exercise studio who were "too uptight to give a guy a chance on a date."[31]

To both male and female critics, feminism appears unnecessary as well as destructive. "American women are the most fortunate human beings who have ever lived. No one has it better," claim Venker and Schlafly, unencumbered by factual support. Never mind that the United States ranks only seventeenth in the World Economic Forum's survey of 58 countries on various measures of gender equality, including economic participation and opportunity, political empowerment, educational attainment, and health and well-being.[32] Nor does it matter that a majority of American women believe that society generally favors men over women and that "all things considered, men continue to have it better in life than women do," that close to half of American women (46 percent) report experiencing sex discrimination, or that over half of women (56 percent) think that women get fewer opportunities than men for good jobs.[33] According to Venker and Schlafly, "if women today are discriminated against, the Equal Employment Opportunity Commission (EEOC) an aggressive federal agency, will take their case."[34] This will come as news to the chronically underfunded EEOC, which, in the year their book was published, received 99,947 complaints and could file only 261 lawsuits.[35]

How large a group these critics represent is difficult to estimate. As the polls cited earlier make clear, their views on the women's movement do not resonate with the large majority of Americans. Nor do most individuals want to return to traditional male breadwinner–female homemaker gender roles. Those who do totaled only 18 percent in a Pew survey, down from 30 percent in 1987, and they disproportionately represent an aging group.[36]

Still, the demonization of activists has clearly carried a cost. In study after study, many women have continued to describe feminists as "shrill," "rude," "aggressive," "angry," "bitter," "strident," "whining," "castrating," "extremist," "anti-male," and "anti-family."[37] As one young woman explained her "I'm not a feminist but" stance: "I just think that everybody is equal but I don't go around bashing men . . . I like men."[38] Yet so, of course, do many feminists. Few deny their debts to men, and leading women's studies texts feature no absence of male heroes. Judging from the acknowledgments in feminist publications, many authors (this one included) are deeply grateful for the assistance of male partners, colleagues, and editors, and few of these feminists seem to believe that they are sleeping with the enemy, metaphorically or otherwise.

Still, the reputation of man-hating has stuck, as has the image of anti-feminine. Pop star Taylor Swift attracted widespread attention in denying that she was a feminist because she didn't "really think about things as guys versus girls."[39] Lady Gaga also famously denied being a feminist because "I hail men, I love men. . . ."[40] Feminists are also seen as "having let themselves go physically": "ugly," "fat," and "hairy."[41] "There are a lot of homely women in Women's Studies," Christina Hoff Sommers observed.[42] According to talk show host Rush Limbaugh, the point of feminism is "to allow unattractive women easier access to the mainstream."[43]

So, too, the subject matter of feminism encourages some women to keep their distance. They would prefer not to think about the prevalence of sexual violence or to imagine themselves as victims.[44] A reader of one of my publications on domestic violence put the point directly: "Why don't you ever write about happy women?"

Even if individuals don't personally have negative associations with the women's movement, they often believe that others do, which gets in the way of embracing the identity.[45] A wide variety of research documents the social penalties experienced by women who challenge sexism.[46] Concerns about guilt by association may help explain singer Beyoncé's ambivalent acknowledgment that she guessed she was a "modern-day feminist" because she believed in equality, but noted that the "the word can be very extreme." "Why do you have to label yourself anything?" she asked, and added that she was "happily married" and loved her husband.[47] Sarah Palin's flip-flop on feminism during her vice-presidential campaign reflected a similar aversion to being typecast. Her statement to Katie Couric that "I'm a feminist who believes in equal rights" raised so many eyebrows in conservative circles that within a month she walked it back. When Brian Williams asked if she was a feminist, she responded, "I'm not gonna label myself."[48]

How to respond to this image problem has been a matter of long-standing dispute. A 2013 *Atlantic* article rehashed the debate—either preach to a feminist choir or avoid alienating a more mainstream audience.[49] While moderates have often sought to distance themselves from radical causes and tactics, many activists have been unapologetic.[50] "This is a revolution, not a public relations movement," Gloria Steinem famously insisted.[51] Jessica Valenti, in *Full Frontal Feminism: A Young Woman's Guide to Why Feminism Matters*, advised readers to recognize the image problem and then just get over it. "Yeah, someone's going to call you a lesbian. Someone's going to say you're a fat ugly dyke. Suck it up."[52] Other leaders saw an easier fix, at least with respect to the term "feminism." Organizations like MomsRising deliberately avoid use of the word.[53] Noreen Farrell, president of Equal Rights Advocates, thought that feminists should simply not "use a word that has been co-opted by the right." Joan Williams, director of the Center for WorkLife Law at UC Hastings College of the Law, agreed. "Sure, the demonization of the term is a symptom of the problem, but I'm not interested in fighting about words, so I don't use it much." Sheryl Sandberg took a different view. "I think progress doesn't turn on identifying as feminists. But I think it would be better . . . if we retake the term and use it and embrace it. . . . The word feminism, in my understanding, is rooted in the understanding that things aren't equal. So by embracing that word we are acknowledging that we're not done yet and we're willing to be for that change."

I'm a Feminist but . . . : Third Wave Feminism

Another challenge for women's organizations has emerged from within the movement, from young women described as the "third wave" of feminism. Its leaders use the term to distinguish themselves from the first wave of activists in the nineteenth and early twentieth century, and the second wave of activists who began leading the movement in the 1960s and 1970s. Rebecca Walker popularized the label in a 1992 *Ms.* essay. She was responding to the sexist treatment of Anita Hill during the Clarence Thomas Senate confirmation hearings and to media claims that the United States had entered a "post-feminist" era. "I am not a post-feminism feminist," Walker famously announced. "I am the third wave."[54] Walker, together with Amy Richards, helped launch the Third Wave Foundation, an organization devoted to supporting feminists under 30 years old.

What is, perhaps, most distinctive about third wavers is the lack of a distinctive set of political objectives. These activists are individualistic, inclusive, and conscious of the intersectional nature of identities across race, class, ethnicity, and sexual orientation. The *Bust Guide to the New Girl Order* claims, "We've entered an era of DIY feminism, sistah, do it yourself. . . . Your feminism is what you want it to be and what you make of it. Define your agenda. Claim and reclaim your F-word."[55] This eclectic group defines itself in opposition to the second wave, which third wavers see as "puritanical, dated, dowdy," and elitist.[56] Women of color are among the most frequent critics of second wave feminism; many view the movement as dominated by white middle class women, whose concerns are not those of minority communities.[57] According to third wave activists, the movement needs to extend its focus beyond gender; women's rights "cannot be achieved in isolation, nor can their achievement be enjoyed across, race, class and cultures, without feminist engagement in broader social and economic justice."[58] In comparison to their mother's generation, third wave feminists often claim to be less rigid and judgmental, and more willing to claim sexual pleasure and actively play with images of femininity.[59]

Much of their focus is on personal narratives, collected in multiple anthologies and circulated online, in a style accessible to a broad audience.[60]

These criticisms have spawned their own share of critiques. To many commentators, the target of third wavers is a whitewashed caricature of their own making. It ignores the powerful voices of women of color and the "pro-sex" faction within the second wave.[61] Charges of racial insensitivity have been particularly galling to activists like Gloria Steinem who have often taken pains to share their podium with women of color and to respond to their concerns. In a foreword to a collection of essays by third wave feminists, many of whom faulted their predecessors for lack of inclusivity, Steinem confessed to moments of feeling "like a sitting dog being told to sit. . . . Imagine how frustrating it is to be held responsible for some of the very divisions you've been fighting against. . . ."[62]

Another criticism of third wave feminism is that a framework grounded in generational differences amplifies divisiveness, obscures commonalities, and marginalizes voices that do not fit within narrow time frames.[63] Too much attention is focused on internal rivalries and too little on social inequalities. Class is particularly overlooked, claims Susan Faludi. For "all the lip service that is paid to the 'intersectionality' of race, class and gender, [the movement] has left economic divisions on the cutting room floor. It's more marketable to talk about sex or pop culture."[64]

Some observers are also critical of the atheoretical, apolitical, and anecdotal focus of much third wave work. This approach often seems "more like a literary form than a social movement."[65] According to one overview, the third wave "seems to abandon the idea of creating a social movement as the goal of feminism."[66] To critics, narrative navel gazing is no substitute for collective action, and when "the personal is no longer political" the chances for a progressive policy agenda erode.[67] As Barnard President Debora Spar argues, the abandonment of political objectives is all the more problematic in a culture that has "privatized feminism" and has sought individual solutions to collective dilemmas.[68]

Here again, however, some of the critiques are overstated. Young feminists have not all abandoned activism. As Katha Pollitt has noted, it is just that more of it has moved to the grassroots level and online organizing.[69] Blogs and websites like Feministing have introduced many young women to feminist commentary. The wider range of issues with which these women have engaged also opens new possibilities for coalitions. If, as some research suggests, femininity is a critical part of many women's self-image, the sex-positive tone of many third wave publications and writing may broaden the movement's appeal.[70] So, too, the concerns raised by women of color have made leaders of women's organizations more conscious of the need to reach out to racial minorities and other underrepresented constituencies. The challenge remaining is to use the energy that has inspired third wave women and to forge connections that will encourage political action.

The State of the Movement

To gain a better sense of the state of the women's movement and the challenges that it faces, I interviewed leaders of prominent women's organizations in the fall of 2012 and talked with Sheryl Sandberg in the summer of 2013 in the wake of publicity about her book. These leaders offered varied views about what should be on the agenda for women and how much stands in the way.

An initial question—whether the movement was stalled—elicited responses across the full spectrum. Many leaders felt strongly that it was. "Is there a woman's movement in the US?," asked Nancy Northrup, president of the Center for Reproductive Rights. "I don't know that we have one. We have an organized policy sector. But movement suggests a broader cultural consciousness like what we had in the 1970s, and I don't see that happening. It may be hibernating. I don't have any doubt that it will be back, but it's in hibernation now." Terry O'Neill, president of NOW, agreed:

> We are totally stalled out and we are getting pushback. Women's representation is 17 percent in the Congress and not much better in state legislatures. Women account for just three percent [of] Fortune 500 CEOs. . . . Despite 45 years of advocacy on employment, women are still corralled in the lowest paid jobs with no health and pension benefits. . . . It's also a measure of how bad we've stalled out that we have [had] a vice presidential nominee who believes that women should not be allowed abortions in cases of rape and incest.

Other leaders pointed to lost ground on issues like reproductive rights, or noted that women's numbers had plateaued in workforce participation and positions of public leadership.[71] Joan Williams noted that, at current rates of change, it would take 276 years for women to achieve parity in CEO positions of Fortune 500 companies: "To me that sounds like a stall." "We're stuck in the muck," said Kathryn Kolbert, director of the Athena Center for Leadership Studies at Barnard. "We made great progress on the rights front in the 1970s and life has changed significantly, but progress for women has plateaued in rights, in leadership, and in the ability to contribute equally in social and cultural affairs."[72] Sheryl Sandberg, both in her book and in interviews following its publication, consistently maintained that "our revolution has stalled," and that "we need to acknowledge that we're stalled so we can change it."[73] When I asked Sandberg whether the reception of her book had altered her view, she responded, "What I meant [by stalled] was that women have stopped making progress at the top. So there's been pretty flat progress particularly in U.S. corporations. . . . I will feel better that we are continuing to make progress once those numbers start moving, and that can't happen in the time frame of any one book. . . ."

By contrast, a minority of those interviewed had an optimistic view. Kim Gandy, president of the National Network to End Domestic Violence and former president of NOW, and Eleanor Smeal, president of the Feminist Majority, both pointed to progress on many fronts. Women's votes and women's issues were, as Smeal put it, "front and center" in the 2012 elections. Republican Congressional candidates who had made extreme statements on rape and reproductive rights lost, even though they had been predicted to win before their comments. The Affordable Health Care Act reflected huge gains for women by banning gender discrimination in rates and benefits and guaranteeing coverage of contraception.

Women who worked primarily on international women's issues also stressed areas of progress. Kavita Ramdas, former president of the Global Fund for Women, noted that "we are moving towards a world in which more and more people believe in the equality of women. Also, women's movements globally are pushing for a more inclusive and broader vision of a just and sustainable world." Ann Ferris, president of the International Women's Democracy Center, similarly cited advances, such as the number of women holding public office, and the increase in governmental endorsements of women's agendas. That 187 out of 194 nations in the world have signed CEDAW, the Convention to Eliminate All Forms of Discrimination Against Women, is testament to progress.

From a domestic standpoint, however, the most common view among leaders was that progress for the American women's movement was uneven. "There are always fits and starts," noted Heidi Hartmann, director of the Institute for Women's Policy Research. "You can't expect linear progress." Most important, women had laid the foundations for change in policy organizations and in higher education. "Many more institutions are working on women's issues," she noted. Marcia Greenberger, co-president of the National Center for Women and the Law, made a similar point. "Progress is jagged." Reproductive choice was a case in point. "There has always been majority support for reproductive rights, but it's hard to mobilize people to keep what they have," Greenberger noted. Even so, as opponents have been more successful, pro-choice women have responded. "Efforts to defund Planned Parenthood and the attacks on Sandra Fluke . . . have served as a wake up call. Pro-choice women are speaking up to a much greater extent" said Greenberger. Judith Lichtman, president of the National Partnership for Women and Families, agreed:

> Social change movements wax and wane. There are times when you're pushing the envelope and times when you're holding the line. Who would have thought in the 21st century we would be fighting about access to contraceptives? We are refighting battles that we thought we won. At the same time, a result of this national conversation that one would hope not to be having, is the energizing of women under 35. The attacks have made an enormous difference in reaching women in a demographic group that has been hard to reach.

Experts on social movements take a similar view. As they note, in the typical life cycle of such movements, the initial revolutionary spirit is hard to sustain, and "gradually sentiment grows that the revolution has stalled. . . . We appear to be entering just such a period of pessimism about the gender revolution." But in the long term, there is reason to hope that "forces making for change over the last half century remain in play and will bring about further substantial reductions in gender inequality."[74]

To some extent, the different views concerning progress reflected differences in time frames. Leaders taking the long view saw major, if uneven, progress. "This is a totally different world than when the modern women's movement started," Eleanor Smeal noted. As an example of progress, Kim Gandy pointed to the pay gap, which has shrunk from 59 cents to 77 cents on the dollar. But in recent years, as Heidi Hartmann pointed out, progress has slowed and pay equity legislation has stalled. To Elizabeth Grayer, president of Legal Momentum, part of the reason for the slowdown is that at least domestically "the low hanging fruit has been dealt with. The really big issues are subtler" and solutions more elusive. "We've made great progress, said Noreen Farrell, president of Equal Rights Advocates, "but not for enough women." From a global perspective, fundamental challenges remain at even the most basic level. "We are still dealing with child brides, horrific violence, and mass illiteracy," Smeal pointed out. In short, as Judith Lichtman summarized the situation, "we've come very far but we have very far to go."

What stands in the way? When asked about difficulties in mobilizing women around women's issues, leaders gave a number of explanations, which track those that research and polling data also suggest. One involves the "no problem problem"—the belief that barriers have come down, women have moved up, and that equal opportunity has been secured. "The narrative today," said Northrup, is that "everything is open to you. What are you whining about?" Debbie Walsh, director of the Center for American Women and Politics, pointed out that progress has created its own barriers to further progress. There isn't any sense of urgency. "If you ask the general public, 'Are women well represented in government?' I'm sure they would say 'absolutely.' They have no sense that women are literally only 17 percent of Congress."[75]

Maureen Howard, cofounder of the reproductive rights advocacy group A Is For, agreed. "A lot is taken for granted by this generation. Nobody really believes that rights could be taken away." Kate Kendell, executive director of the National Center for Lesbian Rights, similarly believes that "[s]exism exists, yet people feel like we're over it and don't want to talk about it. Many feel that they don't need to. They're in decent jobs and doing fine. There's a view that we're in a 'post-feminist' society, whatever that means. But what it seems to mean is that we don't want to talk about feminism any more." Much of the published commentary on the women's movement makes a similar point. "Gender fatigue" is the term used by Sylvia Ann Hewlett, president of the Center for Work-Life Policy.[76] Feminism is "everywhere and nowhere," proclaims the title of Professor Jo Reger's 2012 overview.[77] The movement seems less necessary because its norms have been institutionalized in public policy and mainstreamed in public consciousness.[78] In *Manifesta: Young Women, Feminism and the Future*, Jennifer Baumgardner and Amy Richards suggested that "[f]eminism is like fluoride." Women "scarcely notice that [they] have it. It's simply in the water."[79]

One key predictor of whether someone identifies as feminist is an adverse experience that individuals can see as part of a broader pattern of gender inequality.[80] Many women don't perceive difficulties in their lives in those terms. As Terry O'Neill noted, women often "take personal responsibility for systemic problems." So, too, women also lack the sense of relative deprivation that fuels political activism. In terms of overall satisfaction, most research finds that women do not feel worse off compared to men. In Gallup surveys, women and men worldwide are equally likely to say they are thriving, despite widespread gender inequality in employment, personal safety, and physical well-being.[81] The Organisation for Economic Co-operation and Development Better Life Index finds that in the United States, women are somewhat happier than men, giving life a 7.4 grade compared with 6.8 for men.[82] Another study using a different data set finds that men and women average the same in overall life satisfaction, 3.99 on a 6 point scale.[83] The vast majority of even lower income women (87 percent) report general satisfaction with their lives.[84] Another problem in mobilizing women involves differences in their interests and agendas. Linda Basch, president of the National Council for Research on Women, described the difficulties in getting women to coalesce around a unifying set of issues. "People often don't organize or spend personal resources unless they see how it will make a difference in their own lives." Divisions across age, race, class, and ideology have complicated efforts to establish common priorities. It has often been hard to get women of privilege who underwrite women's organizations to care about the problems facing those worst off and most in need of organizational support.[85] Without a strong personal stake or sense of common ground, women already struggling to balance work and family commitments lack sufficient incentives for mobilization. Even those strongly committed to women's issues may feel stretched too thin for personal involvement. Ironically enough, Debbie Walsh noted, because of opportunities made possible by the women's movement, "women have no time for the women's movement."

As research on social movements makes clear, such barriers to mobilization are not unique to feminism. In the typical life history of a social revolution, a sense of urgency proves sustainable for only so long.[86] To maintain commitment, the movement must be capable of attracting money, supporters, media attention, and alliances.[87] A central challenge for organizations that seek collective benefits like gender equality is the common action problem. No individual has a sufficient material stake in the outcome to justify a significant commitment of time and resources.[88] To overcome this barrier, movements need to create a sense of collective identity and solidarity.[89] Yet mature movements can become victims of their own success. Perceptions of group affiliation that are widely but weakly shared become a public good: individuals can support the movement without engaging in concrete actions that advance its objectives. The more diffuse the movement's support, the more difficulty it experiences in finding followers to "pay the dues and do the work."[90] As Herman put it, "We need to get women to do more than push a button on a computer." The National Organization for Women, the largest American feminist organization, claims only 500,000 members, out of an eligible population of 116 million women.

Nor have major foundations seen women's issues as a priority. O'Neill noted that only about 6 percent of funding by nongovernmental organizations goes to women's issues, and "you're not going to fund a revolution on 6 percent." Many leaders expressed frustration at the lack of foundation support and the turf battles that it created among women's organizations that are all chasing the same dollars. As Williams pointed out, "this is another way that bias against women feeds conflict among women."

Of course, organizational membership and foundation dollars are not the only measures of feminism's influence. The women's movement has become less visible because it has been institutionalized in established organizations.[91] Women's issues are addressed in the church, the military, the workplace, and the media. An immeasurable amount of education, advocacy, and activism also takes place on the Internet. Yet despite such efforts, "active intervention to move toward gender equality is not high on the mainstream political agenda."[92] Most commentators agree that the movement lacks the kind of "political traction it needs to effectively influence public policy."[93]

An Agenda for Change

In 2003, the New Women's Movement Initiative brought together some 50 women leaders in a series of meetings to resolve "long-standing divisions . . . and to build relationships, trust and analysis necessary to revitalize U.S. feminism."[94] The leaders represented major advocacy organizations, as well as funders and scholars. A pivotal issue was whether the movement should focus on equal rights or a broader set of issues involving social justice. In opting for a broader focus, leaders recognized a need to "take into account the dynamics of power and privilege that continue to shape women's lives even once legal rights to equality have been won."[95] Giving priority to issues that integrate concerns of race, class, age, sexual orientation, and "other markers of inequality" is a way to ensure attention to the most "marginalized and vulnerable."[96]

The priorities of leaders interviewed for this book reflect that broad focus. The issues most often mentioned are the subject of the chapters to follow: work, family, reproductive rights, violence, and economic security. Cutting across those issues was one central objective: getting more women into positions of leadership. Debbie Walsh, from the Center for American Women and Politics, put the reason bluntly: "women carry the water on women's issues." That's true in the corporate sector as well, Sheryl Sandberg noted. "There's data to suggest that when there are more women in senior leadership positions . . . companies have better policies [on work/family issues]." Of course, as Andi Zeisler, co-founder of *Bitch* magazine, noted, the goal is not to get "just any women. It's [to get] progressive women who identify as feminists."

Whether the women's movement itself faces leadership issues is a matter of some disagreement. Press coverage often notes that, with the exception of Gloria Steinem, no feminist has the kind of national celebrity that could help popularize the movement. As the *New York Times* reported in 2012, "for more than 40 years, Steinem has been the near singular voice of the women's movement." In all that time, "no one has emerged as her successor."[97] Whether anyone *should* do so raises a broader question. According to Zeisler, the media "are looking for the wrong thing. They're looking for a figurehead of a movement that has many faces and many objectives." In her view, there never should have been *a* leader in the first place. "There should have been attention to more of the women doing important work on issues that aren't necessarily sexy issues. The media wants to see [the movement] as a monolith; it isn't one and it hasn't ever been one."

Other heads of women's organizations, however, were troubled by the leadership vacuum. Many pointed to the fragmentation of groups with overlapping agendas and resources that were not "well coordinated."[98] Kate Kendell put it bluntly: "I don't know who is driving this train. If the answer is no one, there's the problem. There's more that could be done with episodic outbursts." The problem is long-standing. For decades, feminists' aversion to hierarchical leadership has prevented the movement from speaking with one voice on women's issues.[99]

A related issue involves the leadership of established women's organizations, which highlights generational tensions within the women's movement. As author Susan Faludi notes, "alongside the battle of the sexes rages the battle of the ages."[100] Younger women have faulted movement leaders for protecting their turf, and being unwilling to mentor successors or to share power.[101] The inability to cede authority has, in Faludi's view, "crippled women's progress." "Time to pass the torch, ladies," advises Valenti.[102] A few national leaders have agreed. One is the former president of NARAL Pro-Choice America, part of what she described as the "post-menopausal middle," who in 2012 stepped aside to make room for a younger leader.[103] But most others have resisted. Robin Morgan, in an open letter to younger women, urged them to build their own base of support, not to expect one to be handed to them. "Speaking for myself, I'm hanging on to my torch, thank you. Get your own damn torch."[104]

More attention clearly needs to focus on leadership succession as well as coordination and inclusion. Funders could encourage coalitions rather than competition for the limited pool of resources available, and could provide greater support for initiatives that unite organizations around a common agenda. Looking for ways to bridge differences across race, class, and sexual orientation should be a priority. More outreach to men is also critical. It is, as Linda Basch noted, "difficult to get them into the room" in both a literal and metaphorical sense. So, too, Joan Williams points out that "so much of the focus has been on women that what we've been missing is that the glue that holds the system together is gender pressure on men." Their conformity to traditional notions of masculinity has reinforced dysfunctional patterns of male aggression and unequal family responsibilities. During the second wave of the women's movement, a common slogan was that "women's liberation is men's liberation too." More men need to believe it.

Women's groups also need to be more effective and proactive in pursuing their own agendas, rather than reacting to agendas set by the Right. Too often, said Smeal, "we don't ask for what is needed. We ask for what we can win." To advance its objectives, the movement must also do better in getting both facts and stories into public debate. Women need a better sense of the stakes concerning economic security, sexual violence, reproductive services, and work/family conflicts. Hearing women like Lilly Ledbetter on equal pay or Sandra Fluke on contraception can help drive home the human costs of policy failures. More outreach to younger women and more efforts to organize at the grassroots level are equally essential. Above all, noted Noreen Farrell of Equal Rights Advocates, "we need to be having this conversation with each other on a regular basis." This book seeks to encourage that conversation and to widen its audience.

On the first day of his administration, President Obama signed into law the Lilly Ledbetter Fair Pay Restoration Act, which extended the deadline for filing Equal Pay Act claims. In underscoring the new Act's importance, he observed that "equal pay isn't just an economic issue for millions of Americans and their families, it's a question of who we are—and whether we're truly living up to our fundamental ideals."[105] The same is true of other issues involving gender equity. Women deserve no less.

2

Employment

Almost a half century has passed since the enactment of equal employment legislation, but the position of women remains far from equal. There has, to be sure, been substantial progress. Women's labor force participation has nearly doubled; they now earn 60 percent of college degrees; their representation in elite professions has grown from under 5 percent to over 30; the wage gap has been cut almost in half; and the percentage of wives out-earning husbands has grown from 4 to nearly 40 percent.[1] Yet we remain far from *The End of Men*, as Hanna Rosin's widely publicized book would have it. The labor force remains gender-segregated and gender-stratified, with women still overrepresented at the bottom and underrepresented at the top. As a former NOW vice president notes, women have been "climbing the corporate ladder for thirty years now. We're well groomed for the executive suites but too often we're all dressed up with no place to go."[2] Only 4 percent of CEOs of Fortune 1000 companies are women, and they earn only about half of what their male counterparts earn.[3]

The discussion that follows explores the reasons behind persistent and pervasive workplace inequalities and the limits of law in addressing them. A central focus is the unconscious gender stereotypes that affect evaluations of women's performance, as well as the responses that might be most effective at the individual, organizational, and policy level.

Unequal Pay

As we approach the fiftieth anniversary of equal pay legislation, we remain a considerable distance from accomplishing its promise. Full-time female workers' annual earnings are 77 percent of men's, a gap that has not substantially changed since 2001.[4] This gap also understates the full extent of inequality, since most women do not work full-time for all of their working lives. One study that looked at total earnings for all women over a 15-year period found a

gender gap of 62 percent.[5] Although women's increasing representation among
college graduates should help to equalize wage rates over the long term, their
underrepresentation in high-paying specialties is slowing progress. Women
account for only 30 percent of math and science degrees and 20 percent of
engineering degrees.[6] Moreover, the pace of progress has slowed considerably
since the 1990s, and at current rates of change it would take another half century to achieve equal pay rates for full-time workers.[7]

Pay gaps are unevenly distributed across different groups of women. For
those with a bachelor's degree or higher, the disparities increase. Female physicians earn only 71 percent of the incomes of their male counterparts, and
female managers earn only 72 percent.[8] In law, over the course of a 40-year
career, women lose an average of $1.5 million.[9] Even in female-dominated pro-
fessions, like nursing and administrative assistance, men earn more.[10] Women
of color have a smaller gap when compared with men of their own race, and a
larger gap when compared with white men. Hispanic women earned just 59
percent as much as non-Hispanic white men, and African American women
earned just 68 percent.[11]

Pay disparities are attributable to multiple factors. Conservative commentators typically stress women's different choices, capabilities, and career
commitment.[12] Women work fewer hours per week and are more likely to take
significant time out of the labor force for family reasons. Only 61 percent of
women are working compared with 75 percent of men, and they are almost
three times as likely to work part-time.[13] Women who take time out from the
paid labor force suffer long-term wage penalties.[14] In one study of lawyers, a
single year out of the workforce correlated with a third lower chance of making
partner and an earnings reduction of 38 percent.[15]

A second reason for the gender gap is that women are clustered in lower-
earning occupations, and lower-paying sectors within occupations. Just over
40 percent of working women are employed in traditionally female occupations, including administrative support, nursing, and childcare; fewer than 5
percent of men work in these jobs. Forty-four percent of working men are in
traditionally male occupations, such as computer programming and firefight-
ing, compared with fewer than 6 percent of women.[16] Women are, for example,
just 13 percent of engineers but 95 percent of secretaries and administrative
assistants.[17] In law, they are 86 percent of paralegals but only 33 percent of lawyers and 16 percent of partners in large firms.[18] Conservative commentators
often argue that women gravitate toward occupations with better working conditions and greater flexibility, and pay a price in lower wages.[19] But the extent
of this tendency is in dispute. Women are also twice as likely as men to cluster
in occupations with poverty-level wages and few offsetting benefits, such as
waitress and house cleaner.[20] Sex segregation in employment both reflects and

reinforces traditional gender roles; "women's work" tends to involve caretaking and support functions rather than better paying manual, technical, and leadership positions. For example, only 2 percent of women have a degree in a high tech field.[21]

Similarly situated women also earn less than men. Even after controlling for a broad range of factors, such as education, experience, training, and family characteristics, most research finds that a gender gap in earnings persists, typically on the order of at least 8–12 percent.[22] At every educational level and in every occupational field, women have lower earnings. Even female dishwashers earn significantly less than males.[23] As women's share in an occupation rises, wages fall.[24] Studies that compare the equivalence of jobs in terms of employee qualifications and the nature of the work also find that female-dominated occupations tend to pay less than male occupations. So, for example, an Illinois job evaluation study determined that registered nurses deserved higher pay than electricians, but found that the nurses were paid $11,000 less. In California, children's social workers (who were predominantly women) were found to deserve salaries equal to those of male probation officers, but were in fact paid $20,000 less.[25]

The devaluation of "women's work" is reflected in a large array of research as well as public opinion surveys.[26] In a 2013 *NBC News/Wall Street Journal* poll, three-quarters of Americans agreed that "generally speaking, women are paid less than men for doing the same kind of work."[27] That perception is reflected not only in the job comparisons noted above but also in experimental settings. There, women pay themselves substantially less than men pay themselves for the same work.[28] Employers similarly believe that men's work is more skilled and justifies higher pay.[29] Research on merit rewards find that women who receive the same performance evaluations as men receive lower salary increases.[30] In one study of transgendered employees, the earnings of women who became men increased slightly, while men who became women experienced a decline in pay of nearly one-third.[31]

Unconscious Bias and Gender Stereotypes

One reason for the undervaluation of women's work involves unconscious gender bias. Social cognition research demonstrates that people unconsciously categorize others according to stereotypical roles and attributes.[32] Stereotypes about the typical man and woman have remained largely unchanged since the 1970s, even when they are out of step with what people believe is appropriate.[33] Unconscious bias persists even among those who are consciously committed to egalitarian principles.

Despite recent progress, women, particularly racial and ethnic minorities, often lack the presumption of competence enjoyed by white men, and need to work harder to achieve the same results.[34] Male achievements are more likely to be attributed to individual capabilities, such as intelligence, drive, and commitment, and female achievements are more often attributed to external factors such as chance or special treatment, a pattern that social scientists label "he's skilled, she's lucky."[35] In a recent example, a *New York Times* profile of Sheryl Sandberg wrote that "[e]veryone agrees she is wickedly smart. But she has also been lucky."[36] A related problem involves "micro-inequities," such as the tendency to reattribute women's comments to men.[37] Ann-Marie Slaughter describes this as the "butterfly syndrome, in which a woman makes a remark that stays on the table like a caterpillar until a man says the same thing and it becomes a butterfly."[38] The more subjective the standard for assessing qualifications, the harder it is to detect such biases. Because subjective criteria are particularly significant in upper-level positions, women are particularly likely to be underrepresented at the top.

Gender stereotypes are especially strong when women's representation does not exceed token levels, and too few counterexamples are present to challenge conventional assumptions.[39] The force of these stereotypes is apparent in experimental situations where male and female performance is objectively equal, but women are held to higher standards, and their competence is rated lower.[40] Résumés are rated more favorably when they carry male rather than female names.[41] Subjects who receive identical employee profiles except for gender give men higher bonuses even if meritocratic values are stressed.[42] In contexts where men can be promoted based on potential, women must demonstrate performance.[43] Researchers also find that standards for evaluation can shift in ways that advantage men. When a male candidate outranks a female in education, education is the criteria judged most important. When he outranks her in experience but not education, evaluators place primary importance on experience.[44] A telling case study in the extent of unconscious bias involves orchestra auditions. When screens were introduced so that the sex of musicians was no longer visible, women's representation in symphony orchestras dramatically increased.[45]

One 2012 study points up the persistence of such bias even among highly educated professionals. Yale researchers asked science faculty at six prominent universities to evaluate an applicant for a lab manager's position. All of the professors received the same description of the applicant, but in half the descriptions the applicant was named John, and in half the applicant was named Jennifer. John was rated more competent and more likely to be hired and mentored than Jennifer, and received a recommended starting salary averaging about $4,000 higher.[46]

The devaluation of women's competence is particularly pronounced for mothers. Having children makes people judge women, but not men, as less qualified and less available to meet workplace responsibilities, and pregnant women are viewed as ill-suited for most jobs, particularly managerial positions.[47] In an experimental setting, a consultant who was described as a mother was rated as less competent than a consultant described as not having children.[48] In a related study, subjects evaluated job applications from equally qualified candidates who differed only in parental status. Mothers were penalized on a host of measures, including perceived competence, commitment, and starting salary. Fathers suffered no penalty and on some measures benefited from parental status.[49] When résumés were sent to employers who advertised job openings, mothers were called back half as often as childless women.[50] Even when mothers were described as exceptional performers, they were rated lower in likability, which produced lower rates of job offers.[51] Motherhood is now a greater predictor of wage inequality than gender in the United States.[52] It is revealing that the term "working father" is rarely used and carries none of the adverse connotations of "working mother." Wharton Business School's Monica McGrath recalls an example of motherhood bias in an executive management meeting that she attended as a consultant. One of the managers present suggested that the woman who was the most qualified candidate for an overseas post probably would not want the job because she had two small children. Meeting participants "actually thought that this was a sensitive remark."[53]

Other cognitive biases compound the force of these traditional stereotypes. Individuals tend to notice and recall information that confirms their prior assumptions; they filter out information that contradicts those assumptions.[54] For example, when employers assume that a working mother is unlikely to be fully committed to her career, they more easily remember the times when she left early than the times when she stayed late. So, too, those who assume that women of color are beneficiaries of preferential treatment, not merit-based selection, will recall their errors more readily than their insights. Similar distortions stem from what psychologists label a "just world" bias.[55] People want to believe that individuals generally get what they deserve and deserve what they get. To sustain this belief, people will adjust their evaluations of performance to match observed outcomes. If women, particularly women of color, are underrepresented in positions of prominence, the most psychologically convenient explanation is that they lack the necessary qualifications or commitment. These perceptions can, in turn, prevent women from getting assignments that would demonstrate their capabilities, and a cycle of self-fulfilling predictions is established.[56] A further problem involves in-group favoritism. Extensive research documents the preferences that individuals feel for members of their own groups. Loyalty, cooperation, favorable evaluations, and the allocation of rewards and opportunities all increase in likelihood for in-group members.[57] Women in traditionally male-dominated settings often remain out of the loop of advice and professional development opportunities.[58] For example, in law, 62 percent of women of color and 60 percent of white women, but only 4 percent of white men, felt excluded from formal and informal networking opportunities.[59]

The result is to prevent outsiders from developing the "social capital" and sponsorship necessary for success in many workplace contexts.[60] The relatively small number of women who are in positions of power often lack the time or the leverage to mentor all who may hope to join them. Differences across race, ethnicity, and culture compound the problem. Men who would like to fill the gaps in mentoring often lack the capacity to do so or are worried about the appearance of forming close relationships with women.[61] In one *Harvard Business Review* study, close to two-thirds of men acknowledged that they avoided sponsoring junior women out of concern that their attention would appear inappropriate.[62] Women of color experience particular difficulties of isolation and exclusion.[63] Individuals in senior positions are sometimes reluctant to provide any negative feedback for fear of seeming racist.[64]

Although a growing number of organizations are attempting to respond by establishing formal mentoring programs and women's networks, not all programs are well designed to level the playing field. Part of the problem is the lack of incentives. Mentoring activities are not well rewarded in many workplaces, and programs that randomly assign relationships may make such activities less pleasant or comfortable, particularly when cross-gender or cross-racial pairings are involved.[65] Too many individuals end up with mentors with whom they have little in common. Senior men often report discomfort or inadequacy in discussing "women's issues," and minorities express reluctance to raise diversity-related concerns with those who lack personal experience or empathy.[66] The result is a "culture of caution," in which individuals in organizations that need change feel unable to talk openly about how to achieve it.[67]

Mentoring program structures present further difficulties. Often they do not specify the frequency of meetings, set goals for the relationship, or require evaluation.[68] Instead, they rely on a "call me if you need anything" approach, which leaves too many women reluctant to become a burden.[69] Other programs demand a minimum amount of contact and "reams of reports," which may make the relationship seem like just one more pro forma administrative obligation.[70] Not surprisingly, informal mentoring relationships confer more overall benefits than formal ones, and too few programs have been structured in ways to narrow the gap.[71]

The Leadership Gap

Unconscious bias also helps account for women's underrepresentation in positions of greatest power, status, and income. Objective qualifications alone cannot account for that gender gap.[72] Indeed, in one survey of more than 7,000 executives, women rated higher than men on 12 of 16 traits identified as important to leadership effectiveness.[73] Yet those capabilities are not matched by leadership opportunities. In academia, women account for a majority of college graduates, but only about a quarter of full professors and university presidents.[74] In law, women are almost half of law school graduates but only 16 percent of the partners of major firms, and 20 percent of Fortune 500 general counsel and law school deans.[75] In management, women constitute one-third of MBA graduates, but less than 4 percent of Fortune 1000 CEOs and 14 percent of officers.[76] At current rates of change, it would take over two and a half centuries to achieve parity in the executive suite.[77]

Part of the problem may be internally driven. As Sheryl Sandberg has famously put it, women do not "lean in."[78] Some research finds that women are slightly less interested in advancing to the next leadership level than men, and as Chapter 3 indicates, women are also more likely to opt out of the workforce for family reasons.[79] But another part of the problem involves the social penalties for women who do lean in. Workplace practices and cultural biases diminish women's sense of themselves as leaders and create barriers to leadership positions.[80] Social science research has long documented the mismatch between qualities associated with leadership and qualities associated with women. Most of the traits that people attribute to leaders are masculine: dominance, authority, assertiveness. These do not seem attractive in women.[81] People rate men higher on leadership ability and more readily accept men as leaders.[82] In studies where people see a man seated at the head of a table for a meeting, they typically assume that he is the leader. They do not make the same assumption when a woman is in that seat.[83]

Women are subject to double standards and double binds. What is assertive in a man seems abrasive in a woman, and female employees risk seeming too feminine or not feminine enough. On the one hand, they may appear too "soft"—unable or unwilling to make the tough calls required in positions of greatest influence. On the other hand, those who mimic the "male model" are often viewed as strident and overly aggressive.[84] Carly Fiorina, former CEO of Hewlett Packard, recalls repeatedly being referred to as either a "bimbo or a bitch."[85] Executive coaches have discovered a market niche in "feminizing" "bully broads."[86] Aggressive women are viewed as unpleasant to work with or for, and have difficulty enlisting respect, support, and cooperation from

coworkers.[87] Attitudes toward self-promotion reflect a related mismatch between stereotypes associated with leadership and with femininity. Women
are expected to be nurturing, not self-serving, and entrepreneurial behaviors
viewed as appropriate in men are often viewed as distasteful in women.[88] As
comedian Margo Thomas quipped, "A man has to be [like Red-baiting Sena-
tor] Joe McCarthy in order to be called ruthless. All a woman needs to do is
put you on hold."[89] An overview of more than a hundred studies finds that
women are rated lower as leaders when they adopt authoritative masculine
styles, particularly when the evaluators are men, or when the role is one typically occupied by men.[90] Female job candidates are also penalized more than
men for attempting to negotiate favorable treatment, and female supervisors
are disliked more than men for giving negative feedback.[91] In effect, women
face trade-offs that men do not. Aspiring female leaders can be liked but not
respected, or respected but not liked, in settings that may require individuals
to be both in order to succeed.

A telling Columbia Business School experiment illustrated the problem.
It gave participants a case study about a leading venture capitalist with out-
standing networking skills. Half the participants were told that the individual
was Howard Roizen; the other half were told that she was Heidi Roizen. The
participants rated the entrepreneurs as equally competent but found Howard
more likable, genuine, and kind, and Heidi more aggressive, self-promoting,
and power hungry.[92] Even the most accomplished women are subject to such
stereotypes. Brooksley Born, now widely acclaimed for her efforts to regulate
high-risk derivatives while chair of the Commodity Futures Commission,
was dismissed at the time as "strident" and a "lightweight wacko."[93] During
her 2008 bid for the presidency, Hillary Clinton was widely criticized as
too aggressive and abrasive, and "Hillary nutcrackers" sold as an evocative
novelty item.[94]

Many women also internalize these stereotypes, which creates a psychological glass ceiling. On average, women appear less willing to engage in self-
promoting or assertive behaviors.[95] As one comprehensive overview of gender
in negotiations puts it, "Women don't ask." Numerous studies have found that
women report lower pay aspirations than men and negotiate less assertively
on their own behalf.[96] In one survey of Carnegie Mellon graduates, men were
eight times more likely to negotiate a starting salary than women.[97] An unwillingness to seem too "pushy" or "difficult," and an undervaluation of their
own worth, often deters women from bargaining effectively for what they want
or need.[98] In workplace settings, the result is that female employees are less
likely than their male colleagues to gain the assignments, positions, and support necessary to advance. In law, 44 percent of women of color, compared
with 39 percent of white women and only 2 percent of white men, reported

being passed over for desirable work assignments.[99] In managerial contexts, decision-makers generally see women as more suited for jobs involving human relations than those involving responsibilities for profits and losses, or other important high-visibility projects.[100] The absence of such job experience is the major reason given by CEOs in the United States and abroad for women's underrepresentation in leadership positions.[101] Yet that is not the only factor, as a recent Catalyst study demonstrated. In its survey of over 4,000 MBAs, even controlling for relevant factors, men started at higher levels than women and received higher pay and more promotions.[102]

Women also lack access to the support and sponsorship available to their male colleagues. Even CEOs acknowledge the persistence of an unintended and unconscious "old boy's network."[103] Surveys of upper-level American managers find that almost half of women of color and close to a third of white women cite a lack of influential mentors as a major barrier to advancement.[104]

The Limits of Law

Part of women's progress in reducing the gender gap in positions and earnings is attributable to the passage of equal employment opportunity legislation. The Equal Pay Act requires equal pay for jobs that are equal in skill effort and responsibility.[105] Title VII of the Civil Rights Act bars discrimination on the basis of sex as well as other prohibited characteristics, including race, religion, and national origin. States generally have comparable statutes. But as ways of equalizing women's treatment in the workplace, all are subject to significant limitations.

Employment discrimination cases are, as research demonstrates, "exceedingly difficult to win."[106] They are also difficult to settle on terms that adequately compensate for the costs of complaining. Fewer than 20 percent of sex and race discrimination claims filed with the federal Equal Opportunity Commission result in outcomes favorable to the complainant.[107] Settlements in these cases are generally modest and only 2 percent of complaints result in victory at trial.[108] About 40 percent of trial wins are only temporary; they are reversed on appeal.[109]

These sobering statistics do not include the vast number of cases in which individuals may have been subject to discrimination but lacked the information or inclination to challenge it. Often, the subjectivity of standards and lack of transparency surrounding hiring, promotion, and compensation decisions, particularly in upper-level employment, make it difficult for individuals to know that they have been subject to bias. In a case that captured public attention, Lilly Ledbetter was the only female production supervisor at a Goodyear plant. For many years she was subject to pay discrimination; her salary was 40 percent lower than that of the lowest paid male supervisor, but she learned of the disparity only through an anonymous memo upon her retirement.[110] Such lack of transparency regarding compensation is common.[111] Some employers, including Goodyear, even ban discussions of salary. As Justice Ginsburg noted in Ledbetter, most pay discrimination is "hidden from sight."[112] After the Supreme Court threw out Ledbetter's claim as untimely, Congress passed the Lilly Ledbetter Fair Pay Act, which extended the statute of limitations but failed to deal with the underlying problem of lack of information about comparable salaries.

So, too, unless and until they assume the costs of suing, women may have little idea of whether they have a suit worth bringing. Not all differential treatment leaves a paper trail, and colleagues with corroborating evidence are often reluctant to expose it for fear of jeopardizing their own positions.[113] Women who are denied promotions seldom know until after discovery in litigation how closely their files resemble those of successful candidates.

Ann Hopkins, an accountant who successfully sued Price Waterhouse, had no specific proof that "sexist comments" had been made about her or any other woman at the firm at the time she filed her complaint.[114] Yet the record ultimately revealed ample evidence of gender stereotypes. Female accountants were faulted for being "curt," "brusque," or "women's libber[s]," or for acting like "one of the boys."[115] Hopkins herself was characterized as someone who "overcompensated for being a woman" by acting "macho" and "overbearing" and who needed "a course at charm school."[116] But several male accountants who achieved partnership had been similarly described as "abrasive," "overbearing," and "cocky."[117] No one suggested charm school for them.

Nancy Ezold, the associate who unsuccessfully sued the Philadelphia law firm of Wolf, Block, Schorr & Solis-Cohen for discrimination after being denied a partnership, learned only after discovery how her performance evaluations stacked up against those of male colleagues who were promoted. She had been characterized as "assertive," preoccupied with "women's issues," and lacking in analytic ability.[118] Yet some of the male associates who became partners had been described as "not real smart," "overly confrontational," "very lazy," and "more sizzle than steak."[119]

Even individuals with convincing evidence of bias are often reluctant to challenge it. One national survey of a thousand workers found that a third of those who reported experiencing unfair treatment did nothing. Only a fifth filed an internal complaint, and only 3 percent took legal action.[120] Other studies find similarly low rates of legal responses.[121] The reluctance to bring formal claims reflects multiple factors. Social science research finds that most individuals deny being subject to discrimination that they know affects their group.[122] People do not like to present themselves as victims; it undermines their sense of control and self-esteem, and involves the unpleasantness of identifying a perpetrator.[123] Other individuals are deterred by the high cost of legal action and the low probability of winning any substantial judgment.[124] The price of a discrimination case can be substantial, both in financial and psychological terms. Ann Hopkins's legal fees for her seven-year suit against Price Waterhouse totaled over $800,000 in current dollars.[125] Even if a plaintiff finds an attorney to take the case on a contingent fee basis, the out-of-pocket litigation expenses can be steep; Nancy Ezold estimated hers at over $225,000.[126]

Plaintiffs also are putting their professional lives on trial, and the profiles that emerge are seldom entirely flattering. In listening to defense witnesses, Hopkins "felt as if my personality were being dissected like a diseased frog in the biology lab."[127] In some cases, complainants' foibles become fodder for the national press. The lead plaintiff who sued Sullivan and Cromwell in one of the nation's first law firm sex discrimination cases had her "mediocre law school grades" aired in the *Wall Street Journal*.[128] A gay associate who sued the same firm three decades later found himself described in *New York Magazine* as a "smarmy," "paranoid kid with a persecution complex."[129] In Ezold's case, a Wolf Block senior partner told *American Lawyer* that she was like the proverbial "ugly girl. Everybody says she has a great personality. It turns out that [Nancy] didn't even have a great personality."[130]

Many women also resist bringing claims of discrimination out of concerns of reputation and blacklisting. Complaining about bias carries the risk of making individuals seem too "aggressive," "confrontational," or "oversensitive"; they may be typecast as a "troublemaker or 'bitch.'"[131] Lilly Ledbetter was berated for "ruining peoples' careers by causing such a mess." According to a supervisor, "You're bad for morale. . . ."[132] Advice from colleagues is generally to "let bygones be bygones," "let it lie, [d]on't make waves, just move on."[133] Those who ignore that advice frequently experience informal retaliation and blacklisting; "professional suicide" is a common description.[134] Studies consistently find that formal complaints of discrimination generally result in worse outcomes than less assertive responses.[135] As one plaintiff's lawyer put it, a "mid- or high-level attorney who decide[s] to sue in connection with a cutback or firing may never eat lunch in [this] town again."[136] Reported cases often bear this out. Hopkins found herself "a pariah in the Big Eight" accounting firms.[137] Darlene Jesperson, a bartender who unsuccessfully sued Harrah's Casino for gender discrimination in its grooming code, failed to find another a job. As her attorney noted, for anyone in the entertainment industry, "Reno is a small town."[138]

A further limitation in legal protections involves their restrictive scope. The Equal Pay Act requires that jobs be substantially similar, and as noted earlier, the segregated nature of the labor market means that most women are in different occupations or hold different job titles than men. Courts and legislatures have consistently resisted efforts to broaden protections along the lines available in many other countries, which mandate comparable treatment for jobs of comparable worth. Moreover, in upper-level employment, even when men and women hold the same job titles, successful equal pay claims are relatively rare.[139] The burden is on the plaintiff to show that she was paid less than a similarly situated male employee. The employer then has a defense if it can show that the wage differential was the result of seniority or merit or "any other factor other than sex." Cases are difficult to establish because courts accept even small differences in duties or responsibilities as proof that women's jobs are not substantially equal to those held by men, or because courts adopt a permissive view of excuses based on factors other than sex.

The difficulties of proving that positions are equal emerged clearly in a case in which the plaintiff was a vice president in charge of her employer's largest division. Her managerial functions were the same as other division heads. Although she was among those with the greatest seniority, she was paid significantly less than the other male vice presidents, and less than several other men who were neither division heads nor corporate officers. The court, however, accepted the company's justification that the other male vice presidents performed work that was "substantially more important to the operation of the company."[140] In another similar case, the trial court dismissed out of hand the notion that a female vice president was underpaid in comparison with other male vice presidents because each was in charge of "different aspects of Defendant's operation; these are not assembly line workers. . . ."[141]

The lack of protection from bias based on sexual orientation is another limitation of gender discrimination law. In a survey of likely 2012 voters by the Center for American Progress, almost three-quarters supported protecting gay and transgender people from workplace discrimination.[142] Yet proposed federal legislation prohibiting such bias, such as the Employment Non-Discrimination Act, has been unsuccessful in Congress for the last decade. Only a minority of states protect gay and lesbian employees from workplace discrimination, and over half the population live in areas without such protection.[143] Although increasing numbers of Fortune 500 companies prohibit discrimination based on sexual orientation, these prohibitions have not been successful in eliminating the practice. Between a quarter and a half of surveyed gay and lesbian employees report experiencing discrimination at work.[144]

Another limitation in legal remedies involves evidentiary hurdles. Title VII claims take two forms. One involves disparate impact. These cases typically require a statistical showing that a facially neutral job requirement or policy disproportionately affected women and was not job- related or justified by business necessity. A second kind of claim involves disparate treatment. These cases require proof that an employer's rules or decisions intentionally treated a woman less favorably than a man because of sex. Both frameworks impose significant obstacles to recovery.

Disparate impact cases generally require a large enough labor force to establish statistically significant underrepresentation. Such proof is unavailable for upper-level positions, where the numbers are too small to establish disproportionate impact. Even where the labor force is large enough to make a statistical showing, courts have been reluctant to find liability unless the practice seems to be a cover for intentional discrimination.[145] In large class actions involving disparate impact, the plaintiffs also may have difficulty showing a common practice that justifies class-wide relief.[146] A case in point is the Supreme Court's 2011 ruling in *Wal-Mart Stores v. Dukes*.[147] There, a class of 1.5 million women workers claimed that Wal-Mart's highly subjective and discretionary system regarding pay and promotion led to systemic bias. The evidence included statistical studies showing that women had greater seniority and higher performance evaluations on average than men, but were paid significantly less. For women in salaried positions, the gap was $14,500 a year. Women were also less likely to be promoted than similarly situated men. At a time when women constituted 67 percent of hourly workers, they accounted for only 14 percent of store managers and 10 percent of district managers. The Supreme Court, however, refused to allow the case to proceed as a class action seeking relief for women as a group. In the view of a majority of Justices, the female plaintiffs had not established a common question of fact; they had not demonstrated a company-wide policy of discrimination or a common source of discrimination.

According to Justice Scalia's majority opinion, "left to their own devices most managers in *any* corporation—and surely most managers in a corporation that forbids sex discrimination—would select sex neutral, performance-based criteria for hiring and promotion that produce no actionable disparity at all."[148] He cites no authority for that proposition, and it is inconsistent with the vast range of social science research on unconscious bias summarized above. As Justice Ginsburg noted in dissent, "managers, like all humankind, may be prey to biases of which they are unaware. . . ."[149] Although the majority left open the possibility of individual suits, such litigation will face all the obstacles noted above. And the Court's ruling made it much more difficult in future cases to bring the kind of class action likely to have systemic impact. At least in Wal-Mart, despite the company's ultimate victory, the adverse publicity connected with the litigation forced a number of constructive changes while the suit was pending: an overhaul of promotion and compensation systems, and creation of a diversity office and global women's leadership council.[150] But the Court's decision creates barriers to future litigation that might produce analogous changes.

Cases alleging disparate treatment face further obstacles. Part of the problem is the mismatch between legal definitions of discrimination and the social patterns that produce it. In order to recover damages, the law forces a choice between two overly simplistic accounts of workplace decision-making. The basis for an employer's decision must be judged either biased or unbiased, its justifications sincere or fabricated. Yet in life rather than law, legitimate concerns and group prejudices are often intertwined, and bias operates at unconscious levels throughout the evaluation process, rather than simply at conscious levels at the time a decision is made.[151] Most of what produces different outcomes, particularly in upper-level employment contexts, is not a function of demonstrably discriminatory treatment that leaves a paper trail. Rather, these outcomes reflect interactions shaped by unconscious assumptions and organizational structures that "cannot be traced to the sexism [of an identifiable] bad actor."[152] Even when a plaintiff locates direct evidence of bias, courts sometimes dismiss the evidence as "stray remarks" that are insufficient to establish liability if the employer can demonstrate some legitimate reason for unfavorable treatment. So, for example, in one case a court found no discrimination where a supervisor stated, "Fucking women. I hate having fucking women in the office." In the trial court's view, this remark, though inappropriate, seemed directed at "women in general" rather than the plaintiff in particular. Her claim failed because she could not establish that gender was the only reason for her lack of promotion and training opportunities.[153]

Nor are many outcomes so blatantly unjust as to satisfy courts' demanding standard that disparities in treatment be "overwhelming," or so apparent as "virtually to jump off the page and slap you in the face."[154] Rather, the subtle, often unconscious forms of bias that constitute "second generation" discrimination problems are often beyond the reach of conventional doctrine.[155]

Strategies for Change

Individual Strategies

A threshold question is what individuals can do to improve their own workplace situations. In general, women need to ask for what they believe is fair, to develop an appropriate style, to seek challenging assignments, to forge mentoring relationships, and to cultivate a reputation for effectiveness. Succeeding in those tasks also requires attention to unconscious biases and exclusionary networks that can waylay careers.

Ask for It is the title of Linda Babcock and Sara Laschever's book on workplace negotiation; like other experts in the field, they provide a wealth of advice on how women can bargain effectively. Asking for it without adequately preparing is asking for it in a different sense. Employees should know as much as they can about how much bargaining power they have, and what constraints their employers face. Being ambitious but realistic, rehearsing their presentation, and knowing their fallback position can boost the odds of success.[156]

Women also need to strike the right balance between "too assertive" and "not assertive enough." Surveys of successful managers and professional consultants underscore the importance of developing a leadership style that fits the organization, promotes "likability," and is one that "men are comfortable with."[157] That finding is profoundly irritating to some women. At an American Bar Association Summit on Women's Leadership, many participants railed against asking women to adjust to men's needs. Why was the focus always on fixing the female? But as others pointed out, this is the world that professional women inhabit, and it is not just men who find overly authoritative or self-promoting styles off-putting. To maximize effectiveness, women need ways of projecting a decisive and forceful manner without seeming arrogant or abrasive. Experts suggest being "relentlessly pleasant" without backing down.[158] Strategies include frequently smiling, expressing appreciation and concern, invoking common interests, emphasizing others' goals as well as their own, and taking a problem-solving rather than critical stance.[159] Successful women such as former Supreme Court Justice Sandra Day O'Connor have been known for that capacity. In assessing her prospects for success in the Arizona state legislature, one political commentator noted that "Sandy . . . is a sharp gal" with a "steel-trap mind, and a large measure of common sense. . . . She [also] has a lovely smile and should use it often."[160] She did.

Formal leadership training and coaching can help in developing interpersonal styles, as well as capabilities such as risk-taking, conflict resolution, and strategic vision. Emerging leadership programs designed particularly for women or minorities provide particularly supportive settings.[161] Profiles of successful leaders can also provide instructive examples of the personal initiative that opens leadership opportunities. These are not women who worked hard, sat back, and expected to be noticed.[162] Michele Mayes, one of the nation's most prominent African American general counsels, recalls that early in her career, after receiving some encouragement from a woman mentor, she approached the chief legal officer at her company and "told him I wanted his job."[163] After the shock wore off, he worked up a list of the skills and experiences that she needed and later recruited her to follow him to his next general counsel job. She never replaced him, but with his assistance she ultimately went on to general counsel positions in other Fortune 500 companies. Women leaders in a variety of contexts similarly stress the need to raise their hands for challenging assignments and to take steps down and sideways on the status ladder in order to get the necessary experience.[164]

Setting priorities and managing time strategically are also critical skills. As Chapter 3 makes clear, establishing boundaries, delegating domestic tasks, and giving up on perfection are essential for those with substantial caregiving commitments. What employees should not sacrifice is time spent developing relationships with mentors and sponsors who can open doors and provide crucial advice.[165] To forge those relationships, women should recognize that those from whom they seek assistance are under similar pressures. The best mentoring generally goes to the best mentees, who are reasonable and focused in their needs and who make sure that the relationship is mutually beneficial.

Women who expect at some point to step out of the paid labor force should not, as Sheryl Sandberg put it, "lean out" before it is necessary. "Don't leave before you leave," she advises.[166] Women who cut back in anticipation of having children foreclose the kind of jobs to which they will want to return after having children. Those who take substantial time out of the paid labor force should find ways of keeping professionally active. Volunteer efforts, occasional paying projects, continuing education, and re-entry programs can all aid the transition back.

Women also must recognize that many of the barriers that they face demand systemic solutions. More employees need to act collectively to further equal workplace opportunities. Participating in women's networks and initiatives and lobbying for legal reforms are the kind of strategies necessary to translate personal commitments into political priorities.

Legal Reforms

One of the most often proposed legal reforms is the Paycheck Fairness Act, which would make it somewhat easier to challenge wage discrimination. The bill would require employers to show that wage disparities are job-related and are based on genuine business needs; would free employees to disclose salary information; would prohibit retaliation against individuals who raise wage parity issues; would assist women in developing negotiating skills; and would support research to understand the causes of persistent gender gaps in employment compensation.[167]

Most scholars, however, believe that more fundamental changes will be necessary to significantly affect wage disparities. One proposal is to require disclosure of wage rates.[168] Another is to pass legislation along the lines of the proposed Fair Pay Act, which would require equal pay for equivalent jobs in terms of skills, effort, responsibility, and working conditions.[169] That approach would rely on systems of job evaluation that have been widely used in both the public and private sectors since World War II.[170] A number of other nations, including Sweden, England, and Australia, require comparable compensation for jobs of comparable worth, and a European Council Directive similarly interprets the principle of equal pay under the European Council Treaty to encompass "the same work or ... work to which equal value is attributed...."[171] In this country, 20 states require comparable pay for jobs of comparable worth in the public sector, based on evaluations of job characteristics and requirements. These requirements have narrowed the gender gap in compensation by 6–8 percent without substantial negative side effects, such as increased unemployment.[172]

To address other forms of gender inequality in employment, state and federal legislatures should ban employment discrimination based on sexual orientation, and courts should adopt more realistic standards of proof that take into account structural factors and unconscious bias. Where evidence of underrepresentation or differential treatment exists, plaintiffs should not have to produce evidence of intentional discrimination. Rather, courts should focus on whether the employer has taken reasonable steps to reduce gender inequities.[173] What has the employer done to guide performance evaluation and promotion decisions, to ensure adequate mentoring for underrepresented groups, and to provide monitoring and accountability concerning equal opportunity issues?

Employers could also be encouraged or required to disclose information concerning such issues. One unintended byproduct of current liability structures is that they deter workplaces from collecting data on potential problems because such material could be useful to plaintiffs in discrimination lawsuits. The consequence is to discourage informed problem-solving that could prevent such lawsuits from arising in the first instance.[174] One way to neutralize this deterrent would be to require employers over a certain size to compile and disclose relevant information on matters such as gender differences in promotion, compensation, mentoring, and professional satisfaction. In the absence of such a requirement, courts and legislatures could create confidentiality safeguards for information that employers collected to improve internal workplace processes. The goal of such legal reforms would be to focus less on the elusive quest for intentional discrimination and to provide more encouragement for employer-generated initiatives to address unconscious bias and structural failures.

Workplace Initiatives

As a threshold matter, employers need to centralize responsibility for developing and overseeing gender equity initiatives. The most successful approaches tend to be task forces or committees with diverse and influential members who have credibility with their colleagues and a stake in the results.[175] This group's mission should be to identify problems, design responses, and monitor their effectiveness.[176] Some employers have found it helpful to have a diversity officer track the progress of women at both an individual and institutional level. These officers can intervene at the first signs of trouble for junior employees, such as negative evaluations or dead-end assignments. Officers can also identify patterns that suggest more systemic problems calling for institutional responses. A related strategy is the use of ombudspersons or issue-specific committees with diverse memberships to address equity-related concerns, such as those involving compensation and performance appraisals.[177]

Whatever oversight structures an employer chooses, one central priority should be the design of effective evaluation and rewards. Supervisors and managers need to lead by example and to be held responsible for their performance on diversity-related issues.[178] The focus should be on results. Performance appraisals that include diversity but lack significant rewards or sanctions are not likely to affect behavior. Nor are all well-intentioned behaviors likely to affect organizational performance. The most comprehensive evaluation of diversity training programs found that they had not been demonstrably effective in advancing women.[179] Part of the problem is that such programs typically focus on individual rather than institutional practices, provide no incentives to implement recommended changes, and sometimes provoke backlash among involuntary participants.[180] Additionally, although mentoring and sponsorship programs have been shown to be one of the most effective ways of enhancing career skills, satisfaction, retention, and advancement, not all programs are well designed to realize their potential.[181] As noted earlier, programs that lack adequate incentives or requirements often fall short.

Such failures point up the need for more monitoring and accountability. A truism in organizational management is that what gets measured gets done.[182] Employers need to know how policies that affect gender equity play out in practice, and individuals need to be held accountable for both their processes and results. Social science research makes clear that individuals are much more likely to perceive discrimination when they see gender disparities presented in aggregate form.[183] That requires collecting both quantitative and qualitative data on matters such as advancement, retention, compensation, satisfaction, mentoring, allocation of assignments, and work/family conflicts. For example, to assess reduced schedule policies, employers need information on utilization rates, effects on promotion, attrition, and work assignments, and satisfaction rates among part-time lawyers, clients, and colleagues. Periodic surveys, focus groups, interviews with former employees, and bottom-up evaluations of supervisors could all cast light on problems disproportionately experienced by women and minorities. A case study in success is the Deloitte Initiative for the Retention and Advancement of Women, which commissioned Catalyst to collect such information; it revealed patterns of gender bias calling for institutional responses.[184]

Monitoring can be important not only in identifying problems, but also in refining solutions. In some instances, it helps just to establish clear criteria for hiring and promotions, and to inform decision-makers that their actions are being monitored.[185] Requiring individuals to justify their conclusions can reduce bias by making them more attentive to the reasons and information supporting their decisions.[186] Monitoring can also enable employers to target their resources and experiment with innovative approaches. For example, pilot projects in group mentoring and electronic mentoring could be assessed to determine their effectiveness in expanding women's support structures.[187] So too, employers could benefit from sharing information in order to benchmark performance and to identify best practices. A model is the agreement by nine elite universities to promote gender equity in science and engineering by "monitoring data and sharing results annually."[188] Even organizations that are competitive in other respects can learn from each other on matters in which all have a stake in improving performance.

Large employers could also do more to level the playing field and to align their corporate social responsibility policies with that objective. For example, Wal-Mart, in the wake of adverse publicity surrounding the *Dukes* sex discrimination lawsuit, announced an initiative to "help empower women across its supply chain." The company pledged to spend $20 billion over the next five years on purchasing goods and services from women-owned businesses, and to establish training programs for 60,000 factory women who supply its stores. It will also help 200,000 women from low-income households in the United States and 200,000 women abroad gain job skills and access to higher education.[189] It should not take a lawsuit to prompt employers to make such proactive efforts.

Above all, supporters of workplace initiatives need to take the long view. All too often, individuals suffer "diversity fatigue" and disengage when their efforts haven't produced immediate results or the results haven't been sustained.[190] Organizational change on these issues is a difficult bumpy process, and it frequently takes a series of small wins to lay the foundations for significant reform.

In biblical times, according to Leviticus 27:3–4, women of working age were valued at 30 silver shekels and men at 50. For some 2,000 years, that ratio did not improve. Then, in the space of a single generation, the gender gap was halved. And what distinguishes this current era is the perception that the ratio needs further change. The challenge remaining is to restructure legal doctrine and organizational policies to promote such progress and to ensure equal opportunity not just in principle, but also in practice.

3

Work and Family

When I was a law student interviewing for summer jobs in the 1970s, a partner told me that there was no "woman problem" at his firm. One of the firm's 60-some partners was a woman, and she had no difficulties reconciling her personal and professional life. The preceding year she had given birth on a Friday and was back in the office the following Monday. These "faster than a speeding bullet" maternity leaves have not entirely vanished. Marissa Mayer, who was appointed CEO of Yahoo while pregnant, recently received front-page news coverage for taking only two weeks of maternity leave and committing to "work throughout it."[1] Mayer's experience is in some sense emblematic of our partial progress. Three decades ago, hiring a female head of a Fortune 500 company, much less a pregnant one, would have been almost unthinkable. But the pressures she faces to shortchange her family, and the criticism she confronts for appearing to do so, suggest progress yet to be made.

"Marriage has changed more in the past 30 years than in the previous 3,000," claims historian Stephanie Coontz.[2] Yet today's workplace structures have not kept pace with family patterns and workforce needs. In 1960, only 20 percent of mothers were in the paid labor force. Today, two-thirds are working outside the home, and 70 percent of children are in households in which every adult is employed.[3] Four-fifths of workers live with family members and have some day- to-day caregiving responsibilities.[4] Over 40 percent of families are headed by a single parent, usually a woman, a number that has more than doubled in the last three decades.[5] Yet policies governing parental leaves, childcare, and working schedules have done far too little to adapt to employees' domestic responsibilities. The United States has the least family-friendly policies in the developed world. It stands alone with only seven other countries—Suriname, Liberia, Palau, Papua New Guinea, Nauru, Samoa, and Tonga—in not guaranteeing paid maternity leave.[6] And American policies concerning childcare, part-time work, and flexible schedules are far less progressive than those of Western Europe. As a consequence, among 22 economically advanced countries, the United States ranks 17 in women's labor force participation.[7] And a majority of American workers report conflict in balancing work, family, and personal life.[8]

So, too, men's family patterns have not kept pace with women's workplace obligations. Although fathers' share of domestic responsibilities has increased dramatically over the last half century, mothers continue to shoulder disproportionate work in the home and to pay a price in the world outside it. The disparities are especially pronounced among those who opt out of the labor force. About a quarter of married women with children under 15 are stay-at-home mothers; fewer than 1 percent of married men with children under 15 are stay-at-home fathers.[9] Over half of working mothers, compared to only 16 percent of working fathers, have taken a significant amount of time off from work to care for a child or family member.[10] Yet as Gloria Steinem has noted, "women will never be equal outside the home until men are equal inside the home."[11]

What Women Want: What Women "Choose"

In her *New Yorker* essay on "Confessions of a Juggler," comedian Tina Fey described the topic of working mothers as a "tap dance recital in a minefield."[12] Ann-Marie Slaughter brought that point home with a 2011 cover story in the *Atlantic* provocatively titled "Why Women Still Can't Have It All."[13] The piece set off a firestorm of commentary, although the basic storyline was frustratingly familiar. Slaughter's personal difficulties in reconciling a high-pressure position in the State Department with a family life in Princeton were one more variation on a well-worn theme: professional women find that high-powered jobs aren't worth the price. For some women, this article resonated with their experience and validated their choices. For others, it set their teeth on edge and reaffirmed traditional gender stereotypes.

Many feminists found the article irritating on several levels. First was the polemical packaging. The cover photo, which pictured an infant in a briefcase, falls into the genre that Jessica Valenti's blog post labeled "[s]ad white babies with mean feminist mothers." The title, "Why Women Still Can't Have It All," was a misleading message even about Slaughter's own experience. By her own account, both before and after her State Department position, she was a professor at Princeton, carrying a full academic load, giving 40–50 speeches a year, writing a book, and raising two sons. If headline writers at the *Atlantic* think "having it all" means more than that, then they are living in a different world than most of us.

A second problem was that the article focused on the experience of a small group of women, which offered a misleading portrait of most women's preferences. More women report wanting to add hours (24 percent) than to subtract hours (9 percent).[14] Ten percent of women heading families are unemployed, and the number is higher among blacks (13 percent) and Hispanics (11 percent).[15] Just 37 percent of women workers want a job with more responsibilities.[16]

A third issue with Slaughter's analysis was its subtext: the implicit message that the noble thing for mothers to do is to sacrifice a "dream" job when its hours are long and a child is going through a troubled patch. For fathers, Slaughter suggested that the trade-off is different. Men, who are not subject to what she labels the "maternal imperative," seem more likely to "choose job at a cost to their family." Women, by contrast, "seem more likely to choose their family at a cost to their job."[17]

As a descriptive matter, however, Slaughter highlights a common dilemma and a common response. Particularly in the professions, hourly requirements have increased dramatically over the last two decades, and what has not changed is the number of hours in the day. Nor are extended hours an exclusive problem of privileged women. Low-wage workers in the garment, restaurant, domestic, home care, janitorial, and similar industries are routinely subjected to mandatory and sometimes uncompensated overtime.[18] Among dual-career couples, the gender pattern that Slaughter describes is clearly apparent. An American Bar Foundation study found that women lawyers were seven times more likely than men to be working part-time or to be out of the labor force, primarily due to childcare.[19] The problem with Slaughter's article is that it does not acknowledge these gender disparities as a problem, rooted in unequal and by no means "imperative" divisions of domestic roles. Slaughter leaves unexamined the double standard of parenting that subjects working mothers but not fathers to the expectation that they should curtail paid work to care for family members. Heidi Hartmann, director of the Institute for Women's Policy Research, notes that "[n]obody says a man isn't a good father if he doesn't stay home with his kids."[20]

Neither does Slaughter acknowledge the extent to which her situation is atypical. She notes in passing that many women have it worse, but doesn't dwell on the implications of her article for those who cannot afford to leave a demanding job, or cannot find a flexible one like her position at Princeton, which provides control over her own schedule. Fewer than 8 percent of women hold high-level traditionally masculine jobs of the sort that Slaughter describes.[21] And non-professional women are much less likely to have access to flexible schedules than those in professional positions.[22] For women who are unable to choose reduced or adjustable schedules, Slaughter's article provides precious little by way of strategies for getting policy changes that she recognizes as necessary.

The problems of excessive or inflexible work demands are widely shared. Over the past three decades, the number of employees who report work–family conflict has increased from a third to almost a half, and slightly more men (49 percent) than women (43 percent) report a problem.[23] High levels of work–family conflict are related to a variety of problems, including depression, anxiety, poor health, employment attrition, and substance abuse.[24]

Women's roles are in increasing tension with workplace realities. Forty percent of women are now the primary or sole breadwinner for their family.[25] Although fewer than a fifth of women think that women should return to their traditional role as full-time homemaker supported by a full-time bread-winner, and only 16 percent of families conform to this pattern, the workplace remains structured around this model.[26] What law professor Joan Williams labels the "ideal worker" remains the full-time, fully committed employee who has no competing responsibilities.[27] This is not a model that fits women's needs during a significant part of their working lives. Slaughter's analysis resonated with many readers because it reflected their preferences. Only a third of women believe that it is ideal for mothers with young children to work full-time; 47 percent think part-time work is ideal; and 20 percent believe no work outside the home is best.[28] Among women who consider themselves career-oriented, about half want to stay home when their children are preschool age and most of the remainder prefer to work part-time. Nearly three-quarters would like to work full-time when their children are school age, but these women frequently need adjustments in their schedules to make that possible.[29] Two-thirds of high achieving women consider flexibility in scheduling important, and it ranks higher than compensation in their priorities.[30] Two-thirds also would prefer more free time to a larger paycheck.[31] Women's preferences are significantly different from men's. Among parents who work full-time, 61 percent of women (compared with only 19 percent of men) would like to work part-time.[32] A majority of Americans think that children are better off if their mothers are home; only 8 percent think that about fathers.[33]

Opting Out

Among women, a common response to work–family conflict is to drop out of the labor force. About a third of mothers with children under 18 do not hold paying jobs, and about a quarter are out of the labor market for a protracted period.[34] Among stay-at-home mothers, 60 percent are poor, and the remainder are split between middle income and professional/managerial women.[35] In a study by the Center for Work-Life Policy of some 3,000 high-achieving

American women and men (defined as those with graduate or professional degrees or high honors undergraduate degrees), nearly four in 10 women reported leaving the workforce voluntarily at some point over their careers. The same proportion reported sometimes choosing a job with lesser compensation and fewer responsibilities than they were qualified to assume in order to accommodate family responsibilities. By contrast, only one in 10 men left the workforce primarily for family-related reasons.[36] Although other surveys find some variation in the number of women who opt out to accommodate domestic obligations, all of these studies find substantial gender differences.[37] Almost 20 percent of women with graduate or professional degrees are not in the labor force, compared with only 5 percent of similarly credentialed men. One in three women with MBAs are not working full-time, compared with one in 20 men.[38]

When researchers ask full-time mothers why they stayed home, only a minority, typically 20–30 percent, cite "a long-standing desire to be a stay-at-home mom" or the "pull" of family. Other common reasons are the cost of childcare, the needs of elderly parents or a disabled family member, the expectations and unavailability of a partner, and the lack of meaningful part-time options, manageable hours, or a flexible schedule.[39] In Pamela Stone's study of high-achieving professional women who opted out of the workforce for some period of time, 90 percent gave work-related reasons, although the gendered division of family responsibilities also played a role. Over half mentioned the husband as a key influence on their decision to quit.[40] In couples where both partners were working long hours, women came to realize that something had to change and their spouse "wasn't going to."[41] At times, this made economic sense, given the differences in earning power between members of dual-earning couples. As one stay-at-home professional put it, there was "too much money at stake" for her husband to reduce his schedule.[42] In other cases, it was a matter of preferences; men couldn't imagine cutting back, and women felt that "*Somebody's* got to be there."[43] For working class women, the problems were often the absence of control over working schedules, inadequate sick days or parental leaves, and salaries too low to cover child- or elder-care costs.[44] As Stone concludes, for most women, opting out is "a response to obstacles to the integration of work and family, not a choice among viable options."[45]

It is, moreover, a response that comes at a significant price. Jack Welch, former CEO of General Electric, put it starkly. "There's no such thing as work–life balance. There are work–life choices, and you make them, and they have consequences." Women who take time off can still "have a nice career," but their chances of reaching the top decline.[46]

Achieving a "nice career" is also more difficult than anticipated for many women who opt out. While the imagery associated with opting out is of easy entrance and exit, the research suggests otherwise. In the Center for Work-Life Policy's survey of some 2,400 high achieving professionals, 89 percent wanted eventually to resume their careers, but a quarter of those who wished to return to work were unable to do so, and only 40 percent found full-time professional jobs.[47] As Sylvia Ann Hewlett and Carolyn Luce summarized the findings, "off ramps are around every curve on the road, but once a woman has taken one, on ramps are few and far between and extremely costly." Although the average woman in their study was out of the labor force only a little over two years, she lost an average of almost a fifth of her earning power, and those who were out three or more years lost over a third.[48] Other research finds even higher losses.[49]

Workforce interruptions are particularly costly in the event of a spouse's death, disability, unemployment, or desire for divorce. Terry Martin Hekker is a case in point. Some three decades ago, she received considerable attention when, at the height of the women's movement, she published a *New York Times* op-ed defending her decision to become a stay-at-home mother. The column morphed into a well-publicized book and brought her brief celebrity as a spokesperson for the joys of full-time motherhood. When, on her fortieth wedding anniversary, her husband asked for a divorce, a new reality set in. The judge who awarded her inadequate alimony for only four years suggested that, at age 67, she seek job training. After exhausting her savings, she became eligible for food stamps. As she noted, not only was she unprepared for the divorce itself, she was "utterly lacking in skills to deal with the brutal aftermath."[50] Her circumstances are by no means uncommon, but many stay-at-home mothers seem unwilling to envision themselves in similar circumstances. As a Harvard law school graduate who gave up her life as a litigator insisted, "I always have my degree and I don't feel like I've made a choice I can't recover from. I just don't worry about [divorce]. . . ."[51] Even in couples whose marriages remain intact, women experience other costs of economic dependency. Their partners generally assume fewer domestic responsibilities and greater decision-making authority.[52] Wives who give up paid work report being suddenly transformed from "being their husband's intellectual equals into the one member of their partnership uniquely endowed with gifts for laundry or cooking and cleaning."[53] Even when they return to the workforce, these traditional patterns often remain intact.[54] Women without their own income also have fewer options in cases of domestic violence or abuse.

Compared with women who work full-time, full-time homemakers experience higher rates of depression, anxiety, and health difficulties.[55] Workforce participation serves as a buffer for the stresses of family life and supplies a sense of identity, as well as social contacts and relationships. Although substantial volunteer work can sometimes provide similar support, many opt-out home-makers opt in to lifestyles of "intensive mothering" that are difficult to recon-cile with substantial competing commitments.[56]

Part-Time Work and Flexible Schedules

Reducing or adjusting schedules is a common alternative to opting out. Flex-ible time schedules include a variety of arrangements. Some involve giving employees control over when they start and end their workday, as long as they work a required number of hours and are present during a specified core period. Another option is the flexible week, which allows employees to work six short days or four long days. Job-sharing and part-time schedules encom-pass a diverse set of accommodations in terms of working hours and location. Some employees combine these options with telecommuting, which enables them to spend a specified period working from home. A few workplaces have abandoned the time clock completely and have switched to a "results only work environment"(ROWE), which measures performance based on whether deadlines are met and objectives are achieved.[57] Such arrangements carry benefits for both employers and employees. As noted earlier, most mothers prefer part-time or flexible schedules to leaving the labor force, and research finds that reduced schedules are associated with various measures of maternal and family well-being.[58] Employers benefit from higher worker sat-isfaction and lower attrition.[59] In one recent study of high potential workers, the majority believed that flexible work arrangements are very or extremely important.[60]

Yet such benefits often go unrealized. In one study, less than a third of em-ployers felt that they had established options for employees to work in a flex-ible manner to a "moderate or great extent."[61] In other studies, over 40 percent of employees reported that they had no control or very little in scheduling their work, and only 4 percent had access to telecommuting options.[62] Some em-ployers also impose requirements of extended hours or mandatory overtime that are incompatible with substantial caregiving commitments. Americans work the longest hours of any industrialized country.[63]

As Joan Williams notes, the conflict between workplace demands and workforce needs is widely shared, but expresses itself differently in different class contexts. Upper-level professional and managerial employees often have some control and flexibility over their schedules, but their overall hours are excessive. Middle-income workers have more manageable hours, but little con-trol or flexibility over their schedules. Low-wage workers not only lack control and flexibility, they also face pressure to work overtime, reduced schedules, rotating shifts, or second jobs. Most working-class and lower-income employees lack adequate leave policies and childcare; many remain, in Williams's phrase, "one sick child away from being fired."[64] Workers with the greatest needs for family support are least likely to find it available.

Professional and managerial employees generally inhabit what sociologist Lous Coser termed "greedy institutions," where extended hours serve as a measure of commitment.[65] Technology tethers employees to their offices and blurs the boundaries between home and work. Expectations of total availability—that employees will be figuratively, if not literally, "sleeping with their smart phones"—have led to widespread dissatisfaction with work–family balance.[66] In law, for example, only a fifth of female lawyers are satisfied with the allocation of time between their personal and professional lives.[67] As one young attorney responded to a bar survey about her quality of life, "This is not a life."[68] Another noted that her sweatshop schedule made it "difficult to have a cat, much less a family."[69] Such schedules undermine productivity as well as satisfaction. A vast literature documents the adverse effects of sleep deprivation and prolonged stress on health and performance.[70] Personal and caregiving relationships can also suffer, as Arlie Hochschild reports in *The Outsourced Life*: busy professionals can now "rent a friend," hire a "potty trainer," or pay an expert to "relate" to their dog.[71]

For working-class and lower-income employees, the problems arise from mandatory overtime, rigid and shifting schedules, lack of proportional pay, and the absence of paid personal or sick leave or other basic protections.[72] Two-thirds of low-income workers are not entitled to flexible schedules, and one study found that about half lack access to the flexibility they need.[73] For these employees, the law imposes few protections; many lose jobs when emergency childcare falls through, or caregiving needs can't be aligned with unilateral schedule changes.[74] A representative case involves Joanna Upton, a single mother with a young son, who was fired because she could not meet the escalating overtime obligations that her supervisor demanded. For several months she was expected to work every Saturday and until 9 or 10 every night. Yet the Massachusetts Supreme Court held that she had no cause of action for wrongful discharge when she declined such overtime.[75] According to the court, no public policy was "directly served by an employee's refusal to work long hours."[76] Nor does the law "mandate work–life balance," as the trial judge declared in a recent discrimination suit brought by the US Equal Employment Opportunity Commission (EEOC).[77]

For many low-wage employees, the primary problem is not lack of part-time options, but involuntary ones. In retailing alone, a third of employees would prefer full-time schedules but are in jobs where employers find it cheaper to rely on part-time workers who lack benefits or wage rates comparable to full-time employees, and whose schedules can be tied to fluctuating labor demands.[78] Such shifting schedules wreak havoc on those with childcare responsibilities or second jobs.

Even workers who are willing and able to limit their schedules encounter problems, often beyond what their employers recognize. Only 9 percent of company representatives, compared with over a third of surveyed employees, report that the use of flexible schedules or leave policies will jeopardize chances for advancement.[79] In Pamela Stone's study of professional women who opted out, two-thirds had tried part-time or flexible arrangements first, but had found them unworkable.[80] Those women are not atypical. For example, in law, although 90 percent of firms offer part-time policies, only 4 percent of lawyers actually use them.[81] Lack of respect, interesting work, and truly manageable hours make policies that look fine on paper break down in practice.[82] One supervisor expressed common views with uncommon candor to a subordinate who had asked for a reduced schedule: "If you want to be a lawyer, be a lawyer. If you want to be a mother, be a mother."[83] Many part time professionals experience "schedule creep": hours escalate, pay is not proportional, and "unexpected emergencies" become expected events.[84] Other women find that requests for schedule accommodation raise concerns about competence and commitment.[85] Some women find that "flexibility stigma," with its accompanying loss of status and authority, is disabling. As one marketing executive explained, "I decided to quit, and this was a really, really big deal. . . . Because I never envisioned myself not working. I just felt like I would become a nobody if I quit. Well I was a sort of a nobody working too. So it was sort of, 'Which nobody do you want to be?'"[86]

Reduced or flexible schedules can also be sabotaged by coworkers who resent having to adjust or compensate for an employee's unavailability.[87] Colleagues who are already working extended hours become understandably irritated if forced to assume additional responsibilities because employers fail to arrange adequate backup coverage. Deborah Epstein, founder of Flex Time Lawyers, has found that backlash is common and the "reason that a lot of work–life balance programs fail."[88] So, too, supervisors with productivity concerns may resist flexible arrangements, and women often feel powerless to insist on accommodation.[89] One woman who needed to telecommute a few times a month when her husband traveled found herself without that option when a new boss arbitrarily vetoed the arrangement. Although none of her clients or colleagues had objected, she was afraid "that if I make any more fuss over this I will jeopardize my bonus and job security." But she found it irritating that the company was ranked among Working Mother's Top 100 companies because its policies looked good on paper.[90]

Low-wage earning women have even less access to flexibility, and then are penalized for using what little they have. Many women report that their employers don't believe them when they miss work due to a child's illness.[91] One mother whose male supervisor wouldn't believe that she had to take her son to the hospital questioned whether "anyone would have thought *he* was lying" if he had called in with a sick child.[92] Other women are treated as irresponsible when they refuse to stay overtime or attempt to use their own sick leave to care for a child.[93] Only half of single mothers report having supervisors willing to accommodate their family needs.[94]

Although both sexes experience resistance to flexible or reduced schedules, the dynamics play out somewhat differently for men and women. Female employees are less likely than men to obtain choices in workplace schedules because they are less likely to occupy upper-level positions where flexibility is more tolerated.[95] However, men may feel less entitled than women to ask for schedule adjustments for family reasons and suffer more flexibility stigma if they do. Although the vast majority of men who work 50- and 60-hour workweeks would prefer to work significantly less, most do not feel that they can cut back without significant costs.[96] Men worry that they will be perceived as lacking commitment to their careers and as insufficiently deserving of advancement.[97]

The research available finds that their perceptions are well-founded. Caregiving is inconsistent with the male breadwinner image and often brands men as "gender deviants."[98] A persistent assumption is that "real men don't work at home."[99] Those who are absent or on reduced schedules due to work–family conflicts have lower performance ratings, and those who take time off suffer even greater financial and promotion costs than their female colleagues.[100] One study found that caregiving fathers experienced the highest rates of mistreatment at work among men, such as being excluded, ignored, insulted, humiliated, or bullied.[101] Another study found long-term wage penalties for men who reduced work hours for family reasons.[102] The result is that far fewer men than women feel able to opt for part-time schedules.[103] In one large scale survey of 12,000 employees, 20 percent of women but only 2 percent of men reported that they had taken time off from work or reduced their work hours due to family reasons.[104] On average, after birth of a child, men increase their hours at work while women decrease theirs.[105]

Family and Medical Leaves

For many employees, the ability to take short-term leaves to care for themselves or a sick relative makes a substantial difference in their ability to stay in the labor force. In recognition of that fact, Congress in 1993 passed the land-mark Family and Medical Leave Act (FMLA). It provides workers covered by the legislation with 12 weeks of unpaid leave to care for a new child or a sick family member, or to recover from their own illnesses. However, the Act includes only employees who work at an establishment with at least 50 em-ployees, who have worked there for at least one year, and who have averaged at least 24 hours a week. The result of these exemptions is to leave about 40 percent of the workforce uncovered.[106] Paid leave is even less available. Only a few states and cities mandate some form of paid family or sick leave, financed by employers or by employee payroll taxes. As a consequence, only 12 percent of employees have access to paid family leave.[107] Nearly 40 percent of private sector employees have no paid sick leave.[108] Those most likely to lack protec-tion are low-income workers who need it most.[109] Only 4 percent of these em-ployees have access to paid family leave, and almost three-quarters lack sick days that they can use to care for a family member who is ill.[110] A quarter of mothers report sending a sick child to school or day care because they could not miss work.[111] Many employers are unsympathetic to the "sick kid excuse." As one retail store supervisor put it, "Don't have them if you can't take care of them."[112]

Even in California, where workers can receive partial pay coverage, only a third took full advantage of the parental leave available. Fear of sacrificing advancement opportunities was the main deterrent.[113] Here again, employ-ees' concerns are not without foundation. Women who return from maternity leave often find their competence and commitment questioned. One attorney, frustrated by the menial work provided on her return, noted, "I had a baby, not a lobotomy."[114]

Although the FMLA is gender-neutral, men are less likely than women to take parental leave.[115] In California, only 29 percent of those who take leave are fathers.[116] Men are also half as likely as women to miss work because of care of a sick child or a breakdown in childcare.[117] Part of the reason is that employ-ers who are reluctant to accommodate mothers are generally even more resis-tant to fathers. Management practices discourage significant paternity leave regardless of official policy.[118]

To be sure, the situation has improved in recent years. The traditional expec-tation, as one law firm administrator put it, was that men with newborn infants would "just go to the hospital, take a look and come right back to work."[119] Now men feel entitled to take some time off, but the average is less than a week.[120] One manager of a large advertising agency indicated that its current practice was for fathers to take two or three days off. "So we sort of say, 'Please be with your family. You need to be with your family now,' knowing that we'll get that time back from them one way or another." Because the average hospital stay after delivery of a child is only one to two days, the company "felt that three days was suitable."[121] Even in companies that offer generous paternity leaves, men are often reluctant to take advantage of them for fear of losing face.[122]

Both social science research and discrimination lawsuits document workplace resistance to involved fathers. In one experimental study, men who asked for a leave to care for a sick child or parents experienced penalties such as demotion, layoffs, reduced pay or responsibilities, and reduced chances of recommendations for promotion, raises, training, or desirable projects.[123] In another similar study, men who took a leave for a child or parent's illness were evaluated more negatively than women who took leave for the same reason.[124] Discrimination lawsuits report attitudes like that of a supervisor who told a father that he should "decide what was more important: his job or his family."[125] A state trooper who wanted leave to care for a newborn while his wife was disabled from delivery complications was told that she had to be "in a coma or dead" for him to qualify as a primary caregiver.[126] An equipment operator whose stepdaughter had cancer was questioned as to why her "real father or her mother [wasn't] taking her to doctor's appointments and the hospital instead of him," and was told that he was "taking advantage of the company."[127] A police officer who took the leave to which he was entitled under the FMLA received a note offering "[c]ongratulations for taking the most time off for having a baby and not actually having the baby."[128] Such discrimination against men also penalizes women. It encourages unequal divisions of family responsibilities in the home, which limits opportunities in the world outside it. As Joan Williams puts it, "if nothing is changing for men, nothing is changing for women."[129]

Discrimination Based on Pregnancy and Family Responsibilities

As the preceding examples suggest, discrimination based on caregiving obligations remains all too common. In recognition of that fact, the EEOC made clear in 2007 that discrimination based on a worker's family caregiving responsibilities or stereotypes about them violated federal law. Two years later the EEOC followed up with best practices for employers to avoid such discrimination.[130] Over the past decade, family responsibility litigation has mushroomed, growing 400 percent between 1999 and 2009, and it provides an important although incomplete strategy to address work–family conflict.[131]

Employees have often been subjected to biases based on "role incongruity": the assumption that they cannot be both a good mother and a good worker.[132] Few supervisors are as explicit as the general counsel of a legal department who said about working mothers, "I don't see how you can do either job well."[133]

However, reported cases reveal that employees were fired on similar assumptions. The biases begin with pregnancy. Job terminations have included a receptionist at a day spa who would reportedly become less "agile," a restaurant worker who was "moody," a waitress who was "too fat," and a bartender who would be unable "to keep up."[134] The supervisor of an administrative assistant told her that her pregnancy was an "inconvenience" to her coworkers and that she wouldn't want to return to work after childbirth.[135] Some workers have been advised that they could "solve [their] problem" with an abortion.[136] Others have been fired after a miscarriage, or delivery complications that required an extension of leave.[137] In some instances, employees who are pregnant or are taking temporary leave are set up to fail by being given unrealistic performance targets.[138] In other cases, they are transferred, demoted, or denied promotions.[139] One supervisor told a female employee that he would not consider her for a promotion because the job would require too much travel for a mother.[140] Another woman lost a chance for advancement on the assumption that she wouldn't want to relocate her family.[141] A school psychologist was informed that she was not a suitable candidate for tenure because she "had little ones at home."[142]

Pregnant employees have also been denied modest accommodations such as seating, more frequent breaks, or exemptions from heavy lifting.[143] Except in a few states, the law provides no remedy. The federal Pregnancy Discrimination Act requires only that workers be treated "the same" as other employees who are "similar in their ability or inability to work."[144] For workers not covered by the federal Family Medical Leave Act, the law also falls short. A typical case involves a Pennsylvania restaurant employee who had worked at an inn for four years before becoming pregnant. In her ninth month, when she asked for two weeks off for childbirth, she was told that if she failed to show up for work on a busy Saturday night, she would lose her job. She didn't work that night, was fired, and was told that there were no jobs open when she sought to be rehired.[145] Similar results can happen when employers have "no fault absenteeism" policies, which penalize employees each time they miss work, regardless of whether the absence reflected a true emergency.[146] Although such policies, along with refusals to provide reasonable accommodation, increase attrition, many employers seem willing to absorb those costs in an economy where low-skilled workers are easily replaced.

Child and Elder Care

Although we typically associate the "traditional" family with full-time mothers, that tradition is relatively recent. For most of recorded history, wealthy women employed nurses, nannies, and governesses; less privileged women worked and often relied on others, including older children, to care for the young.[147] Today, the traditional model is out of step with workforce patterns, but America's childcare system has not caught up. Almost two-thirds of mothers with children under age six are in the labor force.[148] Sixty percent of children under age five, and almost half of infants, are in non-parental care.[149] Despite these patterns, America has no comprehensive system of government-supported childcare. Instead, parents are left to cobble together their own arrangements, which vary considerably in quality and reliability.

For young children, four patterns are common. The first is unpaid care by relatives, friends, and neighbors. The second is care by paid babysitters or nannies. Neither involves any quality control or state oversight, and the expertise of caregivers is highly uneven. Problems also arise if the caregiver becomes sick or is otherwise unavailable. A third arrangement involves family childcare, which providers typically offer from their own homes to a small group of children. Quality is again highly variable and subject to lax oversight, which prompted Yale professor Edward Zigler to label it a "cosmic crapshoot."[150] A fourth model is care in a non-residential center. It is the most reliable and regulated, but also tends to be the most expensive, and is not always available for infants or for parents working non-standard shifts.

For older children, some form of after-school and summer care is necessary when parents are working full-time, but affordable and age-appropriate programs are in short supply.[151] Six million children are left home alone on a regular basis, which creates increased risks of teen pregnancy, substance abuse, sexually transmitted disease, and criminal behavior.[152] Families that cannot afford adequate care often end up with tag-team shifts, in which spouses work opposite shifts to cover childcare while the other parent is at work. Tag teaming puts an obvious strain on marriages, and such parents divorce at three to six times the national average.[153]

This patchwork of programs raises problems of access and affordability. The kind of care most families want is expensive and often elusive.[154] The primary form of government assistance comes through nonrefundable tax credits, but their value is minimal in relation to the costs of quality providers.[155] The annual cost of center-based care is generally more than the annual in-state tuition at public universities.[156] The price for infants and toddlers is even higher, with the average annual cost of center-based care consuming almost 20 percent of average take-home pay.[157] Only 5 percent of workers have access to employer-sponsored childcare, and only 3 percent receive employer caregiving subsidies.[158] Although children of low-income workers, including those on welfare, are in theory entitled to government assistance, only about 14 percent receive it due to inadequate funding.[159] Three-fifths of states also have some prekindergarten programs for at-risk children, tied to parental income, English learning needs, or related criteria, but most programs meet only a small part of the need and many are only part-time.[160] Forty percent of low-income workers pay for child-care themselves, and nearly a third of them spend at least half of their income to do so.[161] The challenges for low-income parents are compounded because two-thirds are caring for children with either learning disabilities or chronic health conditions.[162]

An equally fundamental problem involves quality. In the most comprehensive survey, only 10–15 percent of centers provided care that experts rated as good.[163] Quality of care is fair or poor in a majority of childcare settings.[164] Only a third of infants are in settings that meet recommended standards.[165] The basic difficulty is that neither regulatory structures nor market conditions encourage well-trained service providers. In-home care and, in most states, family care are exempt from government oversight.[166] This nation requires licensing to be a manicurist, but only a dozen states require any training to care for children.[167] Federal childcare grants prescribe only minimum health and safety standards for center care, and states have not always complied with even these weak rules.[168] Because most purchasers lack reliable quality information and focus instead on cost and convenience (proximity and hours of operation), most providers have inadequate incentives to invest in better services. Caregiving, which is an almost exclusively female occupation, has extremely low pay and high turnover, and little opportunity for advancement. Many providers work at or below poverty levels, and could earn more as parking lot attendants watching cars than as caregivers watching children.[169]

This nation pays an enormous price for the failures of its childcare system. As the Institute for a Competitive Workforce notes, "the research is clear. Early learning opportunities for children from birth to age five have great impact on a child's development and build a strong foundation for learning and success later in life."[170] The quality of early care has a lasting effect on children's cognitive, social, and psychological development.[171] Low-income children are particularly likely to benefit from early learning opportunities. Longitudinal studies find that children who receive quality childcare reap long-term advantages in terms of educational attainment and earnings.[172] Society benefits as well. Economists have estimated that the rate of return on early childhood education in terms of reduced crime and enhanced productivity is 16 percent.[173] Women, who assume the major responsibility for childcare, also benefit enormously from reliable and affordable providers. Countries with more young children in preschool programs have less gender inequality in earnings.[174]

Similar issues arise with elder care, and unmet needs will grow more acute as the population ages. The population over 65 is expected to double by 2050, and two-thirds will require some long-term care.[175] Nearly a fifth of those over the age of 65 need help with basic daily activities, and most of those who provide unpaid care for the elderly are themselves employed.[176] A study by the American Association of Retired Persons concerning disabled elderly Americans found that almost three in 10 had unmet needs that they could not afford to address.[177] The value of assistance provided to adults with disabilities living at home has been estimated at over $200 billion, of which 84 percent is unpaid.[178] Nearly half of surveyed employees have missed work due to elder care responsibilities.[179] Family members and other informal providers are the most critical source of care to the elderly, and more than two-thirds of those unpaid caregivers are women.[180]

In addition, 90 percent of those who provide paid home care are women, disproportionately women of color, and are lacking in adequate legal protections.[181] They are excluded from coverage under federal labor law, health and safety statutes, anti-discrimination legislation, and most state worker's compensation statutes. The regulations that do apply are often under-enforced because workers lack information about their rights or are undocumented and are reluctant to complain. The results are low wages, few benefits, and often unsafe or exploitative working conditions.[182] Such circumstances make it difficult to attract a well-qualified workforce.[183]

Here again, the nation pays a substantial price for failure to address unmet caregiving needs. Lack of adequate assistance puts the elderly at increased risk of death, more severe disability, hospitalization, and institutionalization.[184] And society pays part of the cost of the resulting medical expenditures.

The Gendered Division of Household Work

The last half century has seen a significant shift in domestic roles; women's housework has decreased by over an hour a day, while men's has increased by a half hour.[185] We are a considerable distance from the day when, as one corporate executive recalls, "My awareness of childcare was that you picked up the babysitter, you took the babysitter home, and sometimes you couldn't get a baby sitter."[186] However, women continue to assume a disproportionate share of caregiving. They spend over twice as much time on care of children as men, and over three times as much time on household tasks as men.[187] In virtually all families, women do the invisible managerial work of scheduling medical appointments, arranging family and childcare activities, and ensuring transportation.[188] And they provide more than twice as much elder care, not only for their own parents but for their in-laws as well.[189] Women often compensate for the extra workload at home by cutting back on labor force participation. However, according to a recent Pew survey, men average about three hours more of leisure time per week.[190] Unequal distributions of work lead to greater marital conflict, lower levels of marital satisfaction, and higher risks of divorce and depression.[191] A survey of over 200 adults placed sharing household chores as the third most important factor in a successful marriage, behind faithfulness and a satisfying sexual relationship.[192]

Although the allocation of work varies somewhat by race, in general, the greater the relative economic power of men, the less housework they do.[193] When relative earnings are more equal, so are divisions of domestic labor.[194] Women who lack financial independence tend to have less power and more household responsibilities.[195] If women stay home, men cut back their domestic contributions. As some full-time homemakers note, their husbands are "never around," or if around, "simply stop . . . helping."[196] Even in dual-earning families, couples often fall into conventional gender patterns. A father in Phyllis Moen and Patricia Roehling's study explained: "We do a lot of sharing but we have more of what you may call traditional roles. I certainly help out with kids and help with the inside chores but I am basically the outside guy and she is basically the inside person. I do all the traditionally male chores, . . . mow the lawn, shovel the driveway, . . . and that stuff, and she does the meals and all that stuff."[197] Notably, male "stuff" tends to be less time-consuming, more episodic and enjoyable, and easier to schedule at a convenient time than routine female "stuff," like cooking and cleaning.[198] In dual earner couples, mothers of young children are three times more likely than fathers to report interrupted sleep patterns.[199] As the father in Moen's and Roehling's study acknowledged, his wife "does a lot of housework and the organization of maintaining schedules. I am guilty of that. I don't take initiative, but I help out."[200] Men's abdication of household management leaves women as the "designated worriers."[201]

Part of the reason for unequal gender burdens is the resilience of gender stereotypes. Fathers who engage in large amounts of childcare experience exclusion, humiliation, or insults.[202] Men who sacrifice work for family responsibilities report that colleagues consider them "pussy whipped" and "slackers."[203] As one father explained to a task force on work–life balance, it may be "okay [for men] to say that they would like to spend more time with the kids, but it's not okay to do it, except once in a while."[204] In her study of the gender dynamics in high-tech work cultures of Silicon Valley, Marianne Cooper documents men's perception of what is necessary to be a successful "go-to guy."[205] One man explained, "guys try to out macho each other. . . . There's a lot of 'see how many hours I can work.' Other comments included 'He's a real man, he works 90 hours a week. He's a slacker; he works 50 hours a week.'"[206] Another survey participant observed that those who "conspicuously overwork are guys and I think it's usually for the benefit of other guys."[207] None of those Cooper interviewed questioned the necessity of these demands. "I hate to sound like a capitalist," said one man, "but at the end of the day, the company shareholders aren't holding shares so that we can have flexible lives."[208] Another was equally resigned: "I signed up for this life, right . . . and you pay a price if you have a high paying job, or a career you are really fulfilled by. So my price is that I'm exhausted."[209]

Another price is time with family. A vice president who was on the road for a month at a time was identified as someone who "doesn't have two kids and a wife, he has people that live in his house."[210] One man described the "emotionally downsized" life of the CEO of his former start-up company.

> [He] had three kids—4, 7, and 10—nice kids but he never ever sees them. . . . He does triple sevens. He works from 7:00 in the morning until 7:00 in the evening seven days a week. He thought he was [a] good father because once a year he'd go camping for a week with his kids or one day on a weekend he would take them out . . . for two hours and he'd say it's not the quantity of time, it's the quality of time.[211]

Few men see this kind of a commitment as desirable. In a recent survey of some 1,000 white-collar fathers in large corporations, fathers generally saw their role as caring for their child physically and emotionally as well as earning money to meet their child's financial needs. Most of these fathers would have liked to participate more in their children's care. The "new dad" was, as the study's subtitle put it, "caring, committed, and conflicted."[212] In another national survey, three-quarters of fathers worried that their jobs prevented them from being the kind of parents they wanted to be.[213] Yet many have felt that they cannot insist on saner schedules without an unacceptable loss in status. Derek Bok, former president of Harvard University, described a partner in a San Francisco law firm who "was always complaining about how hard he worked, so I asked 'Then why don't you just work 3/5 as hard and take 3/5 the salary?' He was tongue tied. But of course the real reason he couldn't is that then he feared he wouldn't be a 'player.'"[214]

Those fears are widely shared. In one longitudinal study of elite law school graduates, only 1 percent of fathers had worked part-time or had taken parental leave.[215] In another study, by the American Bar Foundation, male lawyers were about seven times less likely than female lawyers to be working part-time or to be out of the labor force, primarily due to childcare.[216] Part of the reason for those disparities is that the small number of fathers who opt to become full-time caregivers suffer even greater financial and promotion costs than female colleagues who make the same choice.[217]

These patterns are deeply rooted in traditional gender roles. Men with family responsibilities generally feel considerable pressure to provide their primary financial support, whatever the personal sacrifices. Yet these long-standing norms are also coming under increasing challenge. More men are expressing a desire for better work–life balance. And examples of those who insist on it are in increasingly visible supply, including at the highest levels. While president, Bill Clinton put off an important trip to Japan so he could help his daughter, then a high school junior, prepare for her midterms.[218] A *New York Times* article titled "He Breaks for Band Recitals" reported that Barack Obama was willing to leave key meetings in order to "get home for dinner by 6" or attend a school function of his daughters. According to senior advisor David Axelrod, certain functions "are sacrosanct on his schedule—kid's recitals, soccer games. . . ."[219] Yet an irony is that President Obama's commitment to a family-friendly schedule in his own life makes it harder for others to do the same. When he adjourns a meeting at 6 and resumes at 8 to allow his dinner break, other participants who don't "live over the shop" end up extending their hours in the office well past their children's bedtimes. Weekends are not necessarily better. Obama's first White House Chief of Staff, Rahm Emanuel, was known for his "Friday-afternoon mantra: 'Only two more workdays until Monday.'"[220]

Here again, workplace norms that disadvantage men also disadvantage women. By discouraging husbands from assuming an equal division of household responsibilities, such norms reinforce gender roles that are separate and by no means equal.

International Comparisons

In assessing the United States' experience on work–life issues, it is useful to compare the progress that Western Europe has made in this area. One of the starkest comparisons concerns family leave. As noted earlier, the United States stands alone among Western industrialized countries in failing to provide paid maternity leave. Of the world's 16 most economically competitive countries, all but the United States guarantee at least 14 weeks of paid leave.[221] The United States also lags behind the 81 countries that provide paid leave that can be taken by new fathers.[222] In Europe, leaves range from 5 to 42 weeks, and are financed through social insurance.[223] In the Nordic countries, parents receive roughly two-thirds of their wages while on leave, subject to caps for high earners. Some nations allow parents to take leave in increments until their child is eight; others allow parents to use some of their leave benefits to pay for childcare.[224] Over 150 countries guarantee workers paid leave to care for themselves when ill, and 76 guarantee parents a minimum amount of paid leave to care for sick children.[225] The United States stands alone among the world's top 20 advanced economies in failing to provide some form of paid sick leave.[226]

The European Union requires member countries to provide a minimum of 14 weeks of paid maternity leave.[227] Practices concerning paternity leave vary among member countries. According to one global survey, 37 countries grant fathers a right to at least three months of paid leave at the birth of a child.[228] The United Kingdom, for example, guarantees couples a year of leave, half of which can be taken by fathers.[229] France provides 16 weeks for mothers and two for fathers. In addition, either parent can take a leave of up to a year any time before the child is three, and also can receive a monthly childrearing stipend.[230] Sweden, which has pioneered efforts toward gender equality in the use of leaves, reserves two of 13 months exclusively for fathers. Under this "use it or lose it" system, 85 percent of fathers take some leave.[231] Iceland has the most egalitarian system, which gives each parent three months of paid leave plus an additional three months that they can divide in any way they choose.[232] After that policy was implemented, the percent of leave days taken by fathers jumped from 3 to 35 percent.[233] Generous leave provisions are not, however, panaceas. An unintended consequence of such policies is that more women stay out of the labor force for extended periods, which leads to greater income inequality and underrepresentation at leadership levels.

European nations also provide far more generous childcare assistance than the United States. Much of Scandinavia guarantees childcare beginning at birth or by the child's first birthday.[234] Denmark provides center-based care for children of working parents from birth to age six. Staff have college educations and receive teachers' wages; the government picks up about four-fifths of the costs. The system is decentralized, and each center has a management board on which parents constitute the majority.[235] In the rest of Western Europe, children generally get care at slightly older ages, typically around three or four years old. Parents bear only a portion of the costs, usually on a sliding scale.[236] Childcare workers are required to have significant training, and the quality of care is high.

The French system, which is often presented as a model for American reform efforts, is voluntary, but almost 100 percent of parents enroll their children. Schools are available for two- to six-year-olds between 8:30 a.m. and 4:30 p.m., with care available at modest cost before and after school. Additional resources are provided to geographic areas with high concentrations of low-income children, with funding for reduced class size and special teacher training. Because the schools are seen as part of the government's early education system, staff have masters' degrees and are paid teachers' wages.[237] For children under two, regional and municipal governments offer a variety of generously subsidized options, including centers and family home care run by licensed providers.[238] The average cost of this high-quality system is only a few hundred dollars more per year per child than the average cost of an American childcare center. The difference is that the government foots the bill, and spends approximately 1 percent of its gross domestic product (GDP) on early childhood education; by comparison, the United States spends only about a fifth of 1 percent of its GDP.[239]

Europe also provides models for reduced and flexible schedules. A European Council directive prohibits treating part-time workers less favorably than full-time workers in terms of pay, benefits, training, and opportunities for advancement.[240] Some nations also require employers to provide part-time opportunities for employees who request them.[241] A review of policies in 20 European nations found that 12 of 20 provide for a gradual return to work after the birth or adoption of a child. In effect, parents can extend job-protected leaves by working part-time. Eight countries allow parents of young children to work part-time or to receive alternative work schedules after they have returned to work. Eight countries also allow parents to refuse schedules that conflict with childcare responsibilities.[242] In 2003, the United Kingdom introduced the first statute giving employees the "right to request" alternative work arrangements, and requiring employers to make a good-faith response to such requests within a given time frame.[243] Other countries have more generous guarantees of alternative work schedules unless implementation would cause serious organizational costs. In these nations, an employee can appeal to an external body to test whether the employer's concerns are significant enough to justify a refusal. The United Kingdom provides no such appeal.[244] However, the large majority of requests are granted, and the law has occasioned little additional cost.[245] The same is true in countries that provide a right to alternative arrangements, and only a tiny number of employer refusals end up in court. In those cases, employers prevail if they present a legitimate business reason for refusing the proposed arrangement, such as inadequate demand for labor during the hours requested.[246] On the whole, the statutes have produced meaningful change, although their influence has been limited by employees' reluctance to request alternative arrangements when they anticipate a hostile response, particularly in upper-level jobs.

An Agenda for Reform

Public opinion polls reveal widespread public support for work–family policies including paid family leave, childcare, and universal prekindergarten education.[247] In one recent poll, nearly 8 out 10 Americans thought that the government should expand access to high quality affordable childcare for working adults.[248] A wealth of research also documents the benefits to employers from such policies in reducing absenteeism and attrition, and increasing loyalty, commitment, productivity, and job satisfaction.[249] But whether these initiatives are always cost-effective for employers, and who should pay for them if they are not, are subject to debate. As one expert noted, "Everyone believes a child deserves early childhood education, but as soon as you ask them to take out their wallet, they balk."[250] That has to change. Better support for working families is critical to the equality of women, the welfare of children, and the productivity of future generations. The basic elements of a reform strategy are clear. Americans need access to more adequate family leaves, child- and elder-care, protection from pregnancy discrimination, and flexible work arrangements.

Models for an effective leave policy are readily available here and abroad. California, Rhode Island, and New Jersey have a paid leave insurance program, financed by employee contributions. Typically, such programs provide most workers with six weeks of partial salary during leaves to care for a new child or a sick family member or domestic partner.[251] An evaluation of California's program found that the vast majority of employers experienced no problems in implementing the statute, and some experienced cost-savings.[252] Several other states have programs that allow women to use temporary disability insurance to cover a portion of lost wages for leave during and immediately after pregnancy. A few states permit workers to use a portion of their own sick days to care for sick children, parents, spouses, or domestic partners. These leave provisions yield multiple benefits. Women who take leave are more likely to return to work and are less likely to rely on public assistance than those who do not.[253] Workers with paid parental leave are also more likely to return to their employer than those who lack such leave.[254] When men take advantage of leave policies, they contribute more of their fair share of housework.[255]

An obvious reform strategy would be to extend the federal Family and Medical Leave Act to include a broader group of workers and to create a national insurance program modeled on successful state programs. Such an initiative could guarantee partial pay, financed by employee contributions, for six weeks for employees to address a serious health condition, or to care for a sick family member or a new child. Alternatively, the federal government could provide grants for states to set up their own insurance schemes along the lines of California's legislation. For short-term leaves, the federal government could set a national paid sick day standard, guaranteeing workers the right to earn paid sick time.[256] Although such proposals have triggered opposition from the business lobby, and elected leaders have been reluctant to support new taxes, it is worth reconsidering those objections.[257] The proposal suggested here would cost about $1.50 a week for median wage earner.[258] Almost every other nation has determined that such a price is well worth paying, and it is by no means clear why the United States should remain an exception.

Government support for childcare makes similar sense. The idea has extended roots. In 1971, a bipartisan group of senators succeeded in getting both houses of Congress to pass a Comprehensive Child Development Act. That legislation would have established both early education and after-school programs financed by parents, based on a sliding scale of contributions pegged to a family's income bracket. President Nixon vetoed the measure on grounds that it "would commit the vast moral authority of the National Government to the side of communal approaches to child rearing."[259] Today that characterization seems quaint. "Communal" center-based care is now the norm for millions of children. And as experts note, "mothers are a large and varied group." It is unrealistic to assume that they are all equally and uniquely willing and able to be their child's only caregiver.[260]

What would a well-run childcare system look like? Experts generally recommend that high-quality programs be universally accessible in diverse settings that give parents choice.[261] Preschools should be available through the public school system, with extended coverage available at a sliding fee based on parental income. After-school programs for older children should be offered on a similar basis. A more modest proposal would be to guarantee quality care to low-income children, who need assistance most, and to provide other families with access to preschool, infant, and toddler programs on a sliding fee basis.[262] In the long run, giving middle class constituencies a personal stake in reform is the surest way to realize a system that delivers both reliability and quality.

So, too, workers who are providing elder care deserve more government and employer assistance. At a minimum, they should have access to partially paid leave to care for sick parents or in-laws. More support services should be available to the disabled elderly to enable them to function independently in community settings, and more protections should be available for elder-care workers.

More protections should also be extended to pregnant workers. Proposed legislation such as the Pregnant Workers Fairness Act would be a step in the right direction.[263] The bill would require employers to make reasonable accommodations for employees facing limitations from pregnancy or childbirth.[264] In the absence of federal legislation, more states and cities could follow the lead of jurisdictions that have enacted pregnancy protection requirements.[265] More vigorous federal enforcement of pregnancy discrimination laws would also help to safeguard employee rights and to change cultural expectations about women, work, and caregiving.

A final set of reform strategies should focus on flexible scheduling options. One promising Congressional proposal is the Flexibility for Working Families Act. Modeled on the United Kingdom's Right to Request law, the Act gives employees the right to apply to their employer for changes in the hours, times, and location of work, and protects them from retaliation for making re-quests.[266] Notably, the statute applies to all employees, not just caregivers, and is designed to reduce the risks and stigma that often accompany alternative scheduling requests. Under the terms of the Act, the employer must meet with the employee within 14 days of the request and then must provide a written decision that explains the reason for any denial. As noted earlier, experience from the United Kingdom suggests that such legislation promotes a more de-liberative decision-making process and greater accommodation of employees' needs without undue expense to employers. Another possible model is the fed-eral Alternative Work Schedules Act, which allows federal agency employees to use flexible or compressed work schedules as long as they do not interfere with efficient operations. The effect has been to increase recruitment, reten-tion, and productivity.[267] Similar results have been documented in the private sector.[268]

For many hourly workers, however, the problem is not simply the absence of flexibility but also the lack of dependability and consistency in the amount and scheduling of work. For these employees, who are often on involuntary and shifting part-time schedules, the solutions may require more regulation and incentives for employers to offer proportional benefits and more predictable working hours. One such incentive might be provided through a national cer-tification system for family-friendly employers.[269] Such an evaluation system could be useful to employees in selecting employers, and to government agen-cies in allocating grants and contracts.

This is not a modest agenda. But neither was social security when initially introduced. What was once dismissed as a radical or utopian concept is now thoroughly entrenched and widely popular. The same is likely to be true of the kind of work–family initiatives proposed here. Employees who are strug-gling to balance competing responsibilities deserve policies that are part of the solution.

4

Sex and Marriage

Just as women are seeking to redesign work to accommodate family, they are also seeking changes in the family and in sexual relationships more generally. This chapter explores controversies involving sexting, hookups, cohabitation, divorce, and same-sex marriage. These controversies shed light on deeper questions about sexual agency and sexual exploitation, the role and responsibilities of marriage, and the diversity of family structures. At stake in these debates are important issues of public policy, and how best to value women's deep-seated needs for intimate relationships.

Hooking Up

Hooking up, which generally refers to sex outside exclusive relationships, has largely replaced dating on college campuses. However, the practice is not as out of control as sensationalist media accounts suggest. Surveys find that 69–84 percent of college students report having had at least one hookup.[1] In one large sample, the median was three; in another, 80 percent of students hooked up, on average, less than once per semester over the course of college.[2] Only slightly over a third of the hookups involved intercourse, and another third involved just kissing.[3] But hookups have not entirely displaced relationships. By their senior year, about three-quarters of women in one large survey reported that they had been in a relationship that lasted at least six months.[4]

Evidence on the benefits of hookups is mixed, but a growing body of research suggests that the practice often reflects men's preferences more than women's.[5] For example, Kathleen Bogle's study found that after freshman year, men and women's goals diverge. Men generally preferred a "no strings attached" approach to a hookup encounter, and many did not want relationships. Many women, by contrast, wanted a hookup encounter "to turn into some semblance of a relationship."[6] In another survey, almost half of women who engaged in hookups reported that the ideal outcome would be a romantic relationship, compared with a third of men. Nearly twice as many women as men were looking for further relationships.[7]

There are a number of reasons for men's and women's differing preferences. The first is that women's sexual satisfaction is higher in relationships than hookups. In one large study, women reported that they enjoyed sex very much in just half of hookups, but in over four-fifths of relationships.[8] That difference may reflect the fact that it takes some time to learn how to please a new partner, and that affection, commitment, and intimacy increase sexual satisfaction.[9] Of course, sex is likely to improve with experience for both partners. However, research also indicates that men feel more motivated to please their partner in relationships than in hookups, so for women, sex improves more. As one male student put it, his partner's orgasm was "more important if it's in a relationship than if it's a one night stand."[10] Another student was even more direct. "In a hook up . . . I don't give a shit."[11] Women, for their part, appeared more ambivalent than men about whether it was acceptable to expect a casual partner to meet their sexual desires. One female student expressed common reservations: "When it's just a hookup, I just feel like I almost don't have the right. . . . [I]t's just not comfortable enough to be like 'You know, hey, this isn't doing it for me.'"[12]

Another reason women's satisfaction may be higher in relationships than in hookups has to do with a lingering double standard. As one woman put it, "Guys can have sex with all the girls and it makes them more of a man, but if a girl does then all of a sudden she's a ho."[13] One large-scale study found that greater numbers of sexual partners are positively correlated with peer acceptance for male adolescents but negatively correlated with peer acceptance for female adolescents.[14] In other research, half of women, compared with only a quarter of men, said they felt disrespect after hooking up.[15] In Bogle's study, men who were highly sexually active themselves sometimes refused to be involved with a woman who behaved the same way. Women were stigmatized for "getting around" too often, or with too many partners.[16] These reputational costs make women more likely than men to experience guilt and shame following hookups, which contributes to increased symptoms of depression.[17] In commenting on the gendered nature of satisfaction with the hookup culture, one male student noted, "It almost seems like the [contemporary scene] is a guy's paradise. No real commitment, no real feelings. . . . I mean this is what guys have been wanting for many years. And women have always resisted, but now they are going along with it."[18]

One reason that some women go along is that they prefer hookups to relationships, which compete for time and attention with friendships and academic pursuits.[19] As one woman told a *New York Times* reporter, "I positioned myself in college in such a way that I can't have a meaningful romantic relationship, because I'm always busy and the people that I am interested in are always busy, too. And I know everyone says, 'make time, make time.' But there are so many other things going on in my life that I find so important that I just, like, can't make time, and I don't want to make time."[20] According to Hanna Rosin, this ability to have only "temporary relationships that do not derail education or career" is profoundly liberating. "To put it crudely, feminist progress right now largely depends on the existence of the hookup culture."[21] In addition, for some women, relationships pose problems of conflict and inequality. Men can be controlling and sometimes abusive, particularly when women seek to end the relationship.[22] Hookups, by contrast, offer the possibility of sex without commitment, and for some women some of the time, that is an attractive alternative.

There are, of course, downsides to deferring relationships. One was highlighted in a widely circulated op-ed by a "Princeton Mom" written to Princeton undergraduate women. "For most of you," she wrote, "the cornerstone of your future and happiness will be inextricably linked to the man you marry, and you will never again have this concentration of men who are worthy of you. Here's what nobody is telling you: Find a husband on campus before you graduate."[23] Many found the advice both sexist and elitist: Why was she writing only to women, not men, and why was she assuming that only a man, and only someone from Princeton, could be "worthy"? But her emphasis on the significance of decisions related to marriage made sense. Sheryl Sandberg has made a similar point: "the most important career choice you'll make is who you marry."[24] As someone who has been happily married for 37 years to a man she met in college, I would be the last to deny the value of forming close relationships during those years. Never again will most college students be surrounded by such an accessible pool of potential spouses, and it is worth thinking twice before deciding to forgo relationships that take time and effort.

Taken as a whole, what does this body of work suggest about what women want in sexual relationships? Although women differ in the level of commitment that they prefer at any given time, they would all benefit from greater equality in both casual and continuing relationships. More sexual reciprocity in hookups, less stigma for sexually active women, and less controlling and abusive behavior in committed partnerships should be priorities in campus conversations and educational programs.

Sexting

Another practice that has become increasingly popular and one that also raises problematic double standards involves sexting—sending sexually suggestive text messages and images over cell phones and the Internet. Between 15 and 20 percent of teens have reported sending or receiving such pictures, and almost half of boys in coed high schools have seen a nude picture of a female classmate.[25] Girls often use sexting as a form of "relationship currency"; it can foster intimacy, entertain friends, and humiliate enemies.[26] Girls are more likely to send sexualized photos than boys, to feel more pressure to do so, and to suffer more adverse consequences as a result. Given a lingering double standard in sexual expression, girls featured in sexts may be labeled as sluts, while boys are perceived as studs. Consequences for girls from distribution of the images may include bullying, sexual harassment, stigma, psychological trauma, and even suicide.[27] Some studies show that teens who engage in sexting are more likely to engage in sexual activities and in risky sexual behaviors than other teens.[28]

In recognition of these harms, at least 20 states have laws against sexting involving minors, which typically treat it as a misdemeanor.[29] Prosecutors have also brought felony charges under child pornography laws, which carry prison sentences of up to 20 years and require registration as a sex offender. In Iowa, for example, an 18-year-old male ended up on the sex offender registry last year after he sent a picture of his penis to the cell phone of a 14-year-old female friend who had requested it. He was convicted of distributing obscene material to a minor.[30] In another case, a district attorney threatened prosecution of girls who posed provocatively in bras if they did not attend a 10-hour class on sexual violence and pornography.[31] As the American Civil Liberties Union (ACLU) attorney representing the girls noted, the facts scarcely justified a "nuclear-weapon-type charge like child pornography against kids who have no criminal intent and are merely doing stupid things."[32] In another case, a 16-year-old girl was adjudicated a delinquent for filming a sexual act with her boyfriend and e-mailing it to another computer. Although the photos were never distributed to a third party, the court ruled that she had no reasonable expectation of privacy regarding the pictures and could be criminally liable.[33]

What makes such cases particularly problematic is the failure of laws and law enforcement officials to distinguish between those who sext images of themselves and those who distribute images of others without their consent. As *Slate* editor Emily Bazelon notes, "it's not that the first kind of sexting is a good idea—it's that kids shouldn't get caught up in the criminal justice system for it, whereas nonconsensual sexting is a different story."[34] Punishing girls for sending sexually provocative images of themselves is what some commentators label a form of "slut-shaming" that perpetuates sexual double standards.[35] It can also inhibit experimentation that is a normal part of adolescent sexual development.[36] To be sure, as one prosecutor put it, society has an interest in "protect[ing] these kids from themselves" and preventing injury to their repu-tations.[37] But the best way to advance that interest is through education about the risks of sexting and sanctions targeting those who distribute sexual images without consent. States should follow the lead of jurisdictions that allow di-versionary programs for minors, which offer educational courses and the op-portunity to have the conviction expunged on completion. Evaluation of those courses should also be a priority. Do they address the underlying double stan-dards that often accompany sexting, and do they effectively communicate its adverse consequences?

Sexting is, of course, not limited to adolescents. The most famous case has involved former New York Congressman Anthony Weiner, who resigned from the House of Representatives in 2011 after information came to light that he had sent sexually suggestive pictures to multiple women and, when ques-tioned, had failed to admit that the pictures were of him.[38] The controversy re-emerged during Weiner's 2013 bid for mayor of New York City, when an online gossip site released evidence that Weiner had continued sexting even after he resigned from Congress.[39] Other celebrities, including Tiger Woods, Billy Bob Thornton, and Kanye West, have also been involved in sexting scandals.[40] Al-though such practices do not raise the same concerns as adolescent sexting, they do raise broader questions about role modeling and judgment in the lives of public figures.

Marriage and Cohabitation

American attitudes toward marriage reflect a striking paradox. Marriage as a social ideal continues to flourish, even as marriage as a social practice contin-ues to decline. Over 90 percent of women and men say they would like to get married someday, over 80 percent are projected to marry, and the wedding industry generates an estimated $50 billion annually.[41] Yet only about half of Americans are married now, down from almost three-quarters in 1960.[42] Al-though over half of the millennial generation says that being a good parent is one of the most important things in life, only about a third (30 percent) say that about having a successful marriage.[43] Much of the difference in marital rates is attributable to cohabitation, which has increased 1,500 percent in the past half century. In 1960, about 450,000 unmarried couples lived together. Today, the number tops over 7.5 million, and more than half of all marriages are preceded by cohabitation.[44] Most of these live-in relationships are rela-tively short-lived. Within three years, 40 percent transition to marriage and slightly over a quarter break up, while only a third continue living together out of wedlock. Cohabitation is the most common among the least well-educated.

For 70 percent of those without a high school degree, cohabitation rather than marriage is their first live-in relationship.[45]

The increase in cohabitation reflects multiple factors: the sexual revolution, the availability of contraception, the financial advantages of joint households, the desire to test compatibility before marriage, and reservations about the commitment and gender roles that marriage may entail.[46] In one survey, two-thirds of participants thought that living together before marriage was a good way to avoid divorce.[47] In another poll, a majority of Americans had positive or neutral views of more unmarried couples living together.[48]

There are, however, some downsides to cohabitation. Many couples end up in joint households through what researchers call "sliding not deciding."[49] Their shift from dating, to sleeping over, to moving in can be a gradual process, not marked by explicit understandings or shared expectations about what the relationship means. For women, it is often a first step toward marriage; for men, it is often a way to test the relationship or delay commitment. As one commentator notes, "sliding into cohabitation wouldn't be a problem if sliding out were as easy. But it isn't."[50] Inertia and the costs of disentangling shared lives often trap individuals into settling too long for a relationship that isn't working. Moving on and looking for a stable marital relationship could bring the range of health and economic advantages long associated with marriage.[51]

For children, the downside of cohabitation can be still greater. The proportion of children born to unmarried parents has grown from about 4 percent in 1940 to close to 40 percent today.[52] Most of the increase in the last two decades has been to cohabiting couples. Twenty percent of women become pregnant within their first year of cohabiting. Half of the resulting childbirths are unintended, and unintended births are correlated with poorer social, economic, and health outcomes for the child.[53] Cohabiting couples also have high levels of instability. Only about 35 percent of unmarried couples, compared to 80 percent of married couples, are living together five years after the birth. More than half of mothers unmarried at birth go on to date or live with other partners by the time the child is five.[54] Such instability is bad for children. Those born to unmarried parents are worse off than children born to married parents in many different domains such as health, cognitive development, and social adjustment.[55] Growing up in a non-marital household is negatively correlated with adult income, health, and emotional stability.[56]

It is, however, difficult to disentangle how much of the correlation is due to cohabitation and how much is attributable to economic circumstances and individual characteristics, such as parental abilities and education. Fewer than 3 percent of unmarried parents have a college degree.[57] But a substantial body of research suggests that there is some causal relationship between the instability of non-marital relationships and adverse outcomes for both children and adults.[58] The norms associated with marriage prescribe behavior that reinforces commitment, trust, and mutual support.

It does not, of course, follow that marriage is always associated with better outcomes. In high-conflict situations, marriage is negatively associated with health and happiness for both adults and children. And remarriage does not confer the same advantage as a first marriage either for adults or children.[59] Moreover, women at the bottom end of the social and economic spectrum confront a lack of partners who can contribute to a stable marital relationship. High levels of incarceration, substance abuse, and unemployment make many low-income men unattractive marriage partners.[60] Low-income women often report that they have not married their child's father because of serious problems such as violence, addiction, criminal conduct, and chronic conflict—problems that are strongly associated with relationship failure and poor outcomes for children.[61] The "man shortage" is particularly problematic for black women, who are only half as likely as white women to be married, and three times as likely never to marry.[62] In large cities, one survey found twice as many single black women as employed black men in the same age range.[63] Seven of 10 black children are born to unmarried parents, and almost four out of 10 black single mothers are poor.[64]

How public policy should deal with these trends has been a matter of dispute. For conservatives, the decline of marriage represents a significant social problem, calling for major social initiatives.[65] Steps in that direction include the marriage promotion programs funded by the states and federal government. In 2001, George W. Bush made strengthening marriage a priority of his administration, and his $1.5 billion Healthy Marriage Initiative began targeting funds to communication skills workshops, websites, and public education campaigns. One such campaign ran an advertisement claiming, "He may not always be charming, but he'll always be your prince; and the wedding is just the icing on the cake."[66] Another featured a billboard with a sleeping newborn beside the words, "For children's sake." Below, in bold letters, ran the message, "Get Married, Stay Married."[67] Several governors have signed proclamations asserting the importance of marriage to the public, and some states have adopted marriage skills as part of high school education, or distributed educational materials to marrying couples.[68] Only a few of these programs have been systematically evaluated. Overall, their effects appear negligible.[69] Public relations campaigns seem particularly pointless, given the high value that the vast majority of Americans already place on marriage.

The Obama administration has appropriately shifted the federal focus away from marriage and more toward responsible fatherhood. Given that over 40 percent of unwed fathers have had no contact with their children in the previous month, that focus serves a valuable social goal.[70] Program objectives include helping low-income fathers obtain employment, maintain child support obligations, and remain involved in their children's lives. Although women as well as men have a stake in the success of these programs, evidence on their effectiveness is mixed and incomplete.[71] Moreover, many states retain a focus on strengthening marriage.[72] Although some may teach useful communication and conflict resolution skills, the most effective use of funds would be not to promote marriage per se but to strengthen the capacity of all family forms to provide a supportive environment.[73]

To that end, anti-poverty, contraceptive access, and universal preschool programs should be a priority. Only a quarter of children born to unmarried parents attended preschool at age three, although they have the most to gain from such enrichment efforts.[74] Low-income families would also benefit from a child assurance system like that available in European countries, where the state makes up the difference if non-custodial parents cannot afford to pay minimum child support.

Some commentators also recommend following the lead of other nations that treat committed caretaking relationships like marriage for certain purposes. For example, Canadian law bars discrimination against unmarried couples and gives those who have lived together for at least a year the same rights as spouses. An influential 2001 report by the Law Commission of Canada recognized that "marriage is no longer a sufficient model to respond to the variety of relationships that exist in Canada today." Other relationships "are also characterized by emotional and economic interdependence, mutual care and concern and the expectation of some duration" and deserve legal recognition.[75] In Australia and New Zealand, unmarried committed couples are also treated the same as married couples for most purposes.[76] In some European nations, unmarried partners can take advantage of registration systems that confer many of the same advantages as marriage. There is a strong argument for extending similar recognition in this country to all committed arrangements that function as family units.[77]

There is an equally strong justification for treating cohabiting couples who have lived together for a significant period like divorcing couples for purposes of property distribution. The American Law Institute Principles of the Law of Family Dissolution suggest an appropriate framework. It presumes that parties who have lived together for three years (or two if they have a child) are functioning like a marriage and should be subject to similar rules of fairness when they split up unless they have made an agreement to the contrary.[78] Such an approach is consistent with popular opinion, which favors treating unmarried committed parties like spouses for purposes of dividing property.[79]

Divorce

Between 40 and 50 percent of first marriages end in divorce, twice the rate of the 1960s, and the likelihood of breakup is even higher for subsequent marriages.[80] Although close to two-thirds of Americans believe that the high rate of divorce is a very serious or fairly serious problem, it is hard to see any policy response that makes sense.[81] Life was scarcely preferable in the "not-so-good old days" before no-fault divorce, when couples had to stay in high-conflict and abusive relationships or fabricate a legal ground for dissolution.

There are, however, appropriate responses to problems in the current regime, in which spousal support is infrequently and inconsistently awarded. In the most recent study, such support was awarded in less than 9 percent of divorces.[82] Because women are more likely than men to have sacrificed their earning capacity to care for the family, women also fare worse than men following a marital breakup.[83] The gender disparities are particularly problematic at the lower end of the socioeconomic spectrum. Women who have divorced in the previous year are twice as likely as recently divorced men to be in poverty.[84]

Spousal support statutes vary across states but typically give trial courts broad discretion. Legislatures often provide a long list of factors for courts to consider, with no rank order between competing considerations. One study found 60 factors mentioned across the states.[85] The ambiguities are compounded by different justifications for an award. To what extent should support depend on fault, need, rehabilitation, ability to pay, the contribution that the recipient made to the relationship, or compensation for forgone opportunities?[86] This doctrinal indeterminacy has led to inconsistent results, and sometimes to manifest injustice in the case of long-standing marriages. A prominent case in point involves Terry Martin Hekker, a woman who received divorce papers on her fortieth wedding anniversary. As noted in chapter 3, the court awarded her support for only four years and suggested that she seek job training at age 67, when it would be discontinued.[87] In other cases, deserving wives don't even seek support out of some combination of guilt, shame, or doubt that they will be successful.[88]

A survey of public opinion found that Americans favor spousal support in far more cases than current practices allow. The most important factors in predicting awards were the income disparity between the parties, the duration of the relationship, and the presence of young children. For example, in hypothetical cases where the couple had been married 22 years, the survey participants awarded support 52 percent of the time, compared with 43 percent for couples married six years. Both rates were significantly higher than those found in actual cases.[89] Women were more likely to award support than men, but neither sex was particularly moved by the plight of displaced homemakers who had sacrificed their earning potential to care for their families but had no young children at home.[90] Similar attitudes help explain the move in some states toward ending permanent spousal support, an initiative that second wives support.[91]

From a policy standpoint, the inconsistency of support awards and the disparity between public attitudes and judicial practices argue for a more determinate standard. Some states have adopted formulas along the lines that the American Academy of Matrimonial Lawyers has proposed, which are based primarily on the disparity in income of the spouses and the duration of the relationship, but that permit deviations for factors such as the presence of young children and the sacrifice of earning potential by one spouse.[92] The American Law Institute has also proposed a similar formula that provides for "compensatory spousal payments" to close the post-marriage income gap between the parties attributable to lost employment opportunities by one spouse as a result of investments in the marriage. It uses length of the marriage as a proxy for those opportunities and increases the amount of the award when a spouse assumed primary caregiving responsibilities.[93] Such proposals would make for fairer and more consistent results than the current regime. However, the resistance of the courts and the public to long-term spousal support underscores the importance of other reforms, advocated in Chapter 3, which would make it easier for women to combine work and family and to reduce their vulnerability upon divorce.

Same-Sex Marriage

By 2013, the year the Supreme Court issued two historic same-sex marriage decisions, 15 states, along with the District of Columbia, recognized same-sex marriage.[94] In one of its decisions, the Court in effect allowed gay marriage in California; the ruling held that opponents of same-sex marriages lacked standing to challenge a lower federal court decision holding unconstitutional California's ban on such marriages.[95] In the other, the Court struck down section 3 of the federal Defense of Marriage Act (DOMA), which had defined marriage for purposes of federal law as the legal union between one man and one woman.[96] Those decisions are consistent with the latest public opinion polls, in which 53–55 percent of Americans support legal recognition of same-sex marriage, up from just a quarter in 1990.[97] However, the fight for same-sex marriage is scarcely over. The Supreme Court decision leaves in place section

2 of the DOMA, which gives states the right not to recognize same-sex marriages. And the vast majority of states have state versions of DOMA, either as a matter of legislation or as part of their constitutions.

Opposition to same-sex marriage builds on several claims. The first is definitional; marriage is widely understood to involve one man and one woman. David Boies, one of the lawyers for the supporters of same-sex marriage in the California case, characterized this claim as "a slogan, a bumper sticker, a tautology. [Opponents] say 'marriage is between a man and a woman.' That's the question. That's not the answer. And they don't have any reasons why that ought to be the answer."[98]

A second argument by opponents of same-sex marriage involves the link between marriage and procreation. Maggie Gallagher, former president of the National Organization for Marriage, claims that:

> [marital] unions are socially necessary in a way that other kinds of unions, however valuable they may be to the people in them, are not. The critical public or "civic" task of marriage is to regulate sexual relationships between men and women in order to . . . increase the likelihood that there will be a next generation that will be raised by their mothers and fathers in one family, where both parents are committed to each other and to their children. . . . Sexual unions of male and female are the only unions that create new life. . . .[99]

This was also a primary argument that litigants advanced in a case challenging the ban on same-sex marriage under the California constitution. In rejecting that argument, the California Supreme Court noted that "the constitutional right to marry never has been viewed as the sole preserve of individuals who are physically capable of bearing children."[100] In fact, thousands of gay and lesbian couples are raising children, and it makes no sense to deny them the stable nurturing environment that opponents associate with marriage. So, too, in the first decision to strike down same-sex marriage bans under state constitutions, the Massachusetts Supreme Court pointed out that opponents "offered no evidence that forbidding marriage to people of the same sex will increase the number of couples choosing to enter into opposite marriages in order to have and raise children."[101]

Another argument by opponents invokes tradition—the long-standing recognition of a man and a woman as the marital unit that is the foundation of society. According to the opponents of same-sex marriage in California, a "social institution that has prevailed continuously in our history and traditions can justly be said to be rational *per se*."[102] But as the California Supreme Court pointed out, many forms of discrimination that have been rooted in tradition are now recognized as violating constitutional requirements of equal protection of the law. "It is instructive to recall that the traditional well established rules and practices of our not so distant past (1) barred interracial marriage; (2) upheld the routine exclusion of women from many occupations and official duties; and (3) considered the relegation of racial minorities to separate and assertedly equivalent public facilities and institutions as constitutionally equal treatment."[103]

A further argument by opponents is that recognition of same-sex marriages somehow threatens the well-being of families. One celebrated advertisement ominously intoned: "There's a storm cloud gathering. . . . Some who advocate for same-sex marriage . . . want to bring the issue into my life. My freedom will be taken away. . . . Those advocates want to change the way I live."[104] But marriage licenses are not a finite resource, so it is difficult to see how extending freedom to marry to gay and lesbian couples will take any freedom away from other couples. In Evan Wolfson's apt phrase, there is "enough marriage to share."[105] As many commentators argue, broadening the constituencies that can take advantage of marriage can ultimately strengthen the institution.[106]

A variation on opponents' claim is that the threat to families lies in sending a message of normalcy. From their perspective, legalizing same-sex marriage "would give sanction and approval to the creation of a motherless or fatherless family. . . . It would mean the law was neutral as to whether children had mothers and fathers."[107] But why shouldn't the state be neutral? Opponents have introduced no evidence that the well-being of children is jeopardized by being raised in "motherless" or "fatherless" same-sex couples. To the contrary, research overwhelmingly suggests that "the development, adjustment, and well-being of children with lesbian and gay parents do not differ markedly from that of children with heterosexual parents."[108]

There is, in short, no compelling justification for the state to limit marriage to heterosexual couples. And there is a strong moral and constitutional case for viewing marriage as one of the fundamental rights that cannot be abridged without a compelling state interest. Marriage confers a host of concrete economic and symbolic benefits. Although a growing number of states grant domestic partners the same benefits as marriage, this civil union does not carry the same social significance as marriage, and to many gay and lesbian couples, it seems a second-class status. As the Massachusetts Supreme Court recognized, "Civil marriage is at once a deeply personal commitment to another human being and a highly public celebration of the ideas of mutuality, companionship, intimacy, fidelity, and family. Without access to marriage, one is excluded from the full range of human experience."[109]

There is, however, debate within the gay and lesbian community about whether the best response to that exclusion is to seek access to marriage or

challenge its primacy. The debate was sparked by a famous essay by Paul Et-
tlebrick, then legal director of Lambda Legal Defense and Education Fund.
She argued that

> marriage will not liberate us as lesbians and gay men. In fact, it will
> constrain us, make us more invisible, force our assimilation into the
> mainstream, and undermine the goals of gay liberation. Marriage
> runs contrary to two of the primary goals of the lesbian and gay move-
> ment: the affirmation of gay identity and culture; and the validation of
> many forms of relationships. . . .
>
> Justice for gay men and lesbians will be achieved only when we
> are accepted and supported in this society *despite* our differences
> from the dominant culture and the choices we make regarding our
> relationships. . . . I do not want [to] be known as "Mrs. Attached-To-
> Somebody-Else." Nor do I want to give the state the power to regulate
> my primary relationship.[110]

How many gays and lesbians share such views is unclear, but surveys show
that fewer of them want to marry than heterosexual individuals.[111] Underlying these reservations about the same-sex marriage movement are several
concerns. The first is that gay marriage "dilutes the strength of our community by breaking down the systems of support and accommodation lesbians
have built over the decades . . . —the kind of support where friends (not just
a single partner or 'spouse') are family and a great source of strength and support . . . where . . . there are infinite possibilities beyond the one woman plus
one woman model."[112] Similarly, Columbia Law professor Katherine Franke
worries that in "important ways the success of today's marriage rights movement is premised on a promise of discipline, respectability, and obeisance to
a set of civilizing norms that portray those who fall short of those norms as an
embarrassment, or worse, undeserving of the full and equal blessings of civic
belonging. . . ."[113] Other commentators similarly see marriage as "like death by
casserole."[114] "I don't want to deny anybody the right to marriage," explained
one lesbian to a *New York Times* reporter. "But I don't really want it to exist."[115]
To these commentators, marriage is a "poor match for the varied family forms
that exist not only among gay families but straight ones; marriage normalizes
social relations, which queer people should seek to upset."[116]

A second concern is that the priority placed on same-sex marriage has diverted attention from other critical issues:

> Instead of planning our ceremonies, we should shift the focus and plan
> a more just world. . . . [I]t's time to move on and use our vast talents

to fight better fights . . . these including reducing the gap between the rich and poor; battling HIVAIDS; providing affordable health- and childcare; creating jobs; decreasing guns on the streets; lowering the prison population; and decreasing prejudice and discrimination of every kind and against anybody.[117]

Yet whatever their view on such priorities, both lesbian and straight women can unite around the agenda put forth by a coalition of activists in "Beyond Same-Sex Marriage: A New Strategic Vision for All Our Families and Relationships." It sought a "new vision for securing governmental and private institutional recognition of diverse kinds of partnerships, household, kinship relationships and families." From this perspective, same-sex marriage should be seen as part of a "larger effort to strengthen the stability and security of diverse households and families."[118]

In short, the struggle for gay marriage is not just about gays and not just about marriage. It is, as law professor Nancy Polikoff puts it, also about "valuing all families," and ensuring that all such relationships have a "legal framework for economic and emotional security."[119] The struggle is also about homophobia. In a famous commercial opposing same-sex marriage, a mother is standing at a kitchen counter when her daughter rushes in and says, "Guess what I learned in school today." She then shows her mother a children's book and explains that she learned "how a prince married a prince, and I . . . can marry a princess."[120] As a horrified mother flips through the book, the viewer learns that this has already happened in Massachusetts. Yet one way to interpret this commercial is flatly at odds with what its sponsors intended. Children in Massachusetts are learning the virtues of tolerance and the value of diversity. What has happened in that state is exactly what should happen in a democracy committed to liberty and justice for all.

| 5 |

Reproductive Justice and Economic Security

Women's efforts to control their fertility date back some four thousand years, and their attempts to ensure economic security have always been central to the survival of the species. What is distinctive about contemporary American struggles is that what women want is now within reach. Technology has made possible women's control over their reproductive destiny, and our national wealth has made possible a basic safety net for those least able to provide one for themselves. Our failure to realize these possibilities reveals political obstacles that deserve closer scrutiny.

Roe Revisited

In its landmark 1973 decision *Roe v. Wade*, the Supreme Court declared that the Fourteenth Amendment's guarantee of liberty implied a right of privacy "broad enough to encompass a woman's decision whether or not to terminate her pregnancy."[1] Four decades' experience has taught that what the Constitution protects in principle, society can deny in practice. An array of legal restrictions, funding limitations, and clinic terrorism have made abortion inaccessible to many who need it most. A series of conservative Supreme Court appointments have made the *Roe* decision itself increasingly vulnerable. To understand the roots of the current controversy, some historical background is useful.

In the decades preceding *Roe,* social attitudes and practices had grown increasingly out of step with legal prohibitions on abortion. Women's increasing labor force participation and non-marital sexual activity had increased the number of unwanted pregnancies. Ignorance, lack of planning, or pressure from male partners made many women ineffective contraceptive users. The result was about a million abortions annually, few of them legal.[2] Procedures could be painful and dangerous when performed hastily by unskilled practitioners. Some estimates suggested that as many as 10,000 women died each year as a result of botched abortions, and thousands more suffered serious physical injuries. Abortion became a rallying issue for feminists, who popularized the slogan, "Men don't get pregnant, they just pass the laws." On the eve of the *Roe v. Wade* ruling, a majority of Americans thought that the abortion decision should be left to the woman and her physician.[3]

So the Supreme Court held. Under the Court's analysis, restrictions on abortion required justification by a compelling state interest. One such interest, protecting maternal health, became compelling only after the first trimester, the point at which mortality rates from abortion became higher than mortality rates from childbirth. The state's interest in protecting fetal life became compelling at viability, in the third trimester, when the fetus had the capability of meaningful life outside the womb. After that point, the state could prohibit abortion except when necessary to protect the health or life of the mother.

The *Roe* decision set off some of the most sustained and strident controversies that the Court has ever experienced. Opposition came from all points on the political spectrum. The religious Right found the decision without moral justification. Many moderates found it without constitutional justification, and critics on the Left complained that the Court had offered the wrong justification.

In part, the controversy stemmed from the Court's explicit effort to avoid "resolving the difficult question of when life begins."[4] Yet by determining that the fetus was not entitled to protection before viability, the Court necessarily concluded that the unborn before that point were not "persons" within the meaning of the Constitution. This conclusion was unacceptable to many individuals, particularly Catholics and Christian fundamentalists who believed that life begins at conception. Other commentators who did not share the pro-life position nonetheless believed that the Court gave it too little recognition in *Roe*. As Harvard law professor Cass Sunstein put it, the Court went "so far so fast" that the decision appeared a "bolt from the blue" and fueled an anti-abortion backlash.[5] If the Court had proceeded more cautiously, and had allowed states more latitude for working out legislative compromises, many commentators, including Supreme Court Justice Ruth Bader Ginsburg, believe that *Roe's* backlash might have been averted.[6]

To some critics, the court's decision was equally problematic on doctrinal grounds. Critics objected that the Court's trimester framework was "legislative" and that neither it, nor the Court's privacy argument, was grounded in the Constitution's text, history, or structure.[7] Even those who supported the result in *Roe* were critical of an approach dependent on an unstable technological rationale. Within a decade after the decision, medical advances were calling into question the trimester framework. Abortions were safer than pregnancy throughout the second trimester, and viability was occurring earlier than the decision had anticipated.[8]

Other commentators were troubled by the Court's reliance on a privacy rationale for the abortion right. Some, including Justice Ruth Bader Ginsburg and Yale law professor Reva Siegel, believed that the Court should have relied on equality arguments.[9] As Siegel notes, "restrictions on abortion do not merely force women to bear children: powerful gender norms in this society ensure that almost all women who are forced to bear children will raise them as well. . . ."[10] Those parental responsibilities fall disproportionately on women and contribute to their unequal status and opportunities. And scholars such as Georgetown law professor Robin West have noted that the privacy argument fails to identify what is at stake for women in the right to choose an abortion:

> Women need the freedom to make reproductive decisions not merely to vindicate a right to be left alone but often to strengthen their ties to others; to plan responsibly and have a family for which they can provide, to pursue professional or work commitments made to the outside world, or continue to support their families and communities. At other times the decision to abort is necessitated not by a murderous urge to end life, but by the harsh reality of a financially irresponsible partner, a society indifferent to the care of children, and a workplace incapable of accommodating or supporting the needs of working parents. At many other times the need to abort follows directly from a violent sexual assault. When made for any of these reasons, the decision to abort is not one made in an egoistic private vacuum . . . [but] within a web or interlocking, competing, and often irreconcilable responsibilities and commitments.[11]

Yet in evaluating these critiques, Yale law professor Jack Balkin has a point: "Given the legal and moral difficulties of the issue, it was perhaps too much to expect that the Court would get it right the first time under almost anyone's standards of what getting it right might mean."[12] Moreover, although conventional accounts paint "*Roe* rage" as a response to "judicial overreaching," considerable historical evidence demonstrates that political opposition to the expansion of abortion rights preceded the decision.[13] Other factors besides the ruling contributed to the mobilization of opponents, including the association of feminism with abortion rights, the backlash against feminism, the realignment of Republican party politics, and the Catholic Church's response to changing public opinion on the issue.[14] Comparative research also underscores certain features of the American political process that led to the prolonged controversy over abortion, such as low-turnout elections that are responsive to organized single-issue interest groups, and the availability of multiple legislative and judicial venues for conflict.[15]

Anti-Abortion Activism

Whatever the causes, the politicization of abortion has taken a heavy toll. Since the 1980s, anti-choice activists have bombed or burned over 100 clinics, vandalized over 400, and killed seven staff.[16] About a quarter of clinics report incidents of severe violence annually.[17] In 2009, George Tiller, the nation's leading provider of late-term abortions, was gunned down while attending church.[18] "Operation Housecall" organizes activists to target doctors' homes for harassment, and other groups use websites and media campaigns to run slogans like "Some doctors deliver babies. Some doctors kill babies."[19] The doctor who has attempted to replace Tiller has been stalked by protesters and identified on the Internet as a "mass murderer." She has received constant hate mail, such as a letter warning her that activists "know where you shop, who your friends are, what you drive, where you live. You will be checking under your car every day—because maybe today is the day someone places an explosive under it."[20] Partly in response to such activism, the number of doctors willing and qualified to perform abortions has steadily decreased. Only a minority of medical education programs offer abortion training.[21] Even in obstetrics and gynecology, a majority of residency training programs provide no instruction in first-trimester abortions and only 14 percent of OB/GYNs perform them.[22] Even some physicians willing and able to provide abortion services cannot do so because of formal and informal policies restricting abortion provision by their private group practices, employers, and hospitals.[23] Only five states allow qualified nurses to provide first trimester surgical abortions.[24] The consequence of all these restrictions is that over 85 percent of counties have no abortion provider, and four states have just one.[25]

Anti-abortion activists have also succeeded in passing a broad array of restrictive statutes designed to make abortion more costly and less accessible. In one year alone, states considered some 570 laws and passed over 90.[26] When assessing the constitutionality of such restrictions, the Supreme Court has modified the trimester framework of *Roe*, and has permitted limitations on the abortion right as long as they do not impose "undue burdens."[27] That approach has allowed a wide range of constraints. Thirty-five states require that women receive counseling before they can obtain an abortion. Most of these states specify the information that must be given, which covers subjects such as fetal development, fetal pain, and the medical and psychological risks of abortion.[28] Kansas, for example, requires doctors to inform a woman that she is terminating the life of a "whole separate, unique, living human being."[29] Some of this information is inaccurate or incomplete, or relevant only to procedures other than the one the woman is undergoing.[30] For example, South Dakota requires doctors to inform patients seeking abortions that they face an increased risk of suicide after the procedure, despite the fact that research claiming to link mental health and abortion has been "decisively debunked."[31] Some counseling programs link abortion with increased risks of breast cancer, which is unsupported by the evidence.[32] Such compelled disclosures raise obvious First Amendment problems, and violate principles of informed consent.[33] Although courts have struck down a few of these provisions, many persist. A survey by the House Committee on Oversight and Government Reform found that almost 90 percent of federally funded centers gave out false information concerning the link between abortion, breast cancer, infertility, depression, and stress disorders.[34]

Eight states require that women seeking abortions submit to an ultrasound, and that doctors show them the image.[35] Ultrasounds performed during the first trimester require a device to be inserted into the vagina in order to capture a clear image and heartbeat. Texas explicitly mandates a vaginal ultrasound; a similar requirement was withdrawn in Virginia after commentators analogized it to state-imposed rape.[36]

More than half of states also have TRAP laws—Targeted Regulation of Abortion Providers.[37] These statutes seek to force clinic closures by imposing expensive requirements, such as demanding that doctors have admitting privileges at nearby hospitals and that clinic facilities meet building standards similar to those of hospitals. It is impossible for some abortion doctors to gain admitting privileges because they fly in from out of state, and the requirement is unnecessary because hospitals admit patients in emergencies without requiring a physician to have such privileges. Meeting burdensome building standards drives up costs or forces closures because some clinics are unable to comply at existing facilities.[38] In North Carolina, the General Assembly passed a TRAP bill that would close 15 of the 16 abortion facilities in the state.[39] Texas enacted a law that, if enforced, could close all but five of the state's 42 clinics.[40] Regulations governing the height of clinic rooms and the width of hallways have nothing to do with patient safety and everything to do with restricting access; other medical offices that perform even riskier procedures than abortion are not required to meet such standards.[41]

Almost three-quarters of states require women seeking abortions to wait a specified period of time between when they receive counseling and when they obtain the procedure, sometimes as long as 72 hours. These waiting periods increase the expense and difficulty for women who do not live close to an abortion provider. Researchers find that such laws have decreased the rate of abortions and have increased the number that occur in the second trimester, particularly among women who do not have ready access to an out-of-state clinic.[42]

Bans on funding for abortions create another obstacle to choice. Fewer than a fifth of states subsidize all or most medically necessary abortions for poor women.[43] No federal funds can be used to subsidize abortions for women in poverty, except when necessary to save the life of the mother or to end pregnancies resulting from rape or incest.[44] The Supreme Court has upheld that funding prohibition, despite findings that childbirth would sometimes pose serious risks to women's physical and mental health and result in fetuses born with severe abnormalities.[45] As part of the final negotiations over the Affordable Care Act, President Obama agreed to issue an executive order continuing that ban for funds available through the Act.[46] In anticipation of the establishment of state-level healthcare exchanges to assist purchases of private insurance under the Act, almost half of states have enacted restrictions on abortion coverage.[47] Although some courts and commentators characterize such funding bans as trivial hardships or as legitimate revenue-saving measures, neither characterization is consistent with women's experience. Forcing those in poverty to pay for abortions is not a trifling matter; the average cost in some areas is more than an entire monthly welfare payment for a family of three.[48] As many as one-fifth to one-third of poor women cannot obtain abortions that they seek because of lack of resources.[49] Nor are funding prohibitions a rational means of conserving taxpayer dollars. Abortion costs far less than childbirth, which is now fully subsidized for low-income women.

Another strategy of anti-abortion activists involves "personhood amendments." The national group "Personhood USA" has campaigned in over 20 states to amend state constitutions or to enact legislation to protect fetal life.[50] Such amendments typically define "person" as "every human being from the moment of conception," and, depending on the precise wording, might encompass emergency contraception and oral birth control. These campaigns are costly for all concerned. In Mississippi alone, Personhood USA spent over a million dollars in an almost successful effort to amend the state's Bill of Rights.[51] The resources of pro-choice groups are stretched thin in attempting to respond to personhood initiatives as well as state statutory restrictions on 50 fronts.

A further category of restrictions involves prohibitions on late-term abortion except to save the life or protect the health of the mother. Thirty-nine states have such prohibitions.[52] Although only about one in 10 abortions occurs after the first trimester, the reasons for delay are often compelling: the woman was the victim of rape or incest, or she discovered severe fetal abnormalities that couldn't have been detected sooner.[53]

A related restriction involves bans on partial-birth abortions, a method of extracting an intact fetus (known as intact D & E) that politicians and the public found particularly offensive.[54] In *Gonzales v. Carhart*, the Supreme Court upheld a federal act prohibiting such abortions, with no exception for procedures necessary for the woman's health. In justifying that omission, the Court relied on Congressional findings that the procedure was never medically necessary. Yet as the dissent in *Carhart* noted, both the Congressional and trial court record included evidence to the contrary; leading medical associations provided statements that intact D & E carries meaningful safety advantages over other methods. As the dissent also noted, the act did nothing to preserve fetal life; the alternative procedure, non-intact D & E, "could equally be characterized as 'brutal,' . . . involving as it does 'tearing a fetus apart' and ripp[ing] off 'its limbs.'"[55]

Even more troubling was the theory on which the Court sustained the act. Writing for the majority, Justice Kennedy stated:

> Respect for human life finds an ultimate expression in the bond of love the mother has for her child. The Act recognizes this reality as well. . . . While we find no reliable data to measure the phenomenon, it seems unexceptionable to conclude some women come to regret their choice to abort the infant life they once created and sustained. . . . Severe depression and loss of esteem can follow.[56]

The majority's reasoning appears to be that because maternal love would prevent some women from having partial-birth abortions if they truly understood the procedure, Congress could ban it entirely. But as critics of the opinion noted, the "appropriate remedy to the problem Justice Kennedy identifies would be informing the woman about the nature of intact D & E, not preventing the women from choosing whether to undergo the procedure. . . . The law forecloses choice rather than informing it."[57]

To other commentators, the Court's unsupported paternalism was reflective of a worrisome change in rhetorical strategy of the anti-abortion movement generally. Activist David Reardon explains the shift toward a "pro-woman" strategy:

> While committed pro-lifers may be more comfortable with traditional "defend the baby" arguments, we must recognize that many in our

society are too morally immature to understand this argument. They must be led to it. And the best way to lead them to it is by first helping them to see that abortion does not help women, but only makes their lives worse.[58]

Borrowing this strategy, the Americans United for Life named its model statute prohibiting abortions after 20 weeks the "Women's Health Defense Act."

This emphasis on women's well-being represents a shift from early anti-abortion rhetoric, which often painted women as irresponsible, selfish, or both. For example, in *Doe v. Bolton*, the companion case to *Roe,* Justice White's dissent asserted: "At the heart of the controversy in these cases are those recurring pregnancies that pose no danger whatsoever to the life or health of the mother but are nevertheless unwanted for any one or more of a variety of reasons—convenience, family planning, economics, dislike of children, the embarrassment of illegitimacy, etc." From this perspective, *Roe* was objectionable because it valued the women's "convenience, whim, or caprice . . . more than the life or potential life of the fetus."[59]

The shift in strategy from *Doe* to *Carhart* reflects the realization by anti-abortion activists that a different approach was necessary. As Phyllis Schlafly once put it, "If you keep doing what you've been doing, you'll keep getting what you've been getting."[60] By stressing women's "natural" regret concerning the abortion decision, the religious Right hoped to appeal to a wider public. According to James Dobson, of Focus on the Family, "Because of unfair media bias and influence from radical feminists, much of the public views the pro-life movement as being insensitive to the needs of women."[61] Conservatives' arguments centering on women's health seek to counter that perception. Groups such as Concerned Women for America are increasingly stressing women as "abortion's second victims."[62] In *Making Abortion Rare*, David Reardon explained to allies that the solution to "bad publicity is to always—ALWAYS—place our arguments for the unborn in the middle of a pro-woman sandwich. . . . Accepting the fact that the middle majority's concerns are primarily focused on the woman is a prerequisite to developing a successful pro woman/pro life strategy. Rather than trying to reduce public sympathy for women, we want to increase it and align it with our own outrage at how women are being victimized."[63] To that end, advocates stress abortion's claimed links with breast cancer and "post-abortion syndrome," which assertedly subjects women to guilt, anxiety, post-traumatic stress disorder, increased risks of suicide, sexual dysfunction, and substance abuse. Although such claims have been widely disavowed by the medical community, they remain common in anti-abortion advocacy and counseling.[64]

This "women-centered" strategy is apparent in a report by a South Dakota Task Force to Study Abortions that was designed to justify highly restrictive policies. Over half of the Report focuses on the state's interest in prohibiting abortion to protect women.[65] The Task Force refers to testimony of some 1,950 women and concludes that "virtually all of them stated they thought their abortions were uninformed, coerced, or both."[66] According to the report, abortion clinics affirmatively misrepresent the procedure by telling pregnant women that they are carrying nothing but "tissue" and by failing to explain that abortion would terminate the life of a "living human being."[67] Women are also allegedly pressured into having abortions by clinics and by "unjust and selfish demands of male sexual partners."[68] Echoing Justice Kennedy's unsupported assertions in Carhart, the Report concludes that "it is simply unrealistic to expect that a pregnant mother is capable of being involved in the termination of the life of her own child without risk of suffering significant psychological trauma and distress."[69] Minority members of the Task Force objected that the majority had excluded from the Report all inconsistent testimony about women's experience with abortion, and had rested its conclusions on a "sexist, insulting, condescending and inaccurate stereotype of women."[70]

Just as anti-abortion forces have shifted strategies, pro-choice advocates need to rethink ways to capture the moral and political high ground. Nearly one in three women will have an abortion, yet only 41 percent identify themselves as "pro-choice."[71] Over a third of those who support Roe call themselves "pro-life."[72] Part of the problem for "pro-choice" advocates may stem from the label itself. Linguist George Lakoff argues that "choice" is too "consumerist," and other research suggests that it is an inadequate way of describing the financial and social imperatives that make abortion necessary.[73] In one study, about three-quarters of women said that the reason they terminated a pregnancy was inability to afford a baby, and almost half cited reluctance to be a single mother or problems in their relationships.[74] For millions of Americans, the decision to have an abortion is an exercise not simply of individual choice but of moral responsibility: it reflects a deep-seated commitment not to bring a child into the world without adequate financial and family support. Women's rights advocates need to emphasize that commitment. Planned Parenthood has moved in that direction and has abandoned its use of pro-life and pro-choice labels in favor of a more nuanced approach that takes into account the complexity of women's individual situation.[75] At the same time, women's rights groups need to convey the urgency of this issue in the face of constant challenges. Many young women take abortion for granted. One poll found that the majority of women under 35 who are registered to vote feel that there is little threat to abortion rights.[76] These women need to better understand the constraints on access, particularly for poor women who can least afford unintended motherhood.

The challenges in finding common ground are substantial. No issue of importance to the women's rights movement has so deeply divided women. Dispute centers on the morality of abortion, the law that should govern it, and the significance of the issue. Almost half of Americans (47 percent) think that having an abortion is morally wrong, with women slightly more disapproving (49 percent) than men (46 percent). But ideology is more important than gender in predicting positions on abortion. Among Republicans, 63 percent think abortion is morally wrong; among Democrats, only 39 percent agree.[77] When asked whether abortions should be legal, about a quarter of Americans (28 percent) think it should always be legal; about half (52 percent) think it should sometimes be legal, and a fifth think it should always be illegal.[78] In polls telling participants that *Roe v. Wade* established a woman's right to an abortion at least in the first three months of pregnancy, between 63 and 70 percent said the Supreme Court should not overturn the decision, 24–29 percent said it should, and the remainder were unsure.[79] However, over a third of Americans do not know what *Roe* was about, and among millennials, only 44 percent know that the case involved abortion.[80] Although over half of women (54 percent) said the issue of abortion would be very important to their 2012 presidential vote (compared with 36 percent of men), a 2013 poll found that far fewer Americans (18 percent of women and men) viewed the issue as critical to the nation.[81]

Given the divisiveness of the abortion issue, both sides could benefit by looking for common ground. In his Notre Dame commencement speech, President Obama stressed the importance of finding such unifying issues. "So let us work together to reduce the number of women seeking abortions. Let's reduce unintended pregnancies. Let's make adoption more available. Let's provide care and support for women who do carry their children to term."[82] A serious commitment to that effort will require rethinking our policies toward pregnancy, birth control, and the feminization of poverty.

Punishing Pregnant Women

When Regina McNight, a young African American woman, suffered an unexpected stillbirth, she was convicted of homicide by child abuse on grounds that she had used cocaine during her pregnancy. She was sentenced to 12 years in prison. In 2008, the South Carolina Supreme Court overturned her conviction based on ineffective counsel at trial. Her attorney failed to establish that the state had relied on outdated research and had failed to call experts who would have testified about "recent studies showing that cocaine is no more harmful to a fetus than nicotine use, poor nutrition, lack of prenatal care, or other conditions commonly associated with the urban poor."[83] To avoid re-trial, McNight pleaded guilty to manslaughter and was sentenced to the eight years she had already served.

The case exemplifies a broader trend to punish pregnant women for drug and alcohol use, particularly low-income women of color.[84] A major-ity of states impose sanctions on women whose newborns test positive for controlled substances.[85] One survey by Lynn Paltrow and Jeanne Flavin of some 400 cases of arrests, convictions, and detentions of women for conduct during pregnancy found that most were brought under criminal statutes such as child endangerment or child abuse. Although some con-victions have been overturned because these statutes are not intended to encompass fetuses, women continue to be arrested and to plead guilty to avoid the risk of trial.[86] A few jurisdictions have relied on other legislation. For example, Missouri's Abortion Act includes a preamble stating that life begins at conception. Although the statute includes an explicit provision protecting pregnant women from punishment, prosecutors have used the law to arrest pregnant women for using alcohol and drugs, including mari-juana.[87] A 2006 Alabama law prohibits a "responsible person" from expos-ing a child to "an environment in which he or she . . . knowingly recklessly or intentionally causes or permits a child to be exposed to, . . . a controlled substance, chemical substance or drug paraphernalia." Although the law was intended to protect children from the dangers of methamphetamine labs, a 2012 *New York Times* article reports broader application, including some 60 prosecutions of new mothers for drug use since the law was passed. The minimum sentence is 10 years.[88] Sixteen states also consider substance abuse during pregnancy to be child abuse under civil child welfare statutes, and three consider it grounds for civil commitment. In 14 states, healthcare professionals must report suspected drug use by pregnant women.[89] Even women who are no longer using drugs can be confined for failure to take anti-addiction medication.[90]

A large group of women are at risk of prosecution under such statutes. Government statistics indicate that about 5 percent of pregnant women use illicit drugs, 11 percent use alcohol, and 16 percent use tobacco.[91] Al-though cocaine was once considered to be the most harmful form of sub-stance abuse, many of its supposed symptoms have since been linked to poor nutrition, inadequate prenatal care, and other drugs. Considerable recent evidence indicates that cocaine's effects are less severe than those of alco-hol and are comparable to those of tobacco.[92] Yet cocaine use is far more likely than alcohol or tobacco use to be a basis for prosecution. In Paltrow and Flavin's study, 84 percent of cases of prosecution or other intervention involved illicit drugs, mainly cocaine.[93] Such selective prosecution reflects class and racial biases that are also evident in reporting practices. In one study, black women were 10 times more likely than white women to be reported to governmental authorities for substance use, despite similar rates of addiction.[94] In another survey of New York hospitals, those serving low-income women were much more likely than those serving wealthier patients to test new mothers for drugs, and to turn positive results over to child protection authorities.[95]

Virtually every leading health organization, including the American Medical Association, the American Academy of Pediatrics, the American Public Health Association, and the American Society on Addiction Medicine, has opposed prosecution.[96] As they note, the primary effect of punitive policies is to force substance abuse underground and to deter women from seeking drug treatment and prenatal care.[97] A case in point comes from South Carolina, after the State Supreme Court upheld a woman's child abuse conviction for using cocaine while pregnant. In the year following the decision, the state's drug treatment programs witnessed an 80 percent drop in the admission of pregnant women. As the director of one treatment facility explained, "Women are doing one of three things. They're getting abortions, having babies over the . . . state line or not seeking prenatal care."[98] Incarcerating pregnant women also does little to ensure a healthy birth because drugs are often available in prison, and prenatal care is frequently inadequate.[99]

Experts universally agree that a preferable alternative is a public health approach that stresses education and treatment. Yet some women have even been arrested despite the fact that they were voluntarily participating in drug treatment.[100] In other cases, women facing prosecution had sought assistance but were unable to find a program that would accept them.[101] In one New York study, 87 percent of drug treatment programs rejected pregnant Medicaid patients addicted to crack cocaine, even though these were the women most at risk for prosecution.[102] Although recent federal legislation has expanded subsidies for drug treatment programs, including those that target substance abuse during pregnancy, much more needs to be done.[103] Funding is often minimal even though treatment is more effective and less expensive than incarceration.[104] Only nine states require drug treatment facilities to give priority to pregnant women, and only four prohibit facilities from discriminating against those women.[105] That has to change, and a promising approach is to integrate substance abuse treatment into standard prenatal programs.[106] Society has a compelling interest in protecting fetal health, but the most effective way to do so is by respecting the needs of women as well.

Birth Control

Although the Supreme Court seemingly settled the issue of Americans' right to contraceptives 50 years ago, questions resurfaced in the run-up to the 2012 election.[107] The Senate narrowly defeated Republican-proposed legislation that would have permitted any employer to exclude contraceptive coverage from its employee health insurance plans based on moral or religious objections. When Sandra Fluke, a Georgetown law student, was denied the opportunity to testify on an otherwise all-male panel considering the proposed legislation, she was denounced by right-wing commentators. Rush Limbaugh called her a "slut" who "wants to be paid to have sex," and asserted that she was "having sex so frequently that she can't afford all the birth-control pills that she needs."[108] Public outrage caused over 100 advertisers to withdraw ads from his program.

In commenting on the funding controversy, humorist Calvin Trillin devoted one of his Deadline Poet columns to "Contraception (of All Things)":

> Republicans are bashing birth control,
> As candidates far-rightward scurry.
> The voters haven't heard such talk in years.
> We're going backward in a hurry.[109]

At the same time, opponents of contraception coverage took to the courts. By 2013, more than 45 lawsuits had been filed asserting religious objections to a requirement in the Affordable Care Act that employers include birth control in employee health insurance plans.[110] The Supreme Court has granted review of two of those cases.[111]

Similar controversies erupted over Republican efforts to defund Planned Parenthood. Arizona representative Jon Kyl claimed on the floor of the House that "90 percent of what Planned Parenthood does is abortions." When informed that the actual figure was around 3 percent, his office released a statement saying that his claim was "not intended to be factual."[112] Commentator Glenn Beck stated that "only hookers" used Planned Parenthood; in fact, one in five women has visited a PP clinic.[113] Although federal defunding efforts were unsuccessful, similar campaigns have been effective in some states.[114] In explaining his vote to slash subsidies, one New Hampshire Executive Council member stated, "If they want to have a good time, why not let them pay for it?"[115] Lack of access to birth control is one reason that unintended pregnancy has grown by almost 30 percent over the last two decades.[116] About 40 percent of unintended births are unwanted and the remainder are mistimed.[117]

Partly in response to that concern, the federal Food and Drug Administration recently approved the sale of emergency contraceptives over the counter to all women and girls over age 15 without a prescription. That decision raises a broader question: Why not permit access to all oral birth control over the counter? Other countries permit such sales, and the pill presents fewer risks than many other medicines sold without a prescription, including pain pills like Motrin, which can cause stomach bleeding.[118] The American College of Obstetricians and Gynecologists has recommended that oral contraceptives be available over the counter and believes that, with a packaging insert about proper use and precautions, they could be used safely.[119] Enhancing access to contraceptives is one way to reduce the rate of unintended pregnancy and the necessity of abortion.

Adolescent Pregnancy

Other restrictions on access to birth control involve adolescents, who account for a disproportionate number of abortions. The United States has the highest adolescent pregnancy rates in the developed world.[120] Part of the reason involves limitations on teens' access to accurate facts regarding reproductive issues. For the last 15 years, the federal government has supported pregnancy prevention programs for adolescents that teach about abstinence only. Under federal regulations, these programs must instruct students that abstaining from sex is "the only certain way to avoid out-of-wedlock-pregnancy, sexually transmitted diseases, and other associated health problems," and that "sexual activity outside of marriage is likely to have harmful physical and psychological effects."[121] Although much of the funding for these programs expired in 2009 and 2010, it was renewed as part of the Affordable Health Care Act. Supporters of abstinence-only education argue that the "most effective oral contraceptive yet devised is the word no," and that the "only safe sex is no sex."[122] Some programs couple their message with religious themes. Their "reasons to wait" include "God wants us to be pure," and their advice includes "pretend Jesus is on your date."[123]

Critics of this approach do not object to encouraging student resistance to unwanted sex, but they also believe that teens should have accurate information about reproductive issues. As they note, research on abstinence programs consistently finds widespread errors, and no evidence of effectiveness in delaying sexual activity.[124] Restricting access to birth control information reduces birth control practices, not sex. In one survey by the staff of the House of Representatives Committee on Government Reform, four-fifths of abstinence program curricula contained false, misleading, and distorted information about reproductive health, such as misstatements about the ineffectiveness of condoms in preventing sexually transmitted disease, or the link between abortions and sterility.[125] Comprehensive sex education programs, by contrast, have increased responsible sexual behavior, reduced pregnancy, and have not encouraged sexual activity.[126]

Inadequate access to birth control information and assistance carries a substantial price. Teens in the United States on average begin having sexual intercourse at 17 years of age, about the same time as teens in Germany and the Netherlands. Yet the United States has nine times the adolescent pregnancy rate of the Netherlands and five times that of Germany.[127] Americans under 25 are the fastest growing category of new HIV infections, and one in four teenage girls has a sexually transmitted disease.[128] Abstinence-only education also carries a cost in reinforcing gender stereotypes and marginalizing gays and lesbians. Girls get lessons such as not to wear clothing that will invite "lustful thoughts": as one program put it, "watch what you wear. If you don't aim to please, don't aim to tease."[129] And in states that prohibit same-sex marriage, gay and lesbian relationships are devalued by federal regulations requiring abstinence programs to teach that a "mutually faithful monogamous relationship in the context of marriage is the expected standard of human sexual activity."[130]

Equally problematic are requirements in 37 states for parental notification or consent to adolescent abortion.[131] The Supreme Court has upheld such requirements provided that states have available a bypass procedure permitting exemptions.[132] Under this procedure, judges must authorize an abortion for a minor who demonstrates that she is mature and capable of making her own informed decision, or that the abortion would be in her best interests. In principle, consent and notification procedures seem like a reasonable way of fostering family communication about a crucial issue. But in practice, such policies fall short. They do not increase the likelihood that adolescents will restrict their sexual activity, consult their parents about birth control, or use contraceptives effectively.[133] Minors who wish to avoid parental notification may rely on ineffective or dangerous methods, go out of state, or take advantage of bypass procedures.[134] Or they delay until it is too late.

Even in states without parental notification and consent requirements, most teens voluntarily consult at least one parent.[135] When teens choose not to do so, they usually have a good reason, such as fear of violence or being kicked out of the house.[136] In theory, the bypass process should handle those cases. In practice, as one study concludes, the procedure is "anything but effective, confidential, or timely."[137] Courts almost never have defensible grounds for denying an abortion. It is virtually impossible to identify circumstances in which a minor is too immature to make reproductive decisions for herself, but her best interest involves having a child that she does not want. Yet that does not prevent courts from imposing substantial obstacles to adolescent applicants. In some cases, courts have required teens to attend pro-life counseling sessions from a crisis pregnancy center in order to obtain a waiver of parental consent requirements.[138] In other cases, courts have submitted teens to intrusive or punitive questions, such as "How will you feel about having a dead baby?"[139] Many adolescents have difficulty finding out about the bypass procedure or how to satisfy its requirements; others have difficulty arranging or paying for the multiple trips required to obtain the parental consent waiver, satisfy the waiting period, and obtain the abortion.[140]

Some court and clinic personnel are surprisingly ignorant about the bypass procedure. In one survey of Alabama courts, 25 counties were unprepared to handle requests for information, and 6 counties were unwilling to implement the law.[141] It sometimes took 11 or 12 phone calls to reach someone who had information about the process. Incomplete and erroneous answers were common. Clerks' offices often failed to explain that minors were entitled to a court-appointed lawyer, and some were even unaware that a bypass was possible.[142] Typical responses were "We've never had a case like that. I don't want to get your hopes up. I don't think the court would give permission," or "I'm sorry, there's not any such thing."[143] Some clerks' offices referred applicants to other counties. As one explained, "Our judge doesn't do it: he doesn't believe in it." In another case, even though a doctor had recommended the abortion for medical reasons, the judge "still would not grant it." He was "anti-abortion."[144]

When it comes to policies on adolescent pregnancy, the place we most need education is among adult policymakers. Parental consent requirements should be eliminated or, failing that, bypass procedures should be made more accessible and less traumatic. Better education programs are necessary, as are efforts to address our culture's perverse mix of permissive and prudish social signals. The media bombards teens with sexual images but rarely portrays responsible contraceptive behavior.[145] Masculinity is linked with sexual conquest and femininity with sexual attractiveness. Yet many schools preach chastity, and public policy impedes access to contraception and abortion. The costs are substantial. Almost two-thirds of families headed by teen mothers live in poverty.[146] Compared with peers who delay childbearing, teen mothers have less education, are less likely to be married, and are more likely to have children with greater risks of criminal activity, behavioral problems, and low educational achievement.[147] What is open to question is whether adolescent motherhood is a cause of those disadvantages, or just a continued reflection of the inadequate education and employment options that precede it.[148] In either case, some more effective societal response is clearly in order.

The time has come to stop blaming teens, who want "too much too soon" in sexual relationships, and to rethink policies that offer too little too late in birth control information and assistance. Policymakers want adolescents to "just say no" to sex and childbirth, but offer too few opportunities for saying yes to something else. Particularly for many low-income women, whose educational and employment opportunities are highly limited, early motherhood offers status and meaning that are otherwise unavailable. If we want to make serious headway in responding to the problems of adolescent pregnancy, we should be focusing less on morality and more on poverty. As one 2012 study concluded, "to address teen childbearing in America will require addressing some difficult social problems: in particular, the perceived and actual lack of economic opportunity among those at the bottom of the economic ladder."[149]

Poverty

During the 2012 presidential campaign, discussion of poverty was noticeable only for its absence. According to a study by Fairness and Accuracy in Reporting, substantive discussion of poverty figured in less than one percent of campaign news reports.[150] References to women and poverty were rarer still, although women constitute the majority of poor adults in America. More than one in seven women, 16.3 percent, live below the poverty line, compared with 13.6 of men.[151] Among women age 65 or older, 10.7 percent live in poverty, compared with 6.2 percent of men. Almost twice as many households headed by women are poor (31.2 percent) compared with households headed by men (16.1 percent).[152] Poverty rates are particularly high for black women (25.9 percent), Hispanic women (23.9 percent), and Native American women (27.1 percent).[153] Poverty is associated with a host of problems, including food insecurity, homelessness, poor education, and chronic illness.

In 1996, America's response to poverty underwent a major shift. Vowing to "put an end to welfare as we know it," President Clinton signed into law the Personal Responsibility and Work Opportunity Reconciliation Act. The Act replaced federal entitlements to income support with Temporary Aid to Needy Families (TANF) Block Grants to the states, which sought to assist recipients' transition to work. The underlying premise of reform was in some sense nothing new. It was a return to the distinction between the "deserving" and "undeserving" poor that long characterized American welfare programs.[154] What was new was the equation of "deserving" with working, a link that was fortified by requirements that recipients engage in approved work activities within two years of receiving benefits. States were not allowed to use TANF funds to pay benefits to families who had been on welfare more than five years. Nor could these funds go to support legal immigrants for five years after their arrival.[155] Block grants were designed to be used for job training, childcare assistance, and marriage promotion.

Welfare reform was in large part a response to long-standing criticisms that an entitlement system based solely on need discouraged work and rewarded out-of-wedlock childrearing. Critics argued that without a distinction between the deserving and the undeserving poor, indigent parents would have inadequate incentives to take responsibility for providing for themselves and their families.[156] One benefit of reform is that recipients are no longer demonized as shirkers; they are now part of the working poor and their poverty cannot be simply be attributed to their own shiftlessness.[157]

Other impacts of welfare reform have been mixed. In the first decade of implementation of the Act, the number of welfare recipients declined, and paid employment and earnings among low-income single mothers increased. Caseloads peaked in the pre-reform era at 5.1 million families; 12 years later, the number of families on cash assistance dropped to 1.9 million.[158] However, some of that improvement may have been the result of general gains in the economy during the first five years following welfare reform. Other factors may have been the five-year ceiling on benefits, and the culture of denial that prevailed in many welfare offices. Workers had an incentive to keep people off the rolls because block grants weren't tied to caseloads: the fewer the recipients, the more money states had to use for purposes other than benefits.[159] Positive trends slowed after 2001, and poverty increased in the wake of the economic crisis.[160] The number of families in extreme poverty, those living on $2.00 a day or less per person, grew 67 percent between 1996 and 2011.[161]

The financial downturn that began in 2008 posed new challenges for the welfare system. Because the federal block grant system provided no additional funding to meet growing needs, and the stimulus package included no increases for TANF, many state and local governments proved unable to address economic hardship. The central rationale of welfare reform, that all able-bodied parents should work, was inconsistent with the declining job market. Economic vulnerability expanded as a growing number of formerly middle-class parents proved unable to meet basic subsistence needs, although they often had too many assets to qualify for assistance.[162]

By 2011, the fifteenth anniversary of welfare reform, the poverty rate for families was about the same (12.5 percent) as it had been when reform began. The number of Americans living in extreme poverty had increased.[163] Benefits fell below 50 percent of the poverty line in all states. The median TANF benefit for a family of three was about a third of the poverty level.[164] Although poverty and unemployment rates for single mothers were at their highest levels in at least 20 years, the percentage of families on assistance had declined.[165] Welfare caseloads had fallen 60 percent since 1996.[166] The result was that only 28 percent of the poor were receiving welfare, compared with 75 percent in 1995.[167] For single parent families, welfare payments do significantly less to reduce poverty in the United States than in other comparable countries.[168] The American poverty rate is twice the European average.[169] According to the Organization for Economic Cooperation and Development, the United States has the fourth highest poverty rate among 34 OECD countries.[170] Many American families have reported insufficient food, housing, utilities, and healthcare, and the inadequacy of assistance has kept women trapped in violent relationships.[171]

The expectation of welfare reform that recipients of temporary aid would transition out of poverty remains unmet. Studies find that between 50 and 75 percent of poor families remain poor.[172] One survey of 40,000 households found that about one-third of women who were no longer on welfare had to cut the size of meals, or skip meals, and about half either often or sometimes ran out of food and couldn't afford to buy more.[173]

Multiple problems plague the implementation of welfare reform. One is the absence of decently paying jobs at the skill levels of those in need. When recipients do find work, they often lose their eligibility for childcare subsidies and Medicaid before they earn enough to pay for those services.[174] A second problem is that many states do not consider college attendance as meeting work requirements; the number of recipients enrolled in college has dropped since reform, even though post-secondary education is the surest long-term path out of poverty.[175] Difficulties in understanding welfare requirements pose other problems. About half of those eligible for some benefits don't get them, partly because of unawareness that they may qualify for childcare help, health insurance, and food stamps.[176] Because welfare subsidies come nowhere close to meeting recipients' basic needs, most rely on unreported income. If detected, that income can subject them to substantial penalties, including bans on further assistance.[177]

Other problems involve work-family conflicts. The number of poor families needing childcare assistance vastly exceeds the supply available.[178] As Chapter 3 notes, lack of backup care, coupled with the irregular hours and inflexible schedules of many low-wage jobs, compounds the difficulties. Children often suffer due to the lack of supervision and additional responsibilities in caring for younger siblings, which in turn impairs school performance.[179] Tragedy can also result when children are left alone so that parents can meet work requirements. In one New York case, two children perished in a fire when their mother left them to make her late night shift at McDonald's and the babysitter and father failed to arrive in time.[180]

The hardships are greatest for the 10–20 percent of recipients at the bottom of the income scale. Their circumstances have worsened since reform. These individuals have problems such as substance abuse, mental health or learning disabilities, domestic violence, inadequate education, and criminal records, which keep them from earning a living wage.[181]

Even those who manage to transition to full-time work remain a considerable distance from true economic security. Jason DeParle's *The American Dream* chronicles a number of examples. One, who looks to be a success story, is Angie Jobe. After a seven-year struggle, she managed to land a job as a nurse assistant and became able to support her family without welfare. But her commute begins at 5:30 a.m., she often needs to work double shifts and overtime, and sometimes still cannot pay her utility bill. Her daughter, who spent much of her childhood caring for siblings, got pregnant and dropped out of school at age 17 to take a low-wage job as a checkout clerk.[182]

Yet, despite major problems in the welfare system, the climate for reform is unpromising. Cash-strapped states and a deficit-conscious Congress have shown no enthusiasm for enhancing the safety net of the poor, who lack influence in the political process.[183] For example, "the consensus among lawmakers is not *whether* food stamps should be reduced, but by how much."[184] The consensus position was to cut $8 billion over the next decade.[185]

There has been equally little interest in addressing the nation's growing income inequality. During the Occupy Wall Street movement of 2011, a number of spin-off groups, such as Women Occupying Wall Street and Women Occupy, pointed out how women disproportionately bear the costs of inequality because they are underrepresented at the top and overrepresented at the bottom of the economic hierarchy.[186] Since the 1980s, the after-tax income of the top one percent of the nation's earners nearly tripled, while the after-tax income of the bottom 80 percent declined.[187] The 400 richest Americans now have more wealth than the entire bottom half of the population.[188]

It is, of course, true, as defenders of the current system observe, that income inequality is not a direct cause of poverty: "The rich, in other words, are not the reason why the poor are poor."[189] But neither is it true that poverty bears no relationship to inequality, or that its current extent is the natural outgrowth of a market system that rewards individual differences in talent and hard work. Rather, "money breeds power and power breeds more money."[190] Income inequality translates into political inequality, and political influence affects the tax, revenue, and distributional policies that in turn advantage the wealthy. Income inequality also translates into inequality in life chances. Economic status affects many factors that influence capacity to succeed in a market system, such as education, nutrition, health, and housing. A child born into the bottom one-fifth of the economic spectrum in the United States has only about a 17 percent chance of making it into the upper two-fifths.[191] Upward mobility in America is more constrained than in most comparable nations.

Two-thirds of the public believe that wealth is unfairly distributed.[192] The challenge remaining is to translate that perception into political action that will reduce the hardships of the "have nots." While there are no simple solutions, neither do we lack for promising policy proposals. Any meaningful reform agenda needs to recognize, as Georgetown professor Peter Edelman puts it, that "poverty has many faces." An "elderly widow with a limited work history and no extended family has very different needs than an eighteen-year-old high school dropout looking for a job."[193] A range of strategies is necessary to take account of that diversity in experience.

One obvious place to start is adjusting TANF grants to reflect increased needs, and to reverse the trend in the most recent TANF reauthorization vote that left the poorest states worst off.[194] Raising the minimum wage and indexing it to inflation would also help, since women constitute two-thirds of minimum wage workers.[195] The rate has only been increased three times in the last 30 years, and the current level will not lift a full-time year-round worker out of poverty.[196] In the absence of a federal increase, we need state and local initiatives.[197] Minimum wage and overtime protection should also be extended to cover domestic and home care workers, who are almost entirely female and who currently receive protection in only a third of the states.[198] Expanded educational and employment options are still more critical. Pursuing a college degree should count toward meeting work requirements for welfare recipients. In-kind assistance needs to be available for all who are eligible: currently only one in seven mothers receives childcare to which she is entitled, and only one in four eligible families receives housing assistance.[199] More effective partnerships between schools, colleges, employers, and community organizations should aim to prepare low-income students for the decently paying jobs that are projected to be most available. Governments that are cutting vocational education programs should rethink their priorities; the cuts may save money in the short run, but the long-term costs are more substantial.

How to pay for these initiatives is a matter on which reasonable people can disagree. But at least part of the answer is a more equitable tax structure. The 2012 legislation preventing further tax breaks for the wealthiest Americans is a step in the right direction, but much more needs to be done. As Edelman concludes, "the only way to improve the lot of the poor is by requiring the rich to pay more of the cost . . . of governing the country that enables their huge accretion of wealth."[200] To make that possible, the women's movement needs to focus more attention on issues of poverty and inequality. It needs to challenge stereotypes of the undeserving poor and work in alliance with other grassroots and policy groups committed to more just distributive policies.[201]

Social Security

Gender inequalities "become glaring in retirement, especially for those from communities of color and those who live to an advanced age. For too many women, retirement is the culmination of an entire career—an entire lifetime—of pay and income inequality."[202] That is the conclusion of *Breaking the Social Security Glass Ceiling*, a comprehensive joint report of the National Committee to Preserve Social Security and Medicare Foundation, the Institute for Women's Policy Research, and the NOW Foundation. The report found that, because of the gender gap in pay and women's interrupted labor force participation due to work-family conflicts, gender "disparities aggregate" and become pronounced during women's later years. The consequence is both substantially lower Social Security income for women than men, and greater dependence on that income. Retired women's benefits are only about three-quarters those of their male counterparts.[203] Only slightly over a quarter of women age 65–74 have pensions, compared with over 40 percent of men.[204]

The stakes in Social Security reform are substantial. A woman who reaches age 65 can expect to live an additional 20 years.[205] A disproportionate number of those women will live in or near poverty. Almost half of elderly unmarried women depend on Social Security for 90 percent or more of their total income.[206] To improve older women's safety net, a variety of reforms have been proposed.[207] One of the most important is to provide credit for time spent in caregiving. Until now, the only partial compensation for such work has occurred through spousal benefits, which do not provide full benefits and which do not assist unmarried caregivers, or spouses who divorce before 10 years of marriage. Proposed legislation, such as the Social Security Caregiver Credit Act, would provide a more equitable way of acknowledging care. A variety of more technical provisions should be adjusted to promote gender equity and to ensure an adequate standard of living for the elderly.[208] If reforming Social Security is part of the negotiations over addressing the debt crisis, we need to do it in ways that do not penalize those who need help most.

=====

The political challenges of all of these issues are substantial. Women are divided by class and ideology, and those most in need of reform have least leverage in the political process. But the stakes in these debates are too substantial to ignore. Ronald Reagan once famously quipped that "we fought a war on poverty and poverty won."[209] The battle lines are still drawn and we cannot settle for defeat.

Sexual Abuse

"A little bit nutty and a little bit slutty." That was how journalist David Brock described Anita Hill after her Senate testimony concerning sexual harassment by Supreme Court nominee Clarence Thomas. Such descriptions, sometimes more tactfully expressed, are common in cases involving sexual abuse. Victims as much as perpetrators are on trial. A common assumption in cases of harassment, domestic violence, and rape, is that women provoke or exaggerate the conduct at issue.

Sexual Harassment

Workplace Harassment

For centuries, women were harassed, but the law offered neither a label nor a remedy. Female employees spoke of having "difficulties" with a coworker, and the difficulties were always hers, not his. All that changed in the 1980s when the Equal Employment Opportunities Commission and the courts began recognizing sexual harassment as a form of prohibited sex discrimination.[1] What has not changed is the frequency of the problem. Catharine MacKinnon puts it bluntly: "So far as is known, men sexually harass women as often as they did before sexual harassment was illegal."[2] Researchers find that abuse has not diminished since they started collecting data in the late 1970s.[3] Nor has its gendered nature. The vast majority of victims are female and the vast majority of perpetrators are male.[4] Estimates of the number of women who have experienced sexual harassment range from 30 to 80 percent, depending on who is asked and how the term is defined.[5] What has changed is the frequency of formal complaints, which have doubled over the last decade. However, these complaints represent only a fraction of abuse. Victims report only about 5–15 percent of harassment, and less than 3 percent of cases end up in litigation.[6] A textbook case involved San Diego mayor Bob Filner, who was accused of groping and kissing women against their will. Eighteen women eventually came forward with allegations of sexual harassment, but only one filed a lawsuit or formal complaint.[7] Major barriers to reporting include guilt, shame, fears of retaliation and loss of privacy, an unwillingness to jeopardize working relationships, and doubts that an effective response to a complaint will be forthcoming.[8] As one woman put it, "You have to either ignore it, or become the most unliked person: 'Here comes the fun police.'"[9]

Those concerns are not unfounded. Some surveys suggest that most complainants experience retaliation, and believe that complaining made the situation worse.[10] Winning a suit is difficult and expensive. The law recognizes two forms of sexual harassment: (1) quid pro quo harassment, in which the harasser requires sexual contact or favors as a condition of employment, and (2) hostile environment harassment, in which the victim experiences unwelcome sexual conduct that has the purpose or effect of interfering with an individual's performance or creating an intimidating, hostile, or offensive work environment.[11] Individuals face serious evidentiary hurdles in establishing either form of abuse.

Federal and most state employment law does not permit suits against the individuals directly responsible for harassment; complainants must instead sue their employers.[12] And in cases where employers take no "adverse action," such as firing the complainant, they have an affirmative defense to liability if they can establish that they "exercised reasonable care to prevent and correct promptly any sexually harassing behavior" and that the complainant "unreasonably failed to take advantage of any preventive or corrective opportunities. . . ."[13] Surveys of lawsuits raising such a defense find that virtually all an employer needs to do to avoid liability is to promulgate a policy banning sexual harassment and to establish a viable grievance procedure.[14] Indeed, some researchers conclude that an employer would be imprudent to do more, such as provide a hotline for complaints, since this would encourage reporting, which eliminates the affirmative defense.[15] Although reporting is the option of last resort for complainants, and few take advantage of the opportunity, most courts treat any failure to complain promptly as unreasonable, and a bar to liability.[16] "Generalized fears" of retaliation do not justify such a failure.[17] Yet women often have understandable reasons to delay or avoid reporting. They don't want to seem humorless or hypersensitive, or make an uncomfortable situation worse. Many wait to see if the situation escalates. Courts, however, often consider any delay in reporting fatal to the plaintiffs' claim; a delay of even eight days has been held to be too late.[18]

Employees who satisfy the prompt complaint rule still face significant challenges in convincing courts that the offensive conduct was sufficiently severe and pervasive to justify liability. Although conservative critics sometimes argue that "a wink or a leer can be money in the bank," a survey of reported cases find otherwise.[19] Often the situation needs to be "hellish" before courts will find it actionable.[20] Cases that have fallen short suggest the gap between what judges and women find tolerable. One example involved a male worker who made a series of abusive comments to an African American employee, including the instruction to "suck my dick, you black bitch," as he dropped his pants and held his genitals. The court granted summary judgment without trial in favor of the defendant. Although acknowledging that the man's conduct was "deplorable and even offensive, humiliating, and threatening," the trial judge concluded that it was not sufficiently "severe or pervasive to . . . create an abusive working environment."[21] Another case that a trial court found insufficiently "egregious" involved a supervisor who made comments about a woman's sex life, asked when she had had sex, intimated that they should have an affair, groped, grabbed, and hugged her, and accused her of mental problems when she asked him to stop.[22] Also insufficient were claims that an assistant manager had touched the plaintiffs' breasts while making suggestive comments, offered to take her to a local hotel to have a "good time," and patted her buttocks. In the court's view, although the behavior was loathsome and inappropriate, it was too "sporadic and isolated" to justify liability.[23] Although over 90 percent of Americans agree that deliberate sexual touching definitely or probably constitutes harassment, courts have frequently granted summary judgment for defendants in cases involving such conduct.[24]

Some courts have been so dismissive of plaintiffs' claims that they have reversed a jury's awards of damages. In one such case, after the plaintiff refused a supervisor's advances, he subjected her to a series of abusive requests, created a poster portraying her as the president of the "Man Hater's Club of America," and asked her to type a draft of the tenets of the "He Men Women Hater's Club." In reversing a jury finding for the plaintiff, the court acknowledged that the conduct was "boorish, chauvinistic, and decidedly immature" but not so "severe and extreme that a reasonable person would find that the terms or conditions of [her] employment had been altered."[25]

The requirement that plaintiffs prove that harassment is unwelcome has also been problematic because it opens the door to intrusive pretrial discovery. Questions about promiscuity, marital fidelity, and use of profanity are designed to deter plaintiffs from bringing claims or to force an inadequate settlement.[26] A typical example involved a plaintiff who was fired after complaining about sexual overtures from a representative of one of her employer's largest customers. The defendant questioned her about extramarital affairs and sexually transmitted diseases, and even sought to force her to submit to an AIDS test. Although the court ultimately refused to admit much of this evidence, the plaintiff endured significant humiliation during the pretrial discovery process.[27] Yet defense attorneys often defend such practices as necessary to discourage frivolous complaints, so that plaintiffs do not assume that "making a sexual harassment complaint will be a breeze."[28]

Another limitation of current law is that it fails to cover harassment that is not specifically based on sex. Some one-third of surveyed American workers report experiencing bullying behavior, defined as verbal or psychological forms of hostile workplace conduct that persists for at least six months.[29] Unlike European law, American statutes fail to provide a remedy for such abuse. Some courts also have strained to characterize harassing behavior as not sexual in nature. In one case, a federal court of appeals held that the repeated use of the term "sick bitch" was not a "gendered" term. "In its normal usage," said the court, "'bitch' is simply a pejorative term for a woman."[30] Why that did not make it "gendered" was left unexplained.

A further limitation of sexual harassment law involves office romances that create problems of bias and subtle coercion. Surveys generally reveal that about 40 percent of employees have dated someone from work, and 20 percent of affairs are between superiors and subordinates.[31] Only about a third of employees report that their employer has a policy on office romances.[32] Yet around two-thirds of female employees and three-fifths of male employees believe that affairs between supervisors and subordinates create perceptions of favoritism and diminish respect for the supervisor.[33] A well publicized case in point involved David Letterman, who had serial sexual relationships with staff, a practice that even he acknowledged as "creepy."[34]

In short, current harassment law asks too much of complainants and too little of perpetrators or their employers. Courts should adopt a less restrictive view, informed by social science research, about what reasonable persons consider severe and pervasive. Close cases should proceed to a jury, and should not be dismissed by judges based on their own subjective perceptions. Courts should also modify employer liability standards in light of what research shows about victims' behavior. Juries should have the option to decide whether a victim's failure to report harassing conduct promptly was reasonable under the circumstances. Intrusive inquiries into plaintiffs' other sexual behavior should be impermissible.

Employers should also do more to prevent harassing conduct, including bullying that has no sexual content. To that end, they need to know more about the proactive strategies that are most effective. Despite the millions of dollars that are invested in sexual harassment training, we lack evidence that it significantly reduces abusive behaviors.[35] The few studies to date yield inconclusive results. Some find no long-term improvements in attitudes, and others indicate that poorly designed programs can entrench gender stereotypes, encourage male backlash, and perpetuate the very biases that they are designed to confront.[36] Recent experience with California's mandatory training law illustrates the risks. Some programs highlight trivial examples of harassment and exaggerate the risk of personal liability for unintended offenses. According to one program, statements such as "you look nice in that dress," or acts of chivalry like holding a door open, fall into a "dangerous grey areas." Even inadvertent offenders can reportedly risk losing not only their "reputation," but also their "home, car, and life savings" in harassment lawsuits. Too many individuals may end up seeing these required programs and their exaggerated risks of liability as overblown reactions to oversensitive feminists, who should get a life, not a law. As one male supervisor put it in his evaluation, "This appears to be a course designed by idiots for idiots."[37]

Schools

Federal civil rights law prohibits sexual harassment in educational institutions that receive federal funds. Yet despite several decades of enforcement efforts, such abuse is persistent and pervasive. In one study by the American Association of University Women, almost half of middle and high school students had been sexually harassed in the preceding year, and only 9 percent had told any adult at school.[38] About three-fifths of college students also report experiencing unwelcome sexual behavior.[39] The incidents range in seriousness. Journalists have a field day with occasional overreactions, like a six-year-old suspended for a smooch, or a complaint involving a Goya painting of a nude.[40] But the cases that are reported to school authorities generally reveal serious repeated abuse, and female students are disproportionately targeted.[41] They are taunted, threatened, and assaulted; lesbians and gays are particularly vulnerable.[42] Depression, insomnia, absenteeism, and impaired school performance are common results. Some campuses have experienced suicides; others have been subject to widespread publicity for unresponsiveness to harassment and assaults.[43]

The problems are compounded by a liability structure that gives schools incentives to avoid knowledge of abuse. In cases involving harassment of a student by a school employee, schools are liable only if they have actual knowledge of the misconduct and respond with "deliberate indifference."[44] In cases of peer harassment, schools are liable only for "deliberate indifference" to known harassment where the school exercises "substantial control over the harasser," and the conduct is so "severe, pervasive, and objectively offensive that it can be said to deprive the victims of access to the educational opportunities or benefits provided by the school."[45] These limitations on liability encourage a "see no evil" mindset that locates responsibility anywhere and everywhere else. A preferable alternative would be to hold schools accountable for

negligence: for failing to establish reasonable policies, procedures, and training or to respond effectively to conduct that they knew or reasonably should
have known was abusive.

Institutions of higher education should also be responsible for creating
more adequate policies regarding faculty–student relationships. Only a small
minority have banned sexual relationships between teachers and students
under their supervision.[46] Common assumptions are that "the urge to merge
is powerful," "they're trying to ban love!," and "consensual relationships are
none of the university's business."[47] Such views understate the harms of such
conduct. Faculty whose self-image and self-interest are at stake may underes-
timate the pressures that students experience. Regardless of the professor's
intentions, students may believe that their acceptance or rejection of sexual
overtures will have academic consequences. One study found that close to
three-quarters of those who had rejected a faculty member's advances considered them coercive; of those who had sexual relationships with faculty, about
half indicated that some degree of coercion was involved.[48] If the professor has
any advisory or supervisory authority over the student, both the fact and appearance of academic integrity are in question. The potential for unconscious
bias in evaluations, recommendations, and mentoring is inescapable. Even if
the faculty member does not in fact offer or deliver special advantages, others
may suspect favoritism. The reputation of both parties may be compromised.
Faculty–student sexual involvement that poses potential conflicts of interest
should be treated accordingly.

Sex in Cyberspace

The anonymity and ease of online harassment has widened its scope. Between
20 and 40 percent of youth ages 12–17 report experiencing some form of cyber
bullying.[49] A majority of adolescent and adult targets are women, and they are
often subject to distinctively gendered abuse, including pornographic images,
threats of sexual violence, false rumors about promiscuity, and postings of
their home addresses with the suggestion that they should be raped.[50] The
nonprofit organization Working to Halt Online Abuse finds that almost three-
quarters of individuals reporting cyber harassment are female.[51] The extent of
sexual aggression was apparent in a University of Maryland study of attacks associated with the chat medium Internet Relay Chat. Users with female names
received, on average, 100 "malicious private messages" with sexually explicit
or threatening language; users with male names averaged fewer than four.[52]

On campus, online misogyny is a common occurrence. In one widely publicized incident, Cornell students posted anatomically explicit and derogatory
remarks about women on a male-only bulletin board. They also circulated an

obscene caricature of a female candidate for student office, as well as a parody titled "Top 75 Reasons Why Women (Bitches) Should Not Have Freedom of Speech."[53] At Yale, athletic teams and fraternities circulated an anonymous e-mail with photos of incoming freshman women, ranked by how drunk the writer would need to be to sleep with them.[54] Two Yale law students also were vilified on AutoAdmit, an Internet discussion board, and then "Google-bombed" so that threads containing defamatory statements appeared as one of the first search results returned by Google. Among the posts were claims that one or the other of the women had "huge fake tits and is universally hated," had engaged in a lesbian affair with a Yale administrator, had bribed her way into Yale Law School, had engaged in drug use and "bashing gay people," and had "whored around like a feral cat."[55] Commentators on the site maintained that the women had no right to ask for removal of the posts. As one put it, "If these girls can't handle a little humor, how can they handle life?"[56]

Online vilification can have significant consequences. It can damage reputations and lead to serious mental health problems and even suicide.[57] It can also suppress expression. The group Anonymous devotes efforts to silencing feminists on the web and claims credit for closing over a hundred sites and blogs. Group members hack and spam online accounts, post doctored pictures showing female bloggers in obscene poses, and saturate their video blogs with sexually violent pictures.[58] One consequence is that women retreat from chat rooms and gaming communities, shut down blogs and websites, and close comments on blog posts.[59] When women started Rapebook, a page designed to tackle "misogyny on Facebook," the founders were threatened with rape and death, and were bombarded with pornographic images.[60] Friends and potential employers have ready access to defamatory comments. Online vilification also deters women from making sexual assault complaints. In an incident in Torrington, Connecticut, two 13-year-old girls were bullied and harassed online after they reported being raped by two 18-year-old football players. Online posters repeatedly referred to the girls as "snitches" and "whores."[61]

Posts providing addresses and sexual comment have also led to offline stalking.[62] As Chapter 5 notes, online demonization of abortion providers and clinic users has sometimes had tragic consequences; a number of doctors have been murdered after being targeted by "wanted" posters on websites of pro-life groups. Women entering abortion clinics have also been photographed and identified online in efforts to discourage others from seeking abortion services.

Part of what perpetuates the problem is the denial that cyber abuse is a serious problem. Serious harassment is often trivialized as "frivolous frat boy rants," "bad taste," or "playground silliness."[63] Law enforcement agents have sometimes declined to pursue cyber attacks on the grounds that women can "just turn off their computers."[64]

We need better responses. Much more can and should be done through existing criminal law and tort prohibitions to hold individuals accountable for online threats and abuse.[65] But the problem is deeply rooted, and needs to be addressed at more than the legal level. First Amendment protections for speech make categorical prohibitions impossible; the only solution is cultural. Anonymous cyber harassment reflects and reinforces sexism that has become costly to express openly. We cannot combat online abuse without dealing with the fundamental sources of sexual violence and subordination.

In commenting on the state of contemporary harassment law, MacKinnon concludes that it has had important but limited effect:

> Sexual harassment is still not actionable every place it occurs; zero tolerance is the rule virtually nowhere, resistance is far from safe or costless.... Institutions are often recalcitrant in taking responsibility and are often absolved of liability when they are oblivious. Victims seldom receive the support they deserve. Complaining about sexual harassment can be more injurious, if also more self-respecting, than suffering in silence.[66]

All that needs to change. And change is possible only if we demand it.

Domestic Violence

The Trivialization of Abuse

In a widely publicized case, members of a men's right rights group sued to stop Minnesota commissioners from using government funds to support domestic-violence programs. Activists claimed that feminists "hyped" the idea that women need protection, which they characterized as "ideological tripe."[67] The suit failed, but the attitudes expressed reflect the culture's frequent trivialization of domestic violence. Stores sell T-shirts with slogans such as "50,000 battered women and I still eat mine plain." The 2013 National Rifle Association Convention featured a mannequin target called "The Ex" that simulates bleeding when someone shoots it.[68] Such callousness is also apparent in the euphemisms used to describe domestic abuse. Prominent examples include those on display in the prosecution of O. J. Simpson for the murder of his wife. Simpson had a history of brutal domestic assaults, which he described as "get[ting] physical." His lawyer, Johnnie Cochran, referred to the beating that led to Simpson's earlier conviction as an "unfortunate incident." A juror was equally forgiving of the incident, which he saw as part of the normal "ups and downs with spouses and girlfriends."[69]

A similar trivialization of injuries is apparent in many male batterers' description of their crimes:

> I didn't really hit her or nothing. I just threw her down.
> She bruises easily.
> They're not heavy blows or anything like that.
> I didn't kill her or anything.[70]

Other men see their abuse as an understandable response to their partner's conduct.

> She makes me so angry when she won't do what I want her to do.
> It's not supposed to be that way. A girl is supposed to get along with a man.
> She was the provoker.
> [She] yelled at me, haggled with me, and lectured me. . . . If [she] could just give in, the whole mess could be avoided.
> It was over sex. It happened because I was trying to motivate her. And she didn't seem too motivated.[71]

In one study, 60 percent of batterers attributed some responsibility for their conduct to the victim.[72]

Similar attitudes have also figured in judicial decisions. Some give a "domestic discount" in sentences for marital assaults.[73] In one celebrated example, a Florida judge heard testimony about a husband who doused his wife with lighter fluid and set her on fire. The judge responded by singing "You light up my wife," to the tune of "You Light Up My Life."[74]

The Frequency, Causes, and Consequences of Domestic Violence

To be sure, the last quarter century has witnessed significant progress against domestic violence, particularly since passage of the 1994 Violence Against Women Act, reauthorized most recently in 2013. Battered women's shelters, specialized domestic violence courts, and offender treatment programs have been established. Mandatory arrest laws have been passed, and law enforcement has increased. Yet while the amount of domestic violence has been reduced, the proportion of women victimized by partner abuse has not substantially declined. An estimated quarter of women in the United States have experienced physical or sexual violence by an intimate partner or acquaintance at some point in their lifetime.[75] Approximately one-sixth of women have experienced stalking.[76] Over 90 percent of female homicide victims are killed by men with whom they have had a relationship.[77] The United States has the highest rate of spousal homicide in the industrialized world.[78] Close to half of all homeless women and children have left violent situations.[79] Countless other women are victims of non-physical abuse designed to intimidate, such as threats, isolation, and control over necessities. Indeed, some evidence suggests that such non-physical abuse can be at least as harmful as physical assaults.[80] In addition to physical injuries, women suffer trauma, anxiety, social isolation, vandalism, theft, and harassment. Economic costs include medical and shelter expenses and loss of jobs because of absenteeism. Estimates of the price of domestic violence exceed $10 billion annually.[81]

Women are more vulnerable to domestic violence than men. Whether women are as physically aggressive as men has been disputed, but most research indicates that women are less likely than men to inflict significant injury and are more often responding to violence than initiating it.[82] Women are the victims in three out of four murders of intimate partners, and domestic violence is the leading cause of death for pregnant women.[83] African American women and Native American women are at the highest risk of intimate partner homicide.[84] Immigrant women are also particularly vulnerable to abuse, because they are often unfamiliar with local laws and support programs, and are reluctant to contact police.

Theories about the causes of domestic violence stress multiple factors. Psychological theories blame childhood abuse and personality disorders, including psychopathologies and excessive need for control. Sociological theories emphasize the extent to which violence is learned behavior, which responds to cues from families and the cultural environment. Many batterers engage in other criminal conduct, so the dynamics of domestic abuse are not always unique to that setting.[85]

A common response to such patterns is "Why doesn't she just leave?" The answer, too often, is that she has nowhere safe to go. The time when women are most likely to suffer injuries in an intimate relationship is when trying to end it. Forty percent of protective orders are violated. And at least 30 percent of victims who pursue legal action are re-assaulted during the process of prosecution.[86] In one study, married women who separated from their husbands were nearly four times more likely to report that their husbands had raped, physically assaulted, and/or stalked them than women who lived with their husbands.[87] Poor women are particularly vulnerable to abuse because their lack of financial resources and employment skills makes them economically dependent on the relationship.[88] At the same time, violence and stalking impairs their ability to work, which perpetuates that dependence.

Other theories of why women stay in abusive relationships involve cultural factors that legitimate abuse or prioritize marriage, doubts that escape is possible, and cycles of violence, including a "honeymoon" phase in which batterers' remorse and kindness lull women into believing that the abuse will cease.[89] Yet many law enforcement officials still blame women for failing to end violent relationships. Expressing common frustration with uncommon candor, one judge told a woman seeking a protective order, "If you go back one more time, I'll hit you myself."[90]

Inadequacies in Responses to Domestic Violence

What is it that women want regarding domestic violence policy? At a minimum, the agenda includes adequate shelters and support programs, effective prevention and offender treatment strategies, and law enforcement policies that respect women's own choices. The current system falls short in all three respects. Support programs for victims come nowhere close to meeting the need. Some shelters in urban areas turn down as many as 5,000 requests a year.[91] Those refused assistance often have nowhere safe to go. One domestic violence advocate in Oregon reported being asked if she knew a safe bridge that women could sleep under.[92] The system offers least to those who need help most: low income, non-white, elderly, disabled, and immigrant women.[93]

A second cluster of problems involves the inadequacy of state efforts to prevent violence. In too many jurisdictions, domestic matters are not a high priority, and recent budget cutbacks have exacerbated the problem. A textbook illustration is the tragedy at issue in a prominent Supreme Court case, *Castle Rock v. Gonzales.* According to the facts of the complaint, which the Court accepted for purposes of the decision, the ex-husband of Jessica Gonzales violated a civil restraining order when he abducted their three daughters, who were playing in the family's front yard.[94] Gonzales contacted the police six times between 7:30 p.m. and 1:00 a.m. the next morning in an effort to get her husband arrested. In a visit to the police station to file an incident report, Gonzales pleaded with the officers to look for her husband, who had a history of violence. The officer who took the report made "no reasonable effort to enforce the [restraining order] or locate the three children. Instead he went to dinner." The ex-husband subsequently arrived at the police station and opened fire on officers. They shot back, killing him in the exchange, and then discovered the dead bodies of his daughters in his pickup truck.

Although Colorado has a mandatory arrest law for violations of restraining orders, the Supreme Court held that Gonzales was not entitled to sue the state for failure to enforce the statute.[95] She then brought suit before the Inter-American Commission on Human Rights, affiliated with the Organization of American States. She claimed that the United States had violated her rights under the American Declaration of the Rights and Duties of Man, which guaranteed her right to be free from gender-based violence and discrimination.

State Department lawyers responded that the Declaration imposes no duty to prevent crimes inflicted by private individuals and that police officers had acted reasonably on the information available. The Commission rejected that argument. It found that the state's law enforcement system had failed to exercise "due diligence" to protect the Gonzales children and their mother from domestic violence, which violated "the State's obligation not to discriminate and to provide for equal protection before the law under the American Declaration."[96] Accordingly, the Commission recommended that the United States hold responsible those who failed to enforce the protective order and "adopt multifaceted legislation at the federal and state levels, or reform existing legislation to protect women and children from imminent violence and to ensure effective implementation mechanisms."[97]

The *Gonzales* case is not unique. But it should not take an order by the Inter-American Commission on Human Rights to impose accountability on those who act with deliberate indifference to women's repeated requests for assistance. Another example of what goes wrong is *May v. Franklin County Commissioners*, in which the victim called the police three times to report domestic violence by her boyfriend. The second call was coded only a low priority, despite reported threats and noise suggesting an assault in the background. The third call resulted in a police visit, but when the officer received no answer at the door and heard no sounds of struggle, he left without further action. The victim's dead body was discovered the following day. Yet the federal court held that the Constitution's Due Process Clause only serves to protect people from the state, and not to ensure that it protects them from each other.[98]

A similar tragedy occurred in *Pinder v. Johnson*. There, Carol Pinder was assaulted and threatened by an ex-boyfriend, Don Pittman. She told the arresting officer that Pittman posed a future threat and that he had recently been released from prison after serving time for attempted arson at her residence. When she asked if it would be safe for her to return to work that evening, the officer assured her that Pittman would be locked up overnight because a county commissioner would not be available to rule on the charges until morning. Instead, the officer brought Pittman before the commissioner that evening and charged him only with misdemeanors involving trespass and destruction of property. The magistrate released Pittman on his own recognizance and warned him to stay away from Pinder's home. Pittman ignored the warning, and set fire to the house. Pinder was at work, but her three children were at home asleep and died of smoke inhalation. A federal court dismissed Pinder's suit against the police department on the ground that it had no obligation to protect her family from the violence.[99] Other courts have come to similar conclusions, and this doctrine begs for reform along the lines that the Inter-American Commission recommended.[100]

Changes are also needed in laws concerning stalking and domestic violence in the workplace. Bureau of Justice studies find that about 3.4 million individuals, three-quarters of them women, report being subject to stalking, defined as conduct causing reasonable persons to fear for their safety.[101] An estimated 75–95 percent of those who are subject to domestic violence report related problems at work.[102] Problems include assaults, stalking, harassing or threatening phone calls, destruction of work products, and lateness or absenteeism due to physical injuries, legal proceedings, and disruption of childcare and transportation arrangements. American companies lose an estimated $3 billion to $5 billion annually in absenteeism, turnover, lowered productivity, and medical expenses resulting from domestic violence.[103] A common response is to penalize or terminate employees who are victims, which compounds their problems and reinforces economic dependence on abusers. Workplaces that do not provide adequate security compel many women to leave their jobs out of safety concerns. A recent case in point involved a San Diego teacher who was fired from a religious school because her ex-husband could place students and staff in danger. School officials did, however, promise to "continue to pray" for the teacher and her family.[104]

Although about half of victims report losing a job after experiencing domestic violence, only a small number of states have laws protecting them from job discrimination.[105] Law enforcement officials also fail to address stalking that occurs in the course of ongoing relationships.[106] That has to change. Employers need to work with victims to find reasonable solutions that do not punish them for dynamics they cannot control. Changes are also needed in judicial attitudes toward tort suits for employers' failure to take reasonable measures in response to foreseeable violence. These are now difficult cases to win. In *Carroll v. Shoney's*, for example, the court denied relief to the estate of a murdered woman, which sued her restaurant employer for negligence.[107] The woman, who had been beaten by her husband, informed her assistant manager about the abuse and asked him to call the police if her husband came to the restaurant. When the husband arrived and made threats, the police escorted him from the premises, but released him after the restaurant did not press charges. The following day, management rejected the woman's requests to be excused from work and promised to call the police if the man showed up. He did, and shot her in the head before law enforcement officials could be alerted. The majority of the Alabama Supreme Court held that the restaurant was not liable because the murder was not foreseeable. The dissent, by contrast, noted that while that particular consequences could not have been anticipated, some general harm could have been expected, and the defendant had increased the risks by placing the woman at the front counter.[108]

Strategies to increase workplace protections are urgently necessary. A top priority should be state or federal legislation along the lines of the proposed Security and Financial Empowerment Act, which would prohibit discrimination based on domestic violence, guarantee eligible employees time off to address domestic violence issues, and ensure unemployment compensation for those who lose jobs as a result of domestic violence.

Of similar importance is rehabilitation. Since the late 1970s, many jurisdictions have adopted batterer treatment programs in prisons or as alternatives to incarceration. Such programs aim to change attitudes and improve anger management skills. Yet most men referred to these programs do not complete them.[109] And despite their prevalence, surprisingly little data is available on their long-term effectiveness. Much of the existing research is conflicting or hampered by small and non-random samples.[110] Some of the most systematic evidence indicates significant recidivism rates.[111] Other research is clear that offenders who feel that they were treated unfairly by the criminal justice system are more likely to offend again.[112] According to one National Institute of Justice report, "Although interventions are proliferating, there is little evidence that they work."[113] We need to know more about what can enhance defendants' sense of fairness and motivation to change. As one expert put it, "the field of batterer intervention is still in its infancy."[114] Particularly given the significant backlash against domestic violence programs among men's rights groups, there is an urgent need for better data on what can promote changes in male attitudes and behaviors.[115]

Reliable information is also lacking on the effectiveness of other violence prevention and remedial initiatives. For example, some police agencies participate in programs designed to increase outreach to specific populations and to reduce teen violence. Little is known about the impact of these efforts.[116] What we do know underscores the need for effective interventions. Close to one in 10 high school students report being physically hurt by a boyfriend or girlfriend in the preceding year.[117] These youths are more likely to do poorly in school and to suffer from mental health and substance abuse problems.[118] Perpetrators of teen violence may also carry those patterns into future relationships. Among adult victims of rape, stalking, or violence by an intimate partner, almost a quarter of women first experienced some form of partner violence when they were adolescents.[119] The Centers for Disease Control and Prevention have recently launched pilot projects in high-risk urban communities aimed at promoting healthy teen dating relationships.[120] We need more such projects, along with comprehensive evaluations that can identify interventions that work. We also need increased support for programs that we know are successful. Holistic family justice centers that address all of victims' needs for legal and social services can assist abused parties in escaping the conditions that perpetuate abuse.[121]

A final cluster of problems in domestic violence policy involves the failure of the criminal justice system to empower women in decisions that so substantially affect their lives. About half the states have mandatory arrest policies that require police officers to arrest a suspect if there is probable cause to believe that an assault or battery has occurred, without regard to the victim's consent or objection.[122] A related initiative has been mandatory or no-drop prosecution policies, which require prosecutors to pursue domestic violence cases regardless of the victim's wishes. In some jurisdictions, when a defendant is charged with a crime involving domestic violence, prosecutors routinely request a protection order, which prohibits all contact with the victim, again regardless of the victim's preference. These orders function as what one researcher labels "state-imposed de facto divorce."[123] Although the parties may remain formally married, the state has criminalized any contact between them. Even when the victim requests dissolution of the order in the hope of reconciliation, the court may deny the request.

Supporters of mandatory policies argue that they are the best way to force law enforcement officials to take domestic violence seriously. By denying victims a role in the decision, a mandatory approach assertedly deters future abuse and reduces the exposure of victims to pressure and retaliation from the abuser.[124] Whether mandatory policies have such effects is, however, unclear. Some studies find little deterrent impact, increased risk of retaliation, and decreased likelihood that victims will contact police or service providers.[125] Other research finds that arrests deter further abuse.[126] In essence, we know that mandatory arrest policies increase the frequency of arrests, but not how often they translate into successful prosecutions or enhanced safety for victims.[127] What is clear is that arrest and prosecution works best with those who have most to lose from criminal sanctions. The risks of repeat violence are greatest among those who have least to lose: those who are unemployed, poorly educated, unmarried, and have a criminal record already.[128]

Evidence concerning women's views on mandatory policies is also mixed. Some studies suggest that most women want their abuser prosecuted, and support mandatory arrests and no- drop policies.[129] Other research finds that most victims do not want prosecution, due to fear of retaliation, financial dependence, emotional involvement, family and community pressure, or doubt that the proceeding would make things better.[130] An estimated 60–80 percent of victims either recant their testimony or refuse to testify at trial.[131] For many women, interventions over which they have no control can erode their sense of efficacy and autonomy, which have already been compromised by the violence itself. Mandatory prosecution can also deny victims the opportunity to threaten prosecution as leverage to end abuse.[132] In some jurisdictions, victims have even been jailed for refusing to testify after filing an abuse complaint.

The problems are compounded when courts deny victims' requests to dissolve restraining orders or to issue protection orders that permit non-abusive contact. For understandable reasons, judges prefer to err on the side of keeping protections in place; no one wants to have terminated an order for a woman "found face down in the morning."[133] Yet refusing to defer to women's own risk assessments may discourage them from filing requests for restraining orders in the first instance, and denies them bargaining leverage that may help end the abuse.[134] An increasing number of studies find that some women are able to stop the violence and preserve their relationships.[135] Women deserve an opportunity to try.

Directions for Reform

Taken together, such findings suggest several directions for reform in law and public policies. Increasing women's control and long-term safety should be guiding principles; to that end, victims' preferences should receive greater deference. Initiatives to increase workplace protection should be higher priorities.[136] Specialized domestic violence courts that include training for court personnel and court-based advocates for victims can improve law enforcement responses.[137] More jurisdictions should implement newly developed strategies for assessing dangerousness and protecting victims.[138] Additional experimentation should be undertaken with "restorative justice programs" in which the parties involved in an offense help resolve how to deal with it. Goals of such programs are victim empowerment, offender accountability, and restoration of losses.[139] Attention also needs to focus on sanctions. A Department of Justice review indicated that more stringent sentences, including jail, work release, and electronic monitoring, had some effect in deterring further abuse.[140] Equally important is developing more effective prevention strategies and rehabilitation programs for batterers. Schools in other nations have done a better job of integrating materials aimed at reducing violence, and similar efforts should be institutionalized and evaluated in this country.[141] Programs that bring prominent athletes into schools and communities to discuss violence issues are a promising strategy.[142] In effect, the law should do more to protect and empower women, but we should not rely only on law to alter norms that perpetuate abuse and trivialize its consequences.

Rape

In a television broadcast during the 2012 Missouri Senate campaign, candidate Todd Akin was asked whether abortion should be legal in cases of rape.

He responded: "It seems to me, first of all, from what I understand from doctors, that's really rare. If it's a legitimate rape, the female body has ways to try
to shut that whole thing down."[143] The comment immediately went viral, and
was widely credited with costing him the election. What attracted national
outrage was not simply Akin's bizarre belief about reproductive biology,
which was news to the 32,000 women who every year experience pregnancy
following rape.[144] At issue also was the far more common notion that only
some rapes are "legitimate." That same attitude underpinned a 2011 House
bill aimed at permanently banning federal funding for abortion, which included an exception for victims of "forcible rape." Widespread opposition
prompted deletion of the term "forcible." However, the attitudes under-
pinning it may have remained unaffected, as Akin's comment reflected. In
a similar case, a Wisconsin state legislator responded to questions about a
case involving a 14-year-old girl's charge of rape by a 17-year-old boy. "Some
girls, they rape so easy," the legislator said. According to the district attorney
prosecuting the case, it involved a forcible sexual assault and no evidence of
consent.[145]

The Frequency and Causes of Rape

According to governmental and crime center research, nearly 1 in 5 American
women and 1–3 percent of American men have experienced an attempted or
completed rape. About 12 percent of victims are 10 years old or younger.[146]
The United States has the second highest rate of reported rape of countries for
which data are available.[147]

Explanations for rape cluster in three main categories: individual, sociobio-
logical, and cultural.[148] Those that stress individual characteristics find that
many rapists are attracted to power; they want the feeling of domination, ad-
venture, and status that comes from coercing sex. Other men are motivated
by anger; rape serves to punish or avenge some wrong by a particular woman,
women in general, or another perceived adversary. Most rapists blame their
victims, and some blame situational influences such as peer pressure or drug
and alcohol abuse. Exposure to family violence during childhood increases the
probability that men will become sexually violent as adults.[149]

Sociobiologists offer evolutionary explanations: male intercourse with a
large number of fertile females has "favorable reproductive consequences."
For men who have difficulty attracting willing partners, coercive sex is "adap-
tive" and will be favored by natural selection.[150] Critics note that this account
does not explain the substantial variation in rape rates across time and culture,
or the frequency of sexual assaults involving men, non-vaginal intercourse, or
female victims too young or too old to bear children.

Cultural explanations stress the eroticization of male aggression in popular films, television, fiction, and video games. Such explanations also underscore the role of male-dominated institutions such as the military, fraternities, and athletic teams in fostering attitudes that legitimate sexual coercion. Surveys of college campuses found that male athletes, who constituted 3–15 percent of the male student body, were responsible for 20–25 percent of rapes.[151] In a case all too emblematic of fraternity views, the Yale chapter of Delta Kappa Epsilon had its pledges chant "No means yes, yes means anal" in front of dorms housing women.[152] The frequency of rape in the military has attracted increased attention in the wake of Department of Defense estimates that one in four female service members has been sexually assaulted.[153] Over the last quarter century, more than half a million uniformed men and women have experienced rape or attempted rape.[154] Reports of rape continue to rise sharply, despite the military's assurances that it has zero tolerance for sexual assaults.[155] As an army nurse told the co-chair of a new bipartisan caucus on military sexual assault, "I'm more afraid of my own soldiers than of the enemy."[156] Her fears are well-founded. At hearings before the House Committee on Oversight and Reform, Representative Jane Harman noted that "women serving in the U.S. military are more likely to be raped by a fellow soldier than killed by enemy fire. . . ."[157]

Rape Reporting and Rape Myths

The normalization of male aggression is reflected in the exceptionally low rates of sanctions for rape. Of major felonies, rape is the least reported, least indicted, and least likely to end in conviction.[158] According to Bureau of Justice Statistics, only about a third of rapes and attempted rapes are reported.[159] Other research suggests that fewer than 10 percent of sexual assaults will result in a conviction and fewer than 3 percent will result in incarceration.[160] In the military, of an estimated 26,000 assaults occurring in 2012, only 11 percent were reported and only 238 resulted in convictions.[161] Underlying these low conviction rates are certain "rape myths" that are widely shared by judges, juries, and law enforcement officials: that only certain men (i.e., psychopaths) rape; that women invite rape by their appearance and behavior; and that women fantasize or fabricate rape, motivated by revenge, blackmail, guilt, or embarrassment. The following examples are illustrative:[162]

- In explaining why he voted to acquit William Kennedy Smith of acquaintance rape, a juror stated that Smith was "too charming and too good-looking to have to resort to violence for a night out."[163]

- According to Camille Paglia, a "girl who lets herself get dead drunk at a fraternity party is a fool. A girl who goes upstairs alone with a brother at a fraternity party is an idiot. Feminists call this 'blaming the victim.' I call it common sense."[164]
- A witness to the rape of a drunken teenager claimed that he didn't believe it was rape because "it wasn't violent."[165]
- A Toronto police officer told a group of college women that if they wanted to avoid sexual assault, they should avoid dressing like "sluts." The comment went viral and triggered "slutwalks" in more than 70 cities around the world, with women dressed in bras, halter tops, and garter belts.[166]

Part of what perpetuates rape myths are the atypical but celebrated cases in which victims do fabricate assaults. Estimates of the number of false charges vary widely, but most estimates place the number around 2–3 percent, which is no higher than for other offenses.[167] Yet these cases receive widespread publicity. One example was the black exotic dancer who falsely accused two white Duke students of raping her while she was providing entertainment at a lacrosse team banquet. The police used flawed photo identification procedures that featured only suspects, and the prosecutor who was running for re-election exploited the class and racial aspects of the case to court black voters. He was later disbarred for withholding exculpatory evidence. The case was a travesty of procedural due process, and the result would have been far worse had a defense attorney not unearthed the exonerating evidence while sifting through some 1,800 pages of data and documents. As a consequence, the university ended up settling liability claims brought by the students it had suspended during the flawed investigation.[168]

In another celebrated case involving claims by a Guinean hotel maid, Nafissatou Diallo, the district attorney declined to prosecute due to inconsistencies in the woman's testimony. According to her initial account of the incident, she was cleaning a room in the Sofitel Hotel in New York when she was raped by the director of the International Monetary Fund, Dominique Strauss-Kahn.[169] She claimed that Strauss-Kahn pushed her onto the bed and forced her to have oral sex.[170] After he left the suite and Diallo resumed cleaning, she encountered her supervisor who asked why she was upset. Diallo described the rape, and the hotel subsequently called 911. Forensic evidence at the scene confirmed the sexual encounter, and police arrested Strauss-Kahn. However, lies and inconsistencies in the victim's account soon began to surface. She had made false statements on a tax return and asylum application, and had given inconsistent accounts of the Sofitel incident to police, prosecutors, and media. In a taped conversation that she had with a friend who had been convicted in a sting operation, she reportedly stated something to the effect that Strauss-Kahn "had a lot of money" and that she "knew what she was doing."[171] In explaining their decision to drop charges, prosecutors stated, "If we do not believe her beyond a reasonable doubt, we cannot ask a jury to do so."[172]

Strauss-Kahn, for his part, acknowledged a "moral failing" in having sex with Diallo, but insisted that it was consensual. When the press asked him about another assault charge brought by a journalist who had been interviewing him (a charge barred by the statute of limitations), Strauss-Kahn admitted that he had made advances but claimed that he had stopped when they were rejected. Despite his reputation as an aggressive womanizer, Strauss-Kahn also insisted that he "had respect for women."[173] That claim is likely to be disputed in civil cases brought by Diallo and the French female complainant. To women's rights advocates, what is troubling about the case is less the result than the likelihood that it will fuel public perceptions of rape complainants as "gold diggers" and will reinforce victims' concerns that they will be "dragged through the mud" if they report an assault. The effect will be to compound the difficulties of holding rapists accountable.[174]

Victimizing Victims

A recent, highly publicized prosecution of WikiLeaks founder Julian Assange illustrates the costs for rape complainants. According to a leaked Swedish police report, two women claimed that they had unwanted unprotected sex with Assange. One woman complained that Assange had prevented her from reaching for a condom while they were having sex. A second woman claimed that after having protected sex with Assange, she woke to find him having sex with her without a condom. After discovering their common experience, the women decided to insist that Assange get tested for sexually transmitted diseases. They went to a police station for advice, and gave statements that led prosecutors to charge Assange with third-degree rape. The women have been vilified on the Internet and face regular death threats.[175]

Another common pattern in rape cases is the portrayal of victims who drink as irresponsible sluts who deserve what they get. As a campus police officer told one student, "women need to stop spreading their legs like peanut butter or rape is going to keep on happening until the cows come home."[176] Similar attitudes were apparent in the notorious rape in Steubenville, Ohio, where a drunk 16-year-old was sexually assaulted and molested by two high school football players while other classmates texted videos and gleeful descriptions of the incident.[177] In commenting on other incidents in which law enforcement officers blamed rape on victims' dress or drinking, one rape crisis center advocate commented, "I thought we'd left all that behind us years ago."[178]

Villifying victims is also common in military cases where service members who have been drinking before being assaulted are charged with drunk and disorderly conduct and conduct unbecoming an officer while their assailants escape sanctions.[179] In one recent scandal involving the Naval Academy, a complainant who reported a serial rape faced disciplinary action for underage drinking; her alleged assailants, three Naval Academy football players, were permitted to complete their last season.[180] Other problems involve invasive questioning of rape victims, which is permitted in military but not civilian proceedings. In a 2013 hearing, defense lawyers grilled a Naval Academy complainant for three days about her sexual habits, including whether she wore a bra.[181]

The problem is compounded in the military by a structure that gives commanding officers the power to determine whether to institute charges and what sanctions to impose. According to statistics provided to Congress, commanders reduced as many as a third of sexual abuse punishments.[182] In two recent cases, Air Force generals set aside jury convictions for sexual assault, in one instance reasoning that the defendant could not be guilty because he was a "doting father and husband."[183] Sex offenders are also given an option of resignation in lieu of court-martial; if they admit guilt and leave the military, all charges are dropped.[184] In an incident that speaks volumes about attitudes at the upper levels of the military, the officer in charge of sexual assault programs for the air force was recently arrested in a Virginia parking lot for sexual battery.[185]

Despite recent reform efforts, it is the victim's conduct, as well as the assailant's, that is on trial in rape proceedings. Jurors' perception of the "moral character" of the complainant has traditionally been the single most important factor affecting outcomes.[186] Women who are judged to have "led the man on" are unsympathetic victims. As a Maryland Supreme Court justice put it, "When an adult woman goes to a man's room, [she] certainly [has] to realize that they [are] not going upstairs to play Scrabble."[187] Blaming the victim came to the forefront of public attention in the Steubenville trial. In the local community and on the web, many held the girl responsible for "put[ting] the football team in a bad light and put[ting] herself in a position to be violated."[188] "That whore was asking for it," agreed one Twitter poster.[189] In a similar case in Michigan, a high school girl pressed rape charges against a star basketball player despite the advice of their principal. He expressed concern that the allegations could ruin the assailant's chances of recruitment by a Division 1 university. As word of the charges spread, the victim became the target of an intensive cyber-bullying and harassment campaign that portrayed her as a liar and a "whore" who was trying to bring down an innocent athlete.[190] Even underage complainants face such slurs. In a 2013 Montana case, a judge sentenced a schoolteacher to only 30 days in prison for raping a 14-year-old student on the grounds that she was "older than her chronological age" and was "as much in control of the situation" as the man who pled guilty.[191] In another case, an 11-year-old victim of a gang rape was described as wearing makeup and fashions more appropriate to woman in her twenties. [192]

Although the passage of rape shield laws bars evidence about the complainant's sexual history from admission at trial except under limited circumstances, these laws do not prevent prosecutors from considering such evidence in determining whether to press charges. Nor do shield statutes prevent nongovernmental actors or the media from disclosing compromising material. Particularly in celebrity cases, information about the victim's sexual history is often freely available in the press and on the Internet. In the rape prosecution of basketball star Kobe Bryant, for example, the complainant's address and telephone number, as well as details about her sex life, quickly surfaced. She was the target of several death threats and frequent harassment. One extensive review of cases concludes that rape shield laws have not been effective in undermining the unofficial but pervasive "chastity requirement" imbedded in traditional rules of credibility and consent.[193]

Acquaintance Rape

The trivialization of sexual assault and the victimization of victims are most apparent in cases involving acquaintances. A major problem is the mismatch between media images of shocking, violent rapes and the kinds of sexual coercion common in most assaults.[194] According to government statistics, about 7 in 10 rapes or sexual assaults against women are by someone known to the victim. Among college women, about four-fifths of rapes and sexual assaults involve acquaintances, and almost 90 percent involve no weapon. Women have been taking drugs or alcohol in about 40 percent of the rape cases. Only 12 percent report them to law enforcement officials, usually because they do not think it was serious enough or because they anticipate harsh or dismissive treatment by others in the justice system.[195] In one poll, half the students surveyed graded their school a C or lower in handling sexual assault, and less than 10 percent gave their school an A.[196] A textbook illustration of the problem surfaced in a widely publicized Amherst student's account of her campus rape, in which a sexual assault counselor told her that "pressing charges would be useless, he's about to graduate, there's not much we can do. Are you SURE it was rape? It might have been a bad hookup ... you should forgive and forget."[197] In a similar case at Occidental, an administrator reportedly told a complainant not to worry about safety because she had met the rapist and "he didn't seem like the type of person who would do something like that."[198] A report from the Center for Public Integrity found that only 10–25 percent of students found responsible for campus assault are expelled.[199] Many face lenient sanctions, such as as requiring the offender to watch a 23 minute educational video on sexual violence and write a two page reflection paper.[200]

Much of the problem in dealing with acquaintance rape involves distinguishing coercive from consensual sex. Cases are often complicated by substance abuse, common cognitive tendencies to resolve doubts in ways that favor self-interest, and social contexts in which inconsistent understandings coexist. Men whose interest lies in having sex are likely to perceive ambiguous or conflicting signals as consent. Women who come to regret the experience are likely to recall making their opposition clear. The issue then becomes who should bear the risk of misunderstandings, and how much responsibility women have for not clearly communicating their preferences. Research on public opinion and juror attitudes makes clear that most Americans are reluctant to convict in acquaintance rape cases where victims acted "irresponsibly" in leading men on.[201] A common complaint is that overly inclusive definitions of rape give women unreasonable control to define, after the fact, what is or is not acceptable, consensual sex.[202] In one survey, 50 percent of male athletes believed that almost half of women who report rape are lying.[203] Yet empirical research suggests that such fears are overstated. Close to half of surveyed women are unwilling to label forced sex between acquaintances as rape, even when it meets the statutory definition.[204]

The common assumption that date rapes or "nonviolent" rapes do not involve serious harm is similarly inconsistent with the evidence. Data from the National Crime Center and Department of Justice indicate that most rapes do not involve physical injury apart from the assault itself, but that they often produce debilitating and enduring psychological trauma.[205] Acquaintance rape is no less harmful than other assaults because it calls into question a woman's behavior, judgment, and sense of trust in ways that acts of strangers do not.

Another contested issue in campus rapes involves the burden of proof. According to the federal Office of Civil Rights, the appropriate standard is a "preponderance of evidence," which is the rule established under Title IX for violations of civil rights law.[206] More stringent standards have been rejected in light of colleges' lack of criminal law enforcement techniques and sanctions, as well as the "he said/she said" nature of many sexual assault complaints.[207] Male students, however, often see the situation differently. At Stanford, law students opposed to moving to a preponderance of evidence test commented:

- Doesn't the question come down to what kind of citizens we want universities to create? Do we want to train them to assume guilt . . . [and cast] away a student on a 50 percent plus one preponderance standard in a classic "he said she said" case?

- Making it easy to get a false conviction does not improve the safety of accusers or others on campus. It makes us all vulnerable to being punished based on false accusations.[208]

Missing from these students' comments is any consideration of the costs of an unrealistically demanding standard; it makes female students less willing to incur the humiliation and possible retaliation and stigmatization that frequently accompany reporting sexual assault, and keeps the vast majority of victims from coming forward.[209]

Marital Rape

A final context in which law has proven inadequate to deal with sexual assault involves marital rape. Over three-fifths of states treat rape among married couples less severely than other sexual assaults.[210] Many states make marriage a defense for lesser degrees of sexual assault, such as sex with someone who is incapacitated or unconscious.[211] Fifteen states grant immunity from prosecution to married rapists unless certain requirements are met, such as a prompt complaint, extreme force, and living separately from the spouse, strictly defined.[212] Some legislative reforms have broadened the marital rape exception by extending it to parties living together without being legally married.[213]

The traditional arguments for a marital rape exemption is that it encourages reconciliation, protects privacy, and discourages "vindictive wives" from fabricating claims of assault to gain leverage in divorce cases.[214] No research, however, finds that wives are prone to make false charges.[215] What the evidence does show is that psychological injuries to women who have been raped are greatest from sexual assaults by a husband or a relative. In one study, 52 percent of women raped by a husband reported long-term effects, a proportion greater than for women raped by a stranger (39 percent), by an acquaintance (25 percent), or by a friend, date, or lover (22 percent).[216] To protect women's bodily integrity and sexual self-determination, rape in marriage should be treated no differently than other sexual assaults.

Reform Strategies

Much of the contemporary debate over rape reform has focused on broadening the definition of what constitutes an offense. Some commentators believe that the law should require affirmative consent, as do three states currently, although they recognize assent through conduct as well as words.[217] One possible approach would be to follow Canada's example, which requires "the voluntary agreement of the complainant to engage in the sexual activity in question." Consent is not present if "the accused induces the complainant to engage in the activity by abusing a position of trust, power or authority." Nor does an accused have a defense of consent if the belief involved "recklessness or willful blindness," or the accused did not take "reasonable steps . . . to ascertain that the complainant was consenting."[218]

There are obvious difficulties with some aspects of these proposals. It is not likely that most prosecutors, judges, or juries would be comfortable labeling someone a sex offender for proceeding in the face of silence.[219] Nor is it clear how much would be accomplished by shifting to a standard of affirmative consent. Parties would still engage in "he said/she said" battles over whether consent was freely given. It bears note that the wave of rape reform that occurred in the late 1970s and 1980s, which was partly designed to make rape easier to prove, did not in fact increase reporting, arrest, or conviction rates.[220] Doctrinal change in the absence of shifts in cultural attitudes has limited impact. Still, to the extent that the law can affect those attitudes, some reform seems appropriate. At a minimum, reckless indifference to a woman's preferences or abuse of a position of trust or power should be classified as a form of sexual misconduct short of rape. And marital rape should be treated as such.

The law can also serve to make institutions more accountable for the way they respond to sexual assault. Widely publicized Title IX complaints and lawsuits by students and alumni against colleges have led to far-reaching investigations and multiple changes in the way that administrations have responded to sexual assaults.[221] For example, a lawsuit forced the University of Colorado at Boulder to take responsibility for a football recruiting program that encouraged sexual assault of female "ambassadors" who were expected to show recruits "a good time" while on campus.[222]

Media coverage can also be useful in forcing change. The adverse publicity following an Amherst student's exposé of her rape case prompted a comprehensive review and reform of campus sexual assault policy.[223] A documentary, "The Invisible War," about sexual assault in the military, together with widespread media coverage, has led to new rules for handling such abuse, as well as the introduction of federal legislation.[224] Promising proposals for the military include creating an independent prosecutor to handle sex abuse cases, and removing senior commanders' power to reverse a verdict.[225]

The media has also exposed problems surrounding "rape kits" and medical exams. Following a sexual assault, women victims often agree to an exam that yields such a kit: a collection of hair, semen, and skin cell samples. Prosecutors can check the DNA extracted from these kits against a criminal DNA database, and a match can lead to successful prosecutions. Serial offenders account for the vast majority of rapes, so kit evidence can be a crucial law enforcement tool. However, between 180,000 and 400,000 kits remain unanalyzed due to lack of resources.[226] Moreover, although legal provisions are theoretically available to cover medical expenses for kits, victims themselves are often left responsible. For example, the City of Wasilla, Alaska, required victims to pay for their own rape kits while Sarah Palin was mayor.[227] A lack of insurance or other funds to cover expensive emergency room care can deter victims from seeking kits, despite their importance for criminal prosecutions.[228]

In an attempt to eliminate at least some of the vast accumulation of forensic evidence sitting untested on police shelves, Chicago feminists began raising money to have rape kits privately tested. The publicity accompanying that activism inspired legislative attention, and in 2010, Illinois became the first state with a law mandating rape kit testing procedures. The law does not, however, designate funding for its provisions, causing critics to question its potential impact in the face of overwhelmed labs and budgetary constraints. Such partial reform efforts point up the need for greater attention to unfunded kits.

The portrayal of rape in popular culture can also provide occasions to raise awareness of the social norms that trivialize sexual assault. The dust-up over comedian Daniel Tosh's rape jokes is a case in point. When a heckler at a comedy club shouted that rape jokes were never funny, he responded that it would be hilarious if she were gang raped on the spot. The heckler then reported the incident on Tumblr, and after Tosh tweeted a lukewarm apology, the blog post went viral. The most thoughtful responses made the point that while no subject, including rape, should be taboo from comedy, jokes need to be constructed in ways that do not mock victims or trivialize their injuries.[229]

We also need rape education that begins in elementary school and continues through college. The labeling of boys as "studs" and girls as "sluts" at early ages not only fosters double standards, it also encourages sexual miscommunication. When women feel pressure to fake resistance in order to avoid seeming promiscuous, men will feel entitled to disregard it, and the dangers of unjust accusations and coercive sex will persist. Special peer-to-peer educational initiatives should target groups that account for a disproportionate number of sexual assaults, such as athletes and members of fraternities and the armed services. As is true with domestic violence and sexual harassment, more research is necessary about what forms of prevention and education are effective. The limited evidence available casts doubt on the adequacy of the brief rape awareness programs that are common in campus outreach efforts.[230] The stakes in this agenda are substantial, not only for the appalling number of women who experience rape, but also for the still far greater number of women who fear it and limit their lives to avoid it.

Trafficking

Trafficking is organized crime's second most profitable venture, lagging just behind drugs and generating on the order of $32 billion in annual profits.[231] According to the International Labor Organization, some 212 million individuals, four-fifths of them women and children, are subject to forced labor or sexual servitude.[232] The United States government estimates that about 17,500 individuals are trafficked into this country each year, so this is a domestic issue that needs to be addressed through a global lens.[233]

Trafficking encompasses a range of crimes, including sex tourism, involuntary servitude, forced prostitution, child marriage, and rape. Much of the industry involves duping, kidnapping, or purchasing women and girls for the sex trade. Some victims or their families are deceived by promises of jobs such as waitresses, au pairs, clerks, actresses, and exotic dancers.[234] Women and children are also drugged or kidnapped and smuggled across national borders. Many are then sold into child marriages or to brothels and kept against their will.[235] Typically, they are taken to a city or foreign country where they lack marketable skills, passports, and familiarity with the language. Many are threatened with assault, murder, or prosecution if they try to escape. Children who are abused or orphaned as a result of HIV and armed conflict may also end up in brothels.[236] Once victims have entered the sex trade, the stigma that they encounter further restricts their employment and marriage options; many face ostracism if they return to their original communities.[237]

Trafficking also supports a rapidly expanding sex tourism industry. A growing number of American companies offer "sex tours" to countries such as Thailand and the Philippines, where purchasers have ready access to brothels.[238] A California travel agency ad promised: "Sex Tours to Thailand, Real Girls, Real Sex, Real Cheap. These women are the most sexually available in the world. Did you know you can actually buy a virgin girl for as little as $200?" The agency offered a prize to the man who had sex with the most girls on the tour.[239] Nicholas Kristof profiles one of those "real girls." Long Pross was a 13-year-old sold into slavery, and painfully stitched up to look like a virgin four times. If she protested, she was subject to electric shocks and beatings. While recovering from a painful abortion, she pled for rest and enraged the brothel owner, who gouged out her eye. The infection and disfigurement that resulted was what finally enabled her escape.[240] The poverty that propels many women into sex tourism also supplies a rationalization for their male customers. In justifying his sexual transactions with 14- and 15-year-old girls in Mexico and Columbia, one American man noted: "If they don't have sex with me, they may not have enough food. If someone has a problem with me doing this, let UNICEF feed them. I've never paid more than $20 to these young women, and that allows them to eat for a week."[241] Similar rationalizations, along with the revenue and corruption generated by sex tourism, encourage officials in many impoverished countries to tolerate child prostitution.[242]

To respond to sex trafficking, experts have advocated three strategies: prevention, punishment, and protection. Prevention focuses on expanding female education and employment opportunities, reducing poverty in the countries that supply the global trade, and distributing better information to vulnerable groups about traffickers' techniques and the legal remedies available to victims.[243] Punishment involves increased sanctions against traffickers and countries that fail to impose them. Protection focuses on aiding victims who cooperate with law enforcement. All of these approaches are well-intentioned in principle but ineffective in practice. Inadequate resources are the primary but not the sole problem.[244] In the United States, the government has authority to withhold nonhumanitarian nontrade-related foreign assistance to countries that are not making significant efforts to comply with anti-trafficking standards. However, countries have rarely been subject to such sanctions, despite widespread evidence of noncompliance.[245] Relatively few successful prosecutions have targeted traffickers or tourists and tourism companies that violate child sex trafficking prohibitions.[246] And relatively few victims have been granted remedies under federal legislation that authorizes visas and support services for those who assist trafficking investigations. Barriers include victims' inability to provide usable information to law enforcement and their fear that they or their families will be subject to retaliation if they cooperate.[247]

We can and must do better in terms of resources and enforcement. One promising initiative is New York's establishment of specialized courts designed to identify individuals accused of prostitution who have been subject to trafficking. The courts treat these women as victims in need of services rather than criminals deserving of punishment. Those victims who complete a treatment program can have their charges reduced or dismissed.[248]

President Obama, in signing a 2012 Executive Order strengthening policies against trafficking by federal contractors, noted that trafficking "ought to concern every person because it's a debasement of our common humanity.... It ought to concern every nation, because it endangers public health and fuels violence and organized crime.... Our fight against human trafficking is one of the great human rights causes of our time, and the United States will continue to lead it."[249] The challenge remaining is to make good on that commitment.

=====

Although this chapter has focused on the legal issues surrounding sexual abuse, any effective reform strategy must go far deeper. We should continue to use incidents like Akin's statement about "legitimate" rape and the Toronto police officer's comments about women "dress[ed] like sluts" to force focus on the prevalence of sexual assault and the need for better responses. Among those responses should be increased emphasis on violence prevention and education. At relatively early ages, children begin absorbing traditional assumptions about the legitimacy of male sexual aggression and the trivialization of its consequences.[250] We need to alter those assumptions and encourage victims to come forward with a different message.

7

Appearance

Beauty may be only skin deep, but the costs of its pursuit often go far deeper.[1] We all know that looks matter, but few of us realize how much. Seldom do we recognize the price we pay in time, money, and psychological well-being, or the extent to which our beauty biases compromise meritocratic principles. That is not to discount the positive aspects of beauty, including the pleasure that comes from self-expression or the health benefits that result from actions prompted by aesthetic concerns. Nor is it to suggest that discrimination based on appearance is on the same footing as other social problems this book has identified, such as poverty, rape, domestic violence, and unequal pay. But the costs of our cultural preoccupation with attractiveness are much greater than we commonly assume. Of all the major issues that the women's movement has targeted, those related to appearance have shown among the least improvement. In fact, by some measures, such as the rise in eating disorders, cosmetic surgery, and dissatisfaction with body image, the problem has grown worse. As the Introduction noted, almost half of American women are unhappy with their bodies, a percentage higher than a quarter century ago.[2] After money, appearance is women's greatest source of dissatisfaction.[3] Much of the reason lies in the guilt, shame, and discrimination that social pressures impose.

Although women by no means speak with one voice on this issue, there is some common ground about the need for social change. A better understanding of the injustices associated with appearance is a necessary step toward the pursuit of shared values.

The Costs of Appearance

The significance of attractiveness comes as no surprise, but the extent of its advantages is not as obvious. Less attractive individuals are less likely to be viewed as smart, happy, interesting, likable, successful, or well adjusted.[4] Not only are the less attractive treated worse, their unfavorable treatment can erode self-confidence and social skills, which compounds the disadvantages.[5] Appearance also skews judgments about competence. Resumes and essays get less favorable evaluations when they are thought to belong to less attractive individuals.[6] Overweight individuals are seen as having less effective work habits and less ability to get along with others.[7] Less attractive teachers get less favorable course evaluations from students, and less attractive students receive lower ratings in intelligence from teachers.[8] Attractive CEOs receive higher salaries and their companies have higher share values than those run by less attractive counterparts.[9] A meta-analysis that aggregated findings of over a hundred studies found that although less attractive individuals are perceived as less competent, the actual correlation between physical appearance and intellectual competence is "virtually zero."[10] Although the relative importance of appearance varies by occupation, less attractive individuals are generally less likely to be hired and promoted, and they earn lower salaries.[11] Penalties are apparent even in fields like law and higher education, where appearance bears no demonstrable relationship to job performance.[12] About 60 percent of overweight women report experiences of employment discrimination.[13] The extent of irrational bias is apparent in one experimental study finding that body weight significantly affected people's choices of prospective teammates in a trivia contest. Participants gave up about 11 IQ points to have a thin rather than overweight teammate.[14]

Given these consequences, it makes sense for individuals to be concerned about their appearance. Still, the extent of the concern is striking. Almost 90 percent of women consider how they look to be very important or somewhat important to their self-image; a third rank it as the most important contributor, above job performance and intelligence.[15] Over half of young women report that they would prefer to be hit by a truck than be fat, and two-thirds would rather be mean or stupid.[16] How much effect appearance has on overall quality of life is subject to debate, but considerable evidence suggests that most people overestimate its importance.[17] Much of the effort that women now invest in their appearance might be better spent on family, friends, volunteer work, and other activities that contribute to their personal growth and sense of social responsibility.

The costs of our cultural preoccupation with appearance are considerable. The global investment in grooming totals over $100 billion, and Americans alone spend over $40 billion a year on diets.[18] Barnard president Debora Spar estimates that she spends "282 hours a year on basic maintenance. Over the course of a forty year career I will spend 10,080 more hours than the average guy sitting next to me—nearly five working years—trying to make myself look presentable."[19]

For many women, much of their investment falls short of its intended effects or is induced by misleading claims. The weight loss industry is a case in point. Ninety-five percent of dieters regain their weight within one to five years.[20] Yet in the fact-free fantasy land of diet markers, miracle products abound. Claims that the Federal Trade Commission has targeted include:

- gel·ä·thin topical gel reduces fat and cellulite deposits on contact;
- Siluette Patch, made from seaweed, eliminates fat deposits and causes rapid weight loss without dietary changes;
- Xena RX diet pill with green tea extract blocks up to 40 percent of the absorption of fat;
- Hanmeilin Cellulite Cream with Chinese herbs causes up to 95 pounds of weight loss and eliminates fat and cellulite with "No Will Power Required";
- Himalayan Diet Breakthrough, a pill containing Nepalese Mineral Pitch, causes as much as 37 pounds of weight loss in eight weeks without diets or exercise.[21]

Consumers squander millions of dollars on such products because most Americans assume that manufacturers could not make these claims without a factual basis.[22] Yet resource limitations have prevented state and federal regulatory agencies from keeping up with the barrage of misleading advertisements regarding diet and cosmetic products.[23]

Enforcement of product safety standards has been similarly inadequate. Eighty percent of the approximately 10,000 ingredients used in cosmetics and personal care products have never been assessed by the federal Food and Drug Administration.[24] An Environmental Working Group survey found that nearly 400 products sold in the United States contained chemicals prohibited in other countries, and that over 400 had contents considered unsafe by American industry standards.[25]

Our preoccupation with appearance carries other health risks, including eating disorders, yo-yo dieting, and cosmetic surgery.[26] From a health perspective, the current obsession with thinness is misdirected; it compromises reproductive and work capacity, and predicts higher rates of sickness.[27] Except at extreme levels, weight is less important than fitness in preventing disease and prolonging life.[28] Concerns about appearance are also linked to depression, anxiety, and low self-esteem.[29] Even fashion footwear carries a cost; high heels are a major contributor to serious back and foot problems.[30] Hillary Clinton learned that fact the hard way. One Christmas season during the Clinton presidency, after standing for hours in receiving lines at holiday parties, she became bedridden with back pain. A specialist concluded that she "shouldn't wear high heels again." "Never?" Clinton asked. "Well, yes never," he responded, and added, "With all due respect ma'am, why would you want to?"[31]

Alison Wolf, in *The XX Factor*, offers a reason. High heels are a form of signaling, a demonstration that the wearer spends her time "on soft carpets not pounding the city streets. . . ."[32] Perhaps, but if men can signal wealth and status without help from uncomfortable footwear, why can't women?

The Injustice of Discrimination

Part of the discrimination against less attractive individuals stems from inaccurate stereotypes. For example, about two-thirds of Americans believe that people are fat because they lack self- control.[33] In many employers' view, "if you can't control your own contours . . . how can you control a budget and staff?"[34] Experts, however, agree that weight is not simply a matter of willpower; rather, it reflects a complex interaction of physiological, psychological, socioeconomic, and cultural factors.[35] Genetically determined set-points work to keep bodies within a predetermined range; furthermore, when dieters reduce their caloric intake and increase their exercise, their metabolism slows down to compensate and makes any weight loss difficult to sustain. The problems are compounded by sedentary occupations and "toxic environments" that lack recreational opportunities and encourage unhealthy food choices.[36]An equally unfounded assumption is that the stigma associated with being overweight serves a justifiable function by shaming individuals into shedding unhealthy pounds. In fact, such bias is counterproductive. Around 80 percent of those enrolled in weight loss programs respond to stigma by eating more or giving up their diets.[37]

Discrimination on the basis of appearance carries both individual and social costs. It undermines self-esteem, diminishes job aspirations, and compromises efficiency and equity. Assumptions that overweight individuals are lazy, undisciplined, or unfit are a case in point. In one all-too-typical example, an obese woman failed to receive a job as an airport bus driver because a company doctor concluded that her weight would prevent her from effectively protecting passengers in an accident. The doctor subsequently acknowledged that the woman had no health problems and that he had performed no agility tests; he simply assumed that she was unfit because he had watched her "waddling down the hall" to her exam.[38] In a similar case, Jennifer Portnick, a 240-pound aerobics instructor, was denied a franchise by Jazzercise, a national fitness company, on grounds that she lacked the "fit" image that the company was attempting to project. But Portnick was in fact fit. She worked out six days a week, taught back-to-back exercise classes, and had no history of performance problems or lack of students. She simply wanted to be "judged on my merits, not my measurements."[39] Because San Francisco is one of a small number of jurisdictions that prohibits discrimination based on height and weight, she was able to bring a formal complaint. After a ruling in her favor and an outpouring of publicity in her support, the company changed its policy. Another well-publicized case involved sex discrimination claims by two former "Borgata Babes," cocktail waitresses at the Atlantic City Borgata Hotel and Casino. The two "Babes" agreed, as part of their employment contract, to keep a "height and weight appropriate" "hourglass figure." Enforcement of the policy contributed to eating disorders and related mental and physical health difficulties.[40]

One other cost of discrimination on the basis of appearance is the exacerbation of economic and racial inequality. Appearance both reflects and reinforces class privilege. Prevailing beauty standards disadvantage individuals who lack the time and money to invest in attractiveness. Fashion, makeup, health clubs, weight loss products, and cosmetic procedures all come at a cost. Discrimination based on weight is particularly problematic from a class standpoint. Low-income and minority individuals have disproportionate rates of obesity. As one expert puts it, there is some evidence that "poverty is fattening," and an "even stronger case [that] . . . fatness is impoverishing."[41] Many poor people live in nutritional deserts—areas with no readily accessible grocery stores that sell fresh fruits and vegetables.[42] These areas also tend to lack public recreational facilities and schools with adequate physical education programs.[43] The bias that overweight individuals confront then compromises their educational, employment, and earning opportunities. So too, although images of beauty are growing somewhat more diverse, they still reflect the legacy of racial privilege. Light skin, straightened hair, and Anglo-American features carry an economic and social advantage.[44] Those who look less "white" have lower incomes and occupational status after controlling for other factors.[45] They are also less likely to shape cultural images. In commenting on the absence of diversity on fashion runways, a *Washington Post* story put the take-away in the title: "Once Again, White Is the New White."[46]

Discrimination on the basis of appearance also compounds gender inequality by reinforcing a double standard and a double bind for women. They face greater pressures than men to be attractive and greater penalties for falling short; as a consequence, their self-worth is more dependent on looks.[47] Overweight women are judged more harshly than overweight men and are more susceptible to eating disorders and related psychological and physical dysfunctions.[48] About 90 percent of cosmetic surgery patients are female, with all the financial costs and physical risks that such procedures pose.[49] Yet even as the culture expects women to conform, they often face ridicule for their efforts.

A case in point was the comment from a *Boston Herald* columnist about the appearance of a prominent politician: "There seemed to be something humiliating, sad, desperate and embarrassing about Katherine Harris, a woman of a certain age trying too hard to hang on."[50] The "certain age" was 43.

In employment contexts, women can be penalized for being too attractive as well as not attractive enough. In upper-level positions that have been historically male-dominated, beautiful or "sexy" women encounter the "boopsie" effect; their attractiveness suggests less competence and intellectual ability.[51] Even in lower-level positions, women who are too alluring can be victims of their own success. In a recent Iowa case, a dentist fired his attractive hygienist at his wife's insistence. The state court found no discrimination on the curious theory that she was fired "not because of her gender but because she was a threat to the marriage of her employer."[52] To avoid the "boopsie" effect, the army has been advised to use photos of "average looking women" when illustrating stories about female soldiers; women who are too pretty are not perceived as competent for combat roles.[53]

Aging women also face a double standard. Men can gain gravitas with their years; women face marginalization. The preoccupation with female appearance reinforces gender stereotypes and encourages evaluation of women in terms of attractiveness rather than character, competence, hard work, or achievement.[54]

The devaluation and sexualization of women based on appearance is particularly apparent for women in leadership positions. On Condoleeza Rice's first day as national security adviser, the *New York Times* ran a profile discussing her dress size (6), taste in shoes ("comfortable pumps"), and hemline preferences ("modest").[55] After becoming secretary of state, her appearance in high boots when visiting troops in Germany inspired portrayals as a dominatrix in political cartoons and comedy routines.[56] Kamala Harris, California's attorney general, received front page coverage when President Barack Obama described her as "by far the best-looking attorney general in the country."[57] Tennis champion Marion Bartoli was portrayed on national media as someone who was "never going to be a looker."[58] As first lady and then as a political candidate, Hillary Clinton faced a barrage of criticism as frumpy, fat, and "bottom heavy."[59] As secretary of state, when a man at a town hall meeting in Kyrgyzstan asked her which designers she wore, an exasperated Clinton responded, "Would you ever ask a man that question?"[60] Shortly after Marissa Mayer was appointed CEO of Yahoo, a Forbes article described her as "attractive, well coifed, and poised under pressure," and characterized her reputation as being the "hottest CEO ever," and one of the "sexiest geek girls" of Silicone Valley.[61] Although Supreme Court Justices have never been known for being eye candy, no male nominee to the Court has attracted comments like those directed at

Elena Kagan; to talk show host Michael Savage, she looked "as if she belongs in a kosher deli."[62]

I got a personal glimpse into the phenomenon I was describing after publicizing my book *The Beauty Bias*. It was surprising how many men took time to send me comments like "You ugly cunt," or "Let's take up a collection to buy the professor a burka and improve the aesthetics at Stanford."

It is not only men who divert attention from women's substance to appearance. Carly Fiorina got national coverage during a California Senate race for comments about her opponent's hair. Unaware that she was speaking into an open microphone, Fiorina stated, "[My friend] Laura saw Barbara Boxer briefly on television this morning and said what everyone says, 'God what is that hair?' Sooooo yesterday."[63] It speaks volumes about our national preoccupation with female appearance that Sarah Palin's campaign paid more for her makeup specialist than her foreign policy advisor.[64] Recent research finds that describing a female politician in terms of appearance, even when the commentary is favorable, leads people to rate her as less likable, effective, and qualified.[65]

Women also suffer from grooming standards that sexualize the workplace and subject them to demeaning or harassing treatment. Examples include the Bikini Expresso, a drive-through coffee bar with waitresses in sheer babydoll negligees; the Heart Attack Grill, featuring women in "naughty nurses" costumes; the "Valet of the Dolls" parking service with a "wild" and "sexy" all female staff; and a Hooter's restaurant that issued uniforms in only three sizes: small, extra small, and extra extra small.[66] Employees who challenge such requirements are seldom successful. A typical case involved Harrah's Reno Casino. It required female bartenders to wear makeup and nail polish and to have their hair "teased, curled or styled." Male bartenders needed only short haircuts and fingernails that were "neatly trimmed."[67] A federal court of appeals rejected a female bartender's sex discrimination claim on the ground that she had not introduced proof that the grooming standards imposed disproportionate burdens of time and expense on women. But did anyone, except apparently some federal judges, need expert testimony comparing the average time and money required for trimming finger nails with that required for applying makeup and styling hair? As one dissenting judge pointed out, cosmetics "don't grow on trees."[68] Makeup and manicure requirements may seem trivial, but the broader principle is not. Holding only women to standards of sexual attractiveness perpetuates gender roles that are separate and by no means equal. As another dissenting judge noted, the assumption underlying the casino's grooming policy was that women's "undoctored faces compare unfavorably to men's."[69]

Also problematic are grooming codes that unnecessarily restrict expression of racial, religious, and cultural identity. For example, some courts have upheld prohibitions on head scarves and cornrows.[70] From judges' perspective, these issues have seemed a matter "of relatively low importance."[71] But that has not been the view of historians who have studied the issue, employees who have been willing to litigate it, and managers who have fought back.[72]

Although individual examples of appearance discrimination often seem insignificant, their cumulative effect is anything but. Such prejudice undermines equal opportunity, exacerbates stigma, erodes self-esteem, restricts self-expression, and reinforces disadvantages based on class, race, ethnicity, and sex. But how women should respond is a matter of long-standing debate.

Conflict and Consensus

In 1968, protestors at the Miss America pageant gained national attention by announcing a boycott of all products related to the competition, and depositing bras, girdles, curlers, false eyelashes, and women's magazines into a "Freedom Trash Can."[73] Building on the premise that the "personal is political," activists shed a range of conventions along with their undergarments. Unshaved legs and unadorned faces became a symbol of "liberation." The public reception was generally less than enthusiastic. In many quarters, feminists were seen as "dowdy, frumpy moralizers," who hated men because they could not attract them.[74]

Over time, both the critics of appearance standards and the critics of these critics became more nuanced. Many feminists have struggled to find ways of reconciling their personal attachment to femininity with their political commitments to equality. Beginning in the 1990s, third wave feminists sought to reclaim conventional emblems of femininity, such as sexualized clothing and stiletto heels. Yet although women do not speak with one voice on issues of appearance, some grounds for consensus emerge. The challenge is to build on shared values in pursuit of progressive change.

Critics of current attitudes toward appearance stress their costs. In her widely publicized account, *The Beauty Myth*, Naomi Wolf argued that women's absorption with looks "leeches money and leisure and confidence."[75] Because women are held to unattainable ideals, their task is boundless. Almost all areas of the female body are in need of attention. The result is to focus women's efforts on self-improvement rather than social action. An overemphasis on attractiveness diminishes women's credibility and diverts attention from their capabilities and accomplishments. In the long run, these are more stable sources of self-esteem and social power than appearance. Prevailing beauty standards also place women in a double bind. They are expected to conform, yet condemned as vain and narcissistic for attempts to do so. Neither should they "let themselves go," nor look as if they were trying too hard not to. Beauty must seem natural, even when it can only be accomplished through considerable unnatural assistance.

Most disturbing of all is the effect of these criticisms on individuals' own self-esteem. Many women who recognize beauty norms as oppressive feel humiliated by the inability to escape them. They are ashamed for feeling ashamed. With self-deprecating irony, Eve Ensler recounts her own struggles. "What I can't believe is that someone like me, a radical feminist for nearly thirty years, could spend this much time thinking about my stomach. It has become my tormentor, my distractor; it's my most committed relationship."[76]

By contrast, other women stress the pleasure and self-determination associated with appearance. Surveys of women who have had cosmetic surgery generally find that at least four-fifths are happy with the results.[77] Other studies involving beauty products and services find considerable satisfaction with such purchases. Cosmetics make many individuals feel more "credible" and "professional." Time spent shopping or in spas and salons provides pleasure and opportunities for female bonding.[78] Even high heels can boost self-esteem and give women a psychological as well as literal leg up.[79] In one widely circulated *Playboy* article, Jan Breslauer, a former Yale feminist theory professor, further insisted that having a "boob job" expressed feminist principles—"a woman's right to do what she wants with her body." It "made me focus on how far I've come. . . . I have arrived at the point where I can go out and buy myself a new pair of headlights if I want. . . . And if somebody asks if they're [mine, I can] tell them, 'Yes, I bought them myself.'"[80]

Yet at least some of the satisfaction that women take in enhancing their appearance is a response to cultural pressure, shame, and humiliation. One cosmetic surgery patient expressed a common view: "I wish I could have said 'To hell with it. I am going to love my body the way it is,' but I had tried to do that for fifteen years and it didn't work."[81] For many women, the goal has been not beauty but normalcy—fixing an aspect of their appearance that they "just really hate."[82] Other women simply do not "want to look [their] age," or feel embarrassed by "flabby" thighs or "sagging knockers."[83]

These desires are a logical response to market messages. Over a century ago, a collection of essays from *Harper's Bazaar*, *The Ugly-Girl Papers*, stressed the importance of self- improvement in chapters titled "Women's Business to Be Beautiful," and "Hope for Homely People."[84] Today, the basic message of most women's magazines remains the same. A sample of cover features includes "Get a Sexy Body" (*Cosmopolitan*); "The Cost of Looking Good" (*Vogue*); "Swallow This: New Beauty Pills" (*Marie Claire*); "Look Younger by Morning" (*Harper's Bazaar*); "Wynonna's Weight Loss Secrets" (*Ladies Home Journal*); "Easiest Ways to Lose 10 lbs : No Diet, No Exercise, Seriously" (*Good Housekeeping*). Even niche magazines often have a liberal sprinkling of such assistance. Evangelicals get "Pray Your Weight Away," and "More of Jesus, Less of Me"; older women get "Top Tricks to a Flawless Face" and "59 Ways to More Radiant Skin."[85] Such advice, coupled with female images of airbrushed, surgically enhanced perfection, feed women's anxieties. Less than 5 percent of American women are in the same weight category as actresses and models, and three-quarters of women who are at or below normal weight believe that they should lose some.[86]

In short, although appearance is an opportunity for self-determination, it is shaped by cultural pressures. In one study of makeup in the workplace, virtually all the participants believed that they had a choice about whether to use cosmetics. But they also believed that women who decline to wear makeup "do not appear healthy, heterosexual or credible."[87] Even women who report satisfaction with cosmetic surgery are often highly critical of the culture that led them to take that step. Their choice is less the expression of authentic preferences than "the lesser of two evils."[88] As one feminist explained, "Plastic surgery is a bit of a sellout, but I don't think it means I have to skewer myself on the feminist spike. . . . The personal may be political, but the personal is also personal. . . . I know that aging naturally is the more honorable way to go but I'm not there to be honorable to my gender. I've done quite a lot of that in my life."[89] Jan Breslauer defends her implants along similar lines. Sexism "isn't going to change any time soon. Here's the choice: you can rail at an imperfect world or go get yourself a great pair of bazongas." As long as "women are judged by their jugs . . . it's sometimes better to acknowledge that the injustice exists and get on with your life."[90]

The difficulty for women on issues of appearance is that many individuals who opt for cosmetic enhancement feel well served by the result. But the cumulative effect of their decisions is to reinforce standards that make it harder for other women to opt out. What some individuals find expressive and pleasurable, others find expensive and burdensome.

Yet whatever their position on these issues, women can unite around certain shared values. In the world that women want, appearance would be a source of pleasure, not of shame. Individuals would be able to make decisions about whether to enhance their attractiveness without being judged politically incorrect or professionally unacceptable. In order for appearance to be a source of enjoyment rather than anxiety, it must not dictate women's self-worth.

Getting from here to there presents no small challenge, but refocusing the feminist critique is an obvious place to start. It has not helped the political agenda or public image of the women's movement to denounce widely accepted beauty practices or those who won't get with the program. Greater tolerance is in order, along with recognition that women are not similarly situated in their capacity for resistance. Not everyone has the luxury of being able to say "screw you" to the cosmetics industry. In my job as a law professor, no one cares whether I use mascara. My appearance can resemble that of the dowdy academic in Randall Jarrell's novel, *Pictures from an Institution*, who looked as though "her clothes had come together by chance, and involved her, an innocent onlooker, in the accident."[91] For television's legal commentators, such as Greta Van Susteren, the circumstances are far different, and the condemnation she received for her surgical upgrade seemed misdirected. "From Plain Greta to Foxy Babe," ran a headline in the *New York Daily News*, and almost 2 million viewers tuned in to check out her first post–eye lift performance.[92] But why center criticism on her choice rather than on the preferences of viewers and network executives that made the choice seem necessary?

Yet Van Susteren herself missed an opportunity to make that point. Rather, she took the opposite tack. In attempting to put a better face on her facelift, Van Susteren commented, "I've made it safe for other people."[93] But she also made it less safe for those who want media limelight without "fixing" their features. Still, denouncing her decision as unfeminist is unlikely to alter the norms that encourage it, or to enlist participants in a reform effort. As Jessica Valenti notes, "Having a feminist judge you for what you look like or choose to do aesthetically is no different from having a sexist man do it. Except for the damage it does to the movement."[94] Focusing attention on personal decisions rather than collective practices asks too much of individuals and too little of society.

An Agenda for Change

What then should we ask of society? Whatever their other differences, most women would rally behind an agenda that promoted more attainable, healthy, and inclusive ideals. Our aspirational standards should reflect greater variation across age, weight, race, and ethnicity, and our grooming requirements should reflect greater tolerance for diversity and self-expression. Judgments about appearance would be less important. Women would not be held to higher standards than men. Nor would women's self-esteem be tied to appearance rather than accomplishment. Judgments based on attractiveness should not spill over to educational and employment contexts where they have no socially defensible role. More effort should focus on encouraging healthy lifestyles and addressing the weight-related problems that prompt discrimination.

Legal Reforms

In pursuing that agenda, an obvious place to start is to prohibit discrimination based on appearance. In one national poll, 16 percent of workers reported that they had been subject to such bias, a percentage that is slightly greater than those reporting gender or racial prejudice (12 percent).[95] Most women do not believe that employers should have the right to discriminate based on looks.[96] The reasons are straightforward. Such discrimination compromises principles of individual dignity and equal opportunity to the same extent as other forms of bias that are now illegal. Yet only a small number of jurisdictions explicitly ban discrimination based on appearance.[97] What accounts for the difference in treatment?

To many observers, appearance discrimination seems a rational response to customer preferences. Employees' attractiveness can often be an effective selling point, and part of a strategy to "brand" the seller through a certain look. According to a spokesperson for the Borgata Hotel Casino & Spa, its weight limits and periodic "weigh-in" requirements for "Borgata Babes" cocktail wait-resses responded to market demands: "Our customers like being served by an attractive cocktail server."[98] Analogous assumptions evidently underpinned the order by a L'Oreal cosmetics store manager to "[g]et me somebody hot" for a sales position, Abercrombie & Fitch's policy of hiring sexually attractive, "classic American" salespersons, and the preference by certain bars and res-taurants for staff that are "young" and "trendy," or not "too ethnic."[99] "So You Want to Hire the Beautiful," ran the title of a *Business Week* column. "Well, Why Not?"[100]

The reason is the one that courts have advanced in rejecting customer preferences as a defense to claims involving race or sex discrimination. Those preferences generally reflect and reinforce precisely the attitudes that society is seeking to change. During the early Civil Rights era, Southern employers often argued that hiring blacks would be financially ruinous; white custom-ers preferred white employees. Airlines similarly defended their refusal to hire male flight attendants on grounds that male business travelers generally preferred being served by female stewardesses.[101] In rejecting such customer preference defenses, Congress and the courts recognized that the most effec-tive way of combating bias was to deprive people of the option to indulge it. By the same token, it should be illegal for employers to discriminate on the basis of appearance except where it is essential to the occupation, such as modeling, acting, or sexual entertainment.

The same logic applies to grooming codes. Courts have generally permitted sex-specific grooming requirements if they reflect accepted community stan-dards, involve no fundamental rights, or impose no disproportionate burdens on women or men.[102] But this permissiveness toward requirements such as makeup, high heels, and sexually alluring uniforms ignores the social costs of sexual stereotypes. Customers who want what a Hooters' spokeswoman de-scribed as a "little good clean wholesome female sexuality" are no more worthy of deference than the Southern whites in the 1960s who didn't want to buy from blacks, or the male airline passengers in the 1980s who liked stewardesses in hot pants.[103] As long as Hooters markets itself as family-friendly and offers a children's menu, it cannot credibly claim that it is selling sex rather than burgers, and that waitresses with cleavage are a business necessity.

A related justification for discrimination based on appearance is that it often reflects other relevant traits, such as industriousness, sociability, and good hygiene.[104] Yet what is objectionable about many sex-specific appearance requirements is not that they prescribe neatness, which courts could allow under sex-neutral standards, but that they reinforce sex stereotypes and unnecessarily restrict self-expression. Neither empirical research nor common sense suggests that women who decline to wear nail polish or high heels are less industrious. Indeed, in the case against Harrah's Casino, the bartender who lost her job for lacking appropriate makeup and styled hair had consistently received glowing evaluations from supervisors and customers during her 20-year service.[105]

A final cluster of arguments against prohibiting appearance discrimination is pragmatic. To many commentators, the preference for attractiveness appears natural and immutable in a way that other forms of bias do not. Attempting to ban discrimination based on such deeply rooted preferences strikes these observers as impractical and imprudent. In their view, "some aspects of what we consider physically attractive are ... hardwired.... [T]he taste for physical beauty is unfair. But legal intervention is unlikely to eliminate it."[106]

Some commentators have also worried that such intervention risks trivializing other more serious forms of bias. In their view, allowing appearance-discrimination claims under civil rights and disability laws will undermine these statutes' effectiveness in assisting individuals with more severe disadvantages. Richard Ford voices a common objection:

> [T]here are practical limits of human attention and sympathy.... And a business community united in frustration at a bloated civil rights regime could become a powerful political force for reform or even repeal. ... The growing number of social groups making claims to civil rights protection threatens the political and practical viability of civil rights for those who need them most.[107]

Mario Cuomo put the point succinctly in debates over a proposed New York law banning discrimination based on appearance. This was "one law too many."[108]

Part of the problem is that attractiveness and grooming standards fall along a continuum. How would employers or courts determine when an individual is unattractive enough to warrant protection? Critics worry that appearance discrimination laws will result in "litigiousness run wild," impose "untold costs" on businesses, and erode support for other legislation prohibiting "truly invidious discrimination."[109] As one trial judge noted, courts "have too much to do" to become embroiled in petty grooming code disputes about where women can and can't wear pants.[110]

Although such concerns are not without force, neither do they justify the prevailing tolerance for appearance discrimination. An initial difficulty lies in critics' assumption that prejudice based on appearance is more natural and harder to eradicate than other forms of bias. In fact, considerable evidence suggests that in-group favoritism—the preferences that individuals feel for those who are like them in salient respects such as race, sex, and ethnicity—are also deeply rooted.[111] *Plessy v. Ferguson*, the shameful 1896 Supreme Court decision that affirmed "separate but equal" racial policies, assumed that segregation was a natural desire.[112] Yet that desire has proven open to change, partly through legal interventions. Legislation such as the Americans with Disabilities Act also has had powerful positive effects on attitudes about the capacities of disabled individuals.[113] And in less than a decade, views on gay and lesbian relationships have shifted dramatically, partly in response to laws that have helped to publicize injustice and normalize same-sex orientation.[114] Similar initiatives on appearance discrimination could result in similar shifts in popular opinion and practices.

Prohibiting such discrimination is also unlikely to erode support for other civil rights legislation. Jurisdictions with such prohibitions, including San Francisco and Santa Cruz, California, Madison, Wisconsin, and the District of Columbia, are not known for backlash against anti-discrimination policies. There are, to be sure, limits to how far these policies can be extended without diminishing their moral force. But no evidence suggests that we have reached that limit. Neither is it likely that prohibitions on appearance discrimination would unleash a barrage of loony litigation. The few jurisdictions that have such laws report relatively few complaints. Cities and counties average between zero and nine a year, and Michigan averages about 30, only one of which ends up in court.[115] Given the costs and difficulties of proving bias, and the qualifications built into current legal prohibitions, their enforcement has proven far less burdensome than opponents have feared.

Of course, legal requirements that ask too much of human nature may lack moral authority and may undermine the legitimacy of legal institutions. But many laws that have been widely ignored or resisted at the outset have gradually acquired legitimacy and have reshaped public values. Indeed, much of American civil rights legislation is a case in point. Although stigma and evidentiary difficulties will prevent most victims of appearance-related bias from coming forward, the same is true in other discrimination contexts. Even laws that are notoriously underenforced can serve a crucial role in influencing public norms, deterring violations, and affirming social ideals.

Law can also do more to address misleading and risky cosmetic and weight loss products. Traditionally, as a Federal Trade Commission official acknowledged, "appearance-enhancement claims ... [have not been] high on our prosecution list."[116] Rather, government agencies have relied on public education and efforts to encourage media voluntarily to decline advertisements making fraudulent claims.[117] Such approaches have proven demonstrably inadequate. Also worrisome are the ads for "cosmeceuticals"—cosmetic products that include chemicals that aren't regulated by the federal Food and Drug Administration. Government agencies need more resources and authority to protect consumers, as well as stiffer sanctions for misleading claims.

Individual, Business, and Policy Initiatives

Another cluster of strategies should center on individual activism. Women can boycott products, join protests, organize lobbying campaigns, and write letters, op-eds, and blogs. On the relatively infrequent occasions when a critical mass of individuals has engaged in such efforts, their complaints have produced results. Marketers have pulled ads, employers have changed policies, and local governments have passed legislation.[118] San Francisco's ordinance prohibiting height and weight discrimination is a product of such efforts. The activism responded to an advertisement by a fitness center featuring a space alien and a caption reading "When they come, they'll eat the fat ones first." Protesters showed up at the center in alien costumes wearing signs that said "Eat Me" and "This Gym Alienates Fat People." Activists also demanded hearings before the San Francisco Human Rights Commission to explore examples of appearance discrimination and appropriate legal remedies. The result was an ordinance prohibiting discrimination based on height and weight.[119]

Businesses that contribute to appearance-related problems should also assume more responsibility for solutions. One cluster of strategies should seek to promote more diverse, healthy, and realistic images of attractiveness. Fashion, advertising, publishing, and broadcast industries could develop codes to address the issue. One obvious first step would be to follow the lead of some European countries that have banned excessively underweight models whose health is at risk.[120] Employers could also do more to discourage bias based on appearance. As a threshold matter, they could give employees a greater role in developing policies on dress, grooming, and other appearance-related issues. Involving workers could help raise awareness of the injustice of discrimination and the values of self-expression. Employees play such a role in other nations, and survey research indicates that almost two-thirds of American workers would like to have more influence over decisions that affect their workplace conduct.[121] Including appearance as a prohibited form of bias in official anti-discrimination policies and training programs could also raise awareness about stereotypes, stigma, and the price of prejudice. In addition, employers could do more to support workers in making healthy choices that affect appearance. A growing number of large businesses are providing wellness programs that include information, counseling, and access to healthy food and fitness facilities.

More policy efforts should also focus on preventing unhealthy appearance-related behaviors, such as those contributing to obesity and eating disorders. Examples include regulation of children's advertising; use of zoning laws and financial incentives to reduce "nutritional deserts" in low-income communities; greater support of recreational programs; and more educational initiatives aimed at combatting appearance bias and raising public awareness of fraudulent advertising claims.[122]

Finally, the food and cosmetics industries could do more to promote health and reduce costs associated with appearance. At a minimum, they should supply more complete and accurate product information. Except in fast-food restaurants required to post nutrition and calorie content, customers may find it impossible to discover this information. When former Food and Drug Commissioner David Kessler asked one restaurant's employees what was in the menu items he ordered, typical responses were: "We can't tell you that," or "I'm not sure I'm allowed to say."[123] Even more troubling is what marketers do in fact say about certain food and cosmetic purchases. Many health-related claims are, as one industry expert put it, "an exercise in creative writing."[124] Some junk food is even labeled "heart healthy" because it is fried in polyunsaturated fat.[125] Rather than mask the content of unhealthy products, sellers could do more to improve the taste of nutritional alternatives. As one report on market trends noted: "Healthy indulgence is a vast opportunity that is undeveloped by the food and drinks industry."[126] A socially responsible business community would help consumers make good nutritional choices, not delude them about unhealthy alternatives.

====

No one advocating change in American attitudes toward appearance should be naive about all that stands in the way. Discrimination on the basis of looks is deeply rooted and widely practiced, and there are obvious limits to how much legal and policy strategies can affect it. But the same has been true for other forms of discrimination. And the last half-century leaves no doubt that legal prohibitions and public activism can promote significant change. Surely the values at stake are worth the effort. The kind of attention that women once gave to the state of their souls they now give to the state of their bodies.[127] Too often, the result is far from constructive. The financial, psychological, and physical price of appearance demands closer attention and collective action. Appearance must be seen not only as an aesthetic issue, but as a legal and policy one as well.

8

The Politics of Progress

During one of the 2012 presidential debates, Mitt Romney famously empha-
sized his efforts while Massachusetts governor to identify qualified women to
serve in his administration. In his recollection, his staff reportedly collected
"binders full of women."[1] Romney's artless phrase reflects a long-standing problem of women's underrepresentation in political leadership. How to get women
out of binders and into office, and what difference that would make, are questions central to the women's movement.

The Underrepresentation of Women in Political Leadership

Until the last several decades, women in political office were notable for their
absence. The only positions in which they held significant representation
were on library and school boards.[2] Overt prejudice was pervasive. When the
Gallup poll began asking whether voters would support a qualified woman
for president in 1937, only a third said yes.[3] In the 1970s, only two women
served as governors and one as a senator. About 90 percent of state legislatures
and over 95 percent of Congress were male.[4] Today, the political landscape
looks quite different. Voters and interest groups no longer discriminate against
women, but their underrepresentation remains persistent and pervasive.[5]
Ninety-five percent of Americans would vote for a qualified woman for president. However, in elective office, American women account for just 18 percent
of Congress, 24 percent of state legislatures, 10 percent of governors, and 12
percent of mayors of the nation's 100 largest cities.[6] Almost half the states have
yet to elect a woman Senator or Governor.[7] Given current rates of change, it
would take close to 100 years to equalize men's and women's representation in
Congress.[8] At the local level, women's underrepresentation can be just as bad.
A 2013 profile of Los Angeles leadership found that men occupied seven out of
eight of the city's top positions.[9] At the party level, the Republicans confront

a shortage of women in leadership. Only 8 percent of House Republicans are women, and the Senate has only four female Republicans. Women are also absent from a long list of potential 2016 GOP presidential contenders.[10] From a global perspective, the United States ranks 78th in the world for women's representation in political office, below Tajikistan, Slovakia, Bangladesh, and Saudi Arabia.[11]

The problem is not performance. Researchers consistently find that when women run for office, they are just as effective in terms of fundraising and electability.[12] In experimental situations, Americans rate female candidates no worse than males, and the media no longer discriminates against women in the amount or nature of coverage.[13] The main difficulty is that women are less likely than men to run for office. Other problems are that they face more competition in primaries, and tend to run later in life due to family responsibilities, which makes it difficult to gain the experience necessary for the highest offices.[14]

In accounting for the gender gap in political representation, political scientists Jennifer Lawless and Richard Fox surveyed some 3,900 potential candidates and identified recurrent barriers:

- Women perceive the electoral environment as highly competitive and biased against female candidates.
- Women are much less likely than men to see themselves as qualified for office.
- Potential female candidates are less competitive, less confident, and more risk averse than their male counterparts.
- Women are less likely than men to receive suggestions and encouragement to run for office.
- Women react more negatively than men to many of the demands of modern campaigns.
- Women have disproportionate family responsibilities that interfere with the time required for successful political careers.[15]

Although women in fact do as well as men when they run for office, the perception among women is otherwise. Seven out of 10 women in Lawless and Fox's study thought that female candidates do not raise as much money as similarly situated males, and a majority thought that women did not win as often.[16] Charlotte Whitman, the first female mayor of Ottawa, famously maintained that "[w]hatever women do, they must do twice as well as men to be thought half as good. Luckily, this is not difficult."[17] Most American women think she's right, except for the part about it not being difficult. Despite similar credentials, men in the Lawless and Fox study were 60 percent more likely than women to assess themselves as "very qualified" to run for office, and women were more than

twice as likely as men to rate themselves as "not at all qualified."[18] Women also
rated themselves lower on character traits of political relevance such as being
confident, competitive, risk-taking, entrepreneurial, and thick-skinned.[19] In
addition, women had more negative feelings than men toward certain aspects
of campaigning, such as fundraising, going door to door to meet constituents,
possibly needing to engage in a negative campaign, losing privacy, and sacrificing time with family.[20] Compared with men, women were less likely to
receive encouragement to run for political office, both from political officials
and activists, and from family and colleagues.[21] Women also shouldered disproportionate family obligations. In dual-career couples, they were six times
more likely than men to bear responsibility for the majority of household tasks,
and about 10 times more likely to be the primary childcare provider. Women
worked about the same hours as men but spent two-thirds more time on childcare.[22] But just as being married with children presents problems, so too does
being unmarried and childless. In the view of many voters, a woman who does
not want children does not seem quite normal.[23] So, whatever their family situation, traditional gender role expectations make running for office more challenging for women.

Comparative research also reveals certain structural features of the American political system that work against women. Female candidates do better in
nations where party control is strong and politicians are "more or less inter-
changeable representatives of party platforms."[24] By contrast, in the United
States, where politicians depend more on personal visibility and credibility as
legislative players, often by establishing seniority, women do less well. They
suffer greater penalties for interrupting their political career or starting it later
due to family responsibilities, and their aversion to key aspects of campaigning
disproportionately deters them from seeking office.[25] In addition, women face
more primary challenges, perhaps because they are perceived as more vulnerable than men.[26] Whatever the reason, they confront a more difficult primary
terrain, which may discourage all but the most qualified candidates from running for office.

Women may also be deterred by the heightened scrutiny and gendered criticism that they receive as candidates. A case in point was the media's release of
sexually suggestive college pictures of congressional candidate Krystal Ball.[27]
Texas gubernatorial candidate Wendy Davis has faced criticism for neglecting
her children while a student at Harvard Law School.[28] Almost all the Senate
women have stories of being kept out of rooms, clubs, and caucuses, and of
being patronized, propositioned, and scolded for abandoning their children.[29]
As Chapter 7 notes, women's appearance also attracts special scrutiny. Hillary Clinton's preference for pantsuits has received widespread comment,
including television star Tim Gunn's observation that she "dresses like she's

confused about her gender."[30] Representative Michele Bachmann was criticized for wearing too much makeup to a political debate.[31] Vice presidential candidate Sarah Palin faced severe criticism over the costs of her wardrobe and her makeup expert.[32] Studies show that any comments made about a female candidate's appearance, regardless of their content, negatively influence public opinion.[33]

Women may also be discouraged from running by media portrayals of female candidates as less intelligent or mainstream than male candidates. Politicians including Sarah Palin, Nancy Pelosi, and Hillary Clinton have been characterized as "crackpots" and "lunatics."[34] In the 2013 New York mayoral race, lesbian Christine Quinn was described as "bossy," "combative," and "not enough feminine."[35]

These patterns suggest the need for responses on several levels. Political parties could do more to recruit women and dispel the myth that they are less electable. More efforts could focus on encouraging and training the next generation of women leaders. So, for example, the Center for American Women and Politics supports college and university summer institutes that teach college women the value of civic engagement and the importance of having women in positions of political leadership. Another initiative, Elect Her: Campus Women Win, attempts to convince more female college students to gain experience by running for student government. Emerge America is a national program that trains Democratic women to run for office. However, it operates in only 10 states, and has not targeted those where women are most underrepresented.[36] More funding and outreach by such programs could feed the pipeline for future officeholders. More individuals also could contribute to funds like Emily's List, which provides support to Democratic female candidates. And more positive, less gendered portrayals of female politicians in the press and entertainment media can create role models that encourage political ambition. Those strategies take on special importance if, as is often assumed, electing women is a reliable way of advancing women's interests.

The Difference That "Difference" Makes

In announcing her candidacy for the US Senate, Blanche Lambert Lincoln explained that she was running because "nearly one of every three senators is a millionaire, but there are only five mothers."[37] Her assumption that gender difference makes a difference is widely shared. About two-thirds of Americans think that the country would be better off if we had more women in political office.[38] The argument for women's increased representation rest on two premises. The first, based on descriptive representation, is that the presence of women in political leadership is important in and of itself on symbolic grounds, and can help confer legitimacy on governing institutions. A second premise, based on substantive representation, is that the participation of women will increase the likelihood that women's interests will be adequately represented.

The assumption that women would and should represent women's distinctive interests is a relatively recent phenomenon. Early female politicians tended to avoid identification with women's issues.[39] California Senator Barbara Boxer wryly described the traditional approach of female candidates: "You never mentioned being a woman . . . you hoped nobody noticed."[40] Contemporary female politicians are more likely to see themselves as representing women, but with limited consensus on what that representation entails.[41] Women do not speak with a single voice, and what constitutes "women's interests" is not always self-evident. Yet, as the preceding chapters make clear, it is often possible to find common ground around issues central to women's well-being concerning work, family, violence, reproduction, and economic security. The question remaining is whether putting more women in office is a reliable way of advancing that agenda.

Research on the difference that gender difference makes is mixed. Most research finds few gender differences in leadership style or approach.[42] However, a large body of scholarship suggests that women's representation matters in getting women's issues onto the agenda. Both in Congress and state legislatures, women are more likely than their male colleagues to address women's issues and to rank those issues as priorities.[43] Some studies suggest that increased women's representation leads to more women-friendly policies in state-by-state comparisons.[44] By contrast, other research finds no consistent relationship between greater gender equality in political representation and greater gender equality in social policies or outcomes.[45] Party affiliation is more important than gender in predicting votes on women's issues, and ideology is more important than gender in predicting sponsorship of legislation on these issues.[46] Conservative Republican women often play leading roles in speaking out against legislation on issues like abortion and equal pay. When asked if Congress would be more likely to pass the Paycheck Fairness Act if there were more women members, Representative Rosa DeLauro's short answer was "No." It matters who those women are. "We've never been able to engage the Republican women," DeLauro explained. "As a matter of fact, they're the people who get up on the floor and speak against [the act]."[47] As politics has grown more polarized in recent years, it has become increasingly difficult to get women to cross party lines in support of women's issues. Coalitions are likely only on uncontroversial proposals, such as expanded treatment for autistic children of military service members or violence against women in the military.[48] Moderate Republican women are in a particularly difficult position: it is hard to advance within the party and influence its agenda without toeing the conservative line on gender-related matters.[49]

What lessons emerge from the mixed findings on gender differences? One is the need to increase recruitment and support of candidates who will make women's issues a priority.[50] Those candidates need to be men as well as women; male sponsors have made a critical difference in advancing gender-related concerns, and broadening the pool of potential leaders on these issues should be a central priority.[51] To make that possible, more women must target their votes and dollars at those willing and able to advance women's interests. A second lesson is the importance of a strong women's movement that can help create public support for political initiatives. Cross-national research finds that the presence of such a movement is a better predictor of women's rights policies than women's proportional representation in legislatures.[52] A third lesson is the need to address more effectively the needs of particularly disadvantaged subgroups. Research confirms what common sense suggests: women's groups, like other public interest organizations, tend to focus on concerns of their funding base. Less attention goes to issues that disproportionately affect those disadvantaged by race, class, sexual orientation, or related factors.[53] In one study of women's rights organizations, a staff member put it bluntly: welfare reform is "really just not our cup of tea."[54] To alter those priorities, women's organizations need to find more ways of making issues of concern to the disadvantaged also of concern to more privileged women.

The Gender Gap

A century ago, Rheta Childe Dorr's *What Eight Million Women Want* envisioned a world in which women's "special capabilities" were brought to bear on the work of governing. The result, she asserted, would be that the "city will be like a great, well-ordered comfortable sanitary household. There will be no slums, no sweatshops, no sad women and children toiling in tenement rooms. . . . All the family will be taken care of, [and] taught to take care of themselves. . . ."[55] Supporters of women's suffrage similarly cast women as municipal housekeepers, whose "high code of morals" would "purify politics."[56] Disillusionment quickly set in when women achieved the vote and no consistent gender differences in voting patterns emerged. Until the 1980s, there were only occasional gender gaps in presidential races, and these did not reflect concerns about women's rights. For example, Herbert Hoover received a disproportionate number of women's votes because, like the majority of women, he supported Prohibition.[57]

In recent years, the gender gap has grown more consistent and pronounced, and has favored Democratic candidates and platforms. It has also given some leverage to female politicians willing to fight for women's issues.[58] Compared to men, women voters are more likely to support spending on social services and an active role for government in assisting the poor, and less likely to support military intervention.[59] In the 2012 election, women favored Obama over Romney by 11 points (55 percent to 44 percent), insuring his victory. What accounts for that gap and what it means for a progressive women's agenda provide a useful case study in the mobilization of women.

In the run-up to the 2012 election, Democratic Representative Carolyn Maloney announced that the Republican "war on women is stunning in scope, appalling in its indifference and outrageous in its arrogance."[60] Although other liberals were more rhetorically restrained, the "war on women" was a constant theme, and Republicans offered a steady stream of supporting material. First was the party platform, which one of its drafters called the "most conservative in modern history."[61] Among its planks were:

> Opposition to abortion even in cases of rape, incest, or threats to the health of the mother;
>
> Support for a "human life" amendment to the constitution and legislation that "makes clear that the Fourteenth Amendment's protections apply to unborn children";
>
> Opposition to gay marriage and civil unions;
>
> Reform of welfare and social security programs in ways that would cut back assistance.[62]

As Maine's Republican Senator Susan Collins noted, "the platform seems designed to alienate a lot of moderate women. I don't get it."[63]

Mitt Romney largely echoed the platform positions, and also opposed funding for Planned Parenthood as well as federally mandated insurance coverage for contraception. Although he attempted to cast himself as a moderate on abortion by supporting exceptions for rape, incest, and saving the life of the mother, as columnist Katha Pollitt asks, "what kind of moderate wants to criminalize 93 percent of all abortions?"[64] In the absence of a "woman-friendly" policy record to promote, Romney's campaign fell back on promises about the economy and efforts to "war[m] up his image by emphasizing his role as a devoted father and husband."[65] He was partly successful. In all the coverage of the gender gap, a little discussed fact was that Romney won a majority of white women's votes (56 percent). It was Obama's overwhelming support among women of color, particularly blacks (96 percent) and Hispanics (76 percent), that gave him the edge.[66] In this as in other elections, differences among women based on race, religion, and economic status were much larger on average than differences between women and men.[67]

Although it is clear that women voters generally report different preferences and priorities than men, it is less certain how much importance women attach to "women's issues" or how much pressure politicians face to address them. In the run-up to the 2012 election, women were more likely than men to say that they preferred a bigger government with more services (45 percent versus 36 percent). Almost three-quarters of women cited education as a top priority compared with only slightly over half of men (72 percent versus 57 percent). More women also cited helping the poor as a top priority (58 percent versus 46 percent).[68] When asked what they considered the most important issue for women in the election, female voters in swing states cited abortion first (39 percent), followed by jobs (19 percent), healthcare (18 percent), the economy (16 percent) and equal rights, pay, and opportunities (15 percent). Men cited jobs (38 percent), the economy (37 percent), the federal budget and deficit (10 percent), healthcare (10 percent) and taxes (6 percent).[69] It does not, however, appear that Obama feels pressure to make women's issues a central priority in his second term. Apart from passage of the Paycheck Fairness Act, an initiative on early childhood education, and an increase in the minimum wage, the Obama administration has pressed for almost none of the other reforms that the preceding chapters have identified.[70] Nor have Republicans shown much interest in altering their hard-line stance, or in elevating women to positions of influence.[71] When House Speaker John Boehner announced an all-male list of 2012 committee chairs, the ensuing outcry forced appointment of just one woman to head a relatively inconsequential committee on which she had never served.[72]

Financial Support for Women's Issues

There are also gender gaps in women's political contributions. Men generally give about two-thirds of itemized donations when measured by number of donors and amount of funds contributed.[73] As a consequence, women reap fewer of the opportunities for access, influence, and positions that accompany financial support.

That gap in political involvement is to some extent offset by women's greater charitable activity. Some half dozen studies in recent years have found that women donate more than men and are more likely to participate in charitable organizations.[74] Yet relatively little of women's giving goes to support women's issues. Women's advocacy is not among the top 10 areas of female support, and little of the 9 percent of charitable funding that goes to "youth and family organizations" goes to groups working for legal reforms. As one director of a youth law center put it, donors "like children, not lawyers."[75] The same is true of foundations. Well under 10 percent of foundation funding supports programs for women and girls, and little of that funding goes to advocacy organizations.[76] Donors' desires for "measurable impacts" and "newer, hotter" issues work against groups that focus on long-term changes in public policy and social attitudes.[77] The National Organization for Women runs on about $2 million a year, roughly 2 percent of the budget of major environmental organizations.[78] Some efforts are under way to alter this landscape. For example, the Women's Funding Network includes about 160 foundations that commit to making three-quarters of their grants to projects led by women.[79] But much more needs to be done to channel funding to the groups that are best positioned to advance gender equality.

An Agenda for Change

What will it take to get what women want? First, it will take a better understanding of the complexities in defining the agenda. What distinguishes feminism as a movement is the claim to speak for women as a group. What limits feminism as a political force are the practical challenges of doing so, and bridging the diversity in women's experiences, backgrounds, and concerns. It is common for activists to acknowledge the intersections of gender with race, ethnicity, class, and sexual orientation. It is less common for women to bridge those differences in pursuit of common goals. More women need to be convinced that we cannot adequately improve the lot of women without challenging all the sources of subordination with which gender interacts. As Audre Lorde noted, "It is not our differences which separate women, but our reluctance to recognize those differences and deal effectively with the distortions which have resulted. . . ."[80]

A second problem to be confronted is the lack of social consensus that there is a significant problem. Most Americans do not think there are more advantages in being a man than a woman in today's society.[81] To many Americans, the laws against sex discrimination and the presence of women in prominent positions look like evidence that the "woman problem" has been solved. This "no-problem" problem and the sense of complacency that it engenders have themselves become obstacles to broader change.

A third challenge lies in the gap between legal rights and daily realities. Equal opportunity in law is necessary but not sufficient to guarantee equal opportunity in fact. To take some obvious examples, women's constitutional right to reproductive liberty is limited by lack of information, funding, accessible services, and anti-abortion activism. The right to be free from discrimination at work is limited by problems of proof and disincentives to file formal claims. The right to compete for equal workplace advancement is also affected by lack of affordable childcare and disproportionate family responsibilities. Women need not just equal rights but equal respect and equal recognition of values traditionally associated with women. That, in turn, demands changes in laws and policies. Women need an expanded set of rights, such as paid parental leave, reasonable accommodations in schedules, equal pay for jobs of comparable value, and bans on discrimination based on sexual orientation. They also need a change in funding priorities: more resources should be available for childcare, battered women's shelters, comprehensive sex education, and reproductive assistance. Poor women need access to abortions and to welfare support that meets basic subsistence needs. States need more effective prevention and treatment programs for sexual violence.

Of equal importance are changes in workplace structures. Women need not only equal treatment in existing institutions but fundamental changes in the way those institutions are adapting to work/family conflict. Employers need to do better in policies and practices concerning family and medical leave, and flexible and part-time schedules. To make this agenda possible, more women must see personal difficulties as social problems calling for collective action.

Women also need changes in cultural norms. They need to challenge the gender stereotypes that devalue the competence and commitment of working mothers and that penalize assertive behavior in women leaders. They also need to address the ways that society trivializes and tolerates sex-based aggression. As Arianna Huffington puts it, members of the women's movement today are "not just fighting for a space in the world, we're fighting to change it."[82]

This is not a modest agenda. But neither does it seem hopelessly unrealistic. In the space of just two generations, gender roles and expectations have been fundamentally transformed. The vast majority of Americans believe that women and men are entitled to equal opportunities. The challenge now is to recognize our distance from that goal, and to build a movement capable of reaching it. No just society can afford the inequalities that women still face in status, power, income, and physical security. In 1908, newspaper editor William Allen White advised women in America to "raise more hell and fewer dahlias." It remains good advice.

NOTES

Introduction

1. William F. Buckley, Resolutions on the Side of Yale's Survival, in Let Us Talk of Many Things: The Collected Speeches (Roseville Cal: Prima Lifestyles. 2000), 149–150.
2. Janet Lever and Pepper Schwartz, Women at Yale: Liberating a College Campus 243 (Indianapolis, Indiana: Bobbs Merrill, 1971).
3. Lever and Schwartz, Women at Yale, 243.
4. Lever and Schwartz, Women at Yale, at 186–188.
5. Deborah L. Rhode, Justice and Gender (Cambridge, MA: Harvard University Press, 1985), 301; Mary A. Boutilier and Lucinda San Giovanni, The Sporting Woman (Champaign, IL: Human Kinetics Publishing, 1983), 32–42.
6. Warren, Women Athletes Tell of Fight for Respect, Yale Daily News, Nov. 30, 1989, 3.
7. Karen Berger Morello, The Invisible Bar: The Woman Lawyer in America (New York: Random House, 1986), 219.
8. Deborah L. Rhode, Speaking of Sex: The Denial of Gender Inequality (Cambridge, MA: Harvard University Press, 1998), 56; Marilyn A. Hulme, Mirror Mirror on the Wall: Biased Reflections in Textbooks and Instructional Materials, in Ann O'Brien Cavelli, ed. Sex Equity in Education: Readings and Strategies (Springfield, IL: C. C. Thomas, 1988); Myra Sadker and David Sadker, Failing at Fairness: How America's Schools Cheat Girls (New York: Scribners, 1994), 72, 124–131.
9. Jane Austen, Northanger Abbey (London: MacDonald, 1818), 108.
10. Deborah L. Rhode, Equal Rights in Retrospect, Journal of Law and Inequality 1 (1983): 1, 43.
11. Ruth Bader Ginsburg, Reflections on Arizona's Pace-Setting Justices: William Hubbs Rehnquist and Sandra Day O'Connor [comments], Arizona Law Review, 49 (2007): 8.

Chapter 1

1. Jane Mansbridge, Beyond Adversary Democracy (Chicago: University of Chicago Press, 1983).
2. Jennifer L. Pozner, The Big Lie: False Feminist Death Syndrome, Profit, and the Media, in Rory Dicker and Alison Piepmeier, Catching a Wave: Reclaiming Feminism for the 21st Century (Boston, MA: Northeastern University Press, 2003), 31; See Kay Ebeling, The Failure of Feminism, Newsweek, November 19, 1990; Ginia Bellafonte, Is Feminism Dead? Time, June 29, 1998.

3. Sally Quinn, Feminists Have Killed Feminism, Los Angeles Times, January 23, 1992, B7; Jennifer Baumgardener and Amy Richards, Manifesta: Young Women, Feminism and the Future (New York: Farrar, Straus, and Giroux, 2000), 122.

4. Lisa Miller, The Retro Wife, New York Magazine, March 17, 2013.

5. Dorothy Dunbar Bromley, Feminist–New Style, Harper's Monthly Magaine, October 1927, 552.

6. Nancy Gibbs and Jeanne McDowell Berkeley, How to Revive a Revolution, Time, March 9, 1992, 56 (quoting Steinem).

7. Claudia Wallis, Onward Women!, Time Magazine, December 4, 1989, 80 (77 percent); Lorraine Dusky, Ms. Poll, Feminist Tide Sweeps In as the 21st Century Begins, Ms. Magazine, Spring 2003, 56 (citing Peter Harris Research survey finding three-quarters felt women's movement was helpful and 83 percent approved it).

8. Paula Kamen, Feminist Fatale: Voices From the "Twentysomething" Generation Explore the Future of the "Women's Movement" (New York: Donald I. Fine, 1991), 30 (citing New York Times 1989 poll finding that 58 percent of Americans and 67 percent of women said strong movement was needed); CBS News, Women's Movement Worthwhile, February 11, 2009, http://www.cbsnews.com/2102-500,160_162-965,224.html (finding that 48 percent felt movement was necessary).

9. Lorraine Dusky, Poll: Feminist Tide Sweeps In as the 21st Century Begins, Ms. Magazine, Spring 2003, 56 (77 percent of women and 70 percent of men); CBS News, Poll: Women's Movement Worthwhile, February 11, 2009 (65 percent of women and 58 percent of men); Emily Swanson, Poll: Few Identify as Feminists, But Most Believe in Equality of Sexes Huffington Post, April 16, 2013 (citing Huffington Post/You Gov Poll).

10. Swanson, Poll (citing Huffington Post/YouGov poll finding 23 percent of women); Eleanor Smeal, The Feminist Factor, Ms. Magazine Winter 2013, 27 (Lake Research poll finding 55 percent of women voters); The Barrier That Didn't Fall, The Daily Beast, November 18, 2008 (citing Penn, Schoen, and Berland interview data finding 14 percent) CBS News, Women's Movement Worthwhile (finding quarter of women); Jennifer Robison, Feminism—What's in a Name?, Gallup, September 3, 2002, http:www.gallup.com/poll/6715/feminism-whats-name.aspx.

11. Yankelovich, 1998 Time/CNN.

12. The Barrier That Didn't Fall.

13. See Hyde, The Deep Divide; Jason Schnittker, Jeremy Freese, and Brian Powell, Who Are Feminists and What do They Believe?: The Role of Generations, American Sociological Review 68 (2003): 607 (listing studies); Deborah A. Abowitz, The Campus "F" Word: Feminist Self-Identification (and Not) Among Undergraduates, International Journal of Sociology of the Family 34 (2008): 43; Shannon Houvouras and J. Scott Carter, The F Word: College Students' Definitions of a Feminist, Sociological Forum 23 (2008): 234.

14. Janice D. Yoder, Ann Tobias, and Andrea F. Snell, When Declaring "I Am a Feminist" Matters: Labeling Is Linked to Activism, Sex Roles 64 (2011): 9. See also Schnittker, Freese, and Powell, Who Are Feminists, 607 (noting the linkage between identify and actions).

15. Wallis, Onward Women.

16. Ann N. Costain, Inviting Women's Rebellion: A Political Process Interpretation of the Women's Movement (Baltimore, MD: Johns Hopkins University Press, 1992), 47.

17. Laura Shapiro, Sisterhood Was Powerful, Newsweek, June 20, 1994, 68 (quoting Firestone and Atkinson).

18. Rhode, Justice and Gender, 75.

19. Katie J. M. Baker, Does It Matter if Marissa Mayer Doesn't Think She's a Feminist, Jezebel, July 18, 2012 (quoting Mayer).

20. Renee Schreiber, Righting Feminism: Conservative Women and American Politics (New York: Oxford University Press, 2008), 45.

21. Kathryn Jean Lopez, F-Word, Failing, National Review Online, April 11, 2011 (quoting Venker). See Suzanne Venker and Phyllis Schlafly, The Flipside of Feminism: What Conservative Women Know—and Men Can't Say (New York: WND Books, 2011).

22. Lauren Barbato, Misogyny and Elder Abuse, Ms. Magazine, Spring 2012, 16.

23. Meghan Daum, Rush Limbaugh's Blind Spot, Los Angeles Times, March 8, 2012, A19.

24. Daum, Rush Limbaugh's Blind Spot (citing other characterizations of Fluke and other critiques by Limbaugh).

25. Henry P. Belanger, Meet the Men's Rights Movement, The Good Men's Project, http://goodmenproject.com/ethics-values/meet-the-mens-rights-movement/.

26. Michael Kimmel, Angry White Men: American Masculinity at the End of an Era (New York: Nation Books, 2013), 21.

27. Paul Elam, Feminist Apocalypse, http://failuresforgodesses.blogspot.com/2010/05/sobering-article-by-paul-elam.html.

28. Men's Rights Movement vs. Feminism, post by adamblanch, http://www.squidoo.com/mens-rights-movement-vs-feminism. For an overview, see Judith Newton, From Panthers to Promise Keepers: Rethinking the Men's Movement (Lanham, MD: Rowman & Littlefield, 2004).

29. Arthur Goldwag, Southern Poverty Law Center, Leader's Suicide Brings Attention to Men's Rights Movement (Spring 2012), http://www.splcenter.org/get-informed/intelligence-report/browse-all-issues/2012/spring/a-war-on-women.

30. Arthur Goldwag, Southern Poverty Law Center, Leader's Suicide Brings Attention to Men's Rights Movement (Spring 2012), http://www.splcenter.org/get-informed/intelligence-report/browse-all-issues/2012/spring/a-war-on-women.

31. Kimmel, Angry White Men, 172.

32. World Economic Forum, Women's Empowerment: Measuring the Global Gender Gap (2011).

33. Pew Research Center, On Pay Gap, Millennial Women Near Parity-For Now, December 11, 2013; John Halpin and Ruy Teixeira, Battle of the Sexes Gives Way to Negotiations, in Heather Boushey and Ann O'Leary, eds., The Shriver Report: A Woman's Nation Changes Everything (Washington, D.C.: Center for American Progress, 2009), 407; NBC News, Wall Street Journal Poll, April 2013; Pew Research Center for the People and the Press, American Values Survey, 2012, http: www.people-press.org/values-questions/q40aa/women-get-fewer-opportunities-than-men-for-good-jobs/.

34. Venker and Schlafly, The Flipside of Feminism, 47–48.

35. EEOC All Statutes, FY 1997-Fy2012, http:www.eeoc.gov/eeoc/statistics/enforcement/all.cfm. EEOC Litigation Statistics, FYI 1997 through FY2012, http:www.eeoc.gov/eeoc/statistics/enforcement/litigation.cfm.

36. PEW Research Center, The Decline of Marriage and Rise of New Families, November 18, 2010.

37. Molly Worthen, Single Mothers with Family Values, New York Times, October 27, 2013, Wk 6; Hyde, The Deep Divide, 268; Paula Kamen, Feminist Fatale: Voices from the "Twentysomething" Generation Explore the Future of the "Women's Movement" (New York: Donald I. Fine, 1991), 23; Carolyn Sorisio, A Tale of Two Feminisms: Power and Victimization in Contemporary Feminist Debate, in Leslie Heywood and Jennifer Drake, eds., Third Wave Agenda: Being Feminist, Doing Feminism (Minneapolis: University of Minnesota Press, 1997), 134; Houvouras and Carter, The F Word, 249; Susan Bolotin, Voices from the Post Feminist Generation, New York Times Sunday Magazine, October 17, 1982, 29; Reger, Everywhere and Nowhere, 35.

38. Pamela Aronson, Feminists or "Postfeminists"? Young Women's Attitudes Toward Feminism and Gender Relations, Gender and Society 17 (2003): 900, 916.

39. Ramin Setoodeh, Taylor Swift Dishes on Her New Album, "Red," Dating Heartbreak, and "Grey's Anatomy," The Daily Beast, October 22, 2012, http://www.thedailybeast.com/articles/2012/10/22/taylor-swift-dishes-on-her-new-album-red-dating-heartbreak-and-grey-s-anatomy.html?utm_source=feedburner&utm_medium=feed&utm_campaign=Feed%3A+thedailybeast%2Farticles+%28The+Daily+Beast+-+Latest+Articles%29.

40. N. Williams, Is Lady Gaga a Feminist or Isn't she?, Ms. Blog, March 11, 2010, http://msmagazine.com/blog/2010/03/11/is-lady-gaga-a-feminist-or-isnt-she/.

41. Pozner, The Big Lie; Jessica Valenti, Full Frontal Feminism: A Young Woman's Guide to Why Feminism Matters (Emeryville, CA: Seal Press, 2007), 8; Anna Quindlen, Public and Private: And Now, Babe Feminism, New York Times, January 19, 1994, A21 (quoting Christina Hoff Sommers); Kamen, Feminist Fatale, 23; Claudia Wallis, Onward Women, Time, December 4, 1989.

42. Tad Friend, Yes (Feminist Women Who Like Sex), Esquire, February, 1994, 55 (quoting Sommers).

43. Valenti, Full Frontal Feminism, 8 (quoting Limbaugh).

44. Baumgardner and Richards: Manifesta, 61; Anna Quindlen, Babe Feminism, January 19, 1994.

45. Pia Peltola, Melissa A. Milkie, and Stanley Presser, The "Feminist" Mystique: Feminist Identity in Three Generations of Women, Gender and Society 18 (2004): 122, 139.

46. For examples, see Alexander M. Czopp and Margo J. Monteith, Confronting Prejudice (Literally): Reactions to Confrontations of Racial and Gender Bias, Personality and Social Psychology Bulletin 29 (2003): 532; sources cited in Deborah L. Brake and Joanna L. Grossman, The Failure of Title VII as a Rights-Claiming System, North Carolina Law Review 86 (2008): 859, 901.

47. Maureen O'Connor, Beyoncé Is a Feminist, I Guess, New York Magazine.com, April 4, 2013, http://nymag.com/thecut/2013/04/beyonc-is-a-feminist-i-guess.html.

48. Bonnie Erbe, Sara Palin's Feminist Flip-Flop, U.S. News and World Report, October 28, 2008.

49. Abigail Rine, The Pros and Cons of Abandoning the Word "Feminist," The Atlantic, May 2, 2013, http://www.theatlantic.com/sexes/archive/2013/05/the-pros-and-cons-of-abandoning-the-word-feminist/275511/.

50. Hyde, Deep Divide, 291.

51. Nancy Gibbs and Jeanne McDowell, How to Revive a Revolution, Time, March 9, 1992, 56 (quoting Steinem).

52. Jessica Valenti, Full Frontal Feminism, 14.

53. Eliza Strickland, Mother's Work, S.F. Weekly, December 6, 2006.

54. Rebecca Walker, Becoming the Third Wave, Ms. Magazine, January 1992, 39. Others had used the term earlier. See Henry, Not My Mother's Sister, 22.

55. Astrid Henry, Solitary Sisterhood: Individualism Meets Collectivity in Feminism's Third Wave, in Jo Reger, ed., Different Wavelengths, 83.

56. Henry, Not My Mother's Sister, 7, 11.

57. Jessica Valenti, Who Stole Feminism, The Nation, September 29, 2010; Henry, Not My Mother's Sister, 166.

58. Nancy A. Naples, Confronting the Future, Learning from the Past, Feminist Praxis in the Twenty-First Century, in Reger, Different Wavelengths, 215, 222, 231.

59. R. Claire Snyder, What Is Third-Wave Feminism? A New Directions Essay, Signs 34 (2008): 175, 179.

60. For overviews, see Kathleen Kelly Janus, Building Bridges and Finding Common Feminist Ground: The Role of the Next Generation in Shaping Feminist Legal Theory, Duke Journal of Law and Gender Policy 20 (2013): 255; Snyder, What Is Third Wave Feminism?; Leslie Haywood and Jennifer Drake, Introduction, in Leslie Heywood and Jennifer Drake, Third Wave Agenda: Being a Feminist, Doing Feminism (Minneapolis: University of Minnesota Press, 1997), 1.

61. Snyder, What Is Third Wave Feminism, 179–180; Henry, Not My Mother's Sister, 33; Naples, Confronting the Future, 218–222. For the inability of wave theories to capture black feminist history, see Kimberly Springer, Third Wave Black Feminism? Signs 27 (2002): 1059, 1061–1106; Reger, Everwhere and Nowhere, 22.

62. Gloria Steinem, Forward, in Rebecca Walker, ed., To Be Real: Telling the Truth and Changing the Face of Feminism (New York: Anchor Books, 1995).

63. Snyder, What Is Third Wave Feminism?, 178; Naples, Confronting the Future, 221; Henry, Not My Mother's Sister, 5; Stacy Gillis and Rebecca Munford, Genealogies and Generations: The Politics and Praxis of Third-Wave Feminism, Women's History Review 13 (2004), 176; Jo Reger, Introduction, in Reger, Different Wavelengths, xxvii.

64. Susan Faludi, Sandberg Left Single Mothers Behind, CNN.com, March 13, 2013.

65. Bridget J. Crawford, Toward a Third-Wave Feminist Legal Theory: Young Women, Pornography and the Praxis of Pleasure, Michigan Journal of Gender and Law 14 (2007): 99, 126. See also Rory Dicker and Alison Piepmeier, Catching a Wave: Reclaiming Feminism for the 21st Century (Boston, MA: Northeastern University Press, 2003), 91; Reger, Everywhere and Nowhere, 5.

66. Snyder, What Is Third Wave Feminism?, 186.

67. For concerns about the personal as no longer political, see Karen Lehrman, The Lipstick Proviso: Women, Sex, and Power in the Real World (New York: Doubleday, 1997), 5.

68. Debora Spar, Wonder Women: Sex, Power, and the Quest for Perfection (New York: Farrar, Straus and Giroux, 2013), 235–236.

69. Katha Pollitt, Feminist Mothers, Flapper Daughters?, The Nation, October 18, 2010, 9.

70. Hyde, The Deep Divide, 39 (almost half of women polled said being feminine was central to what they liked about being a woman).

71. Maggie Crosby, ACLU of Northern California; Debbie Walsh, director, Center for American Women in Politics; Linda Basch, president, National Council for Research on Women.

72. Leslie Bennetts, Women and the Leadership Gap, The Daily Beast, March 5, 2012 (quoting Kolbert).

73. Sheryl Sandberg, Lean In: Women, Work, and the Will to Lead (New York: Knopf, 2013), 7; PBS NewsHour, Is the Advice for Women in Sheryl Sandberg's "Lean In" Elitist or Universal? March 12, 2013, http://www.pbs.org/newshour/bb/social_issues/jan-june13/sandberg_03-12.html.

74. Francine D. Blau, Mary C. Brinton, and David B. Grusky, The Declining Significance of Gender?, in Francine D. Blau, Mary C. Brinton, and David B. Grusky, eds., The Declining Significance of Gender (New York: Russell Sage, 2006), 3.

75. Dana Bash, Despite New Female Faces in Congress, Numbers in Decline, CNN, November 10, 2010 (quoting Walsh).

76. NPR Staff, Want More Gender Equality at Work? Go to an Emerging Market, NPR Morning Edition, April 22, 2013, http://www.npr.org/2013/04/22/177511506/want-more-gender-equality-at-work-go-to-an-emerging-market (quoting Hewlett).

77. Jo Reger, Everywhere and Nowhere: Contemporary Feminism in the United States (New York: Oxford University Press, 2012).

78. Sylvia Walby, The Future of Feminism (Cambridge, UK: Polity Press, 2011), 148–149; Jo Reger, Everywhere and Nowhere, 5–7.

79. Baumgardner and Richards, Manifesta, 17.

80. Other key predictors are higher education and liberal political views. Joan K. Buschman and Silvo Lenart, "I Am Not a Feminist, But . . .": College Women, Feminism, and Negative Experiences, Political Psychology 17 (1996): 59, 69. Laurie A Rhodebeck, The Structure of Men's and Women's Feminist Orientations: Feminist Identity and Feminist Opinion; Gender and Society 10 (1996): 386, 398, 397; Janice McCabe, What's in a Label: The Relationship Between Feminist Self Identification and "Feminist" Attitudes Among U.S. Women and Men, Gender and Society 19 (2005): 480.

81. http:www.gallup.com/poll/155462/Women-Men-Woprldwide-Equally-Likely-Thriving.aspx.

82. OECD Better Life Index, http://www.oecdbetterlifeindex.org/topics/life-satisfaction.

83. Chris M. Herbst, "Paradoxical" Decline? Another Look at the Relative Reduction in Female Happiness, 32 Journal of Economic Psychology 773 (2011).

84. Anna Greenberg, David Walker, Alex Lundry, and Alicia Downs, Failure to Adapt to Changing Families Leaves Women Economically Vulnerable, in Olivia Morgan and Karen Skelton, The Shriver Report: A Woman's Nation Pushes Back from the Brink (Washington, D.C.: Center for American Progress and Palgrave Macmillan, 2014), 407.

85. Interview with Noreen Farrell, Equal Rights Advocates.

86. Francine D. Blau, Mary C. Brinton, and David B. Grusky, The Declining Significance of Gender, in Francine D. Blau, Mary C. Brinton, and David B. Grusky, eds., The Declining Significance of Gender (New York: Russell Sage Foundation, 2006), 3.

87. John McCarthy and Mayer Zald, The Enduring Vitality of the Resource Mobilization Theory of Social Movements, in Jonathan H. Turner, ed., Handbook of Sociological Theory (New York: Kluwer Academic, 2002), 533.

88. Bert Klandermans, The Demand and Supply of Participation: Social Psychological Correlates of Participation in Social Movements, in David A. Snow, Sarah A. Soule, and Hanspeter Kriesi, eds., The Blackwell Companion to Social Movements (Malden, MA: Blackwell Publishers, 2003), 360, 362.

89. Debra Friedman and Doug McAdam, Collective Identity and Activism: Networks, Choices, and the Life of a Social Movement, in Aldon Morris and Carol McClurg Mueller, Frontiers in Social Movement Theory (New Haven, CT: Yale University Press, 1992), 156.

90. Friedman and McAdam, Collective Identity, at 164.

91. Suzanne Staggenborg and Verta Taylor, Whatever Happened to the Women's Movement, Mobilization: An International Journal 10 (2005): 37, 43.

92. Philip N. Cohen, The "End of Men" Is Not True: What Is Not and What Might Be on the Road Toward Gender Equality, Boston University Law Review 93 (2013):101, 123.

93. Linda Burnham, The New Women's Movement Initiative (August 16, 2007), quoted in Kristin Kalsem and Verna L. Williams, Social Justice Feminism, UCLA Women's Law Journal 18 (2010): 132.

94. Linda Burhham, The New Women's Movement Initiative (August 1, 2007), http://www.cew.umich.edu/sites/default/files/BurnhamFinalProject.pdf.

95. Burnham, New Women's Movement.

96. Burnham, New Women's Movement.

97. Sarah Hepola, Gloria Steinem, A Woman Like No Other, New York Times, March 18, 2012, S1.

98. Interviews with Heidi Hartman, Elizabeth Grayer, Kate Kendall.

99. Ann N. Costain, Inviting Women's Rebellion: A Political Process Interpretation of the Women's Movment, (Baltimore, MD: John Hopkins University Press, 1992), 138.

100. Susan Faludi, American Electra: Feminism Ritual Matricide, Harpers, October 2010, 29, 31.

101. Kristin Rowe-Finkbeiner, The F-Word: Feminism in Jeopardy (Emeryville, CA: Seal Press, 2004), 29 (quoting Susan Scanlan); Kamen, Feminist Fatale, 97; Katha Pollitt, Amber Waves of Blame, The Nation, June 15, 2009, 10.

102. Valenti, Full Frontal Feminism, 166; Suzanne Beechey, When Feminism Is Your Job: Age and Power in Women's Policy Organizations, in Jo Reger, Different Wavelengths: Studies of the Contemporary Women's Movement (New York: Routledge, 2005), 117, 128–131.

103. Amanda Marcotte, NARAL President Steps Aside, Wants More Young Leaders, Slate.com May 11, 2012 (quoting Nancy Keenan).

104. Rowe Finkbeiner, The F-Word, 175 (quoting Morgan).

105. Barack Obama, Speech upon the Signing of the Lilly Ledbetter Fair Pay Restoration Act, January 29, 2009, in Lilly Ledbetter with Lanier Scott Isom, Grace and Grit: My Fight for Equal Pay and Fairness at Goodyear and Beyond (New York: Crown, 2012), 243.

Chapter 2

1. For changes in women's labor force participation, see U.S. Department of Labor, Bureau of Labor Statistics, Changes in Men's and Women's Labor Force Participation rates (January 2007); Paula England, The Gender Revolution: Uneven and Stalled, Gender and Society 24 (2010): 149, 152. For women's historic representation in the professions, see Deborah L. Rhode, Perspectives on Professional Women, Stanford Law Review 40 (1988): 1163, 1173. For current representation, see National Committee on Pay Equity, Fact Sheet 2010, Professional Women: Vital Statistics, http://www.pay-equity.org/PDFs/ProfWomen.pdf. For wives out earning spouses, see Liza Mundy, The Richer Sex (New York: Simon & Schuster, 2012), 249–250.

2. Beth Corbin, Women Go Center Stage in Affirmative Action Debate, National Now Times, May–June 1995, 1, 3.

3. Catalyst, Women CEOs of the Fortune 1000 (New York: Catalyst, 2013). For pay gaps, see US Bureau of Labor Statistics, Highlights of Women's Earnings in 2011, Table 2; Deborah Thompson Eisenberg, Shattering the Equal Pay Act's Glass Ceiling, SMU Law Review 63 (2010): 17, 25.

4. Carmen DeNavas-Walt, Bernadette D. Proctor, and Jessica C. Smith, Income, Poverty and Health Insurance Coverage in the United States: 2012 (Washington, D.C.: U.S. Census Bureau, 2013), 7, table 1. Women's median weekly earnings are higher, about 82 percent of men's. U.S. Department of Labor, Bureau of Labor Statistics, Highlights of Women's Earnings in 2011 (Washington, D.C.: Bureau of Labor Statistics, October 2012). See Institute for Women's Policy Research, About Pay Equity and Discrimination (2012), http://www.iwpr.org/initiatives/pay-equity-and-discrimination. For the stability in the gap, see Heather Boushey, A Woman's Place is in the Middle Class, in Olivia Morgan and Karen Skelton, The Shriver Report: A Woman's Nation Pushes back from the Brink (Washington, D.C.: Center for American Progress and Palgrave Macmillan, 2014), 51.

5. Heidi Hartmann, Stephen J. Rose, and Vicky Lovell., How Much Progress in Closing the Long-Term Earnings Gap, in Francine D. Blau, Mary C. Brinton, and David Grusky, The Declining Significance of Gender? (New York: Russell Sage Foundation, 2006), 125, 129.

6. Julie Siebens and Camille L. Ryan, U.S. Census Bureau, Fields of Bachelor's Degrees in the United States (2009), 5, table 2.

7. See Francine D. Blau and Lawrence M. Kahn, The U.S. Gender Pay Gap in the 1990s: Slowing Convergence, Industrial and Labor Relations Review 60 (2006): 45; Institute on Women's Policy Research, Institute for Women's Policy Research, Quick Figures, (Washington, D.C., September, 2013).

8. U.S. Bureau of Labor Statistics, Highlights of Women's Earnings in 2011, Table 2; Deborah Thompson Eisenberg, Shattering the Equal Pay Act's Glass Ceiling, SMU Law Review 63 (2010): 17, 25.

9. Jessica Arons, Lifetime Losses: The Career Wage Gap, Center for American Progress (2008), http://www.americanprogressaction.org/issues/women/report/2008/12/08/5343/lifetime-losses-the-career-wage-gap/.

10. Eisenberg, Shattering the Equal Pay Act's Glass Ceiling, 27.

11. AAUW, The Simple Truth about the Gender Gap (Washington, D.C.: AAUW, 2013), 11.

12. Diane Furchtgott-Roth, Women's Figures: An Illustrated Guide to the Economic Progress of Women in America (Washington, D.C.: AEI Press, 2012), 19, 22; Kingsley R. Browne, Biological Sex Differences in the Workplace: Reports of the "End of Men" are Greatly Exaggerated (As Are Claims of Women's Continued Inequality), Boston U. L. Rev. 93 (2013): 769, 794; Warren Farrell, Why Men Earn More: The Startling Truth behind the Pay Gap—and What Women Can Do about It (New York: Amacom, 2005).

13. U.S. Department of Commerce and the Executive Office of the President, Council on Women and Girls, Women in America: Indicators of Social and Economic Well Being (2011), 27.

14. David Leonhardt, Financial Careers Come at a Cost to Families, New York Times, May 27, 2009, at B1 (29 percent pay gap for professionals who had taken time out).

15. Mary C. Noonan and Mary Corcoran, The Mommy Track and Partnership: Temporary Delay or Dead End?, The Annals of the American Academy of Political and Social Science 596 (2004): 130, 146.

16. AAUW, The Simple Truth about the Gender Gap, 15.

17. Institute for Women's Policy Research, The Gender Wage Gap by Occupation (April 2011) at http://www.iwpr.org/publications/pubs/the–gender–wage–gap–by–occupation–updated–april–2011.

18. U.S. Department of Labor: Women in the Labor Force: A Databook, table 11 (U.S. Department of Labor, December 2011); ABA Commission on Women in the Profession, A Current Glance at Women in the Law (September, 2012).

19. Carrie Lukas, There Is No Male-Female Wage Gap, Wall Street Journal, April 12, 2011, A15; Farrell, Why Men Earn More, xx–xi.

20. Institute for Women's Policy Research, The Gender Wage Gap by Occupation (2012).

21. Claire Cain Miller, Curtain Is Rising on a Tech Premiere with (as Usual) a Mostly Male Cast, New York Times, October 5, 2013, B1.

22. See Equal Pay for Equal Work?: New Evidence on the Persistence of the Gender Pay Gap: Hearing Before the S. J. Economic Committee, 111th Congress (2009), 3–4 (statement of Randy Albelda); AAUW, Behind the Pay Gap (2007) http://www.aauw.org/research/behind–the–pay–gap/ (finding unexplained gap of 5 percent one year after graduation and 12 percent 10 years after graduation); Francine D. Blau and Lawrence M. Kahn, The Gender Pay Gap: Have Women Gone as Far as They Can? Academy of Management Perspectives 21 (2007): 7, 12 (finding unexplained gap of 9 percent); Deborah Thompson Eisenberg, Money, Sex, and Sunshine: A Market-Based Approach to Pay Discrimination, Arizona State Law Journal 43 (2011): 951, 972–982 (reviewing studies); U.S. Congress Joint Economic Committee, Invest in Women, Invest in America: A Comprehensive Review, Women in the U.S. Economy (Washington, D.C.: Government Printing Office, 2010) (statement of Randy Albelda, reviewing studies), 75 See Reshma Jagsi et al., Gender Differences in the Salaries of Physician Researchers, Journal of American Medical Association 307 (2012):2410.

23. Deborah L. Rhode and Joan C. Williams, Legal Perspectives on Employment Discrimination, in Faye J. Crosby, Margaret S. Stockdale, and S. Ann Ropp, eds., Sex Discrimination in the Workplace: Multidisciplinary Perspectives (Malden, MA: Blackwell Publishing, 2007): 235, 239.

24. Philip N. Cohen and Suzanne M. Bianchi, Marriage, Children, and Women's Employment: What Do We Know?, Monthly Labor Review 22 (December 1999): 22; Stephanie Coontz, The Myth of Male Decline, New York Times, September 30, 2012, SR1.

25. See National Committee on Pay Equity, Real Life Example of Equivalent Jobs, http://www.pay-equity.org/PDFs/EquivalentJobs.pdf. For the devaluation of women's work, see Philip N. Cohen and Matt L. Huffman, Individuals, Jobs, and Labor Markets: The Devaluation of Women's Work, American Sociological Review 68 (2003): 443, 457.

26. For a sample of work, see sources cited in Barbara F. Reskin and Denise D. Bielby, A Sociological Perspective on Gender and Career Outcomes, Journal of Economic Perspectives 19 (2005): 71, 83. For women's tendency to value their work less, Virginia Valian, Why So Slow?: The Advancement of Women (Cambridge, MA: MIT Press, 1998), 156–157. For employers' tendency to offer less money to women, see Deborah Eisenberg, Money, Sex and Sunshine, Arizona State Law Journal 43 (2011): 951, 994. See also Hartmann, Rose, and Lovell, How Much Progress in Closing the Long-Term Earnings Gap, 137.

27. NBC News Wall Street Journal Survey, April, 2013, http://online.wsj.com/article/SB10001424127887324695104578417020376740796.html.

28. Deborah L. Brake and Joanna L. Grossman, The Failure of Title VII as a Rights-Claiming System, North Carolina Law Review 86 (2008): 859, 893.

29. Reskin and Bielby, A Sociological Perspective, 83.
30. Emilio J. Castilla, Gender, Race, and Meritocracy in Organizational Careers, American Journal of Sociology 113 (2008): 1479, 1483, 1485.
31. Kristen Schilt and Matthew Wiswall, Before and After: Gender Transitions, Human Capital, and Workplace Experiences, B.E. Journal of Economic Analysis and Policy (2008): 1–2, 6, 13.
32. Cecilia L. Ridgeway, Gender as an Organizing Force in Social Relations: Implications for the Future of Inequality, in Francine D. Blau, Mary C. Brinton, and David B Grusky, eds., The Declining Significance of Gender? (New York: Russell Sage Foundation, 2006): 268; K. Anthony Appiah, Stereotypes and the Shaping of Identity, California Law Review 88 (2000): 41; Linda Hamilton Krieger, The Content of Our Categories: A Cognitive Bias Approach to Discrimination and Equal Employment Opportunity, Stanford Law Review 47 (1995): 1161.
33. Ridgeway, Gender as an Organizing Force, at 268, 280.
34. For competence, see Eli Wald, Glass Ceilings and Dead Ends: Professional Ideologies, Gender Stereotypes, and the Future of Women Lawyers at Large Law Firms, Fordham Law Review 78 (2010): 2245, 2256; Cecilia L. Ridgeway and Paula England, Sociological Approaches to Sex Discrimination, in Crosby, Stockdale, and Ropp, eds., Sex Discrimination in the Workplace, 189, 195. In national surveys, half to three-quarters of female lawyers believe that they are held to higher standards than their male colleagues. Rhode and Williams, Legal Perspectives on Employment Discrimination, at 235, 245. Even in experimental situations where male and female performance is objectively equal, women are held to higher standards, and their competence is rated lower. Martha Foschi, Double Standards in the Evaluation of Men and Women, Social Psychology Quarterly 59 (1996): 237.
35. Janet K. Swim and Lawrence J. Sanna, He's Skilled, She's Lucky: A Meta-Analysis of Observers' Attributions for Women and Men's Successes and Failures, Personality and Social Psychology Bulletin 22 (1996): 507; Jeffrey H. Greenhaus and Saroj Parasuraman, Job Performance Attributions and Career Advancement Prospects: An Examination of Gender and Race Effects, Organizational Behavior and Human Decision Processes 55 (1993): 273, 276, 290. Jennifer Crocker, Brenda Major and Claude Steele, Social Stigma, in Daniel T. Gilbert, Susan T. Fiske, and Gardner Lindzey, eds., Handbook of Social Psychology (New York: McGraw Hill, 1998), 504–553; John F. Dovidio and Samuel L. Gaertner, Stereotypes and Evaluative Intergroup Bias, in Diane M. Mackie and David L. Hamilton, eds., Affect, Cognition, and Stereotyping (San Diego, CA: Academic Press, 1993), 167–193; Martha Foschi, Double Standards for Competence: Theory and Research, Annual Review of Sociology 26 (2000): 21–42; Krieger, The Content of Our Categories, 1161–1248; Cecilia L. Ridgeway, Interaction and the Conservation of Gender Inequality: Considering Employment, Contemporary Sociology 62 (1997): 218.
36. Rebecca J. Rosen, In the New York Times, Sheryl Sandberg Is Lucky, Men Are Good, The Atlantic, February 7, 2012.
37. For examples, see Jeremiah A. DeBerry, Best Practices for Integrating Diverse and Women Laterals, New York Law Journal, February 3, 2014.
38. Ann-Marie Slaughter, Foreword, in Joan C. Williams and Rachel Dempsey, What Works for Women at Work (New York: New York University Press, 2014), xvi.
39. Virginia Valian, Why So Slow? 39–40; Galen V. Bodenhausen, C. Neil Macrae, and Jennifer Garst, Stereotypes in Thought and Deed: Social-Cognitive Origins of Intergroup Discrimination, in Constantine Sedikides, John Schopler, and Chester A. Insko, eds., Intergroup Cognition and Intergroup Behavior (Mahwah, NJ: Lawrence Erlbaum Associates, 1998); Robin Ely, The Power in Demography: Women's Social Constructions of Gender Identity at Work, Academy of Management Journal, 38 (1995): 589–634.

40. Martha Foschi, Double Standards in the Evaluation of Men and Women, Social Psychology 59 (1996): 237; Jacqueline Landau, The Relationship of Race and Gender to Managers' Rating of Promotion Potential, Journal of Organizational Behavior 16 (1995): 391.

41. Linda Babcock and Sara Laschever, Women Don't Ask: Negotiation and the Gender Divide (Princeton, NJ: Princeton University Press, 2003) 94; Rhea E. Steinpreis, Katie A. Anders and Dawn Ritzke, The Impact of Gender on the Review of the Curricula Vitae of Job Applicants and Tenure Candidates: A National Empirical Study, Sex Roles 41 (1999): 509; Joan C. Williams, Reshaping the Work Family Debate: Why Men and Class Matter (Cambridge, MA: Harvard University Press, 2010), 93; David Neumark, Sex Discrimination in Restaurant Hiring: An Audit Study, The Quarterly Journal of Economics 111 (1996): 915 (finding that when male and female job testers with similar résumés approach employers, women's probability of getting hired is 50 percent lower than men's).

42. Emilio J. Castilla and Stephen Benard, The Paradox of Meritocracy in Organizations, Administrative Science Quarterly 55 (2010): 543.

43. See sources cited in Williams, Reshaping the Work Family Debate, 94 and Williams and Dempsey, What Works for Women at Work, 25-26.

44. E. L. Uhlman and G. L. Cohen, Constructed Criteria: Redefining Merit to Justify Discrimination, Psychological Science 16 (2005): 170; Michael I. Norton et al., Casuistry and Social Category Bias, Journal of Personality and Social Psychology 87 (2004): 817.

45. Claudia Goldin and Cecilia Rouse, Orchestrating Impartiality: The Impact of "Blind" Auditions on Female Musicians, American Economic Review 90 (2000): 715.

46. Corinne A. Moss-Racusin, et al., Science Faculty's Subtle Gender Biases Favor Male Students, Proceedings of the National Academy of Sciences of the United States of America, 109 (2012), www.pnas.org/cgi/doi/10.1073/pnas.1211286109.

47. For motherhood, see Amy J. C. Cuddy, Susan T. Fiske, and Peter Glick, When Professionals Become Mothers, Warmth Doesn't Cut the Ice, Journal of Social Issues 60 (2004): 701, 709; Kathleen Fuegen and Monica Biernat, Elizabeth Haines, and Kay Deaux, Mothers and Fathers in the Workplace: How Gender and Parental Status Influence Judgments of Job-Related Competence, Journal of Social Issues 60 (2004): 737, 745; Claire Etaugh and Denise Folger, Perceptions of Parents Whose Work and Parenting Behaviors Deviate from Role Expectations, Sex Roles 39 (1998): 215. For pregnancy, see Glick and Fiske, Sex Discrimination, 171.

48. Amy J. C. Cuddy, Susan T. Fiske, and Peter Glick, When Professionals Become Mothers, 701.

49. Shelley J. Correll, Stephen Benard, and In Paik, Getting a Job: Is There a Motherhood Penalty?, American Journal of Sociology 112 (2007): 1297.

50. Correll, Benard, and Paik, Getting a Job.

51. Women in the Workplace: A Research Roundup, Harvard Business Review, September 2013, 88.

52. Stephanie Coontz, Progress at Work, but Mothers Still Pay a Price, New York Times, June 9, 2013, Sr5.

53. Madeleine Kunin, The New Feminist Agenda: Defining the Next Revolution for Women, Work and Family (White River Junction, VT: Chelsea Green Publishers, 2012), 165.

54. Ridgeway, Gender as an Organizing Force, at 279; David L. Hamilton and Jeffrey W. Sherman, Stereotypes, in Robert S. Wyer, Jr., and Thomas K. Srull, eds., Handbook of Social Cognition 2 (Hillsdale, NJ: L. Erlbaum Associates, 1994), 1-68; Galen V. Bodenhausen and Robert S. Wyer, Jr., Effects of Stereotypes on Decision Making and Information-Processing Strategies, Journal of Personality and Social Psychology 48 (1985): 267, 281-282.

55. Melvin J. Lerner, The Belief in a Just World: A Fundamental Delusion (New York: Plenum Press, 1980), vii-viii; Virginia Valian, The Cognitive Bases of Gender Bias, Brooklyn Law Review 65 (1999): 1037.

56. Deborah L. Rhode, Balanced Lives: Changing the Culture of Legal Practice (Chicago: American Bar Association Commission on Women in the Profession, 2002), 16; Linda Krieger, The Content of our Categories, 34.

57. Marilyn B. Brewer and Rupert J. Brown, Intergroup Relations in Daniel T. Gilbert, Susan T. Fiske, and Gardner Lindzey, eds., The Handbook of Social Psychology (New York: McGraw-Hill, 1998), 554–594; Susan T. Fiske, Stereotyping, Prejudice and Discrimination, in Daniel T. Gilbert et al., eds., Handbook of Social Psychology (New York: McGraw-Hill, 1998), 357–414; Barbara Reskin, Rethinking Employment Discrimination and Its Remedies, in Mauro F. Guillén, Randall Collins, Paula England, and Marshall Meyer, eds., The New Economic Sociology: Developments in an Emerging Field (New York: Russell Sage, 2000): 218–244; Katharine T. Bartlett, Making Good on Good Intentions: The Critical Role of Motivation in Reducing Implicit Workplace Discrimination, Virginia Law Review 95 (2009): 1893, 1913 (reviewing studies).

58. Ida O. Abbott, The Lawyers' Guide to Mentoring (Washington, D.C.: National Association for Law Placement [NALP], 2000); Belle Rose Ragins, Gender and Mentoring Relationships: A Review and Research Agenda for the Next Decade, in Gary N. Powell, ed., Handbook of Gender and Work (Thousand Oaks, CA: Sage, 1998), 347, 350–362; Catalyst, Women in Corporate Leadership: Progress and Prospects (New York: Catalyst, 1996); Timothy O'Brien, Up the Down Staircase, New York Times, March 19, 2006, A4.

59. ABA Commission on Women in the Profession, Visible Invisibility: Women of Color in Law Firms (Chicago: American Bar Association, 2006).

60. The term comes from Pierre Bourdieu, The Forms of Capital, in John G. Richardson, ed., Handbook of Theory and Research for the Sociology of Education (Westport, CT: Greenwood Press, 1986), 241, 248. See Sylvia Annn Hewlett, with Kerrie Peraino, Laura Sherbin, and Karen Sumberg, The Sponsor Effect: Breaking Through the Last Glass Ceiling, Harvard Business Review Research Report, 2010, 8; Cindy A. Schipani, Terry M. Dworkin, Angel Kwolek-Folland, and Virginia G. Maurer, Pathways for Women to Obtain Positions of Organizational Leadership: The Significance of Mentoring and Networking, Duke Journal of Gender Law & Policy 16 (2009): 89.

61. See Karen L. Proudford, Isn't She Delightful?: Creating Relationships That Get Women to the Top (and Keep Them There), in Barbara Kellerman and Deborah L. Rhode, Women and Leadership: The State of Play and Strategies for Change (San Francisco: Jossey-Bass, 2007) 431; Ragins, Gender and Mentoring Relationships, 361–363.

62. Mirembe Biigwa and Karen Sumberg, Lack of Sponsorship Keeps Women from Breaking through the Glass Ceiling, Harvard Business Review Research Report, 2011.

63. Ella L. J. Edmondson Bell and Stella M. Nkomo, Our Separate Ways: Black and White Women and the Struggle for Professional Identity (Cambridge, MA: Harvard School Press, 2001), 123–132; Bernardo M. Ferdman, The Color and Culture of Gender in Organizations: Attending to Race and Ethnicity, in Powell, Handbook of Gender and Work, 17, 18–26; Catalyst, Women of Color in Corporate Management: Dynamics of Career Advancement, (New York: Catalyst, 1998), 15; David Wilkins and G. Mitu Gulati, Why Are There So Few Black Lawyers in Corporate Law Firms? An Institutional Analysis, University of California Law Review 84 (1996): 493; Deborah L. Rhode, The Unfinished Agenda: Women and the Legal Profession (Chicago: ABA Commission on Women and the Profession, 2001), 16.

64. Martin N. Davidson, The End of Diversity As We Know It (San Francisco: Berrett-Koehler Publisher, 2011), 26.

65. Minority Corporate Counsel Association (MCCA), Mentoring across Differences, http://www.mcca.com/index.cfm?fuseaction=page.viewpage&pageid=666; Leigh Jones, Mentoring Plans Failing Associates, National Law Journal (September 15, 2006): 1.

66. Jones, Mentoring Plans, 1; MCCA, Mentoring across Differences.

67. Davidson, The End of Diversity, 35–36.
68. Minnesota State Bar Association, Diversity and Gender Equity in the Legal Profession, Best Practices Guide, http://www.mnbar.org/committees/DiversityImplementation/DiversityBestPracticesGuideFinal.pdf.
69. Minnesota State Bar Association, Diversity and Gender Equity.
70. Jones, Mentoring Plans, 1.
71. Cindy Schipani et al., Pathways, 89, 112. The key variable is satisfaction with the relationship, which tends to be higher when the relationship arises naturally. See Schipani et al., Pathways, 112; Rhode & Kellerman, Women and Leadership, 30.
72. For studies in law, see Deborah L. Rhode, From Platitudes to Priorities: Diversity and Gender Equity in Law Firms, Georgetown Journal of Legal Ethics 24 (2011): 1041, 1043. For management, see Catalyst, Women "Take Care," Men "Take Charge": Stereotyping of U.S. Business Leaders Exposed (Catalyst, 2005).
73. Women in the Workplace, 88.
74. Center for Educational Statistics, American Council on Education (women account for 57 percent of bachelor's degrees and 62 percent of associate's degrees): The American College President 2012 (March, 2012): Table 283 (women account for 26.4 of college presidents); John W. Curtis, Persistent Inequity: Gender and Academic Employment (Washington, D.C.: American Association of University Professors, 2011) (women are 28 percent of full professors).
75. ABA Commission on Women in the Profession, A Current Glance at Women in the Law.
76. Joann S. Lublin and Kelly Eggers, More Women Are Primed to Land CEO Roles, Wall Street Journal Online, April 30, 201; See also Catalyst 2013 Census of Fortune 500: Still No Progress After Years of No Progress (New York: Catalyst, 2013).
77. Joan C. Williams, The End of Men? Gender Flux in the Face of Precarious Masculinity, Boston University Law Review 93 (2013); 699.
78. Sheryl Sandberg with Nell Scovell, Lean In: Women, Work, and the Will to Lead (New York: Alfred A. Knopf, 2013).
79. Sue Shellenbarger, The XX Factor: What's Holding Women Back?, Wall Street Journal, May 7, 2012, B7: Pew Research Center, Millennial Women Approach Wage Parity with Men-For Now (2013) (60 percent of men and 44 percent of women are the boss or would like to be the boss in their workplace).
80. Herminia Ibarra, Robin Ely, and Deborah Kolb, Women Rising: The Unseen Barriers, Harvard Business Review, September 2013, 65.
81. Rhode and Kellerman, Women and Leadership, 7.
82. Laurie A. Rudman and Stephen E. Kilianski, Implicit and Explicit Attitudes Toward Female Authority, Personality and Social Psychology Bulletin, 26 (2000): 1315. Catalyst, Women "Take Care," Men "Take Charge": Stereotyping of Business Leaders (New York: Catalyst, 2005); Linda L. Carli and Alice H. Eagly, Overcoming Resistance to Women Leaders: The Importance of Leadership Style, in Kellerman and Rhode, Women and Leadership, 127.
83. Virginia Valian, The Cognitive Bases of Gender Bias, Brooklyn Law Review 65 (1999): 1048–1049.
84. See research reviewed in Peter Glick and Susan T. Fiske, Sex Discrimination: The Psychological Approach, in Crosby, Stockdale and Ropp, Sex Discrimination in the Workplace, 170; Rhode and Kellerman, Women and Leadership; 7; Ibarra, Ely, and Kolb, Women Rising, 65.
85. Williams and Dempsey, What Works for Women at Work, 59 (quoting Fiorina).
86. Neela Banerjee, The Media Business: Some "Bullies" Seek Ways to Soften Up; Toughness Has Risks for Women Executives, New York Times, August 10, 2001, C1.
87. For coworkers' attitudes, see Alice Eagly and Steven Karau, Role Congruity Theory of Prejudice Toward Female Leaders, Psychological Review 109 (2002): 574; Donna L. Brooks and Lynn M. Brooks, Seven Secrets of Successful Women (New York:

McGraw-Hill, 1997), 195; Alice Eagly, Achieving Relational Authenticity: Does Gender Matter?, The Leadership Quarterly, 16 (2005): 470; Babcock and Laschever, Women Don't Ask, 87–88.

88. Eagly and Karau, Role Congruity Theory of Prejudice Toward Female Leaders, 111; Todd L. Pittinsky, Laura M. Bacon, Brian Welle, The Great Women Theory of Leadership: Perils of Positive Stereotypes and Precarious Pedestals, in Kellerman and Rhode, Women and Leadership, 101.

89. Sandberg with Scovell, Lean In, 50 (quoting Thomas).

90. D. Anthony Butterfield and James P. Grinnell, "Re-viewing" Gender, Leadership, and Managerial Behavior: Do Three Decades of Research Tell Us Anything?, in Gary N. Powell, Handbook of Gender and Work, 223, 235; Alice H. Eagly, Mona G. Makhijani, and Bruce G. Klonsky, Gender and the Evaluation of Leaders: A Meta-Analysis, Psychological Bulletin 111 (1992): 17; Jeanette N. Cleveland, Margaret Stockdale, Kevin R. Murphy, and Barbara A. Gutek, Women and Men in Organizations: Sex and Gender Issues at Work (New York: Psychology Press, 2000): 106, 107; Rochelle Sharpe, As Leaders, Women Rule: New Studies Find That Female Managers Outshine Their Male Counterparts in Almost Every Measure, Businessweek Online, November 19, 2000, http://www.businessweek.com/stories/2000-11-19/as-leaders-women-rule.

91. Hannah Riley Bowles, Linda Babcock, and Lei Lai, Social Incentives for Gender Differences in the Propensity to Initiate Negotiations: Sometimes It Does Hurt to Ask, Organizational Behavior and Human Decision Processes 103 (2007): 84; Glick and Fiske, Sex Discrimination, 173.

92. Francis J. Flynn, Cameron Anderson, and Sebastian Brion, Too Tough Too Soon: Familiarity and the Backlash Effect, working paper.

93. Michael Hirsh, Capital Offense: How Washington's Wise Men Turned America's Future over to Wall Street (Hoboken, NJ: Wiley, 2010): 1, 12 (quoting Robert Rubin and unnamed staffer).

94. Jeff Gerth and Don Van Natta, Jr., Her Way: The Hopes and Ambitions of Hillary Rodham Clinton (Boston, MA: Little, Brown, 2007), 111.

95. Babcock and Laschever, Women Don't Ask, 88; Carol Hymowitz, Women to Watch (A Special Report); Through The Glass Ceiling: How These 50 Women Got Where They Are—And Why They Bear Watching, Wall Street Journal, November 8, 2004, R1. That point is widely acknowledged in trade publications featuring advice for aspiring women leaders. See Brooks and Brooks, Seven Secrets of Successful Women, 63–65, 147–153; Gail Evans, Play like a Man Win like a Woman: What Men Know about Success That Women Need to Learn (New York: Broadway Books, 2000), 68–87.

96. Hannah Riley Bowles and Kathleen L. McGinn, Gender in Job Negotiations: A Two-Level Game, Negotiation Journal 24 (2008): 393, 2999 (citing studies).

97. Babcock and Laschever, Women Don't Ask, 1.

98. Babcock and Laschever, Women Don't Ask 1–11, 41–44.

99. American Bar Association Commission on Women in the Profession, Visible Invisibility.

100. Christine Silva, Nancy M. Carter, Anna Beninger, Good Intentions, Imperfect Execution?: Women Get Fewer of the "Hot Jobs" Needed to Advance (New York: Catalyst, 2012), 5–7.

101. Sheila Wellington, Marcia Brumit Kropf, and Paulette Gerkovich, What's Holding Women Back, Harvard Business Review (June 2003): 18; International Labor Organization, Breaking Through the Glass Ceiling: Women in Management (2004), 57, http://www.ilo.org/dyn/gender/docs/RES/292/f267981337.

102. Catalyst, The Pipeline's Broken Promise (New York: Catalyst, 2010), 3–4.

103. Boris Groysberg and Katherine Connolly, Great Leaders Who Make the Mix Work, Harvard Business Review, September, 2013, 79.

104. Catalyst, Women of Color (New York: Catalyst, 2000): 13; Catalyst, Women in Corporate Leadership: 37.

105. 29 U.S.C. Section 206(d)(1).

106. Minna J. Kotkin, Outing Outcomes: An Empirical Study of Confidential Employment Discrimination Settlements, Washington & Lee Law Review, 64 (2007): 11, 115 (citing studies)., Laura Beth Nielsen, Robert L. Nelson, and Ryan Lancaster, Individual Justice or Collective Legal Mobilization: Employment Discrimination Litigation in the Post-Civil Rights United States, Journal of Empirical Legal Studies, 7 (2010): 175, 187, 195–196 (noting that only about 2 percent of plaintiffs win in court); Kevin M. Clermont and Stewart J. Schwab, Employment Discrimination Plaintiffs in Federal Court: From Bad to Worse?, Harvard Law & Policy Review 3 (Winter 2009): 3, 13, 35 (noting that compared to other plaintiffs, employment discrimination complainants win a lower proportion of trials and appeals); Kevin M. Clermont and Stewart J. Schwab, How Employment Discrimination Plaintiffs Fare in Federal Court, Journal of Empirical Legal Studies, 1 (2004): 429 (finding low success rates for employment discrimination plaintiffs in federal court).

107. U.S. Equal Employment Opportunity Commission, Enforcement and Litigation Statistics from the U.S. Equal Employment Opportunity Commission, FY 1997 through 20,012, http://www.eeoc.gov/eeoc/statistics/enforcement/.

108. Kotkin, Outing Outcomes, 111 (noting mean recovery of $54, 651); Nielsen, Nelson, and Lancaster, Individual Justice, 187.

109. Clermont and Schwab, Employment Discrimination Plaintiffs, 35.

110. Deborah Thompson Eisenberg, Shattering the Equal Pay Act's Glass Ceiling, SMU Law Review 63 (2010): 17, 64, n. 331; Lilly Ledbetter with Lanier Scott Isom, Grace and Grit: My Fight for Equal Pay and Fairness at Goodyear and Beyond (New York: Crown Archetype, 2012), 241, 179.

111. Deborah Thompson Eisenberg, Money, Sex, and Sunshine: A Market-Based Approach to Pay Discrimination, Arizona State Law Journal 43 (2011): 993, 997; Linda Krieger, The Watched Variable Improves: On Eliminating Sex Discrimination in Employment, in Crosby, Stockdale and Ropp, eds., Sex Discrimination in the Workplace, 295, 310.

112. Lebbetter v. Goodyear Tire and Rubber Co., 550 U.S. 618, 649–650 (2007) (Ginsburg, J., dissenting).

113. Deborah L. Rhode and Joan C. Williams, Legal Perspectives on Employment Discrimination, in Crosby, Stockdale, and Ropp, Sex Discrimination in the Workplace, 243; Riordan v. Kempiners, 831 F. 2d 690, 697 (7th Cir. 1987).

114. Hopkins v. Price Waterhouse, 618 F. Supp. 1109 (D.D.C. 185), aff'd in part and rev'd in part, 825 F. 2d 458 (D.C. Cir. 1987), aff'd in part and rev'd in part, 490 U.S. 228 (1989); Ann Branigar Hopkins, So Ordered: Making Partner the Hard Way (Amherst: University of Massachusetts Press, 1996), 172.

115. Hopkins v. Price Waterhouse, 618 F. Supp. at 1117.

116. Hopkins, So Ordered, 235.

117. Hopkins v. Price Waterhouse, 618 F. Supp. at 1115, 1117.

118. Ezold v. Wolf, Block, Schorr & Solis-Cohen, 751 F. Supp. 1175 (E.D. Pa.1990), reversed, 983 F.2d 509 (3d Cir. 1992), *cert. denied*, 510 U.S. 826 (1993).

119. Ezold v. Wolf, Block, 751 F, Supp. At 1184–1186.

120. K.A. Dixon, Duke Storen, and Carl E. Van Horn, A Workplace Divided: How Americans View Discrimination and Race on the Job (New Brunswick, NJ: John J. Heldrich Center for Workforce Development, Rutgers University, 2002), 15.

121. Laura Beth Nielsen and Robert L. Nelson, Rights Realized? An Empirical Analysis of Employment Discrimination Litigation as a Claiming System, Wisconsin Law Review (2005): 663.

122. Susan Bisom-Rapp, Margaret Stockale, and Faye J. Crosby, A Critical Look at Organizational Responses to and Remedies for Sex Discrimination, in Crosby, Stockdale, and Ropp, Sex Discrimination in the Workplace, 274–275; Faye Crosby, The Denial of Personal Discrimination, American Behavioral Scientist 27 (January–February 1984): 380, 381.

123. Cheryl R. Kaiser and Brenda Major, A Social Psychological Perspective on Perceiving and Reporting Discrimination, Law and Social Inquiry 31 (2006): 801, 808; Crosby, the Denial of Personal Discrimination, 381; see studies cited in Deborah L. Brake and Joanna L. Grossman, The Failure of Title VII as a Rights-Claiming System, North Carolina Law Review 86 (2008): 860, 887–888, 890; and Deborah L. Rhode, Speaking of Sex: The Denial of Gender Inequality (Cambridge, MA: Harvard University Press, 1997), 9.

124. Rhode and Williams, Legal Perspectives on Employment Discrimination, 244.

125. Hopkins, So Ordered, at 384 (noting fees of $500,000 in 1991 dollars). For the conversion to today's dollars, see the U.S. Department of Labor Inflation Calculator, http://146.142.4.24/cgi-bin/cpicalc.pl.

126. Deborah L. Rhode, What's Sex Got to Do with It?: Diversity in the Legal Profession, in Legal Ethics Stories, Deborah L. Rhode and David Luban, eds. (New York: Foundation Press, 2006), 246 ($150,000 in 1993 dollars). For the conversion to today's dollars, see the U.S. Department of Labor Inflation Calculator, http://www.bls.gov/data/inflation_calculator.htm.

127. Hopkins, So Ordered, 197.

128. Fred Strebeigh, Equal: Women Reshape American Law (New York: W. W. Norton, 2009), 193 (discussing litigation against Sullivan and Cromwell).

129. Robert Kolker, The Gay Flannel Suit, New York Magazine, March 5, 2007, http://nymag.com/news/features/28515/.

130. Loren Feldman, What's Sex Got to Do with It: Partnership on Trial, The American Lawyer, November, 1990, at http://amlawdaily.typepad.com/files/partnership-on-trial-november-1990.pdf (quoting Charles Kopp).

131. ABA Commission on Women in the Profession, Visible Invisibility: Women of Color in Law Firms, 20 (aggressive, bitch); Joan C. Williams and Veta T. Richardson, New Millennium, Same Glass Ceiling?: The Impact of Law Firm Compensation Systems on Women, Hastings Law Journal 62 (2010–2011): 630 (confrontational); Nancy M. Reichman and Joyce S. Sterling, Sticky Floors, Broken Steps, Concrete Ceilings in Legal Careers, Texas Journal of Women and Law 14 (Fall 2004): 47, 65 (bitch); Jill L. Cruz and Melinda S. Molina, Hispanic National Bar Association National Study on the Status of Latinas in the Legal Profession, Few and Far Between: The Reality of Latina Lawyers, Pepperdine Law Review 37 (2010): 971, 1019 (rock the boat); American Bar Association Commission on Women in the Profession, The Unfinished Agenda: A Report on the Status of Women in the Profession 21 (2001) (troublemaker, oversensitive). For reputational concerns generally, see Elizabeth H. Dodd, Traci A. Giuliano, Jori M. Boutell, and Brooke E. Moran, Respected or Rejected: Perceptions of Women Who Confront Sexist Remarks, Sex Roles 45 (2001): 567.

132. Ledbetter with Ison, Grace, and Grit, 89, 132.

133. For the advice, see Kolker, The Gay Flannel Suit; ABA Commission on Women in the Profession, Visible Invisibility, 21. For negative consequences following complaints about compensation, see Williams and Richardson, New Millennium, 639.

134. Rhode, Speaking of Sex, 162. See Susan Antilla, After Boom Boom Room, Fresh Tactics to Fight Bias, New York Times, April 2, 2013, A1 (noting reluctance of women to sue because of career repercussions). The problem is true of employment discrimination litigation generally. See Nielsen and Nelson, Rights Realized,; Linda Hamilton Krieger, The Watched Variable Improves: On Eliminating Sex Discrimination in Employment, in Crosby, Stockdale and Ropp, Sex Discrimination in the Workplace, 296, 309–310.

135. Brake and Grossman, The Failure of Title VII, 903.

136. Paul M. Barrett, The Good Black: A True Story of Race in America (New York: Plume, 1998), 59 (quoting George Galland).

137. Hopkins, So Ordered, 166.

138. Deborah L. Rhode, The Beauty Bias (New York: Oxford University Press, 2010), 14 (quoting Jennifer Pizer).

139. Katharine T. Bartlett, Deborah L. Rhode, and Joanna Grossman, Gender and the Law: Theory Doctrine, Commentary, 6th ed. (New York: Aspen, 2013).

140. Stopka v. Alliance of American Insurers, 141 F. 3d 681, 686 (7th Cir. 1998).

141. Georgen-Saad v. Texas Mutual Insurance Company, 195 F. Supp. 2d 853 (W.D.Tex. 2002).

142. Los Angeles Times Editorial Board, Preventing Bias on the Job, Los Angeles Times, June 17, 2012.

143. See Bartlett, Rhode, and Grossman, Gender and Law; Los Angeles Times Editorial Board, Preventing Bias on the Job.

144. Catalyst, Making Change: LGBT Inclusion—Understanding the Challenges (New York: Catalyst, 2007), 18; Los Angeles Times Editorial Board, Preventing Bias on the Job, (summarizing data from by the Williams Institute for Sexual Orientation Law and Public Policy, UCLA); Testimony of M. V. Lee Badgett, Williams Institute, United States Senate Committee on Health, Education, Labor and Pensions, Hearings on S.811, The Employment Non-Discrimination Act of 2011, June 12, 2012.

145. See sources cited in Samuel R. Bagenstos, The Structural Turn and the Limits of Antidiscrimination Law, California Law Review 94 (2006): 1, 2, n. 3, 41.

146. Tristin K. Green, Discrimination in Workplace Dynamics: Toward a Structural Account of Disparate Treatment Theory, Harvard Civil Rights–Civil Liberties Law Review 38 (2003): 91, 142, 153.

147. Wal-Mart Stores, Inc. v. Dukes, 131 S Ct. 2541 (2011).

148. Wal-Mart Stores, Inc. v. Dukes, 131 S Ct. 2541 (2011), at 2554.

149. Wal-Mart Stores, Inc. v. Dukes, 131 S Ct. 2541 (2011), at 2564 (Ginsburg, J., dissenting).

150. Nina Martin, Why the Wal-Mart Case Is So Important to Women, Minorities, New America Media, March 23, 2011.

151. Rhode, Speaking of Sex, 160; Linda Krieger, The Content of Our Categories, 34.

152. Susan Sturm, Second Generation Employment Discrimination: A Structural Approach, Columbia Law Review 101 (2001): 458, 460. See also Bagenstos, Structural Turn, 5.

153. Heim v. State of Utah, 8 F 3d 1541 1546 (10th Cir. 1993).

154. Bullington v. United Airlines, Inc., 186 F. 3d 1301, 1319 (10th Cir. 1999); Deines v. Texas Department of Protective and Regulatory Services, 164 F.3d 277, 280 (5th Cir. 1999). For other cases see Green, Discrimination in Workplace Dynamics, 118.

155. Sturm, Second Generation.

156. Linda Babcock and Sarah Laschever, Ask for It: How Women Can Use the Power of Negotiation to Get What They Really Want (New York: Bantam Dell, 2008), 77.

157. Catalyst, Women in Corporate Leadership, 15, 21; Eleanor Clift and Tom Brazaitis, Madam President: Shattering the Last Glass Ceiling, (New York: Routledge, 2000), 321, 324.

158. Babcock and Laschever, Ask for It, 252–262.

159. Babcock and Laschever, Ask for It, at 252–262.

160. Joan Biskupic, Sandra Day O'Connor: How the First Woman on the Supreme Court Became Its Most Influential Justice (New York: Harper Collins, 2009), 56 (quoting Benie Wynn).

161. Robin Ely, Herminia Ibarra, and Deborah Kolb, Taking Gender into Account: Theory and Design for Women's Leadership Development Programs, Academy of Management Learning and Education (September 2011), 10; Erin White, Female Training Classes Flourish, Wall Street Journal, September 25, 2006, B3. The Leadership Council on Legal Diversity also offers a fellowship program for minorities on the leadership track.

162. Sandberg with Scovell, Lean In, 63.

163. Michele Coleman Mayes and Kara Sophia Baysinger, Courageous Counsel: Conversations with Women General Counsel in the Fortune 500 (SNR Denton LLP, 2011), 82.

164. Mayes and Baysinger, Courageous Counsel, at 69; Shallenbarger, The XX Factor, B 10.

165. Shellenbarger, The XX Factor, B10; Susan A. Berson, The Rules (for Women): Steps May Be Unspoken But They Are Necessary, Successful Partners Say, ABA Journal (January 2012), at 28; Linda Bray Chanow and Lauren Stiller Rikleen, Power in Law: Lessons from the 2011 Women's Power Summit on Law and Leadership (Center for Women in Law, University of Texas School of Law, 2012), 15.

166. Sheryl Sandberg, Why We Have Too Few Women Leaders, Ted Talk, December 21, 2010, http://blog.ted.com/2010/12/21/why-we-have-too-few-women-leaders-sheryl-sandberg-on-ted-com/.

167. http://thomas.loc.gov/cgi-bin/bdquery/z?d112:SN03220:@@@L&summ2=m&.

168. Deborah Thompson Eisenberg, Shattering the Equal Pay Act's Glass Ceiling, SMU Law Review 63 (2010): 17, 65: Eisenberg, Money, Sex and Sunshine.

169. http://thomas.loc.gov/cgi-bin/bdquery/z?d112:SN03220:@@@L&summ2=m&.

170. Rhode and Williams, Legal Perspectives on Employment Discrimination, 257.

171. Directive 2206/54/EC of the European Parliament and of the Council (July 5, 2006).

172. Heidi I. Hartmann and Stephanie Aaronson, Pay Equity and Women's Wage Increases: Success in the States, A Model for the Nation, Duke Journal of Gender Law and Policy 1 (1994): 69, 80; Institute for Women's Policy Research, Pay Equity and the Wage Gap: Success in the States (1995); Deborah L. Rhode, Speaking of Sex, 174.

173. Green, Discrimination in Workplace Dynamics, 147.

174. Sturm, Second Generation Employment Discrimination.

175. Frank Dobbin and Alexandra Kalev, The Architecture of Inclusion: Evidence from Corporate Diversity Programs, Harvard Journal of Law and Gender 30 (2007): 282–283; Jeanine Prime, Marissa Agin, and Heather Foust-Cummings, Strategy Matters: Evaluating Company Approaches for Creating Inclusive Workplaces (Catalyst, 2010), 6; Theresa M. Beiner, Not All Lawyers Are Equal: Difficulties That Plague Women and Women of Color, Syracuse Law Review 58 (2007–2008): 333.

176. Sturm, Second Generation, 475. For an example, see the discussion of Deloitte's Task Force on the Retention and Advancement of Women, discussed in Sturm, Second Generation, at 493.

177. For recommendations of an ombudsperson, see MCCA, Pathways, 38; for recommendations of a diverse committee to address compensation concerns, see Williams and Richardson, New Millenium, 663–664.

178. Rhode and Kellerman, Women and Leadership, 276; Shellenbarger, The XX Factor, B9; Ceclia Ridgeway and Paula England, Sociological Approaches to Sex Discrimination in Employment, in Crosby, Stockdale, and Ropp, eds., Sex Discrimination in the Workplace, 202; Groysberg and Connolly, Great Leaders, 74.

179. Dobbin and Kalev, The Architecture of Inclusion, 279. Frank Dobbin, Alexandra Kalev, and Erin Kelly, Diversity Management in Corporate America, Contexts 6 (Fall 2007): 21, 23–25. See Elizabeth Levy Paluck, Diversity Training and Intergroup Contact: A Call to Action Research, Journal of Social Issues 62 (2006): 577, 583, 591.

180. Tiffani N. Darden, The Law Firm Caste System: Constructing a Bridge Between Workplace Equity Theory and the Institutional Analyses of Bias in Corporate Law Firms, Berkeley Journal of Employment and Labor Law 30 (2009): 117; Katharine T. Bartlett, Making Good on Good Intentions: The Critical Role of Motivation in Reducing Implicit Workplace Discrimination, Virginia Law Review 95 (2009): 1893, 1961, 62; Diane Vaughan, Rational Choice, Situated Action, and the Social Control of Organizations, Law and Society Review 32 (1998); 23, 34; Donna Chrobot-Mason, Rosemary Hays-Thomas, and Heather Wishik, Understanding and Defusing Resistance to Diversity Training and Learning, in Kecia M. Thomas, ed., Diversity Resistance in Organizations (New York: Lawrence Erlbaum Associates, 2008), 23, 23–39.

181. Rhode and Kellerman, Women and Leadership, 30; Alexandra Kalev, Frank Dobbin, and Erin Kelly, Best Practices or Best Guesses: Assessing the Efficacy of Corporate Affirmative Action and Diversity Policies, American Sociological Review 71 (2006), 589.

For the difficulties in institutionalizing sponsorship, see Joanna Barsh and Lreina Yee, Unlocking the Full Potential of Women at Work (New York: McKinsey and Company, 2012), 11. See generally Cindy A. Schipani, et al., Pathways, 89.

182. Maureen Giovannini, What Gets Measured Gets Done: Achieving Results Through Diversity and Inclusion, Journal for Quality and Participation 27 (2004): 21. For the importance of monitoring generally, see Barsh and Yee, Unlocking the Full Potential of Women, 11; Susan Bisom-Rapp, Margaret S. Stockdale, and Faye J. Crosby, A Critical Look at Organizational Responses to Remedies for Sex Discrimination, in Crosby, Stockdale, and Ropp, Sex Discrimination in the Workplace, 273, 287; Krieger, The Watched Variable Improves, 317–319.

183. Krieger, The Watched Variable Improves, 297–298.

184. Sturm, Second Generation Employment Discrimination, 496.

185. Mahzarin Banaji and Anthony G. Greenwald, Blindspot: Hidden Biases of Good People (New York: Delacorte Press, 2013), 106; Emilio J. Castilla, Gender, Race, and Meritocracy in Organizational Careers, American Journal of Sociology 113 (2008): 1479, 1485.

186. Jennifer S. Lerner and Philip E. Tetlock, Accounting for the Effects of Accountability, Psychological Bulletin 125 (1999): 255, 263; Stephen Benard, In Paik, and Shelley Correll, Cognitive Bias and the Motherhood Penalty, Hastings Law Review 59 (2008): 1359, 1381; Martha Foschi, Double Standards and the Evaluation of Men and Women, Social Psychology Quarterly 59 (1996): 237, 247.

187. Under some models of group mentoring, any individual can a join a group, which serves many of the same functions as affinity organizations. See Mara H. Washburn and Alexander W. Crispo, Strategic Collaboration: Developing a More Effective Mentoring Model, Review of Business 27 (2006): 18–24. Kathryn H. Dansky, The Effect of Group Mentoring on Career Outcomes, Group and Organization Management 21 (1996): 5, 9–13. Electronic mentoring (e-mentoring) provides support through online communications including e-mail and chat rooms.

188. Gender Equity in Academic Science and Engineering (2001), reprinted in Stanford University, Building on Excellence: Guide to Recruiting and Retaining an Excellent and Diverse Faculty at Stanford University (2008). For the value of such information sharing, see Sturm, Second Generation Employment Discrimination, 522–538.

189. Andrea Chang, Wal-Mart Announces Women Friendly Initiatives, Los Angeles Times, September 15, 2011.

190. Davidson, The End of Diversity, 41.

Chapter 3

1. Jessica Grose, The Great Yahoo! Baby Debate, Bloomberg Businessweek, October 22–26, 2012.

2. Claudia Dreifus, Where Have You Gone Norman Rockwell: A Fresh Look at the Family, New York Times, June 14, 2005 (quoting Coontz).

3. Joan C. Williams and Heather Boushey, The Three Faces of Work-Family Conflict: The Poor, the Professionals, and the Missing Middle (Center for American Progress and Center for Work Life Law, University of California Hastings College of Law, 2010).

4. Ellen Ernst Kossek, Work and Family in America: Growing Tensions Between Employment Policy and a Transformed Workforce, in Edward E. Lawler and James O'Toole, eds., America at Work: Choices and Challenges (New York: Palgrave MacMillan, 2006), 54.

5. Heather Boushey and Ann O'Leary, eds., The Shriver Report: A Woman's Nation Changes Everything (Washington, D.C.: Center for American Progress, 2009), 76.

6. Jody Heymann with Krsten McNeill, Children's Chances: How Countries Can Move from Surviving to Thriving (Cambridge, MA: Harvard University Press, 2013), 136.

7. Francine D. Blau and Lawrence M. Kahn, Female Labor Supply: Why Is the US Falling Behind? (Bonn, Germany: Institute for the Study of Labor, January 2013), 1.

8. Jerry A. Jacobs and Kathleen Gerson, The Time Divide: Work Family and Gender Inequality (Cambridge, MA: Harvard University Press, 2005), 85.

9. Jonathan Vespa, Jamie M. Lewis, and Rose M. Kreider, United States Bureau of the Census, America's Families and Living Arrangements, 2012 (August 2013), 26; http://www.census.gov/hhes/families/.

10. Pew Research Cnter, Millennial Women Approach Wage Parity with Men—For Now, December, 2013.

11. Patricia Montemurri, Steinem: Every Woman Stands for Feminist Movement, Asbury Park Press (New Jersey), April 7, 2009 (quoting Steinem).

12. Tina Fey, Confessions of a Juggler, The New Yorker, 87.

13. Anne-Marie Slaughter, Why Women Still Can't Have It All, The Atlantic, July–August 2012, 85.

14. Susan J. Lambert, "Opting in" to Full Labor Force Participation, in Bernie D. Jones, Women Who Opt Out: The Debate over Working Mothers and Work-Family Balance (New York: New York University Press, 2012), 91.

15. U.S. Joint Economic Committee, Invest in Women, Invest in America: A Comprehensive Review of Women in the U.S. Economy (December 2010), 54–55.

16. Catherine Rampell, Coveting Not a Corner Office, but Time at Home, New York Times, July 8, 2013, A1; See also Kerstin Aumann and Ellen Galinsky, The Real "Opt Out Revolution" and a New Model of Flexible Careers, in Bernie D. Jones, Women Who Opt Out (New York: New York University Press, 2012), 59.

17. Slaughter, Why Women Can't Have It All, 92.

18. Shirley Lung, Overwork and Overtime, Indiana Law Review 39 (2005): 51, 66–67 and ns 109–125.

19. Ronit Dinovitzer, Robert Nelson, Gabriele Plickert, Rebecca Sandefur, and Joyce S. Sterling, After the JD II: Second Results from a National Study of Legal Careers (Washington, D.C.: NALP Foundation for Law Career Research and Education and the American Bar Foundation 2009), 62.

20. Leslie Bennetts, The Feminine Mistake: Are We Giving Up Too Much? (New York: Hyperion, 2007), 38 (quoting Heidi Hartmann).

21. Joan C. Williams and Jamie Dolkas, The Opt Out Revolution Revisited, in Bernie D. Jones, Women Who Opt Out (New York: New York University Press 2012), 151.

22. Williams and Dolkas, The Opt Out Revolution Revisited, 152.

23. Kerstin Aumann and Ellen Galinsky, The Real "Opt Out Revolution" and a New Model of Flexible Careers, in Bernie D. Jones, Women Who Opt Out (New York: New York University Press, 2012), 69.

24. Phyllis Moen and Patricia Roehling, The Career Mystique: Cracks in the American Dream (Lanham, MD: Rowman and Littlefield, 2005), 86.

25. Pew Research Center, Breadwinner Moms (Washington, D.C.: Pew Research Center, 2013), 1.

26. Pew Research Center, The Harried Life of the Working Mother (Washington, D.C.: Pew Research Center, 2009), 14; United States Census Bureau, America's Families and Living Arrangements: 2010. Table FG1 (Washington D.C.: U.S. Census Bureau).

27. See Joan Williams, Unbending Gender: Why Family and Work Conflict and What to Do about It (New York: Oxford University Press, 2001).

28. Pew Research Center, Mothers and Work: What's "Ideal" (Washington, D.C.: Pew Research Center, 2013).

29. Working Mother Research Institute, What Moms Choose: The Working Mother Report (Working Mother Research Institute, 2011), 15.

30. Sylvia Ann Hewlett and Carolyn Buck Luce, Off-Ramps and On Ramps: Keeping Talented Women on the Road to Success, Harvard Business Review (March 2005), 48.

31. Anita Bruzzese, Survey: More Women Are Choosing Time over Money, USA Today, October 31, 2011, 7b.

32. Pew Research Center, Recession Turns a Graying Office Grayer (Washington, D.C.: Pew Research Center, 2009), 27.

33. Pew Research Center, Breadwinner Moms, 10.

34. Pew Research Center, The Harried Life of the Working Mother, 7 (third); Phyllis Moen and Patricia Roehling, The Career Mystique: Cracks in the American Dream (Lanham, MD: Rowman and Littlefield, 2005), 71–72 (quarter).

35. Joan C. Williams, Reshaping the Work-Family Debate: Why Men and Class Matter (Cambridge, MA: Harvard University Press, 2010), 19.

36. Hewlett and Luce, On-Ramps, 44–45.

37. See sources cited in Deborah L. Rhode and Barbara Kellerman, Women and Leadership: The State of Play, in Barbara Kellerman and Deborah L. Rhode, Women and Leadership: The State of Play and Strategies for Reform (San Francisco: Jossey-Bass, 2007), 4–5.

38. Claudia Wallis, The Case for Staying Home, Time, March 22, 2004, at 51, 53.

39. Working Mother Research Institute, What Moms Choose, 11; Pamela Stone and Lisa Ackerly Hernandez, The Rhetoric and Reality of "Opting Out," in Bernie D. Jones, Women Who Opt Out: The Debate over Working Mothers (New York: New York University Press 2012), 48–50.

40. Pamela Stone, Opting Out? Why Women Really Quit Careers and Head Home (Berkeley: University of California Press, 2007), 62.

41. Stone, Opting Out, 61.

42. Stone, Opting Out, 73.

43. Stone, Opting Out, 69.

44. Stone and Hernandez, Rhetoric and Reality, 55; Working Mother Research Institute, What Moms Choose.

45. Stone and Hernandez, Rhetoric and Reality, 50.

46. Debra Cassens Weiss, Jack Welch: Women Take Time Off for Kids at Their Peril, ABA Journal, July 16, 2009, http://www.abajournal.com/news/article/jack_welch_women_take_time_off_for_kids_at_their_peril/.

47. Hewlett and Luce, Off-Ramps and On-Ramps, 48.

48. Hewlett and Luce, Off-Ramps and On-Ramps, 48, 46.

49. Stephen Rose and Heidi Hartmann, Still a Man's Labor Market: The Long Term Earnings Gap (Washington, D.C.: Institute for Women's Policy Research 2004) (20 percent for a one-year interruption and 30 percent for two- to three-year interruption).

50. Terry Martin Hekker, Paradise Lost (Domestic Division), New York Times, January 1, 2006, Style, 9.

51. Leslie Bennetts, The Feminine Mistake (New York: Hyperion, 2007), 29 (quoting Susan Yardley).

52. Bennetts, The Feminine Mistake, 188, 207.

53. Judith Warner, Ready to Rejoin the Rat Race? New York Times Magazine, August 11, 2013, 29.

54. Warner, Ready to Rejoin the Rat Race, 29.

55. Moen and Roehling, The Career Mystique, 88; Elizabeth Medes, Lydia Saad, and Kyley McGeeney, Stay-at-Home Moms Report More Depression, Sadness, Anger, Gallup, May 18, 2012.

56. Williams, Reshaping the Work Family Debate, 23; Judith Warner, Perfect Madness: Motherhood in the Age of Anxiety (2006); Sharon Hays, The Cultural Contradictions of Motherhood (New Haven, CT: Yale University Press, 1996); Carl Honore, Under Pressure: Rescuing Our Children from the Culture of Hyper-Parenting (New York: Knopf, 2008).

57. Phyllis Moen, Erin Kelly, and Kelly Chermack, Learning from a National Experiment: Studying a Corporate Time Policy Initiative, in Crouter and Booth, Work-Life Policies (Washington, D.C.: Urban Institute Press, 2009), 97; Erin L. Kelly and Phyllis Moen,

Rethinking the Clockwork of Work: Why Schedule Control May Pay Off at Work and at Home, Advances in Developing Human Resources 9 (2007): 487; Cali Ressler and Jody Thompson, Why Work Sucks And How to Fix It; The Results-Only Revolution (New York: Portfolio/Penguin, 2011).

58. Cheryl Buehler and Marion O'Brien, Mothers' Part-time Employment: Associations with Mother and Family Well-Being, Journal of Family Psychology 25 (2011): 895.

59. Laura A. McNall, Aline D. Masuda, and Jessica Nicklin, Flexible Work Arrangements, Job Satisfaction and Turnover Intention: The Mediating Role of Family Enrichment, Journal of Psychology 144 (2010): 61.

60. Catalyst, The Great Debate: Flexibility vs. Face Time (New York: Catalyst, 2013), 4.

61. Marcie Pitt-Catsouphes, Steven Sweet, and Kathy Lynch, with Elizabeth Whalley, Talent Management Study Issue Brief 23 (Boston: Sloan Center on Aging and Work at Boston College, 2009), 1.

62. Jerry A. Jacobs and Kathleen Gerson, The Time Divide: Work, Family and Gender Inequality (Cambridge, MA: Harvard University Press, 2005), 100. Ellen Ernst Kossek and Brian Distelberg, Work and Family Employment Policy for a Transformed Labor Force, in Ann C. Crouter and Alan Booth, Work-Life Policies (Washington, D.C.: Urban Institute Press, 2009), 14.

63. Kossek and Distelberg, Work and Family Employment Policy, 7.

64. Williams, Reshaping the Work Family Debate, 209, 43.

65. Lewis Coser, Greedy Institutions: Patterns of Undivided Commitment (New York: Free Press, 1974); Cynthia Fuchs Epstein, Carroll Seron, Bonnie Oglensky, and Robert Sauté, The Part-Time Paradox: Time Norms, Professional Lives, Family and Gender (New York: Routledge, 1999), 56; Stone, Opt Out, 222. Renee M. Landers, James B. Rebitzer, and Lowell J. Taylor, Rat Race Redux: Adverse Selection in the Determination of Work Hours in Law Firms, American Economic Review 86 (1996): 329.

66. Leslie Perlow, Sleeping with Your Smartphone: How to Break the 24/7 Habit and Change the Way We Work (Cambridge, MA: Harvard Business Press Books, 2012).

67. ABA Young Lawyers Division, Career Satisfaction Survey (American Bar Association, 2000).

68. Cynthia Fuchs Epstein et al., Glass Ceilings and Open Doors, Women's Advancement in the Legal Profession, Fordham Law Review 64 (1995): 291, 385.

69. Suzanne Nossel and Elizabeth Westfall, Presumed Equal: What America's Top Women Lawyers Really Think about Their Firms (Franklin Lakes, NJ: Career Press, 1997), 295.

70. Stanley Coren, Sleep Deprivation, Psychosis, and Mental Efficiency, Psychiatric Times, March 1, 1998, 15; Emily Tanner-Smith and Adam Long, The Stress-Health Connection and Its Implications for Employers, Managed Care Outlook, May 15, 2008, 21.

71. Arlie Hochschild, The Outsourced Self (New York: Henry Holt, 2012), 10–11.

72. Moen and Roehling, The Career Mystique, 91.

73. Williams and Boushey, The Three Faces of Work-Family Conflict, 29; Corporate Voices for Working Families and WFD Consulting, Workplace Flexibility for Lower Wage Workers (2006): 32 table 3, http://www.cvworkingfamilies.org/system/files/lowerwageflexreviewreport.pdf.

74. Williams, Reshaping the Work Family Debate, 46–50.

75. Upton v. J.P.W. Businessland, 682 N.E. 2d 1357, 1358 (Mass. 1997).

76. Upton v. J.P.W. Businessland, 682 N.E. 2d 1357, 1358 (Mass. 1997), 1359.

77. EEOC v. Bloomberg, L.P. 778 F. Supp. 2d 458, 485 (S.D. N.Y. 2011).

78. Steven Greenhouse, A Part-Time Life, as Hours Shrink and Shift, New York Times, October 27, 2012, 1, 20.

79. Kossek and Distelberg, Work and Family Employment Policy, 31.

80. Stone, Opt Out, 121.

81. Paula Patton, Women Lawyers, Their Status, Influence, and Retention in the Legal Profession, William and Mary Journal of Women and the Law 11 (2005): 173, 189.

82. Hewlett and Luce, Off-Ramps, 48.

83. Epstein, Seron, Oglensky, and Sauté, The Part-Time Paradox, 34–35.

84. Stone, Opt Out, 88–89; research cited in Deborah L. Rhode, From Platitudes to Priorities: Diversity and Gender Equity in Law Firms, Georgetown Journal of Legal Ethics 24 (2011):1041, 1057; Joan C. Williams, Canaries in the Mine: Work/Family Conflict and the Law, Fordham Law Review 70 (2002): 221.

85. Pamela Stone and Lisa A. Hernandez, The All-or-Nothing Workplace: Flexibility Stigma and Opting Out among Professional-Managerial Women, Journal of Social Issues 69 (2013):235.

86. Stone, Opt Out?, 92.

87. Hannah Seligson, When the Work-Life Scales Are Unequal, New York Times, September 2, 2012, 5.

88. Seligson, When the Work-Life Scales Are Unequal (quoting Epstein).

89. Ellen Ernst Kossek, Alison E. Barber, and Deborah Winters, Using Flexible Schedules in the Managerial World: The Power of Peers, Human Resource Management 38 (1999): 33, 40.

90. Stone, Opt Out, 218.

91. Lisa Dodson, Stereotyping Low-Wage Mothers Who Have Work and Family Conflicts, Journal of Social Issues 69 (2013): 257, 267.

92. Dodson, Stereotyping Low-Wage Mothers, 267.

93. Dodson, Stereotyping Low-Wage Mothers, 269.

94. Jeff Hayes and Heidi Hartmann, Women and Men Living on the Edge: Economic Insecurity After the Great Recession (Washington, D.C.: Institute for Women's Policy Research, 2011), 68.

95. See sources cited in Jessica A. Clarke, Beyond Equality? Against the Universal Turn in Workplace Protections, Indiana Law Journal 86 (2011): 1219, 1275.

96. Jacobs and Gerson, The Time Divide, 66, 69.

97. Kelly and Moen, Rethinking the Clockwork of Work, 490.

98. Jennifer L. Berdahl and Sue H. Moon, Workplace Mistreatment of Middle Class Workers Based on Sex, Parenthood, and Caregiving, Journal of Social Issues 69 (2013): 341; Laurie A. Rudman and Kris Mescher, Penalizing Men Who Request a Family Leave: Is Flexibility Stigma a Femininity Stigma?, Journal of Social Issues 69 (2013): 322.

99. Epstein, Seron, Oglensky and Sauté, The Part Time Paradox, 35.

100. For lower rewards and performance ratings, see Adam B. Butler and Amie Skattebo, What Is Acceptable for Women May Not Be for Men: The Effect of Family Conflicts with Work on Job-Performance Ratings, Journal of Occupational and Organizational Psychology 787 (2004): 553; Tammy Allen and Joyce Russell, Parental Leave of Absence; Some Not So Family-Friendly Implications, Journal of Applied Social Psychology 39 (1999): 166. For male-female comparisons, see Kenneth G. Dau Schmidt, Marc Galanter, Kaushik Mukhopadhaya, and Kathleen E. Hull, Men and Women of the Bar: The Impact of Gender on Legal Careers, Michigan Journal of Gender and Law 16 (2009): 49, 112–113; Nancy Levit and Douglas O. Linder, The Happy Lawyer (New York: Oxford University Press, 2010), 12–13.

101. Berdahl and Moon, Workplace Mistreatment.

102. Scott Coltrane, Elizabeth Miller, Tracy DeHaan, and Lauren Stewart, Fathers and the Flexibility Stigma, Journal of Social Issues 69 (2013): 279.

103. Joseph A. Vandello, Vanessa E. Hettinger, Jennifer K. Bosson, and Jasmine Siddiqi, When Equal Isn't Really Equal: The Masculine Dilemma of Seeking Work Flexibility, Journal of Social Issues 69 (2013): 303.

104. Coltrane, Miller, DeHaan, and Stewart, Fathers and the Flexibility Stigma.

105. Keith Cunningham-Parmeter, Men at Work, Fathers at Home: Uncovering the Masculine Face of Caregiver Discrimination, Columbia Journal of Gender and Law 23 (2013): 253, 255.

106. Jacob Klerman, Kelly Daley, and Alyssa Pozniak, Family and Medical Leave in 2012: Technical Report (Cambridge, MA: Abt Associates, 2012).

107. United States Department of Labor, Bureau of Labor Statistics, National Compensation Survey: Employee Benefits in the United States, (Washington, D.C.: Bureau of Labor Statistics, March 2013), table 32.

108. Bureau of Labor Statistics, National Compensation Survey (2013); Report of the Joint Economic Committee, Expanding Access to Paid Sick Leave: The Impact of the Healthy Families Act on America's Workers, in Report of the Joint Economic Committee, Invest in Women, 172, and Karen Nussbaum before the United States Joint Economic Committee, Hearing on Balancing Work and Family in the Recession: How Employees and Employers Are Coping, July 23, 2009, reprinted in Report of the Joint Economic Committee, Invest in Women, 217, 219.

109. Ann O'Leary, How Family Leave Laws Left Out Low-Income Workers, Berkeley Journal of Employment and Labor Law 28 (2007): 1, 4.

110. Annamaria Sundbye and Ariane Hegewisch, Maternity, Paternity, and Adoption Leave in the United States (Washington, D.C.: Institute for Women's Policy Research, May 2011), 3 (access to family leave); Heather Boushey and Sarah Jane Glynn, The Effects of Paid Family and Medical Leave on Employment Stability and Economic Security (Washington, D.C.: Center for American Progress, 2012), 11 (duration of leave); Joan C. Williams and Heather Boushey, The Three Faces of Work-Family Conflict (Washington, D.C.: Center for American Progress, 210), 28 (sick leave).

111. Hayes and Hartmann, Women and Men Living on the Edge, 64.

112. Dodson, Stereotyping Low-Wage Mothers, 271.

113. Sylvia Guendelman et al., Utilization of Pay-in Antenatal Leave among Working Women in Southern California, Maternal and Child Health Journal 10 (2006): 63, 71.

114. Nossell and Westfall, Presumed Equal, 72.

115. United States Department of Labor, Wage and Hour Division, the 2000 Survey Report app. A2 (2001).

116. Richard Dorment, Why Mern Still Can't Have It All, Esquire, June/July 2013.

117. Jacobs and Gerson, The Time Divide, 90.

118. Erin L. Kelly, Failure to Update: An Institutional Perspective on Noncompliance with the Family and Medical Leave Act, Law and Society Review 44 (2010): 33, 53.

119. Lotte Bailyn, Breaking the Mold: Women, Men and Time in the New Corporate World (Ithaca, NY: Cornell University Press, 1993), 23.

120. Wen-Jui Han and Jane Waldfogel, Parental Leave: The Impact of Recent Legislation on Parents' Leave Taking, Demography 40 (2003):191, 192. See Klerman, Daley, and Poozniak, Family and Medical Leave, 141 (70 percent of paternity leaves are no more than 10 days).

121. Erin L. Kelly, Failure to Update: An Institutional Perspective on Noncompliance with the Family and Medical Leave Act, Law and Society Review 44 (2010): 33, 57.

122. Lauren Weber, Why Dads Don't Take Paternity Leave, Wall Street Journal, June 12, 2013, http://online.wsj.com/article/SB10001424127887324049504578541633708283670.html.

123. Rudman and Mescher, Penalizing Men, discussed in Stephanie Bornstein, The Law of Gender Stereotyping and the Work-Family Conflicts of Men, Hastings Law Review 63 (2012): 1297, 1335.

124. Julie Holliday Wayne and Bryanne L. Cordeiro, Who Is a Good Organizational Citizen? Social Perceptions of Male and Female Employees Who Use Family Leave, Sex Roles 49 (September 2003): 241.

125. Scott v. Allied Waste Service of Bucks-Mont., 2010 U.S. Dist. LEXIS 136,202 (E.D. Pa. 2010).

126. Knussman v. Maryland, 272 F. 3d 625, 630 (4th Cir. 2001).

127. Aldridge v. Indian Electric Coop, 2008 WL 1,777,480 (N.D. Okl. 2008).

128. Wells v. City of Montgomery, 2006 W.L1133300, 2006 U.S. Dist. Lexis 23,013 (S.D. Ohio, April 25, 2006, 04CV425), quoted in Williams and Boushey, The Three Faces of Work-Family Conflict, 46.

129. Tara Siegel Bernard, The Unspoken Stigma of Workplace Flexibility, New York Times, June 15, 2013, B1 (quoting Williams).

130. EEOC Enforcement Guidance: Unlawful Disparate Treatment of Workers with Care-giving Responsibilities (2007): EEOC, Employer Best Practices for Workers with Care-giving Responsibilities (2009).

131. Joan C. Williams, Jumpstarting the Stalled Gender Revolution: Justice Ginsburg and Reconstructive Feminism, Hastings Law Review 63 (2012): 1267, 1289.

132. Williams and Boushey, The Three Faces of Work-Family Conflict, 30.

133. Trezza v. Hartford, Inc., 1998 U.S. District Lexis 20,206 (S.D.N.Y. 1998).

134. Stephanie Bornstein, Work, Family, and Discrimination at the Bottom of the Ladder, Georgetown Journal on Poverty Law and Policy 19 (2012):1, 16–17; EEOC v. W & O, Inc., 213 F 3d 600, 608 (11th Cir.2000) 9 (Affirming in part and vacating in part); EEOC v. J.H.Hein Corp., U.S. District Lexis 49,609 (N.D. Ind. 2009).

135. Fisher v. Rizzo Brothers Paint Contractors, Inc. 2005 U.S. District lexis 31,901 (E.D. Ky. 2005).

136. Department of Fair Employment and Housing v. Advance Medical Solutions, 2007 CAFHEC Lexis 5, 9 (Cal. F.E.H.C.2007). See Paz v. Wauconda Healthcare and Reha-bilitation Center, 464 F. 3d 659, 661–662 (7th Cir. 2006); Kreider v. Creative Fabrica-tors, Inc., 1997 WL33104348 (1997).

137. Hercule v. Wendy's, 2010 WL 1,882,181 (S.D.Fla., May 2010); Notter v. Hand Protec-tion 1996 US. App Lexis 14,954 (4th Cir. 1996).

138. See cases discussed in Bornstein, Work, Family, and Discrimination, at 36–37.

139. Williams and Boushey, The Three Faces of Work-Family Conflict, 59.

140. Moore v. Alabama State University, 980 F. Supp. 426, 431 (M.D. Ala. 1997).

141. Lust v. Sealy, 383 F.3d 580 (7th Cir.2004).

142. Back v. Hastings on Hudson Union Free School District, 365 F. 3d 107, 120 (2d Cir.2004).

143. Bornstein, Work, Family, and Discrimination, 21–22; Reeves v. Swift Transportation, 446 F. 3d 637 (6th Cir., 2006).

144. 42 U.S. Code Section 2000e(k)(2006).

145. Berry v. Georgetown Inn, Ltd. 2010 Wl 1,784,658 (W.D. Pa. February 2008) (noting jury verdict for employer).

146. Joan C. Williams and Penelope Huang, Improving Work-Life Fit in Hourly Jobs: An Underutilized Cost-Cutting Strategy in a Globalized World (San Francisco: Center for Work Life Law, Hastings Law School, 2011), 44–45; Bornstein, Work, Family, and Dis-crimination, 27.

147. Carol Sarler, It's the Mother of All Myths: Times (of London), June 15, 2006. For an overview of how America's mothers coped, see Sonya Michel, Children's Interests/Mothers' Rights: The Shaping of America's Child Care Policy (New Haven, CT: Yale University Press, 2000).

148. Edward Zigler, Katherine Marsland and Heather Lord, The Tragedy of Child Care in America (New Haven, CT: Yale University Press, 2009), 2.

149. Institute for a Competitive Workforce, Ready, Set, Go! Why Business Should Support Early Childhood Education (Washington, D.C.: Institute for a Competitive Workforce, of the U.S. Chamber of commerce, 2010), 11; Zigler, Marsland, and Lord, Tragedy of Childcare, 4; Dan Clawson and Naomi Gerstel, Caring for Our Young: Child Care in Europe and the United States, Contexts (Winter 2002): 28, 30.

150. Zigler, Marsland, and Lord, Tragedy of Childcare, 7.

151. Moen and Roehling, The Career Mystique, 97–98.

152. Lynne M. Casper and Kristin E. Smith, Dispelling the Myths: Self-Care, Class, and Race, Journal of Family Issues 23 (2002): 716; Zigler, Marsland, and Lord, Tragedy of Childcare, 118; Jerry A. Jacobs and Kathleen Gerson, The Time Divide: Work, Family, and Gender Inequality (Cambridge, MA; Harvard University Press, 2004), 175.

153. Williams and Boushey, Three Faces, 17.

154. Williams and Boushey Three Faces, 46, 57.

155. Meredith John Harbach, Outsourcing Childcare, Yale Journal of Law and Feminism 24 (2012): 254, 288.

156. Children's Defense Fund, The State of America's Children Handbook (2012), 32; Katie McDonough, Childcare Is More Expensive Than College in a Majority of States, Salon. com, November 4, 2013, http://www.salon.com/2013/11/04/child_care+is_more_ expensive_than_college_in_a-majority_-of_states/ (citing report of Childcare Aware of America).

157. National Association of Child Care Resource and Referral Agencies, Breaking the Piggy Bank: Parents and the High Cost of Child Care (Washington, D.C.: National Association of Child Care Resource and Referral Agencies, 2006).

158. Kossick and Distelberg, Work and Family Employment Policy, 14.

159. Zigler, Marsland, and Lord, xiv; see also Children's Defense Fund, Child Care Basics (April, 2005), http://www.childrensdefense.org/child-research-data-publications/ data/child-care-basics.pdf.

160. Institute for a Competitive Workforce, Why Business Should Support Early Childhood Education (Washington, D.C.: Institute for a Competitive Workforce, of the U.S. Chamber of Commerce, 2010), 24, 15; Children's Defense Fund, Child Care Basics, 3.

161. Hannah Matthews, Child Care Assistance Helps Families Work: A Review of the Effects of Subsidy Receipt on Employment (Washington, D.C.: Center for Law and Social Policy, 2006), 2.

162. Lisa Dodson, Tiffany Manuel, and Ellen Bravo, Keeping Jobs and Raising Families in Low-Income America: It Just Doesn't Work (Cambridge, MA: Radcliffe Institute for Advanced Study, 2002), 4.

163. Cost, Quality, and Child Outcomes Study Team, Cost, Quality and Child Outcomes in Child Care Centers. Technical Report, Public Report, and Executive Summary, 2nd ed. (Denver: University of Colorado, 1995); Zigler, Marsland, and Lord, Tragedy of Childcare, 8.

164. Clawson and Gerstel, Caring for Our Young, 33.

165. Jonathan Cohen, The Hell of American Day Care, New Republic, April 15, 2013.

166. Only 13 states license all family care homes that provide care for unrelated children. Zigler, Marsland and Lord, The Tragedy of Child Care, 74.

167. Gail Collins, None Dare Call It Child Care, New York Times, October 18, 2007, See also Children's Defense Fund, Child Care Basics.

168. Zigler, Marsland, and Lord, Tragedy of Child Care, xiii. For the inadequacy of state oversight, see also Suzanne W. Helburn and Barbara R. Bergman, America's Childcare Problem: The Way Out (New York: Palgrave, 2002), 6.

169. Zigler, Marsland, and Lord, Tragedy of Child Care, 11; Clawson and Gerstel, Caring for Our Young, 31.

170. Institute for a Competitive Workforce, Why Business Should Support Early Childhood Education (Washington, D.C.: Institute for a Competitive Workforce of the U.S. Chamber of Commerce, 2010), 24.

171. Institute for a Competitive Workforce, Why Business Should Support Early Childhood Education, 8–9. Deborah Lowe Vandell, Do Effects of Early Child Care Extend to Age 15 Years? Results for the NICHD Study of Early Child Care and Youth Development, Child Development 81 (2010): 737.

172. See research discussed in Madeleine M. Kunin, The New Feminist Agenda (White River Junction, VT: Chelsea Green Publishing, 2012), 110–111; Nicholas D. Kristof, Do We Invest in Preschools or Prisons, New York Times, October 27, 2013, SR 11.

173. James J. Heckman and Dimitriy V. Masterov, The Productivity Argument for Investing in Young Children, Working Paper 5 (Invest in Kids Working Group, Committee for Economic Development, 2004).

174. Organisation for Economic Co-operation and Development, Closing the Gender Gap: Act Now (Organisation for Economic Co-operation and Development, 2012), 212. See also Michelle J. Budig, Joya Misra, Irene Boeckmann, The Wage Penalty for Motherhood in a Cross National Perspective: Relationships with Work Family Policies and Cultural Attitudes Social Policy 19 (Summer 2012): 183.

175. Kunin, The New Feminist Agenda, 204. Robyn I. Stone, Long-Term Care for the Elderly (Washington, D.C.: Urban Institute Press, 2011), 27.

176. Heather Boushey and Sarah Jane Glynn, The Effects of Paid Family and Medical Leave on Employment Stability and Economic Security (Washington, D.C.: Center for American Progress, April 2012), 3.

177. Mary Jo Gibson and Satyendra K. Verma, Just Getting By: Unmet Need for Personal Assistance Services Among Persons 50 or Older with Disabilities (Washington, D.C.: ARPP Public Policy Institute 2006), vi.

178. Gibson and Verma, Just Getting By, 1.

179. Boushey and Williams, Three Faces of Work-Family Conflict, 62.

180. For the critical role of family and other unpaid providers, see Robyn I. Stone, Long-Term Care for the Elderly with Disabilities: Current Policy, Emerging Trends, and Implications for the Twenty-First Century 8–9 (2000), 8–9. Ari N. Houser, Mary Jo Gibson, and Donald L. Redfoot, Trends in Family Caregiving and Paid Home Care for Older People with Disabilities in the Community: Data from the National Long-Term Care Survey (Washington, D.C.: AARP Public Policy Institute, 2010). For gender, see Boushey and Glynn, Effect of Paid Family and Medical Leave, 3.

181. Rhonda J. V. Montgomery, Lyn Holley, Jerome Deichert, and Karl Kosloski, A Profile of Home Care Workers from the 2000 Census: How It Changes What We Know, Gerontologist 45 (2005): 593, 595.

182. Peggie R. Smith, Aging and Caring in the Home: Regulating Paid Domesticity in the 21st Century, Iowa Law Review 92 (2007):1835, 1848. Estimates suggest that attrition rates are as high as 50 percent each year. Paraprofessional Healthcare Institute, Training Quality Home Care Workers (2003), 3.

183. H. Stephen Kaye, Robert J. Newcomer, Charlene Harrington, The Personal Assistance Workforce: Trends in Supply and Demand, Health Affairs 25 (2006): 1113, 1113–1114.

184. Gibson and Verma, Just Getting By, 1.

185. Liza Mundy, Women, Money and Power, Time, March 26, 2012, 31.

186. Carol Lawson, A New Spokesman (Yes Man) for Childcare, New York Times, April 30, 1992, B5.

187. U.S. Department of Labor, Bureau of Labor Statistics, American Tie Use Survey, 2012; Ruth Davis Konigsberg, Chore Wars, Time, August 8, 2011, 47.

188. Jill Filipovic, When Are We Going to Involve Men in Discussions of Work/life Balance?, The Guardian, August 8, 2013, http://www.theguardian.com/commentisfree/2013/aug/08/women-opting-back-in-workforce:Scott Coltrane, Research on Household Labor: Modeling and Measuring the Social Embeddedness of Routine Family Work, Journal of Marriage and the Family 62 (2000): 1208, 1219.

189. Richard W. Johnson and Joshua M. Weiner, A Profile of Frail Older Americans and Their Caregivers, Urban Institute, Occasional paper Number 8 (February 2006).

190. Wendy Wang, The "Leisure Gap" Between Mothers and Fathers (Pew Research Center, October 2013).

191. Scott Coltrane, Research on Household Labor: Modeling and Measuring the Social Embeddedness of Routine Family Work, Journal of Marriage and Family 62 (2000): 1224; Stephanie Coontz, Sharing the Load, Shriver Report, 373–374; Kimmel, Has a Man's World Become a Woman's Nation?, 353; Stephanie Coontz, The M.R.S. and the Ph.D., New York Times, February 12, 2012, SR 6, Lori Gottlieb, Does a More Equal Marriage Mean Less Sex?, New York Times Magazine, February 9, 2014, 27.

192. Pew Research Center, Modern Marriage (July 18, 2007).

193. So, for example, black men do more housework than white men. Michael Kimmel, Has a Man's World Become a Woman's Nation?, in Heather Boushey and Ann O'Leary, The Shriver Report: A Woman's Nation Changes Everything (Washington, D.C.: Center for American Progress, 2009), 349.

194. Moen and Roehling, The Career Mystique, 108; Coltrane, Research on Household Labor, 1220; Coontz, The M.R.S. and the Ph.D., SR 6.

195. Bennetts, The Feminine Mistake, 207, 218.

196. Stone, Opt Out, 183, 189.

197. Moen and Roehling, The Career Mystique, 102.

198. Scott Coltrane, Research on Household Labor: Modeling and Measuring the Social Embeddedness of Routine Family Work, Journal of Marriage and the Family 62 (2000): 1208, 1210.

199. Jennifer Senior, Why Mom's Time Is Different From Dad's Time, Wall Street Journal, January 24, 2014.

200. Moen and Roeling, The Career Mystique, 103.

201. Marianne Cooper, Cut Adrift; Families in Insecure Times (Berkeley, CA: University of California Press, 2014).

202. Rudman and Mescher, Penalizing Men. See also Jennifer L. Berdahl and Sun H. Moon, Workplace Mistreatment of Middle Class Workers Based on Sex, Parenthood and Caregiving (Working Paper, 2012), discussed in Bornstein, The Law of Gender Stereotyping, 1336.

203. Francine Deutsch, Having It All: How Equally Shared Parenting Works (Cambridge, MA: Harvard University Press, 2000), 90; Williams, Reshaping the Work Family Debate, 89.

204. Task Force on Professional Challenges and Family Needs, Boston Bar Association, Facing the Grail: Confronting the Cost of Work-Family Imbalance (Boston: Boston Bar Association, 1999), 15.

205. Marianne Cooper, Being the "Go-To Guy": Fatherhood, Masculinity, and the Organization of Work in Silicon Valley, Qualitative Sociology 23 (2000): 379, reprinted in Naomi Gerstel, Dan Clawson, and Robert Zussman, Families at Work: Expanding the Bounds (Nashville, TN: Vanderbilt University Press, 2002): 5, 10, 13.

206. Cooper, Being the Go-To Guy, 7 (quoting Scott Webster).

207. Cooper, Being the Go-To Guy, 9 (quoting Kirk Sinclair).

208. Cooper, Being the Go-To Guy, 24 (quoting Chris Baxter).

209. Cooper, Being the Go-To Guy, 20.

210. Cooper, Being the Go-To Guy, 21 (quoting Rich Kavelin).

211. Cooper, Being the Go-To Guy, 25 (quoting Rich Kavelin).

212. Brad Harrington, Fred Van Deusen and Beth Humberd, The New Dad: Caring, Committed and Conflicted (Boston College Center for Work and Family, 2011), 10.

213. Dina Bakst, Jared Make, Nancy Rankin, Beyond the Breadwinner: Professional Dads Speak Out on Work and Family (Work and Family Legal Center, June 2011), 3.

214. Joan C. Williams, Reshaping the Work-Family Debate (Cambridge, MA: Harvard University Press, 2010), 89 (quoting Derek Bok).

215. Mary C. Noonan, Mary E. Corcoran, The Mommy Track and Partnership: Temporary Delay or Dead End?, 596 Annals of the American Academy of Political and Social Science 130, 137 (2004).

216. Ronit Dinovitzer, Robert Nelson, Gabriele Plickert, Rebecca Sandefur, and Joyce S. Sterling, After the JD II: Second Results from a National Study of Legal Careers (Chicago: American Bar Foundation; Dallas, TX: NALP Foundation for Law Career Research and Education, 2009), 62.

217. Nancy Levit and Douglas O. Linder, The Happy Lawyer: Making a Good Life in the Law, (New York: Oxford University Press 2010), 12, 13; Kenneth G. Dau-Schmidt et al., Men

Notes to Pages 62–64

and Women of the Bar: The Impact of Gender on Legal Careers, Michigan Journal of Gender and Law 16 (2009): 49, 112–113.

218. Sheryl Gay Stolberg, He Breaks for Band Recitals, New York Times, February 14, 2010, S1, S11.
219. Stolberg, He Breaks for Band Recitals, S10.
220. Todd S. Purdum, Washington, We Have a Problem, Vanity Fair, September 2010, 290.
221. Heyman with McNeill, Children's Chances, 155.
222. Heymann with McNeill, Children's Chances, 138.
223. Janet C. Gornick and Marcia K. Meyers, Families That Work: Policies for Reconciling Parenthood and Employment 40, 319 (New York: Russell Sage, 2005).
224. Gornick and Meyers, Families That Work, at 129.
225. Jody Heymann, We Can Afford to Give Parents a Break, Washington Post, May 14, 2006, B07; Heymann with McNeill, Children's Chances, 147.
226. Martha Burk, The Wisdom of Paid Sick Leave, Ms., Summer 2013, 49.
227. European Union Council Directive 92/85/EEC, article 1, 1992 O.J. (L348), 1, 2.
228. Heymann and McNeill, Children's Chances, 138.
229. Kunin, The New Feminist Agenda, 47.
230. Julie C. Suk, Are Gender Stereotypes Bad for Women: Rethinking Antidiscrimination Law and Work-Family Conflict, Columbia Law Review 110 (2010): 1, 26, 29–30.
231. Katrin Bennhold, In Sweden, Men Can Have It All, New York Times, June 9, 2010, 6.
232. Institute for Women's Policy Research, Maternity, Paternity and Adoption Leave in the United States (Washington, D.C.: Institute for Women's Policy Research, May 2011), 6.
233. Heymann with McNeill, Children's Chances, 138–140.
234. For the Swedish system, see Suk, Are Gender Stereotypes Bad, 37–38.
235. Clawson and Gerstel, Caring for Our Young, 32.
236. Williams, Reshaping the Work-Family Debate, 37.
237. Clawson and Gerstel, Caring for Our Young, 30–31. See also Druckerman, Catching Up with France on Day Care, New York Times, September 1, 2013.
238. Suk, Are Gender Stereotypes Bad?, 32.
239. Clawson and Gerstel, Caring for Our Young, 32.
240. Council of the European Union, Council Directive 97/81/Concerning the Framework Agreement on Part-Time Work Concluded by UNICE, CEEP and the ETUC, European Union, December 15, 1997, 1998 Official Journal L14/9.
241. Institute for Women's Policy Research and the Center for WorkLife Law, Statutory Routes to Workplace Flexibility in Cross-National Perspective (Washington, D.C.: Institute for Women's Policy Research, 2008), 9; Moen and Roehling, The Career Mystique, 176.
242. Institute for Women's Policy Research and the Center for WorkLife Law, Statutory Routes to Workplace Flexibility, 10–15.
243. Employment Act, 2002, c. 22 Section 47 (United Kingdom).
244. Institute for Women's Policy Research and the Center for Work-Life Law, Statutory Routes to Workplace Flexibility, 21.
245. Institute for Women's Policy Research, at 24. See Holya Hooker et al., Institute for Employment Studies, Employment Relations Research Series, No. 58, The Third Work-Life Balance Employee Survey: Main Findings (2007), 57 (finding that 60 percent of requests were fully accepted and 18 percent were partly accepted).
246. Institute for Women's Policy Research and Center for Worklife Law, Statutory Routes to Workplace Flexibility, 25.
247. Jennifer Glass, Work-Life Policies: Future Directions for Research, in Crouter and Booth, Work-life Policies, 237; Kristof, Do We Invest in Preschools?, SR11.
248. Olivia Morgan and Karen Skelton: The Shriver Report: A Woman's Nation Pushes Back From the Brink (Washington, D.C.: Center for American Progress and Palgrave Macmillan, 2014), 28.

249. Williams, Reshaping the Work-Family Debate, 66–70; Jacobs and Gerson, The Time Divide, 159; Boushey and Glynn, The Effects of Paid Family and Medical Leave, 5; Ellen Ernst Kossek and Brian Distelberg, Work and Family Employment Policies for a Transformed Labor Force, in Crouter and Booth, Work-Life Policies, 20; Cynthia A. Thompson and David J. Prottas, Elaborations on a Theme: Toward Understanding Work-Life Culture, in Crouter and Booth, Work-Life Policies, 52; Kossek, Work and Family, 65.

250. Kunin, The New Feminist Agenda, 124.

251. California Unemployment Insurance Code Section 2626.

252. Eileen Appelbaum and Ruth Milkman, Leaves That Pay: Employer and Worker Experiences with Paid Leave in California (Washington, D.C.: Center for Economic and Policy Research, 2011) (89 percent reported a positive effect or no noticeable effect on productivity and 91 percent reported no awareness of abuse), 4.

253. Linda Houser and Thomas P. Vartanian, Pay Matters: The Positive Economic Impacts of Paid Family Leave for Families, Businesses, and the Public (New Brunswick, NJ: Rutgers Center for Women and Work, January 2012), 2; Boshey and Glynn, Effects of Paid Family and Medical Leave, 15.

254. Report of the Joint Economic Committee, Invest in Women, 12.

255. Sarah Beth Estes, Mary C. Noonan, and David J. Maume, Is Work-Family Policy Use Related to the Gendered Division of Housework, Journal of Family Economic Issues, 28 (2007): 527, 538; Kossek and Distelberg, Work and Family Employment Policies, 29.

256. See the proposed Healthy Families Act, hthp://go.nationalpartnership.org/site/DocServer/HFA_Expanded_Overview.pdfdocID = 10,741.

257. Chai Feldblum, Policy Challenges and Opportunities for Workplace Flexibility: The State of Play, in Work-Life Policies, 260, Suk, AntiDiscrimination Law and Work-Family Conflict, 17–18 (discussing federal proposals).

258. Personal Correspondence, Vicki Shabo, National Partnership for Women and Families, November 15, 2013. A more generous program of paid leave of 2 weeks would cost each worker about $10 a month. Kunin, The New Feminist Agenda, 232.

259. Ariel Levy, Lift and Separate, New Yorker, November 16, 2009, 80 (quoting Nixon).

260. Jacobs and Gerson, The Time Divide, 195.

261. Zigler, Marsland, and Lord, The Tragedy of Child Care, 155.

262. Michel, Children's Interests/Mothers' Rights, 280.

263. Jessica Mason Pieklo, Pregnant Workers Fairness Act Introduced in Both House and Senate, RH Reality Check, May 14, 2013, http://rhrealitycheck.org/article/2013/05/14/pregnant-workers-fairness-act-introduced-in-both-house-and-senate/.

264. Pieklo, Pregnant Workers Fairness Act.

265. Shae Collins, NYC Delivers, Ms., Fall, 2013, at 14.

266. Working Families Flexibility Act, H.R. 1274, 111th Congress Section 3(a) (2009).

267. Kossek and Distelberg, Work and Family Employment Policies, 21.

268. Corporate Voices for Working Families, Innovative Workplace Flexibility Options for Hourly Workers (Washington, D.C.: Corporate Voices for Working Families, 2010), 6, 10, 16. See also Erin L. Kelly, Phyllis Moen, and Eric Tranby, Changing Workplace Norms to Reduce Work-Family Conflict: Schedule Control in a White-Collar Organization, American Sociological Review 76 (2011): 265.

269. Ellen Ernst Kossek, Work and Family, 53.

Chapter 4

1. Elizabeth A. Armstrong, Paula England, and Alison C. K. Fogarty, Accounting for Women's Orgasm and Sexual Enjoyment in College Hookups and Relationships, American Sociological Review 77 (2012): 435, 442 (69 percent); Elizabeth A. Armstrong, Laura Hamilton, and Paula England, Is Hooking Up Bad for Young Women, Contexts,

9 (2010): 22, 24 (72 percent); Carolyn Bradshaw, Arnold S. Kahn, and Bryan K. Saville, To Hook Up or Date: Which Gender Benefits?, Sex Roles 62 (2010): 661, 662 (citing surveys ranging from 77 to 84 percent).

2. Armstrong, England, and Fogarty, Accounting for Women's Orgasm, 442: Armstrong, Hamilton, and England, Is Hooking Up Bad, 24.
3. Armstrong, England, and Fogarty, Accounting for Women's Orgasm, 442.
4. Armstrong, England, and Fogarty, Accounting for Women's Orgasm, 442.
5. Kathleen A. Bogle, Hooking Up: Sex, Dating, and Relationships on Campus (New York: New York University Press, 2008); Mark Regnerus and Jeremy Uecker, Premarital Sex in America: How Young Americans Meet, Mate, and Think about Marrying (New York: Oxford University Press, 2011), 139–149, 160–161; Bradshaw, Kahn, and Saville, To Hook Up or Date, Elaine M. Eshbaugh and Gary Gute, Hookups and Sexual Regret among College Women, Journal of Social Psychology 148 (2008): 77; Catherine M. Grello, Deborah P. Welsh, and Melinda S. Harper, No Strings Attached: The Nature of Casual Sex in College Students, Journal of Sex Research 43 (2006): 255; Michael Kimmel, Guyland: The Perilous World Where Boys Become Men (New York: Harper, 2008), 202.
6. Bogle, Hooking Up, 97.
7. Twenty-eight percent hoped for friendships and 17 percent wanted future hookups. Justin R. Garcia and Chris Reiber, Hook Up Behavior: A Biopsychocosocial Perspective, Journal of Social, Evolutionary, and Cultural Psuchology 2 (2008): 192.
8. Armstrong, England, and Fogarty, Accounting for Women's Orgasm, 442.
9. Armstrong, England, and Fogarty, Accounting for Women's Orgasm, 437; F. Scott Christopher and Susan Sprecher, Sexuality in Marriage, Dating, and Other Relationships: A Decade Review, Journal of Marriage and Family 62 (2000): 999 (finding that the quality of the relationship influences sexual satisfaction).
10. Armstrong, England, and Fogarty, Accounting for Women's Orgasm, 456.
11. Armstrong, England, and Fogarty, Accounting for Women's Orgasm, 456.
12. Armstrong, England, and Fogarty, Accounting for Women's Orgasm, 457.
13. Laura Hamilton and Elizabeth A. Armstrong, Gendered Sexuality in Young Adulthood; Double Binds and Flawed Options, Gender and Society 23 (2009): 589.
14. Derek A. Kreager and Jeremy Staff, The Sexual Double Standard and Adolescent Peer Acceptance, Social Psychology Quarterly 79 (2009): 143.
15. Regnerus and Uecker, Premarital Sex in America, 106.
16. Bogle, Hooking Up, 114, 106–108; Hamilton and Armstrong, Gendered Sexuality, 598–599.
17. Bradshaw, Kahn, and Saville, To Hook Up or Date, 644; Grello, Welsh, and Harper, No Strings Attached, 265; Elizabeth L. Paul and Kristen A. Hayes, The Casualties of "Casual" Sex: A Qualitative Exploration of the Phenomenology of College Students' Hookups, Journal of Social and Personal Relationships 19 (2002): 639, 654.
18. Bogle, Hooking Up, 183.
19. Armstrong, Hamilton, and England, Is Hooking Up Bad for Young Women, 25; Regnerus and Uecker, Premarital Sex in America, 111.
20. Kate Taylor, Sex on Campus: She Can Play That Game, Too, New York Times, July 12, 2013.
21. Hanna Rosin, Boys on the Side, Atlantic, August 22, 2012.
22. Armstrong, Hamilton, and England, Is Hooking Up Bad for Young Women, 26; Armstrong and Hamilton, Gendered Sexuality in Young Adulthood, 601.
23. Susan Patton, Letter to the Editor: Advice for the Young Women of Princeton: The Daughters I Never Had, The Daily Princetonian, March 29, 2013.
24. Aimee Groth and Sheryl Sandberg, The Most Important Career Choice You'll Make Is Who You Marry, Business Insider, December 1, 2011, http://www.businessinsider.com/shertyl-sandberg-career-advice-to-women-2011-12.

25. Jane Bailey and Mouna Hanna, The Gendered Dimensions of Sexting: Assessing the Applicability of Canada's Child Pornography Provision, Canadian Journal of Women and Law 10 (2011): 405, 410; Tamar Lewin, Rethinking Sex Offender Laws for Youth: Showing Off Online, New York Times, March 21, 2010; Amanda Lenhart, Teens and Sexting, Pew Internet and American Life Project, December 15, 2009.

26. Lenhart, Teens and Sexting; Alex Morris, They Know What Boys Want, New York Magazine, January 30, 2011; Jim Hoffman, A Girl's Nude Photo, and Altered Lives, New York Times, March 27, 2011, A1.

27. Bailey and Hanna, The Gendered Dimensions of Sexting, 407, 411–421; Emily Bazelon, Yet Another Sexting Tragedy, Chicago Tribune, April 15, 2013, C15.

28. Genevra Pittman, "Sexting" Again Linked to Risky Sex Among Teens, Reuters, September 17, 2012, http://www.reuters.com/article/2012/09/17/us-sexting-again-linked-to-risky-sex-amo-idUSBRE88G0G220120917; "Sexting" Teens Found to Be Up to 82 Percent More Likely to Be Having Sex Compared to the Non-Sexting Teens, New York Daily News, July 4, 2012, http://www.nydailynews.com/life-style/health/sexting-teens-found-tos-82-sex-compared-non-sexting-teens-article-1.1107729#ixzz2buV0SPpz.

29. 2012 Sexting Legislation, National Conference of State Legislatures, December 14, 2012.

30. Joe Holley and Austin Bureau, State Senator's Bill Would Reduce Penalty for Teen Sexting, Houston Chronicle, February 7, 2011, http://www.chron.com/news/houston-texas/article/State-senator-s-bill-would-reduce-penalty-for-1,685,811.php.

31. Miller v. Mitchell, 598 F. 3d 139 (3d Cir. 2010).

32. Sean D. Hamill, Students Sue Prosecutor in Cellphone Photos Case, New York Times, March 26, 2009, at A18 (quoting Witold J. Walczak).

33. A. H. v. State, 949 So. 2d 234 (Fla. Dist. Ct. App. 2007).

34. Bazelon, Yet Another Sexting Tragedy, C15.

35. LiJia Gong and Alina Hoffman, Sexting and Slut-Shaming: Why Prosecution of Teen Self-Sexters Harms Women, Georgetown Journal of Gender and Law 13 (2012): 577.

36. Lynn E. Ponton and Samuel Judice, Typical Adolescent Sexual Development, Child Adolescent Psychiatric Clinics of North America 13 (2004): 497, 508. See Liz Kulze, Why Sexting Laws Are Part of the Problem, Atlantic, December 6, 2012.

37. Comments of Michael McAlexander, Chief Deputy, Prosecutor's Office, Allen County, PA, in "Sexting": Racy Teen Messaging Could Be Illegal, Talk of the Nation, NPR, February 18, 2009.

38. Jonathan Karl et al., Anthony Weiner Announces Resignation from Congress, ABC News, June 16, 2011, http://abcnews.go.com/Politics/anthony-weiner-resign-huma-abedin-return/story?id=13,855,468.

39. Exclusive Image: Anthony Weiner Penis Picture and Timeline, The Dirty, July 25, 2013, http://thedirty.com/2013/07/exclusive-image-anthony-weiner-penis-picture-and-timeline/; see also Mike Zapler and Katie Glueck, Anthony Weiner Kept Sexting after Resignation, Politico, July 24, 2013, http://www.politico.com/story/2013/07/anthony-weiner-apology-94,626.html.

40. Evann Gastaldo, 44 Celebrity Sexting Scandals, Newser, July 27, 2013, http://www.newser.com/story/171561/44-celebrity-sexting-scandals.html; Catharine Smith, 9 Controversial Sexting Scandals, Huffington Post, May 25, 2011, http://www.huffingtonpost.com/2010/03/27/controversial-sexting-pic_n_515,248.html#s75127title=Jesse_James.

41. For desires to marry, see Regnerus and Uecker, Premarital Sex, 169. For projections of marriages, see Andrew J. Cherlin, In the Season of Marriage, A Question: Why Bother?, New York Times, April 28, 2013, SR7. For the wedding industry, see Elizabeth Marquardt et al., The President's Marriage Agenda for the Forgotten Sixty Percent: The State of Our Unions Marriage in America (Charlottesville, VA: National Marriage Project and Institute for American Values, 2012), 1.

42. Aja Gabel, The Marriage Crisis, University of Virginia Magazine, Summer 2012.
43. Wendy Wang and Paul Taylor, Pew Research Center, For Millenials, Parenthood Trumps Marriage, March 9, 2011, http://www.pewsocialtrends.org/2011/03/09/for-millennials-parenthood-trumps-marriage/.
44. Meg Jay, The Downside of Cohabiting before Marriage, New York Times, April 14, 2012, SR4.
45. Casey Copen et al., First Premarital Cohabitation in the United States: 2006–2010 National Survey of Family Growth, National Health Statistics Reports, April 4, 2013.
46. For feminists' reservations about marriage, see Jessica Valenti, My Big Feminist Wedding, The Guardian, April 23, 2009, http://www.theguardian.com/lifeandstyle/2009/apr/24/feminist-wedding-jessica-valenti.
47. Jay, The Downside of Cohabiting.
48. Pew Research Center, The Public Renders a Split Verdict on Changes in Family Structure, February 16, 2011.
49. Jay, The Downside of Cohabiting.
50. Jay, The Downside of Cohabiting.
51. See Marsha Garrison and Elizabeth S. Scott, Legal Regulation of Twenty-First Century Families, in Marsha Garrison and Elizabeth S. Scott, Marriage at the Crossroads (New York: Cambridge University Press, 2012), 303, 307.
52. Sara S. McLanahan and Irwin Garfinkel, Fragile Families: Debates, Facts, and Solutions, in Garrison and Scott, Marriage at the Crossroads, 142.
53. Copen et al., First Premarital Cohabitation.
54. McLanahan and Garfinkel, Fragile Families, 147.
55. McLanahan and Garfinkel, Fragile Families, 152, 154; Kay Hymowitz, Jason S. Carroll, W. Bradford Wilcox, and Kelleen Kaye, Knot Yet: The Benefits and Costs of Delayed Marriage in America, The National Campaign to Prevent Teen and Unplanned Pregnancy, The Relate Institute, and The National Marriage Project at the University of Virginia (2012), 324; Carmen Solomon-Fears, Nonmarital Childbearing: Trends, Reasons, and Public Policy Interventions (Washington, D.C.: Congressional Research Service, 2008), 31. See generally Andrew J. Cherlin, The Marriage-Go-Round: The State of Marriage and the Family in America Today (New York: Knopf, 2009).
56. Garrison and Scott, Legal Regulation, 308; Paul R. Amato, The Impact of Family Formation Change on the Cognitive, Social, and Emotional Well-Being of the Next Generation, Future of Children 15 (2005): 75.
57. McLanahan and Garfinkel, Fragile Families,146.
58. See research summarized in Garrison and Scott, Legal Regulation, 309.
59. See research summarized in Garrison and Scott, Legal Regulation, 309.
60. Ralph Richard Banks, Is Marriage for White People: How the African American Marriage Decline Affects Everyone (New York: Dutton, 2011); Kathryn Edin and Maria Kefalas, Promises I Can Keep: Why Poor Women Put Motherhood Before Marriage (Berkeley: University of California Press, 2005).
61. Edin and Kefalas, Promises I Can Keep; Wendy Sigle Ruston and Sara McLanahan, Father Absence and Child Well-Being: A Critical Review, in Daniel P. Moynihan, Timothy M. Smeeding, and Lee Rainwater, eds., The Future of the Family (New York: Russell Sage Foundation, 2006), 116.
62. Banks, Is Marriage for White People?, 7.
63. Stephanie Coontz, Marriage Is Not Antidote to Poverty, CNN, September 10, 2012, http://www.cnn.com/2012/09/10/opinion/coontz-poverty-marriage.
64. Banks, Is Marriage for White People, 69.
65. Marquardt, The President's Marriage Agenda; Hymowitz, Carroll, Wilcox, and Kaye, Knot Yet.
66. Banks, Is Marriage for White People?, 21.
67. Banks, Is Marriage for White People?, 22.

68. Linda C. McClain, The Place of Families: Fostering Capacity, Equality, and Responsibility (Cambridge, MA: Harvard University Press, 2006), 122.

69. McLanahan and Garfinkel, Fragile Families, 161; Anupa Bir et al., The Community Healthy Marriage Initiative Evaluation: Impacts of a Community Approach to Strengthening Families (Washington, D.C.: Office of Planning Research and Evaluation, U.S. Department of Health and Human Services, November 2012): ES 7–9; 7–5.

70. Robert I. Lerman, Capabilities and Contributions of Unwed Fathers, Future of Children 20 (2010): 63, 74.

71. Carmen Solomon-Fears, Fatherhood Initiatives: Connecting Fathers to Their Children (Washington, D.C.: Congressional Research Service, 2012), 5–9. Philip A. Cowan, Carolyn Pape Cowan, and Virginia Knox, Marriage and Fatherhood Programs, The Future of Children 20 (2010): 205, 218.

72. Paul R. Amato, Institutional, Companionate, and Individualistic Marriages, in Garrison and Scott, Marriage at the Crossroads, 122–123.

73. McLanahan and Garfinkel, Fragile Families; McClain, The Place of Families; Martha Albertson Fineman, Progress and Progression in Family Law, University of Chicago Legal Forum (2004): 1; Nancy D. Polikoff, Beyond (Straight and Gay) Marriage (Boston, MA: Beacon Press, 2008); Melissa Murray, The Networked Family: Reframing the Legal Understanding of Caregiving and Caregivers, Virginia Law Review 94 (2008): 385.

74. McLanahan and Garfinkel, Fragile Families, 157.

75. Law Commission of Canada, Beyond Conjugality: Recognizing and Supporting Close Adult Personal Relationships (2001), 113.

76. Polikoff, Beyond Marriage, 116–118.

77. Polikoff, Beyond Marriage; McClain, The Place of Families; Laura Rosenbury, Friends with Benefits, Michigan Law Review 106 (2007): 189.

78. American Law Institute, Principles of the Law of Family Dissolution, Section 7.02, 954–957.

79. Ira Mark Ellman and Sanford L. Braver, Should Marriage Matter, in Marshal Garrison and Elizabeth S. Scott, Marriage at the Crossroads (New York: Cambridge University Press, 2012), 176.

80. Andrew J. Cherlin, Demographic Trends in the United States: A Review of Research in the 200s, Journal of Marriage and Family 72 (2020): 403; Gabel, The Marriage Crisis.

81. NBC News Wall Street Journal Survey, April, 2013.

82. Judith G. McMullen and Debra Oswald, Why Do We Need a Lawyer?: An Empirical Study of Divorce Cases, Journal of Law and Family Studies 12 (2010): 57, 75.

83. Katherine T. Bartlett, Deborah L. Rhode, and Joanna L. Grossman, Gender and Law: Theory, Doctrine, Commentary, 6th ed. (New York: Wolters Kluwer Press, 2013), 272.

84. Belinda Luscombe, The End of Alimony, Time, May 27, 2013, 48. For divorced women's greater likelihood of poverty, see Diana B. Elliott and Tavia Simmons, Marital Events of Americans 2009 (Washington D.C.: U.S. Census Bureau, 2011).

85. Mary K. Kisthardt, Rethinking Alimony: The AAML's Considerations for Calculating Alimony, Spousal Support, or Maintenance, Journal of American Academy of Matrimonial Law 21 (2008): 61, 64–65.

86. Judith Areen, Marc Spindelman and Philomila Tsoukala, Cases and Materials on Family Law, 6th ed. (New York: Foundation Press, 2012), 1095–1099.

87. Terry Martin Hekker, Paradise Lost (Domestic Division), New York Times, January 1, 2006.

88. Judith G. McMullen, Alimony: What Social Science and Popular Culture Tell Us about Women, Guilt, and Spousal Support after Divorce, Duke Journal of Gender, Law and Policy 19 (2011): 41.

89. Ira Mark Ellman and Sanford L. Braver, Lay Intuitions about Family Obligations: The Case of Alimony, Theoretical Inquiry 13 (2012): 209, 223. For actual cases, see McMullen and Oswald, Why Do We Need a Lawyer.

90. Ellman and Braver, Lay Intuitions, 230, 236.
91. Luscomb, The End of Alimony.
92. McMullen, Alimony, 78–80; Kisthardt, Rethinking Alimony, 78–79.
93. American Law Institute, Principles of the Law of Family Dissolution, Chapter 4 (2002).
94. http://www.ncsl.org/issues-research/human-services/same-sex-marriage-overview. aspx.
95. Hollingsworth v. Perry, 570 U.S. 183 (2013).
96. United States v. Windsor, 570 U.S. (2013).
97. NBC News Wall Street Journal Survey, April 2013; CNN/ORC poll, June 11–13, Polling Report.com. For 1990 figures, see Michael Klarman, From the Closet to the Altar: Courts, Backlash, and the Struggle for Same-Sex Marriage (New York: Oxford University Press, 2013), 218.
98. Daniel Denvir, David Boies on the Fight for Gay Marriage, Salon.com, June 27, 2010.
99. Maggie Gallagher, The Case Against Same Sex Marriage, in John Corvino and Maggie Gallagher, Debating Same-Sex Marriage (New York: Oxford University Press, 2012), 96, 97, 102.
100. In re Marriage Cases, 43 Cal 4th 757, 431 (Cal. 2008).
101. Goodridge v. Department of Health, 798 N.E. 2d 941, 945 (Mass. 2003).
102. Brief for the Petitioners in Hollingsworth v. Perry, 6.
103. In re Marriage Cases, 43 Ca. 4th 757, 451 (Cal. 2008).
104. Distributed by Gallagher's National Organization for Marriage; Corvino, The Case for Same-Sex Marriage, 85.
105. Evan Wolfson, Enough Marriage to Share: A Response to Maggie Gallagher, in Lynn D. Wardle et al., eds., Marriage and Same-Sex Unions: A Debate (Westport, CT: Praeger, 2003), 25–32.
106. Andrew Sullivan, Virtually Normal: An Argument about Homosexuality (New York: Picador, 1996), 202–203; Jonathan Rauch, Gay Marriage: Why It Is Good for Gays, Good for Straights, and Good for America (New York: Henry Holt, 2004), 94.
107. Maggie Gallagher, What Marriage Is For: Children Need Mothers and Fathers, Weekly Standard, August 4–11, 2003, 24.
108. R. U. Paige, Proceedings of the American Psychological Association, Incorporation, for the legislative year 2004, quoted in Corvino, The Case for Same-Sex Marriage, in Corvino and Gallagher, Debating Same-Sex Marriage, 47. That is the view of the American Psychological Association, the American Academy of Child and Adolescent Psychiatry, the Child Welfare League of America, and virtually every other major health and welfare organization and scholarly expert that has examined the data. Corvino, The Case for Same-Sex Marriage, 47. See Timothy J. Biblarz and Judith Stacey, How Does the Gender of Parents Matter? Journal of Marriage and Family 72 (2010): 3.
109. Goodridge v. Department of Public Health, 798 N.E. 2d 941 (2003).
110. Paula L. Ettelbrick, Since When Is Marriage a Path to Liberation, 2 Out/Look, National Gay and Lesbian Quarterly 9 (Fall 1989): 14.
111. According to a 2013 Pew Research poll, 60 percent of lesbian, gay, bisexual, and transgender adults are married or said they wanted to marry, compared with 76 percent of the general population. Cara Buckley, Choosing to Say "I Don't," New York Times, October 27, 2013.
112. Stephanie Schroeder, I Don't Want to Be Part of Your {de}volution, in Audrey Bilger and Michele Kort, eds., Here Come the Brides: Reflections on Lesbian Love and Marriage (Berkeley, CA: Seal Press, 2012), 113–114.
113. Katherine Franke, The Curious Relationship of Marriage and Freedom, in Garrison and Scott, Marriage at the Crossroads, 95.
114. Holly Hughes, I'm Not from Here, in Bilger and Kort, Here Come the Brides, 136.
115. Buckely, Choosing to Say "I Don't" (quoting Stephanie Schroeder).

116. Emily Douglas, We Have to Talk about It, Someday, in Bilger and Kort, Here Come the Brides, 131.
117. Linda Villarosa, Let Them Eat (Wedding Cake), in Bilger and Kort, Here Come the Brides, 119.
118. Polikoff, Beyond Marriage 208. The full statement is at http://www.beyondmarriage.org/full_statement.html.
119. Polikoff, Beyond Marriage, 210.
120. It's Already Happened, http://www.youtube.com/watch?v=7352ZVMKBQM.

Chapter 5

1. Roe v. Wade, 410 U.S. 113 (1973) 706.
2. Lawrence Lader Abortion II: Making the Revolution (Boston: Beacon, 1973), 65; Richard Schwarz, Septic Abortion (Philadelphia: Lippencott, 1968).
3. Deborah L. Rhode, Justice and Gender (Cambridge, MA: Harvard University Press, 1989), 208; Jack M. Balkin, ed., Roe v Wade: An Engine of Controversy, in Jack M. Balkin, What Roe v. Wade Should Have Said (New York: New York University Press, 2005), 6.
4. Roe v. Wade, 410 U.S. at 730.
5. Cass Sunstein, Comments, in Balkin, What Roe v. Wade Should Have Said, 248.
6. Allen Pusey, Ginsburg: Court Should Have Avoided Broad-Based Decision in Roe v. Wade, ABA Journal online, May 13, 2013; Paul Freund, Storms over the Supreme Court, American Bar Association Journal 69 (1983): 1474, 1480; David Brooks, Roe's Birth, and Death, New York Times, April 21, 2005; sources cited in Linda Greenhouse and Reva B. Siegel, Before (and After) Roe v. Wade: New Questions about Backlash, Yale Law Journal 120 (2011): 2029, 2073–2075.
7. John Hart Ely, The Wages of Crying Wolf, A Comment on *Roe v. Wade*, Yale Law Journal 82 (1973): 920–949.
8. Rhode, Justice and Gender, 210.
9. Ruth Bader Ginsburg, Some Thoughts on Autonomy and Equality in Relation to Roe v. Wade, North Carolina Law Review 63 (1984): 375, Reva Siegel, Reasoning from the Body: A Historical Perspective on Abortion Regulation and Questions of Equal Protection, Stanford Law Review 44 (1992): 261.
10. Siegel, Reasoning from the Body, 370.
11. Robin West, The Supreme Court 1989 Term, Foreword: Taking Freedom Seriously, Harvard Law Review 104 (1990): 43, 85.
12. Balkin, Roe v Wade, 23.
13. Robert Post and Reva Siegel, *Roe* Rage: Democratic Constitutionalism and Backlash, Harvard Civil Rights and Civil Liberties Law Review 42 (2007): 373, 410.
14. Post and Siegel, *Roe* Rage, 418; Greenhouse and Siegel, Before (and After) Roe v. Wade, 2077–2080; Linda Gordon: The Moral Property of Women: A History of Birth Control Politics in America, 3rd ed. (Urbana: University of Illinois Press, 2002), 300; Pamela Johnston Conover, The Mobilization of the New Right: A Test of Various Explanations, Western Political Quarterly 36 (1983): 632, 634–635.
15. Drew Halfmann, Doctors and Demonstrators: How Political Institutions Shape Abortion Law in the United States, Britain and Canada (Chicago: University of Chicago Press, 2011), 210–212. See also Gene Burns, The Moral Veto: Framing Contraception Abortion, and Cultural Pluralism in the United States (Cambridge: Cambridge University Press, 2005).
16. Halfmann, Doctors and Demonstrators, 129. See also Ricki Sollinger, Reproductive Politics: What Everyone Needs to Know (Oxford University Press, 2013).

17. Sarah Erdreich, Generation Roe: Inside the Future of the Pro-Choice Movement (New York: Seven Stories Press, 2013), 149.

18. Kate Pickert, What Choice? Abortion-Right Activists Won an Epic Victory in Roe v. Wade. They've Been Losing Ever Since, Time, January 14, 2013, 41.

19. Eyal Press, My Father's Abortion War, New York Times Magazine, January 22, 2006, 59.

20. Amanda Robb, Bringing Abortion Back to Wichita, Ms., Winter, 2013, 12, 13; Mathew Burgoyne, The Means to a Wichita Abortion, Ms., Spring 2011, 15.

21. Eve Spey et al., Abortion Education in Medical Schools: A National Suervey, American Journal of Obstetrics and Gynecology 192 (2005): 640.

22. Erdreich, Generation Roe, 48; Rene Almeling et al., Abortion Training in U.S. Obstetrics and Gynecology Residency Programs, Family Planning Perspectives 32 (2000): 268; Sarah Kliff, Has Violence Deterred Doctors from Performing Abortions? Washington Post, March 6, 2012.

23. Lori Freedman, Uta Landy, Philip Darney, and Jody Steinauer, Obstacles to the Integration of Abortion into Obstetrics and Gynecology Pracitce, Perspectives on Sexual and Reproductive Health 42 (2010): 146.

24. Ian Lovett, California Expands Availability of Abortions, New York Times, October 10, 2013.

25. Pickert, What Choice, 40; Erdreich, Generation Roe, 48.

26. Rachel Benson Gold and Elizabeth Nash, Troubling Trend: More States Hostile to Abortion Rights as Middle Ground Shrinks, Guttmacher Policy Review, Winter 2012; http:www.guttmacher.org/pubs/gpr/15/1/gpr150114.html; L. I. Jackson, A Right-to-Life Movement Reborn, American Bar Association Journal, August 2011, 20.

27. Planned Parenthood of Southeastern Pennsylvania v. Casey, 505 U.S. 833 (1992).

28. See Guttmacher Institute, Counseling and Waiting Periods for Abortion (2012).

29. Associated Press, Planned Parenthood Sues over New Kansas Abortion Law, June 20, 2013, http://www.usatoday.com/story/news/nation/2013/06/20/planned-parethood-lawsuit/2443059.

30. Guttmacher Institute, Counseling and Waiting Periods for Abortion; Jenifer Y. Seo, Raising the Standard of Abortion Informed Consent: Lessons to Be Learned from the Ethical and Legal Requirements for Consent to Medical Experimentation, Columbia Journal of Law and Gender 21 (2011): 357; Erdreich, Generation Roe, 121. See Harper Jean Tobin, Confronting Misinformation on Abortion: Informed Consent, Deference, and Fetal Pain Laws, Columbia Journal of Gender and Law 17 (2008): 112.

31. David Bailey, Appeals Court Upholds South Dakota Abortion Law's Suicide Advisory, Reuters, July 24, 2012, http://www.reuters.com/article/2012/07/24/us-usa-abortion-southdakota-idUSBRE86N1DM20120724. Joerg Dreweke, Study Purporting to Show Link Between Abortion and Mental Health Outcomes Decisively Debunked, (Guttmacher Institute, March 5, 2012), http://www.guttmacher.org/media/nr/2012/03/05/index.html.; Vignetta E. Charles, Abortion and Long Term Mental Health Outcomes: A Systematic Review of the Evidence, Contraception 78 (2008): 436.

32. Solinger, Reproductive Politics, 81.

33. Robert Post, Informed Consent to Abortion: A First Amendment Analysis of Compelled Physician Speech, University of Illinois Law Review (2007): 939; Reva B. Siegel, Dignity and Politics of Protection: Abortion Restrictions under Casey/Carhart, Yale Law Journal 117 (2008): 1694, 1758.

34. Katherine T. Bartlett, Deborah L. Rhode, and Joanna Grossman, Gender and Law: Theory, Doctrine, Commentary (New York: Aspen, 2013), 713; Nancy Gibbs, 1 Woman at a Time, Time, February 25, 2007, 25, 28.

35. Guttmacher Institute, State Policies in Brief: Requirements for Ultrasound (May 2012).

36. Bartlett, Rhode, and Grossman, Gender and Law, 713; Nicholas Kristof, When States Abuse Women, New York Times, March 23, 2012, SR 11.

37. Mary Tuma, Can You Hear Us Now? Ms., Summer 2013, 13.
38. Carole King, War on Women Rages On, Ms., Spring 2013, 13 (describing laws in six states).
39. Abortion Bill Passes General Assembly, Heads to McCroy, WNCN, July 26, 2013, http://www.wncn.com/story/22934322/abortion-legislation-pending-for-nc-lawmakers.
40. Tuma, Can You Hear Us Now, 13.
41. Erdreich, Generation Roe, 65.
42. Theodore Joyce et al., The Impact of Mississippi's Mandatory Delay Law on Abortions and Births, Journal of American Medical Association 278 (1997): 653, 655; Theodore Joyce and Robert Kaestner, The Impact of Mississippi's Mandatory Delay Law on the Timing of Abortion, Family Planning Perspectives 32 (2000): 4.
43. Guttmacher Institute, State Funding of Abortion under Medicaid (2012).
44. That prohibition will be carried forward under the new health care reform act. Halfmann, Doctors and Demonstrators, 192.
45. McCrae v. Califano, 491 F. Supp. 630, 668–690 (E.D.N.Y. 1980); Harris v. McCrae, 448 U.S. 297 354–355 (1980) (Stevens, J., dissenting); Harrus v. McCrae at 345 (Marshall, J., dissenting).
46. Executive Order No. 13.535, 75 Federal Register 15.5909 (March 24, 2010).
47. Guttmacher Insittute, Restricting Insurance Coverage of Abortion (2012).
48. Rhode, Speaking of Sex, 205.
49. Allison Stevens, Hyde's Exit Leaves His Amendment Open to Challenge, Women's eNews, January 7, 2007; American Civil Liberties Union, Public Funding for Abortion (2004).
50. For a description of initiatives, see the Personhood USA website, at http://www.personhoodusa.com.
51. Holly Derr, Voting for Sanity, Ms., Winter 2012, 15.
52. Guttmacher Institute, State Policies in Brief: State Policies on Later Abortions (2012).
53. Other reasons include difficulty making arrangements (often due to restrictive abortion laws), and fear of telling parents or partners. Stephanie Pappas, Study Reveals Who Gets Late-Term Abortions, December 16, 2011, at http://www.livescience.com/17529-trimester-abortions.html.
54. Gonzales v. Carhart, 550 U.S. 124 (2007).
55. 550 U.S. at 1647 (Ginsburg, J., dissenting).
56. 550 U.S. at 1634.
57. Jack Balkin, Gonzales v. Carhart—Three Comments, Balkinization, April 18, 2007.
58. David Reardon, Politically Correct vs. Politically Smart: Why Politicians Should be Both Pro-Woman and Pro-Life, Post Abortion Review 2 (Fall 1994): 3.
59. Doe v. Bolton, 410 U.S. 1279, 221 (White, J., dissenting).
60. Phyllis Schlafly, Principle or Pragmatism? Abortion Politics in the Twenty-First Century, in Teresa R. Wagner, Back to the Drawing Board: The Future of the Pro Life Movement (South Bend, IN: St. Augustine Press, 2003), 163.
61. James C. Dobson, Letter to the Troops: The Grassroots of the Pro-Life Movement, in Theresa R. Wagner, ed., Back to the Drawing Board, 205.
62. Jessica Wadkins, Reaching Abortions' Second Victims, Faamily Voice, January, 1999, 2.
63. David C. Reardon, Making Abortion Rare: A Healing Strategy for a Divided Nation (Springfield: Acorn Books, 1996), 26–27.
64. Ronee Schreiber Righting Feminism, Conservative Women and American Politics (New York: Oxford University Press, 2008), 98–101; Joshua Lang, Unintentional Motherhood, New York Times Magazine, June 16, 2013, 45.
65. Reva B. Siegel, The New Politics of Abortion: An Equality Analysis of Woman Protective Abortion Restrictions, University of Illinois Law Review (2007): 991, 1008, discussing Report of the South Dakota Task Force to Study Abortion (2005).
66. Task Force Report, 38.
67. Task Force Report, 21, 38.

68. Task Force Report, 31–32, 21.

69. Task Force Report, 47–48.

70. Because the majority refused to include the views of the minority in the Task Force Report, the minority separately published its views. South Dakota Task Force to Study Abortion, Report of Minority (2006), 26–27.

71. Pickert, What Choice, 40, 42 (citing 2012 Gallup poll and Guttmacher Institute projection). Other polls find only 15 percent favor outlawing abortion in all circumstances. Nancy L. Cohen, Delirium: How the Sexual Revolution Is Polarizing America (Berkeley, CA: Counterpoint, 2012), 355.

72. Katha Pollitt, Choice Words, The Nation, February 4, 2013, 9 (citing polls).

73. Katha Pollitt, If the Frame Fits, Nation, June 23, 2005 (quoting Lakoff).

74. Lawrence B. Finer et al., Reasons U.S. Women Have Abortions: Quantitative and Qualitative Perspectives, Perspectives on Sexual and Reproductive Health 37 (2005): 110, 112.

75. Changing Language on Choice, The Public Affairs Pulse, Planned Parenthood Newsletter, February, 2013, 1; For the new campaign, see notinhershoes.org.

76. Krisitin Rowe-Finkbeiner, The F-Word: Feminism in Jeopardy (Emeryville, CA: Seal Press, 2004), 53.

77. Pew Research Center, January 9–13, 2013, http://www.pewforum.org/Abortion/roe-v-wade-at-40.aspx.

78. Gallup Poll, May 2–7, 2013, http://www.pollingreport.com/abortion.html.

79. NBC News/Wall Street Journal Poll, January 12–15, 2013, http://www.pollingreport.com/abortion.htm (70 percent); Pew Research Center, January 9–13, 2013, http://www.pewforum.org/Abortion/roe-v-wade-at-40.aspx (63 percent).

80. Roe v. Wade at 40: Most Oppose Overturning Abortion Decision, January 16, 2013, http://www.pewforum.org/Abortion/roe-v-wade-at-40.aspx.

81. Pew Research Center, Roe v. Wade at 40: Most Oppose Overturning Abortion Decision, January 16, 2013, http://www.pewforum.org/Abortion/roe-v-wade-at-40.aspx

82. Commencement Address, Notre Dame University, May 17, 2009, at http://www.nytimes.com/2009/05/17/us/politics/17text-obama.html?pagewanted=all.

83. McNight v. State, 661 S.E. 2d 354, 358 n. 10 (S. C. 2008).

84. Linda Fentimen, In the Name of Fetal Protection: Why American Prosecutors Pursue Pregnant Drug Users (and Other Countries Don't), Columbia Journal of Gender and Law 18 (2009): 647.

85. Linda C. Fentimen, Rethinking Addiction: Drugs, Deterrence and the Neuroscience Revolution, University of Pennsylvania Journal of Law and Social Change, 14 (2011): 233, 237.

86. Lynn Paltrow and Jeanne Flavin, Arrests of and Forced Interventions on Pregnant Women in the United States, 1973–2005: Implications for Women's Legal Status and Public Health, Journal of Health Politics, Policy and Law 38 (2013): 299, 321.

87. Mo. Ann. Stat 1.205 (West 2011); Paltrow and Falvin, Arrests of Women, 324.

88. Ada Calhoun, The Criminalization of Bad Mothers, New York Times Magazine, April 25, 2012.

89. Guttmacher Institute, State Policies in Brief: Substance Abuse During Pregnancy (January, 1, 2013).

90. Erik Eckhom, Case Explores Rights of Fetus Versus Mother, New York Times, October 23, 2013, A1.

91. Department of Health and Human Services, Results from the 2010 National Survey on Drug Use and Health: Summary of National Findings (2010), 20, 29, 43.

92. Susan Okie, Crack Babies: The Epidemic That Wasn't, New York Times, January 27, 2009; Calhoun, Criminalization of Bad Mothers. See also Michael Winerip, Revisiting the "Crack Babies" Epidemic That Was Not, New York Times (May 20, 2013). Deborah A. Frank et al., Growth, Development and Behavior in Early Childhood Following

Prenatal Cocaine Exposure: A Systematic Review, Journal of the American Medical Association 285 (2001):1613, 1613–164.

93. Paltrow and Flavin, Arrests, 315.

94. Dorothy E. Roberts, Race and the New Reproduction, Hastings Law Journal 47 (1996): 935, 947–948; Drug Policy Alliance, Fact Sheet: Women, Prison and the Drug War (2013).

95. Oren Yaniv, Weed Out: More Than a Dozen City Maternity Wards Regularly Test New Moms for Marijuana and Other Drugs, New York Daily News, December 25, 2012.

96. National Advocates for Pregnant Women, Medical and Public Health Statements Addressing Prosecution and Punishment of Pregnant Women, February 22, 2011, http://advocatesforpregnantwomen.org/medical_group_opinions_2011/Medical%20Group%20Positions%202011.pdf.

97. National Advocates for Pregnant Women; see also American College of Obstetricians and Gynecologists, Committee on Ethics, Committee Opinion 321, Maternal Decision Making, Ethics and the Law, Obstetrics and Gynecology 106 (2005):1, 9. American Medical Association Board of Trustees, Legal Interventions during Pregnancy, Journal of the American Medical Association 264 (1990): 2663, 2667; American Academy of Pediatrics, Committee on Substance Abuse, Drug Exposed Infants, Pediatrics 96 (1995): 364, 366–367 ("punitive measures taken toward pregnant women, such as criminal prosecution and incarceration, have no proven benefits for infant health").

98. Emily Figdor and Lisa Keser, Concerns Mount over Punitive Approaches to Substance Abuse among Pregnant Women (New York: Guttmacher Institute, October, 1998), 4.

99. Julie B. Ehrlich and Lynn Paltrow, Jailing Pregnant Women Raises Health Risks, Women's enews, September 20, 2006; Wendy Chavkin, Mandatory Treatment for Drug Use during Pregnancy, Journal of American Medical Association 266 (1991): 1559; The Rebecca Project for Human Rights, Mothers behind Bars (October 2010), 6.

100. Paltrow and Flavin, Arrests, 332.

101. Bartlett, Rhode, and Grossman, Gender and Law, 757.

102. Rachel Roth, Making Women Pay: The Hidden Costs of Fetal Rights (Ithaca, NY: Cornell University Press, 2000), 140.

103. Alcohol Drug Abuse and Mental Health Administration Reorganization Act, 106 Stat. 323, codified as amended in 42 U.S.C.A. Sections 202 300 (West Supplement 2012).

104. Vicki Toscano, Misguided Retribution: Criminalization of Pregnant Women Who Take Drugs, Social and Legal Studies 14 (2005): 360, 364–365 (funding); Julie B. Ehrlich, Breaking the Law by Giving Birth: The War on Drugs, the War on Reproductive Rights, and the War on Women, New York Review of Law and Social Change 32 (2011): 381, 419.

105. Jean Reith Schroedel and Pamela Fiber, Punitive versus Public Use by Pregnant Women, Yale Journal of Health Policy, Law, and Ethics 1 (0012): 217; Guttmacher Institute, State Policies in Brief.

106. A useful model is Kaiser Permanente's Early Start Program which coordinates substance abuse treatment with prenatal care. N. C. Goler, Substance Abuse Treatment Linked with Prenatal Visits Improves Perinatal Outcomes: A New Standard, Journal of Perinatology 28 (2008): 597.

107. Griswold v. Connecticut, 381 U.S. 479 (1965).

108. Brian Stelter, Facing Outcry, Limbaugh Apologizes for Attacking Student over Birth Control, New York Times, March 4, 2012, 17.

109. Calvin Trillin, Contraception (of All Things), The Nation, March 26, 2012.

110. Ethan Branner, A Flood of Suits Fights Coverage of Birth Control, New York Times, January 27, 2013, A11.

111. Sebelius v. Hobby Lobby Stores (docket number 13–354) and Conestoga Wood Specialties Corp. v. Sebelius (docket number 13–356). For an argument that the contraceptive coverage mandate does not violate the constitution's Free Exercise Clause or the Religious Freedom Restoration Act, see Kathryn S. Benedict, When Might Does Not Create

Religious Rights: For-Profit Corporations' Employees and the Contraceptive Coverage Mandate, Columbia Journal of Gender and Law 26 (2013): 58.

112. Katha Pollit, Women: The Bus Rolls On, The Nation, May 2, 2011, 12 (quoting Kyl).
113. Pollitt, Women, 12 (quoting Beck and citing figures).
114. Katha Pollitt, Ban Birth Control? They Wouldn't Dare, The Nation, October 24, 2012, 10.
115. Katha Pollitt, Birth Control: Yesterday, Today, and Tomorrow, The Nation, August 15/22, 2011 (quoting Raymond Wieczorek).
116. Hillary Hammel, Is the Right to Health a Necessary Precondition to Gender Equality? New York University Review of Law and Social Change 35 (2011); 131, 181.
117. Tom W. Smith, American Sexual Behavior Trends, Socio-Demographic Differences, and Risk Behaviors (Chicago, IL.: National Opinion Research Center, 2003): 7.
118. Elizabeth Rosenthal, Is It Time for Off-the-Shelf Birth Control Pills? New York Times, April 21, 2013, SR 4.
119. The American College of Obstetricians and Gynecologists—Committee on Gynecologic Practice, Committee Opinion: Over the Counter Access to Contraceptives, 544 (December 2012).
120. Shari Roan, U.S. Teen Pregnancy Rate Remains Highest in Developed World, Los Angeles Times, January 19, 2012; Planned Parenthood, Pregnancy and Childbearing among U.S. Teens, (2010), http:www.plannedparenthood.org/files/PPFA/pregnancy_ teens_2010-01.pdf.
121. 42 U.S.C. Section 710(b)(2) (2012).
122. Rhode, Speaking of Sex, 210 (quoting Jeremiah Denton and Orrin Hatch, and Rush Limbaugh).
123. Rhode, Speaking of Sex, 210. One federal court struck down a Louisiana program for including religious material in violation of the First Amendment's requirement of separation between church and state. ACLU of Louisiana v. Foster, 2002 U.S. Dist. LEXIS 13778 (July 24, 2002).
124. Minority Staff, Committee on Government Reform, United States House of Representatives, The Content of Federally Funded Abstinence-Only Education Programs (2004); Christopher Trenholm et al., Mathematica Policy Research, Inc., Impacts of Four Title Vi, Section 510 Abstinence Programs Final Report 17 (2007), http://www.mathematica-mpr.com/publications/pdfs/impactabstinence.pdf.
125. Minority Staff, Abstinence-Only Education Programs, 1.
126. Erdreich, Generation Roe, 193; Douglas Kirby, National Campaign to Prevent Teen and Unplanned Pregnancy, Emerging Answers: Research Findings on Programs to Reduce Teen Pregnancy and Sexually Transmitted Diseases (2007), 15–16.
127. Michelle Fine and Sara I. McClelland, The Politics of Teen Women's Sexuality: Public Policy and the Adolescent Female Body, Emory Law Journal 56 (2007): 993, 1000.
128. Julie F. Kay, What's Not Being Said about Sex and Who It's Hurting, http://www.americanprogress.org/issues/education/news/2008/03/27/4082/whats-not-being-said-about-sex-and-who-its-hurting/.
129. Fine and McClelland, The Politics of Teen Women's Sexuality, 1006; Jessica Valenti, Full Frontal Feminism (Emeryville: Seal Press, 2007), 23.
130. 42 U.S.C. Section 710(b)(2) (2012).
131. Guttmacher Institute, An Overview of Minor's Consent Laws (2013); Rachel Rebouche, Parental Involvement Law and New Governance, Harvard Journal of Law and Gender 34 (2011): 175, 179–183.
132. Belllotti v. Baird, 443 U.S. 622 (1979).
133. Sources cited in Rhode, Speaking of Sex, 206.
134. Sources cited in Fine and McClelland, The Politics of Teen Women's Sexuality, 1022–1023; Rhode, Speaking of Sex, 206.
135. Sources cited in Fine and McClelland, The Politics of Teen Women's Sexuality, 1019; Rhode, Speaking of Sex, 206.

136. Sources cited in Fine and McClelland, The Politics of Teen Women's Sexuality, 1020–1021.

137. Rachel Rebouche, Parental Involvement Laws and New Governance, 188. See also Helena Silverstein and Leanne Speitel, "Honey I Have No Idea"; Court Readiness to Handle Petitions to Waive Parental Consent for Abortion, Iowa Law Review 88 (2002): 75.

138. Helena Silverstein and Kathryn Alessi, Religious Establishment in Hearings to Waive Parental Consent for Abortion, University of Pennsylvania Journal of Constitutional Law 7 (2004): 473, 475.

139. Rhode, Speaking of Sex, 206.

140. Rebouche, Parental Involvement, 189–191.

141. Helena Silverstein and Leanne Speitel, "Honey, I Have No Idea": Court Readiness to Handle Petitions to Waive Parental Consent for Abortion, Iowa Law Review 88 (2002): 75, 107.

142. Sliverstein and Speitel, "Honey, I Have No Idea," 94–100.

143. Silverstein and Speitel, "Honey, I Have No Idea," 101.

144. Silverstein and Speitel, "Honey, I Have No Idea," 102–103.

145. Rhode, Speaking of Sex, 210.

146. National Campaign to Prevent Teen and Unplanned Pregnancy, Why It Matters: Teen Childbearing, Education, and Economic Wellbeing, http://www.thenationalcampaign. org/why-it-matters/pdf/Childbearing-Education-EconomicWellbeing.pdf.

147. Planned Parenthood, Pregnancy and Childbearing; Saul D. Hoffman and Rebecca A. Maynard, The Study, the Context, and the Findings in Brief, in Saul D. Hoffman and Rebecca A. Maynard, eds., Kids Having Kids: Economic Costs and Social Consequences, 2nd ed. (New York: Urban Institute Press, 2008), 12, 16, 17, 22; Rebecca A. Maynard and Saul D. Hoffman, The Costs of Adolescent Childbearing, in Hoffman and Maynard, eds., Kids Having Kids, 386.

148. Melissa S. Kearney and Phillip B. Levine, Why Is the Teen Birth Rate in the United States So High and Why Does It Matter? Journal of Economic Perspectives 26 (2012):141, 142 (arguing that teen birth itself does not have much direct economic consequence but is a continuation of a "low economic trajectory").

149. Kearney and Levine, Why Is the Teen Birth Rate in the United States So High, 142.

150. Nicholas D. Kristof, Profiting from a Child's Illiteracy, New York Times, December 9, 2012, SR 9.

151. United States Census Bureau, Income, Poverty and Health Insurance Coverage in the United States, 2011 (Washington, D.C.: Government Printing Office, 2012), 15.

152. U. S. Census Bureau, Income, Poverty, and Health Insurance Coverage, 16–17.

153. National Women's Law Center, Insecure and Unequal: Poverty and Income among Women and Families, 2000–2011 (2012), 3.

154. King v. Smith 392 U.S. 309, 321 (discussing moral character requirements); Mimi Abramovitz, Regulating the Lives of Women: Social Welfare Policy from Colonial Times to the Present, rev. ed. (Boston: South End Press, 1996), 201; Gwendolyn Mink, The Wages of Motherhood: Inequality in the Welfare State (Ithaca, NY: Cornell University Press, 1995), 143–145. See generally Linda Gordon, Pitied but Not Entitled: Single Mothers and the History of Welfare (New York: Free Press, 1994).

155. For discussion, See Jasmin Sethi, Lessons for Social Scientists and Politicians: An Analysis of Welfare Reform, Georgetown Journal on Poverty Law and Policy, 17 (2010): 5, 12.

156. Charles Murray, Losing Ground: American Social Policy 1950–1980 (New York: Basic Books, 1984), at 154–162, 178–181.

157. Marissa Chappell, The War on Welfare: Family, Poverty, and Policies in Modern America (2010), 247.

158. Bartlett, Rhode, and Grossman, Gender and Law, 769.

159. Peter Edelman, So Rich, So Poor: Why It's So Hard to End Poverty in America (New York: The New Press, 2012), 4.

160. U.S. Census Bureau, Income, Poverty and Health Insurance Coverage, 13; Edelman, So Rich, So Poor, xiii; Robert Pear and Erik Eckholm, A Decade after Welfare Overhaul, a Fundamental Shift in Policy and Perception, New York Times, August 21, 2006, at 12.

161. National Poverty Center, Extreme Poverty in the United States, 1996–2011 (February 2012), 2.

162. Amy Goldstein, Welfare Rolls See First Climb in Years, Washington Post, December 17, 2008, at A1; Molly Hennessy-Fiske, Middle-Class Jobless Run into a Welfare Wall, L.A. Times, March 26, 2009, at A1.

163. H. Luke Scaefer and Kathryn Edin, Extreme Poverty in the United States, 1996–2011 (National Poverty Center, February, 2012)1, 3.

164. Sethi, Lessons for Social Scientists and Politicians, 6.

165. For poverty and unemployment rates, see Diana Spatz, The End of Welfare as I Knew It, Nation, January 2, 2012, at 22.

166. Diana Brazzell, Welfare Reform at 15, The Policy Brief, August 25, 2011, http://thepolicybrief.wordpress.com/2011/08/25/welfare-reform-at-15/.

167. Jake Blumgart, Happy Birthday, Welfare Reform, American Prospect, August 19, 2011.

168. Timothy Casey and Laurie Maldonado, Worst-Off-Single Parent Families in the United States (New York: Legal Momentum, December, 2012), 25.

169. Mark R. Rank, Poverty in America is Mainstream, New York Times, November 3, 2013, SR12.

170. Organization for Economic Cooperation and Development, Poverty Rates and Gaps, in OECD Factbook 2013: Economic, Environmental and Social Statistics (Paris: OECD, 2013); Timothy Casey, Too Little Progress: Reflections on Poverty in the United States on the Fiftieth Anniversary of President Johnson's Declaration of a War on Poverty (New York: Legal Momentum, 2014).

171. Legal Momentum, Welfare Reform at Age 15, A Vanishing Safety Net for Women and Children, April, 2011, at 7, http://www.legalmomentum.org/our-work/women-and-poverty/resources--publications/welfare-reform-15.pdf.

172. Chappell, The War on Welfare, 245; Legal Momentum, Welfare Reform.

173. Shawn Fremstad, Recent Welfare Reform Research Findings, Center on Budget and Policy Priorities, at 5 (January 20, 2004), http://www.cbpp.org/1-30-04wel.pdf (citing studies).

174. Dorothy E. Roberts, Welfare Reform and Economic Freedom: Low Income Mothers' Decisions about Work at Home and in the Market, Santa Clara Law Review 44 (2004): 1029, 1044.

175. Noah Zatz, What Welfare Requires from Work, UCLA Law Review 54 (2006): 373, 415 (citing state definitions); Juliette Terzieff, Welfare Clock Should Stop for College Moms (noting that only 10 percent of single mothers hold a degree and number has dropped since reform); Avis Jones-DeWeever et al., Before and After Welfare Reform: The Work and Well-Being of Low-Income Single Parent Families, Institute for Women's Policy Research (2003), at x–xi; http://www.iwpr.org/publications/pubs/before-and-after-welfare-reform-the-work-and-well-being-of-low-income-single-parent-families.

176. Richard Wolf, How Welfare Reform Changed America: 10 Years Later, Success Stories Common but Many Families Still Struggle to Get By, USA Today, July 18, 2006, A1. See also Kaaryn S. Gustafson, Public Assistance and the Criminalization of Poverty 124–145 (2011).

177. Gustafson, Public Assistance, 67–69, 141, 143, 160.

178. Roberts, Welfare Reform, 1047–1048.

179. Pamela Morris et al., Effects of Welfare Reform and Employment Policies on Young Children (Ann Arbor, Society for Research in Child Development, 2005).

180. Nina Berstein, Daily Choice Turned Deadly, Children Left on Their Own, New York Times, October 19, 2003, A1.

181. Pear and Eckholm, A Decade after Welfare Overhaul, 12; Erik Eckholm, A Welfare Law Milestone Finds Many Left Behind, New York Times, August 22, 2006, at 13; Rebecca

M. Blank, Improving the Safety Net for Single Mothers Who Face Serious Barriers to Work, The Future of Children 17 (Fall 2007): 183, 184.

182. Jason DeParle, American Dream (New York: Penguin, 2005), 338, discussed in Bartlett, Rhode, and Grossman, Gender and Law, 771.

183. Blumgart, Happy Birthday.

184. Arthur Delaney, Food Stamp Cuts Set to Kick In, Congress Not Paying Attention, Huffington Post, July 29, 2013, http://www.huffingtonpost.com/2013/07/29/food-stamp-cuts_n_3671142.html.

185. Michael D. Shear, In Signing Farm Bill, Obama Extols Rural Growth, New York Times, February 7, 2014.

186. Sarah Selzer, We Are the Many, Not the Few, Ms., Winter 2012, at 34.

187. Hendrik Hertzberg, Occupational Hazards, The New Yorker, November 7, 2011, at 24 (summarizing a 2011 report of the Congressional Budget Office).

188. Rob Reich and Debra Satz, Ethics and Inequality, Boston Review, November 28, 2011, http://www.bostonreview.net/br-book/occupy-future.

189. Ryan Messmore, Justice, Inequality and the Poor, National Affairs 10 (2012); 108, 117.

190. Edelman, So Rich, So Poor, 161.

191. Julia B. Isaacs, Isabel V. Sawhill, and Ron Haskins, Getting Ahead or Losing Ground: Economic Mobility in America, The Brookings Institution, February 2008, at 19, http://www.pewstates.org/uploadedFiles/PCS_Assets/2008/PEW_EMP_GETTING_AHEAD_FULL(2).pdf; Rana Foroohar, Whatever Happened to Upward Mobility, Time, November 14, 2011, at 28.

192. Bryan Montopoli, Poll: 43 percent agree with views of "Occupy Wall Street," CBS News, October 25, 2011, http://www.cbsnews.com/8301-503544_162-20125515-503544/poll-43-percent-agree-with-views-of-occupy-wall-street/?tag=cbsnewsMainColumnArea.

193. Edelman, So Rich, So Poor, 31.

194. Greg Kaufmann, Welfare Reform—From Bad to Worse, Week in Poverty March 9, 2012. http://www.thenation.com/blog/166705/week-poverty-welfare-reform-bad-worse.

195. Laura Flanders, Demanding Women, The Nation, February 19, 2013, 22.

196. Kaufman, Welfare Reform.

197. Sheila Bapat, Maximizing the Minimum, Ms., Winter/Spring, 2014, 13.

198. National Employment Law Project, Which States Provide Minimum Wage and Overtime to Home Care Workers? (Washington, D.C., 2012).

199. Edelman, So Rich, So Poor, 73–74.

200. Edelman, So Rich, So Poor, 35.

201. For examples, see Women Occupy, A Space to Connect, Share, Learn and Build, http://www.womenocupy.org/ and The Women's Economic Agenda project, http://weap.org/.

202. Institute for Women's Policy Research, National Committee to Preserve Social Security and Medicare Foundation, NOW Foundation, Breaking the Social Security Glass Ceiling, A Proposal to Modernize Women's Benefits (Washington, D.C.: National Committee to Preserve Social Security and Medicare Foundation, 2012).

203. Institute for Women's Policy Research, National Committee to Preserve Social Security and Medicare Foundation, and NOW Foundation, Breaking the Social Security Glass Ceiling, 9.

204. Institute for Women's Policy Research, Six Key Facts on Women and Social Security (Washington, D.C.: Institute for Women's Policy Research, 2011), 2.

205. Annual Report of the Board of Trustees of the Old Age and Survivors Insurance and Disability Insurance Trust Funds (Washington, D.C., 2011), 91.

206. Institute for Women's Policy Research, National Committee to Preserve Social Security and Medicare Foundation, and NOW Foundation, Breaking the Social Security Glass Ceiling, 4.

207. For a comprehensive account, see Institute for Women's Policy Research, National Committee to Preserve Social Security and Medicare Foundation, and NOW Foundation, Breaking the Social Security Glass Ceiling.

208. For examples, see Institute for Women's Policy Research, National Committee to Preserve Social Security and Medicare Foundation, and NOW Foundation, Breaking the Social Security Glass Ceiling.

209. Peter Edelman, Poverty in America: Why Can't We End It, New York Times, July 28, 2012, SR5 (quoting Ronald Reagan).

Chapter 6

1. See 29 C.F.R. section 1604.11 (1985); Meritor Savings Bank v. Vinson, 477 U.S. 57 (1986).

2. Catharine A. MacKinnon, Afterward, in Catharine A. MacKinnon and Reva B. Siegel, eds., Directions in Sexual Harassment Law (New Haven, CT: Yale University Press, 2004), 673.

3. Joanna Grossman, The Culture of Compliance: The Final Triumph of Form over Substance in Sexual Harassment Law, Harvard Women's Law Journal 26 (2003): 3, 5–7.

4. See research cited in Grossman, The Culture of Compliance, 6; Society for Human Research Management, Sexual Harassment Survey (1999), 5 (81 percent of complaints involve female complainants and male perpetrators, 9 percent the opposite, and 10 percent same-sex harassment); Dana Mattioli, More Men Make Harassment Claims, Wall Street Journal, March 23, 2010, D4 (about 84 percent of EEOC complaints are by women).

5. Katharine T. Bartlett, Deborah L. Rhode, and Joanna Grossman, Gender and Law: Theory, Doctrine, Commentary, 6th ed. (New York: Wolters Kluwer, 2013), 332; Theresa M. Beiner, Gender Myths v. Working Realities: Using Social Science to Reformulate Sexual Harassment Law (New York: New York University Press, 2004), 1.

6. Bartlett, Rhode and Grossman, Gender and Law, 333.

7. Jennifer Medina, Denying Accusations of Sexual Harassment, the Mayor of San Diego Resigns, New York Times, August 24, 2013, at A10.

8. Bartlett, Rhode, and Grossman, Gender and Law, 333; Grossman, Culture of Compliance, 51–52.

9. Sabrina Rubin Erdely, The Rape of Petty Officer Blumer, Rolling Stone, February 14, 2013 (quoting Rebecca Blumer), 56.

10. Louise F. Fitzgerald, Suzanne Swan, and Karla Fischer, Why Didn't She Just Report Him? The Psychological and Legal Implications of Women's Responses to Sexual Harassment, Journal of Social Issues 51 (1995): 117, 122–123; Mindy E. Bergman, Regina Day Langhout, Patrick A. Palmieri, et al., The (Un)reasonableness of Reporting: Antecedents and Consequences of Reporting Sexual Harassment, Journal of Applied Psychology 87 (2002): 230, 237.

11. 29 C. F. R. Section 1604.11(a)(1)-(3) (1980).

12. Anthony D. Pignotti, If You Grab the Honey, You Better Have the Money: An In-Depth Analysis of Individual Supervisor Liability for Workplace Sexual Harassment, Ave Maria Law Review 5 (2007): 207.

13. Burlington Industries, Inc. v. Ellerth, 524 U.S. 742, 745 (1998).

14. David Sherwyn, Michael Heise, and Zev J. Eigen, Don't Train Your Employees and Cancel your 1–800 Harassment Hotline: An Empirical Examination and Correction of the Flaws in the Affirmative Defense to Sexual Harassment Charges, Fordham Law Review 69 (2001): 1265, 1294, 1301, 1304; Ann Lawton, Operating in an Empirical Vacuum, The Ellerth and Faragher Affirmative Defense, Columbia Journal of Gender and Law, 13 (2004): 197, 210.

15. Sherwyn, Heise, and Eigen, Don't Train Your Employees, 1301–1304.

16. For the reluctance to complain, see Fitzgerald et al., Why Didn't She Just Report Him?, 120. For the treatment of failure to complain, see Sherwyn, Heise, and Eigen, Don't Train Your Employees, 1286, 1299, Deborah L. Brake and Joanna L. Grossman, The Failure of Title VII as a Rights-Claiming System, North Carolina Law Review 86 (2008): 859, 881.

17. Fierro v. Saks Fifth Avenue, 13 F. Supp.2d 481 (S.D.N.Y. 1998) 482; Joanna Grossman, The First Bite Is Free: Employer Liability for Sexual Harassment, University of Pittsburgh Law Review 61 (1999): 611.

18. Marsicano v. American Society of Safety Engineers, No. 97-C7189, 1998 WL 603,128 (N.D. Ill 1998.)

19. Ronnee Schreiber, Righting Feminism: Conservative Women and American Politics (New York: Oxford University Press, 2008), 75 (quoting Elizabeth Lawson).

20. Perry v. Harris Chernin, Inc. 126 F. 3d 428, 430 (7th Cir. 1995). See Grace S. Ho, Not Quite Rights: How the Unwelcomeness Element in Sexual Harassment Law Undermines Title VII's Transformative Potential, Yale Journal of Law and Feminism 20 (2008): 131, 152.

21. EEOC v. Champion International Corp., No. 93 C 20,279, 1995 WL 488,333, 8 (N.D. Ill. 1995).

22. Lissau v. Southern Food Services, Inc., 159 F. 3d 177, 180 (4th Cir., 1998).

23. Saidu-Kamera v. Parkway Corp, 155 F. Supp. 2d 436, 439 (E.D. Pa. 2001).

24. Beiner, Gender Myths v. Working Realities, 35, 42–43.

25. Duncan v. General Motors Corporation, 300 F3d 928 (8th Cir., 2002).

26. Ho, Not Quite Rights, 150–151.

27. Rodriguez-Hernandez v. Miranda-Velez, 132 F. 3d 848, 856 (1st Cir., 1998).

28. Ho, Not Quite Rights, 151 (quoting defense attorney).

29. Workplace Bullying Institute, results of the 2010 and 2007 WBI U.S. Workplace Bullying Survey, http://www.workplacebullying.org/wbiresearch/2010-wbi-national-survey/.

30. Galloway v. General Motors Service Parts Operations, 78 F. 3d 1164, 1165 (7th Cir. 1996).

31. Sylvia A. Hewlett, The Sponsor Effect: Breaking Through the Last Glass Ceiling, Harvard Business Review Research Report (January 12, 2011): 35.

32. Hewlett, The Sponsor Effect, 41.

33. Hewlett, The Sponsor Effect, 37.

34. Bill Carter and Brian Stelter, Extortion Case Raises Questions for Letterman and His Network, New York Times, October 3, 2009, A1.

35. Grossman, The Culture of Compliance, 48–49; Robert S. Moyer and Anjan Nath, Some Effects of Brief Training Interventions on Perceptions of Sexual Harassment, Journal of Applied Social Psychology 28 (1998): 333, 347; Deborah L. Rhode, Social Research and Social Change: Meeting the Challenge of Gender Inequality and Sexual Abuse, Harvard Journal of Law and Gender 30 (2007): 11, 14.

36. See studies reviewed in Susan Bisom-Rapp, Fixing Watches with Sledgehammers: The Questionable Embrace of Employee Sexual Harassment Training by the Legal Profession, University of Arkansas Little Rock Law Review 24 (2001): 147, 163; Susan Bisom Rapp: An Ounce of Prevention Is a Poor Substitute for a Pound of Cure: Confronting the Developing Jurisprudence of Education and Prevention in Employment Discrimination Law, Berkeley Journal of Employment and Labor Law 22 (2001): 1, 37–38.

37. The examples come from training program materials and evaluations on file with the author.

38. American Association of University Women, Crossing the Line: Sexual Harassment at School (Washington, D.C.: AAUW, 2011), 2, 11, 27. In another study, four-fifths of elementary and secondary students experienced sexual harassment, but only 7 percent reported it. American Association of University Women Educational Foundation, Hostile Hallways; Bullying, Teasing, and Sexual Harassment in Schools (Washington, D.C.: AAUW, 2001), 4, 7.

39. American Association of University Women, Crossing the Line: Sexual Harassment on Campus (Washington, D.C.: AAUW, 2005).

40. Adam Nossiter, Six-Year-Old's Sex Crime: Innocent Peck on Cheek, New York Times, September 27, 1996, A9; Deborah L. Rhode, Sex in Schools: Who's Minding the Adults, in MacKinnon and Siegel, Directions in Sexual Harassment Law, 292, 294.

41. AAUW, Crossing the Line, 2.

42. AAUW, Hostile Hallways, AAUW, Crossing the Line, and sources cited in Deborah L. Rhode, Sex in Schools: Who's Minding the Adults, in MacKinnon and Siegel, Directions in Sexual Harassment Law, 293.

43. William McGurn, Sex and the College Dean, Wall Street Journal, April 26, 2011, A15. For an example, see Nicole Allan, Title IX Investigation into Climate for Women at Yale, Yale Alumni Magazine, May/June 2011, 16.

44. Gebser v. Lago Vista Independent Schoool District, 524 U.S. 274 (1998).

45. Davis v. Monroe County Board of Education, 526 U.S. 629, 633 (1999).

46. See sources cited in Rhode, Sex in Schools, 295.

47. Dan Sabotnik, What's Wrong with Faculty-Student Sex? Response II, Journal of Legal Education 47 (1997): 441, 443; Susan Edelman, CUNY Mulls Ban on Professor-Student Relationships, New York Post, March 21, 2012; Elisabeth A. Keller, Consensual Amorous Relationships Between Faculty and Students: The Constitutional Right to Privacy, Journal of College and University Law 15 (1988): 21, 22.

48. Caroline Forell, What's Wrong with Faculty-Student Sex: The Law School Context, Journal of Legal Education 47 (1997): 1, 41, 49, 57.

49. AAUW, Crossing the Line, 8.

50. Lorraine P. Sheridan and Tim Grant, Is Cyberstalking Different?, Psychology, Crime and Law 13 (2007): 627, 637; Danielle Keats Citron, Law's Expressive Value in Combating Cyber Gender Harassment, Michigan Law Review 108 (2009): 373, 374–375, 378, n 24; Peter Lattman, Student Gets Costly Lesson in Defending Vicious Speech, Wall Street Journal, May 9, 2007, B3.

51. Working to Halt Online Abuse, Cyberstalking Comparison Statistics 2000–2012, http://www.haltabuse.org/resources/stats/Cumulative2000–2012.pdf.

52. Robert Meyer and Michael Cukier, Assessing the Attack Threat Due to IRC Channels, in Proceedings of the International Conference on Dependable Systems and Networks (2006), 469, http://dl.acm.org/citation.cfm?id=1,135,726.

53. Thomas J. De Loughry, Colleges Criticized for Response to Offensive On-Line Speech, Chronicle of Higher Education, December 1, 1995.

54. Allan, Title IX Investigation into Climate for Women at Yale, 16.

55. A copy of the complaint appears at http://online.wsj.com/public/resources/documents/071109aaacomplaint.pdf.

56. Ellen Nakashima, Harsh Words Die Hard on the Web; Law Students Feel Lasting Effects of Anonymous Attacks, Washington Post, March 7, 2007, A1. Comment by Inquiring Mind, June 12, 2007.

57. Alexander Abad-Santos, How Bad Is "Viral" Rape Shame? It Pushes Teenage Girls into Killing Themselves, The Atlantic Wire, April 12, 2013, http://www.theatlanticwire.com/national/2013/04/rape-suicides-audrie-pott-rehtaeh-parsons/64172/.

58. Pat Miller, Another Rape in Cyberspace, Cerise, November 2007; Citron, Combating Cyber Gender Harassment, 383–384.

59. Citron, Combating Cyber Gender Harassment, 380–381.

60. Soraya Chemaly, Facebook's Big Misogyny Problem, The Guardian, April 18, 2013, http://www.guardian.co.uk/commentisfree/2013/apr/18/facebook-big-misogyny-problem, See also http://abcnews.go.com/Technology/oregon-mom-challenges-facebook-rape-posts-target-threats/story?id=18887931#.UZVfRbXviSo.

61. Alexander Abad-Santos, The Problem with Torrington Is the Problem with Rape, Not Twitter, The Atlantic Wire, April 5, 2013, http://www.theatlanticwire.com/national/2013/03/torrington-rape-tweets/63502/.

62. Catherine Holahan, The Dark Side of Web Anonymity, Business Week, April 30, 2008, at 64; Citron, Combating Cyber Gender Harassment, 390.

63. Citron, Combating Cyber Gender Harassment, 396.

64. Attorney General to Vice President, Report on Cyberstalking: A New Challenge for Law Enforcement and Industry (Washington, D.C.: Department of Justice, 1999).

65. Danielle Keats Citron, Cyber Civil Rights, Boston University Law Review 89 (2009): 61. If the parties had a dating relationship, domestic violence statutes may be applicable.

66. Mackinnon, Afterward, 672.

67. Booth v. Hvass, 302 F3d 849 (8th Cir. 2002), cert. den. 537 U.S. 1108 (2003). See the discussion in Molly Dragiewicz, Equality with a Vengeance: Men's Rights Groups, Battered Women, and Antifeminist Backlash (Boston, MA: Northeastern University Press, 2011), 1, 27, 31.

68. Elizabeth Plank, NRA Vendor Sells Ex-Girlfriend Target That Bleeds When You Shoot It, http://www.policymic.com/articles/40049/nra-sells-an-ex-girlfriend-target-that-bleeds-when-you-shoot-it.

69. Frank Rich, The Second Wind, New York Times, October 14, 1995, A19 (quoting Simpson); Ann Jones, I Object, Mr. Cochran: "Being Human" Is Not an Excuse for Wife-beating, New York Times, October 1, 1995, E13 (quoting Cochran); Katha Pollitt, Subject to Debate, The Nation, October 23, 1995, 457 (quoting Michael Knox).

70. Dragiewicz, Equality With a Vengeance, 69–71.

71. Michael Kimmel, Angry White Men: American Masculinity at the End of an Era (New York: Nation Books, 2013), 182; Dragiewicz, Equality with a Vengeance, 74–76.

72. Michelle L. Meloy and Susan L. Miller, The Victimization of Women: Law, Policies, and Politics (New York: Oxford University Press), 103.

73. For examples, see Leigh Goodmark, A Troubled Marriage: Domestic Violence and the Legal System (New York: New York University Press, 2012), 86–87; Deborah L. Rhode, Speaking of Sex (Cambridge, MA: Harvard University Press, 1997), 110–111.

74. Supreme Court of the State of Florida, Report of the Florida Supreme Court Gender Bias Study Commission (Tallahassee: Florida Supreme Court, 1990), 14.

75. Hilary G. Harding and Marie Helweg-Larsen, Perceived Risk for Future Intimate Partner Violence among Women in a Domestic Violence Shelter, Journal of Family Violence 24 (2009): 75–76; National Center for Injury Prevention and Control, Centers for Disease Control, The National Intimate Partner and Sexual Violence Survey, 2010 Summary Report (2010), 1, 39.

76. National Center, National Intimate Partner Survey, 29 (defining stalking as circumstances in which victims felt very fearful, or believed that they or someone close to them would be harmed as a result).

77. Jacquelyn C. Campbell, Prediction of Homicide of and by Battered Women, in Jacquelyn C. Campbell, ed., Assessing Dangerousness: Violence by Batterers and Child Abusers, 2nd ed. (New York: Springer Publications, 2007), 85, 86.

78. Kimmel, Angry White Men, 173.

79. Kimberly Bailey, Lost in Translation: Domestic Violence, "The Personal is Political," and the Criminal Justice System, Journal of Criminal Law and Criminology 100 (2010): 1255, 1281–1282.

80. Margaret E. Johnson, Balancing Liberty, Dignity, and Safety: The Impact of Domestic Violence Lethality Screening, 32 Cardozo L. Rev. (2010): 519, 526; Jennifer Langhinrichsen-Rohling, Top 10 Greatest "Hits": Important Findings and Future Directions for Intimate Partner Violence Research, Journal of Interpersonal Violence 20 (2005): 108, 113.

81. For the most authoritative estimate of the cost, which adjusted for inflation comes to $10.3 billion, see U.S. Centers for Disease Control and Prevention, Costs of Intimate Partner Violence Against Women in the United States (Washington, D.C.: U.S. Centers for Disease Control, 2003); http://www.cdc.gov/ncipc/pub-res/ipv_cost/ipvbook-final-feb18.pdf.

82. See Rana Sampson, Domestic Violence, in Mario R. Dewalt, ed., Domestic Violence: Law Enforcement Response and Legal Perspectives (New York: Nova Science

Publishers, 2010), 6–7; Meloy and Miller, The Victimization of Women, 35–38; D. Kelly Weisberg, Domestic Violence: Legal and Social Reality (New York: Wolters Kluwer, 2012), 35; Nancy Ver Steegh and Clare Dalton, Report from the Wingspread Conference on Domestic Violence and Family Courts (2007), 11; Kimmel, Angry White Men, 190–194.

83. See Callie Marie Rennison and Sarah Welchans, Bureau of Justice Statistics, Special Report: Intimate Partner Violence (NCJ 178,247), May 2000, 1, http://www.bjs.gov/content/pub/pdf/ipv.pdf; Meloy and Miller, The Victimization of Women, 35–38; National Center, National Intimate Partner Survey.

84. Marie Tessier, Intimate Violence Remains a Big Killer of Women, Women's eNews, July 25, 2008, http://womensenews.org/story/crime-policy-and-legislation/080725/intimate-violence-remains-big-killer-women#.UbEVPkDvt8E; Elizabeth M. Schneider, Domestic Violence Law Reform in the Twenty-First Century: Looking Back and Looking Forward, 42 Family Law Quarterly 42 (2008): 353, 361.

85. For an overview, see Sampson, Domestic Violence, at 9.

86. T. K. Logan, Lisa Shannon, Robert Walker, and Teri Marie Faragher, Protective Orders: Questions and Conundrums, Trauma Violence Abuse 7 (2006): 175, 184, 191; Deborah Epstein, Margret Bell, and Lisa A. Goodman, Transforming Aggressive Prosecution Policies: Prioritizing Victims' Long-Term Safety in the Prosecution of Domestic Violence Cases, American University Journal of Gender, Social Policy and the Law, 11 (2003): 465, 476.

87. Patricia Tjaden and Nancy Thoennes, Full Report of the Prevalence, Incidence, and Consequences of Violence Against Women, Findings from the National Violence Against Women Survey, November 2000, https://www.ncjrs.gov/pdffiles1/nij/183781.pdf. For claims that most assaults occur during a relationship rather than after it, see Sampson, Domestic Violence, 11.

88. Angela M. Moe and Myrtle P. Bell, Abject Economics: The Effects of Battering and Violence on Women's Work and Employability, Violence Against Women 10 (2004): 29, 35–36.

89. For an overview of theories and critical accounts of the Battered Women's Syndrome approach to cycles of violence, see D. Kelly Weisberg, Domestic Violence: Legal and Social Reality (New York: Wolters Kluwer, 2012), 48–56.

90. North Dakota Commission on Gender Fairness: A Difference in Perceptions, The Final Report on the North Dakota Commission on Gender Fairness in the Courts, reprinted in North Dakota Law Review 72 (1996): 1113, 1208.

91. Michelle Chen, The Economic Crisis Hits Home, Ms. Magazine, Fall 2010, 15.

92. Goodmark, A Troubled Marriage, 158.

93. Rhode, Speaking of Sex, 115.

94. 545 U.S. 748 (2005). The description of the Supreme Court case and international proceedings draws on Bartlett, Rhode, and Grossman, Gender and Law, 409–410.

95. Castle Rock v. Gonzales, 545 U.S. 748 (2005).

96. Jessica Lenahan (Gonzales) et al. v. United States, Report No. 80/11, Case 12.626, paragraph 5 (Merits, July 21, 2011).

97. Gonzales et al. v. United States, paragraph 201.

98. May v. Franklin County Commissioners, 437 F. 3d 579, 583 (6th Cir. 2006).

99. Pinder v. Johnson, 54 F. 3d 1169 (4th Cir. 1995).

100. For other examples, see Atinuke O. Awoyomi, The State-Created Doctrine Danger in Domestic Violence Cases: Do We Have a Solution in Okin v. Village of Cornwall-on-Hudson Police Department?, Columbia Journal of Gender and Law 20 (2011): 1, 13–34.

101. Elizabeth Olson, Though Many Are Stalked, Few Report It, Study Finds, New York Times, February 14, 2009, A1.

102. See Family Violence Prevention Fund, The Facts on the Workplace and Domestic Violence, http://endabuse.org/userfiles/file/Workplace/Workplace.pdf. Marie Tessier,

More States Give Abuse Victims Right to Time Off, January 16, 2005, http://womensenews.org/story/domestic-violence/050116/more-states-give-abuse-victims-right-time#.Ua5YFkDvt8E. This discussion of stalking and the Caroll v. Shoney case draws on Bartlett, Rhode, and Grossman, Gender and Law, 411–412.

103. Julie Leupold, Execs Aware of Domestic Violence Costs, Womens' enews, February 2, 2003, http://womensenews.org/story/business/030202/execs-aware-domestic-violence-costs#.Ua5YREDvt8E; Moe & Bell, Abject Economics, 34.

104. Simon McCormack, Carie Charlesworth, Teacher, Fired after Being Abused, Huffington Post, June 13, 2013, http://www.huffingtonpost.com/2013/06/13/carie-charlesworth-teacher-fired_n_3,436,716.html.

105. Alison Bowen, Battered New Yorker Sues Employer for Firing Her, July 26, 2007, http://womensenews.org/story/the-courts/070726/battered-new-yorker-sues-employer-firing-her#.Ua5YdUDvt8E. For the inadequacy of legislative protections for victims, see Robin R. Runge, The Evolution of a National Response to Violence Against Women, Hastings Women's Law Journal 24 (2013): 429, 454.

106. Deborah Tuerkheimer, Yale Journal of Law and Feminism 25 (2013): 51, 61, 71–72.

107. Carroll v. Shoney's, Inc, 775 So. 2d 753 (Ala. 2000).

108. 775 So. 2d, 758., 775 So. 2d, 758.

109. Goodmark, A Troubled Marriage, 149. California is an exception. It has a 55 percent completion rate. Doug MacLeod, Ron Pi, David Smith, and Leah Rose Goodwin, Batterer Intervention Systems in California: An Evaluation (Administrative Offices of the Court, 2005), 68.

110. Deborah L. Rhode, Social Research and Social Change: Meeting the Challenge of Gender Inequality and Sexual Abuse, Harvard Journal of Law and Gender 30 (2007): 11, 21 (reviewing studies); Sampson, Domestic Violence, 25.

111. MacLeod, Pi, Smith, and Goodwin, Batterer Intervention Systems in California, 79 (40 percent of program participants were rearrested within 12 months, half for domestic violence).

112. Sampson, Domestic Violence, 125; Deborah Epstein, Procedural Justice: Tempering the State's Response to Domestic Violence, William and Mary Law Review 43 (2002): 1845, 1883.

113. Shelly Jackson, National Institute of Justice, Batterer Intervention Programs: Where Do We Go from Here?, http://www.nij.gov/pubs-sum/195079.htm.

114. Suzanne Batchelor, Programs for Batterers Changing Their Focus, January 30, 2006, http://womensenews.org/story/domestic-violence/060130/programs-batterers-changing-their-focus#.Ua5Y3kDvt8E (quoting Shelly Jackson).

115. Dragiewicz, Equality with a Vengeance.

116. Sampson, Domestic Violence, 20.

117. Centers for Disease Control and Prevention, Youth Risk Behavior Surveillance-United States, 2011, http://www.Cdc.gov/mmwr/pdf/ss/ss6104.pdf.

118. Victoria L. Banyard and Charlotte Cross, Consequences of Teen Dating Violence: Understanding Intervening Variables in Ecological Context, Violence Against Women 14 (2008): 998.

119. National Center for Injury Prevention and Control, Centers for Disease Control and Prevention, National Intimate Partner and Sexual Violence Survey: 2010 Summary Report (2011), http://www.cdc.gov/violencePrevention/pdf/nisvs_report2010-a.pdf.

120. Dating Matters, http://www.cdc.gov/violenceprevention/datingmatters.

121. Suzie Boss, Under One Roof: One-Stop Centers Offer a Safer Future for Victims of Domestic Violence, Stanford Social Innovation Review (Spring 2011): 21.

122. Atinuke O. Awoyomi, The State-Created Danger Doctrine in Domestic Violence Cases: Do We Have a Solution in Okin v. Village of Cornwall-On-Hudson Police Department?, Columbia Journal of Gender & Law 20 (2010): 1, 9.

123. Jeannie Suk, Criminal Law Comes Home: Yale Law Journal 116 (2006): 1.

124. Christopher D. Maxwell et al., National Institute of Justice, Research in Brief: The Effects of Arrest on Intimate Partner Violence: New Evidence from the Spouse Assault Replication Program (2001).

125. For an overview, see Sally F. Goldfarb, Reconceiving Civil Protection Orders for Domestic Violence: Can Law Help End the Abuse Without Ending the Relationship?, 29 Cardozo L. Rev. (2008): 1511, 1537; Laurie S. Kohn, The Justice System and Domestic Violence: Engaging the Case But Divorcing the Victim, New York University Review of Law and Social Change 32 (2008): 191, 218, 235.

126. See research cited in U.S. Department of Justice, Practical Implications of Current Domestic Violence Research: For Law Enforcement, Prosecutors and Judges, in Dewalt, Domestic Violence, 59, 71.

127. Leigh Goodmark, Autonomy Feminism: An Anti-Essentialist Critique of Mandatory Interventions in Domestic Violence Cases, Florida State University Law Review 37 (2009); 1, 35.

128. See Bartlett, Rhode, and Grossman, Gender and Law, 405; Deborah Epstein et al., Transforming Aggressive Prosecution Policies: Prioritizing Victims' Long-Term Safety in the Prosecution of Domestic Violence Cases, American University Journal of Gender, Social Policy and the Law 20 (2003): 465, 476–477.

129. For women's desires on prosecution, see research summarized in Department of Justice, Practical Implications, 71, 100. For research on mandatory policies, see Department of Justice, Practical Implications, and Alisa Smith, It's My Decision, Isn't It?, Violence Against Women 6 (2000): 1384, 1395–1396.

130. Keith Guzik, The Forces of Conviction: The Power and Practice of Mandatory Prosecution upon Misdemeanor Domestic Battery Suspects, Law & Social Inquiry 32 (2007): 41–48; Nancy R. Rhodes and Eva Baranoff McKenzie, Why Do Battered Women Stay?: Three Decades of Research, Aggression and Violent Behavior 3 (1998): 391; Department of Justice, Practical Implications, 101.

131. Kimberly Bailey, Lost in Translation: Domestic Violence, "the Personal is Political": and the Criminal Justice System, Journal of Criminal Law and Criminology 100 (2010): 1255, 1257.

132. Donna Coker, Crime Control and Feminist Law Reform in Domestic Violence Law: A Critical Review Buffalo Criminal Law Review 4 (2001): 801, 805.

133. Tamara L. Kuennen, Analyzing the Impact of Coercion on Domestic Violence Victims: How Much Is Too Much?, Berkeley Journal of Gender, Law and Justice 22 (2007): 2, 25.

134. Goldfarb, Reconceiving Civil Protection Orders, 1501–1505, 1523.

135. Goodmark, A Troubled Marriage, 96.

136. Deborah Epstein, Margaret Bell, and Lisa A. Goodman, Transforming Aggressive Prosecution Policies: Prioritizing Victims' Long-Term Safety in the Prosecution of Domestic Violence Cases, American University Journal of Gender, Social Policy, and the Law, 11 (2003): 465.

137. Department of Justice, Practical Implications, 103; Kathryn Gillespie Wellman, Taking the Next Step in the Legal Response to Domestic Violence: The Need to Reexamine Specialized Domestic Violence Courts from a Victim Perspective, Columbia Journal of Gender and Law, 24 (2013): 444, 464–465.

138. For examples, see Rachel Louise Snyder, A Raised Hand, New Yorker, July 22, 2013, 34–40.

139. Loretta Frederick and Kristine C. Lizdas, The Role of Restorative Justice in the Battered Women's Movement, in James Ptacek, ed. Restorative Justice and Violence Against Women (New York: Oxford University Press, 2010), 43; James Ptacek, Resisting Cooptation: Three Feminist Challenges to AntiViolence Work, in Ptacek, Restorative Justice, 8.

140. Department of Justice, Practical Implications, 109–110.

141. Meloy and Miller, The Victimization of Women, 171.

142. Kimmel, Angry White Men, 198.

143. Naftali Bendavid and Louise Radnofsky, Crucial Senate Race in Uproar, Wall Street Journal, August 21, 2012, A1.

144. Centers for Disease Control, National Center for Injury Prevention and Control, Sexual Violence: Facts at a Glance (Washington, D.C.: 2012): 2.

145. Associated Press, Wisconsin: Prosecutor Says "Rape Easy" Case That Lawmaker Discussed Wasn't Consensual, October 15, 2012, http://www.twincities.com/politics/ci_21780919/wisconsin-prosecutor-says-rape-easy-case-that-lawmaker.

146. National Intimate Partner and Sexual Violence Survey:2010 Summary Report (Atlanta, GA: National Center for Injury Prevention and Control, Centers for Disease Control and Prevention, 2010); surveys cited in Testimony of Susan B. Carbon, Director, Office on Violence Against Women, Rape in the United States, Testimony before the Subcommittee on Crime and Drugs, Committee on the Judiciary, United States Senate, September 14, 2010, http://www.judiciary.senate.gov/hearings/hearing.cfm?id=e655f9e2809e5476862f735da16234b9.

147. United Nations Office of Drugs and Crime, Crime and Criminal Justice Statistics, table on Rape at the National Level (2011).

148. This explanation draws on Bartlett, Rhode, and Grossman, Gender and Law, 614, and Rhode Speaking of Sex, 121.

149. See Diane Scully, Understanding Sexual Violence (New York: Routledge, 1990) and sources cited in Rhode, Speaking of Sex, 121.

150. See Owen D. Jones and Timothy H. Goldsmith, Law and Behavioral Biology, Columbia Law Review 105 (2005): 405.

151. Jeff Benedict, Public Heroes, Private Felons: Athletes and Crimes Against Women (Boston, MA: Northeastern University Press, 1998), 4; Michael Winerip, Stepping Up to Stop Sexual Assault, New York Times, Februrary 9, 2014, E14. See Michelle S. Jacobs, Invisible Criminality: Male Peer Support Groups, Alcohol, and the Risk of Aggressive Sexual Behavior, in Michael L. Seigel, ed., Race to Injustice: Lessons Learned from the Duke Lacrosse Rape Case (Durham, NC: Carolina Academic Press, 2009), 105.

152. Nicole Allan, Confusion and Silence, Yale Alumni Magazine, July/August 2011, http://www.yalealumnimagazine.com/articles/3235.

153. Karisa King, Military Often Scorns Victims of Sex Assault, San Francisco Chronicle, May 19, 2013, A16.

154. Kirby Dick, Don't Trust the Pentagon to End Rape, New York Times, June 3, 2013, A23.

155. Jennifer Steinhauer, Reports of Military Sexual Assault Rise Sharply, New York Times, November 7, 2013, at A2; Julian E. Barnes, Sex-Assault Reports Surge for Military, Wall Street Journal, December 30, 2013, A6.

156. Erdely, The Rape of Petty Officer Bumer, 59.

157. Benedict, Scandal of Military Rape (quoting Harman).

158. Ilene Seidman and Susan Vickers, The Second Wave: An Agenda for the Next Thirty Years of Rape Law Reform, 38 Suffolk University Law Review 38 (2005) 467, 472.

159. Susan S. Carbon, Director, Office on Violence Against Women, Testimony before Subcommittee on Crime and Drugs, Committee on the Judiciary, U.S. Senate, September 14, 2010.

160. Francis X. Shen, How We Still Fail Rape Victims: Reflecting on Responsibility and Legal Reform, Columbia Journal of Gender and Law 22 (2011): 1, 8; Donald Dripps, Rape Law and American Society, in Clare McGlynn and Vanessa E. Munro, Rethinking Rape Law: International and Comparative Perspectives (New York: Routledge, 2010), 231; Monika Johnson Hostler, Making campuses Safer for Women, Wall Street Journal, February 25, 2014, A11.

161. Maureen Dowd, America's Military Injustice, New York Times, May 8, 2013, A23.

162. Some of these examples draw from Bartlett, Rhode, and Grossman, Gender and Law, 629.

163. Lynn Hecht Schafran, The Importance of Voir Dire in Rape Trials, Trial, August 1992, 26.
164. Camille Paglia, Sex, Art, and American Culture: Essays (New York: Vintage, 1992), 51.
165. Jessica Valenti, In Rape Tragedies, the Shame Is Ours, The Nation, May 6, 2013, 10.
166. Rebecca Traister, Ladies, We Have a Problem, New York Times Magazine, July 24, 2011, 9.
167. Rhode, Speaking of Sex, 125; Commonwealth v. Cepull, 568 A 2d 247, 248–249 (PA Super. Ct. 1990). For the range of estimates, see research cited in Jacobs, Invisible Criminality, 120.
168. Dripps, Rape Law, 234–235; Siegel, Race to Injustice; Stuart Taylor, Jr., and K. C. Johnson, Until Proven Innocent: Political Correctness and the Shameful Injustices of the Duke Lacrosse Rape Case (New York: Thomas Dunne Books, 2007).
169. This account of the case draws on Bartlett, Rhode, and Grossman, Gender and Law, 630–631.
170. Christopher Dickey and John Solomon, The Maid's Tale, Newsweek, August 8, 2011, 26, 28 (quoting Diallo).
171. Dickey and Solomon, The Maid's Tale, 31.
172. Scott Turow, Reasonable Doubt and the Strauss-Kahn Case, New York Times, August 27, 2011, at SR 4.
173. Steven Erlanger and Maïa de la Baume, Strauss-Kahn Is Not Charged in French Case, New York Times, October 14, 2011, A1.
174. Cara Buckley, After Strauss-Kahn, Fear of Rape Victim Silence, New York Times, August 25, 2011, A21.
175. See Bartlett, Rhode, and Grossman, Gender and Law, 629; John F. Burns and Ravi Somaiya, Confidential Swedish Police Report Details Allegations Against WikiLeaks Founder, New York Times, December 19, 2010, A8.
176. Caroline Heldman and Danielle Dirks, Blowing the Whistle on Campus Rape, Ms. Winter/Spring, 2014, 35.
177. Tina Susman, Teen Rape Puts Town on Trial, Los Angeles Times, March 10, 2013, A14.
178. Rose Corrigan, Up Against a Wall: Rape Reform and the Failure of Success (New York: New York University Press, 2013), 85–86.
179. Karisa King, How Military Makes Target of Rape Victims, San Francisco Chronicle, May 20, 2013, A5; Erdely, The Rape of Petty Officer Blumer, 60.
180. James Risen, Naval Academy Is Shaken by Student's Report of Rape by Athletes, New York Times, June 1, 2013, A9.
181. Jennifer Steinhauer, Navy Hearing in Rape Case Raises Alarm, New York Times, September 21, 2013, A1.
182. Tom Vanden Brook and Gregg Zoroya, Why the Military Hasn't Stopped Sexual Abuse, USA Today, May 16, 2013, 1A.
183. Brook and Zoroya, Why the Military Hasn't Stopped Sexual Abuse, 1A.
184. Erdely, The Rape of Petty Officer Blumer, 62.
185. New York Times Editorial Board, The Military's Sexual Assault Crisis, New York Times, May 8, 2013, A26.
186. Gary La Free, Rape and Criminal Justice: The Social Construction of Sexual Assault, (Belmont, CA: Wadsworth, 1989); Lynne Henderson, Getting to Know: Honoring Women in Law and in Fact, Texas Journal of Women and Law 2 (1993): 42.
187. State v. Rusk, 424 A. 2d 720, 733–734 (Md. Sup Ct. 1981) (Cole, J., dissenting).
188. Juliet Macur and Nate Schweber, Rape Case Unfolds on Web and Splits City, New York Times, December 16, 2012.
189. Zoe Mintz, Steubenville Tumblr Blog Reveals Horrific Twitter, Facebook Posts That Blame the Rape Victim, International Business Times, March 19, 2013.
190. Jessica Mason, Piklo, Michigan High School Protects Student Athlete at Expense of Alleged Sexual Assault Victim, Reality Check, April 21, 2013, http://rrealitycheck.org/article/2013/04/21/michigan-high-school-protects-student-athlete-at-expense-of-rape-victim/.

191. Jack Healy, Montana Legal Officials Step In on Rape Case Sentence, New York Times, September 7, 2013, A12.

192. Heldman and Dirks, Blowing the Whistle, at 32.

193. Michelle J. Anderson, From Chastity Requirement to Sexuality License: Sexual Consent and a New Rape Shield Law, George Washington Law Review 70 (2002): 51, 74–75, 94–95.

194. Corey Rayburn Yung, To Catch a Sex Thief: The Burden of Performance in Rape and Sexual Assault Trials, Columbia Journal of Gender and Law 15 (2006): 437.

195. The White House Council on Women and Girls, Rape and Sexual Assault: A Renewed Call to Action (Washington: D.C., White House Council on Women and Girls, 2014): 14; Hostler, Making Campuses Safer for Women, A11; National Crime Victimization Study, Violent Victimization of College Students (1995–2002), http://www.ocpa-oh. org/Campus%20Safety/Violent%20Victimization%20of%20College%20Students.pdf.

196. Heldman and Dirks, Blowing the Whistle on Campus Rape, 37.

197. Angie Epifano, An Account of Sexual Assault at Amherst College, The Amherst Student issue, October 17, 2012, http://amherststudent.amherst.edu/?q=article/2012/10/17/account-sexual-assault-amherst-college. See Richard Pérez-Peña, Sexual Assaults Roil Amherst, and College President Welcomes the Controversy, New York Times, November 11, 2012, A19.

198. Richard Pérez-Peña and Ian Lovett, 2 More Colleges Accused of Mishandling Assaults, New York Times, April 19, 2013, A14.

199. Heldman and Dirks, Blowing the Whistle on Campus Rape, 35.

200. Heldman and Dirks, Blowing the Whistle on Campus Rape, 32.

201. See sources cited in Donald Dripps, After Rape Law: Will the Turn to Consent Normalize the Prosecution of Sexual Assault? Akron Law Review 41 (2008): 957, 971–973.

202. See Neil Gilbert, The Phantom Epidemic of Sexual Assault, Public Interest 103 (Spring 1991): 54.

203. Jacobs, Invisible Criminality, 108.

204. See sources cited in Rhode, Speaking of Sex, 123.

205. See sources cited in Rhode, Speaking of Sex, 123.

206. For a letter to Stanford University describing the standard, see http://www.whitehouse. gov/sites/default/files/dear_colleague_sexual_violence.pdf.

207. Mathew R. Triplett, Sexual Assault on College Campuses: Seeking the Appropriate Balance Between Due Process and Victim Protection, Duke Law Journal 62 (2012): 487.

208. Postings to law talk@lists.stanford.edu (December 2011).

209. For reasons that victims fail to report, see Massachusetts Executive Office of Public Safety and Security, Analysis of Campus Rape and Sexual Assault Reports (2012), 12. For the skepticism that deters women from coming forward, see Nanette Asimov, Students Feel Like Sex Assaults Often Taken Too Lightly, San Francisco Chronicle, August 22, 2013, A1.

210. Susan Caringella, Addressing Rape Reform in Law and Practice (New York: Columbia University Press, 2009), 43.

211. Michelle J. Anderson, Marital Immunity, Intimate Relationships, and Improper Inferences: A New Law on Sexual Offenses by Intimates, Hastings Law Journal 54 (2003): 1465, 1470–1475. For provisions in these states, see the Appendix in Anderson, Marital Immunity, at 1537–1574.

212. Anderson, Marital Immunity, 1471–1473.

213. Conn. Gen. Stat. Ann. §53(a)-67(b) (West 2008).

214. Jill Elaine Hasday, Contest and Consent: A Legal History of Marital Rape, California Law Review 88 (2000): 1373, 1486–1892.

215. Hasday, Contest and Consent, at 1489. This account of marital rape draws on Bartlett, Rhode, and Grossman, Gender and Law, 623.

216. Diana H. Russell, Rape in Marriage, rev. ed. (Bloomington: Indiana University Press, 1990), 192, 193.

217. Stephen J. Schulhofer, Unwanted Sex: The Culture of Intimidation and the Failure of Law (Cambridge, MA: Harvard University Press, 2000); Joan McGregor, Is it Rape? On Acquaintance Rape and Taking Women's Consent Seriously (New York: Ashgate Publishing, 2005), 190–193. For discussion of the three states and a proposal to require affirmative consent, see Susan Caringella, Addressing Rape Reform in Law and Practice (New York: Columbia University Press, 2009), 76–78.

218. Criminal Code, R.S.C. 1985, C-46 section 273.

219. Caringella, Addressing Rape Reform, 78–79.

220. Caringella, Addressing Rape Reform, 2.

221. Allen, Confusion and Silence, Pérez-Peña and Lovett, 2 More Colleges Accused of Mishandling Assaults, A14.

222. Simpson v. University of Colorado, Boulder, 500 F. 3d 1170 (10th Cir. 2007).

223. Richard Pérez-Peña, Student's Account Has Rape in Spotlight, New York Times, October 27, 2012, A15.

224. See Thom Shanker, Pentagon Finishing Rules to Curb Sexual Assaults, New York Times, August 8, 2013, A15; Barnes, Sex-Assault Reports Surge for Military, at A6.

225. Julian E. Barnes, Pentagon Pushes Military-Justice Overhaul, Wall Street Journal, April 9, 2013, A5; Lauren R. S. Mendonsa and Lynne Bernabei, Battling Military Sexual Assault, National Law Journal, July 15, 2013, 30 (describing the Military Justice Improvement Act).

226. Stephanie Hallett, How to Stop a Serial Rapist, MS., Summer 2011, at 33; Katherine L. Prevost O'Connor, Eliminating the Rape-Kit Backlog: Bringing Necessary Changes to the Criminal Justice System UMKC L. Rev. 193, 72 (2003): 194–196.

227. Dawn Rae Flood, Rape in Chicago: Race, Myth, and the Courts (Urbana: University of Illinois Press, 2012), 167.

228. Flood, Rape in Chicago, 166.

229. Jeremy Stahl, What Daniel Tosh Has in Common with Michael Richards, Slate, July 13, 2012, http://www.slate.com/blogs/browbeat/2012/07/13/daniel_tosh_is_like_michael_richards_but_not_for_the_reasons_you_think.html.

230. See research summarized in Rhode, Social Research and Social Change, 16–17.

231. U.S. Department of Health and Human Services, About Human Trafficking, 2012, http://www.acf.hhs.gov/trafficking/about/index.html; Steven Seidenberg, Of Human Bondage, ABA J., April 2013; Report of the Director-General Global Alliance Against Forced Labor, paragraph 265 and table 2.1, International Labor Conference (June 6, 2005).

232. U.S. Department of State, Trafficking in Persons Report (2012), 7; U.N. Office on Drugs and Crime, Global Report on Trafficking in Persons Report (2009), 8.

233. Civil Rights Division, United States Department of Justice. Department of Justice Report on Activities to Combat Human Trafficking: Fiscal Years 2001–2005, 9 (2006).

234. U.S. Department of State, Trafficking in Persons Report, 6–11; see also Alexandra V. Orlova, Trafficking of Women and Children for Exploitation in the Commercial Sex Trade: The Case of the Russian Federation, Georgetown Journal of Gender and Law 6 (2005): 157; Peter Landesman, The Girls Next Door, New York Times Magazine, January 25, 2004, at 32.

235. For child marriages, see Jane Kim, Trafficked: Domestic Violence, Exploitation in Marriage, and the Foreign-Bride Industry, Virginia Journal of International Law 51 (2011): 443, 454–465.

236. Julia O'Connell Davidson, Children in the Global Sex Trade (Malden, MA: Polity, 2005).

237. See U.S. Department of State, Trafficking in Persons Report, 6–11.

238. Luchina Fisher, Judge to Rule on Ground-Breaking Sex Tourism Case, Womens' enews September 22, 2003, http://womensenews.org/story/the-courts/030922/judge-rule-ground-breaking-sex-tourism-case.

239. Davidson, Children in the Global Sex Trade, 130.
240. Nicholas Kristof, If This Isn't Slavery, What Is?, New York Times, January 4, 2009, at WK 8.
241. Kathy Steinman, Sex Tourism and the Child: Latin America's and the United States' Failure to Prosecute Sex Tourists, Hastings Women's Law Journal 13 (2002): 53, 62.
242. Steinman, Sex Tourism, 65.
243. U.S. State Department, Trafficking in Persons Report, at 20–36. This account of trafficking draws on Bartlett, Rhode, and Grossman, Gender and Law, 661.
244. Jonathan Todres, Taking Prevention Seriously: Developing a Comprehensive Response to Child Trafficking and Sexual Exploitation, Vanderbilt Journal of Transnational Law 43 (2010): 1; Robert Uy, Blinded by Red Lights: Why Trafficking Discourse Should Shift Away from Sex and the "Perfect Victim" Paradigm, Berkeley Journal of Gender Law and Justice 26 (2011): 204.
245. Susan W. Tiefenbrun, Updating the Domestic and International Impact of the U.S. Victims of Trafficking Protection Act of 2000: Does Law Deter Crime? Case Western Reserve Journal of International Law 38 (2006–2007): 249, 286.
246. U.S. State Department, U.S. Accomplishments on Combating Trafficking (February 2012) (65 convictions in 2011). Seidenberg, Of Human Bondage, 54; Camelia M. Tepelus, Social Responsibility and Innovation on Trafficking and Child Sex Tourism: Morphing of Practice into Sustainable Tourism Policies? Tourism and Hospitality Research 8 (2008): 98, 103.
247. U.S. Department of Justice, Attorney General's Annual Report to Congress and Assessment of U.S. Government Activities to Combat Trafficking in Persons (2010), 30 (only 2,617 victims received certification for visas from 2001 to 2010), 30. See Lise Olsen, Visa Problems Put Sex Trafficking Victims' Lives in Limbo, Houston Chronicle, November 24, 2008; Jayashri Srikantiah, Perfect Victims and Real Survivors: The Iconic Victim in Domestic Human Trafficking Law, Boston University Law Review 87 (2007): 157, 178–180.
248. Mary G. Leary, Sex Trade Court Holds Hope for the Oft-Blamed, National Law Journal, Ocotber 7, 2013, at 26.
249. White House, Fact Sheet: The White House Announces Efforts to Combat Human Trafficking at Home and Abroad (2012).
250. Rhode, Speaking of Sex, 128.

Chapter 7

1. This chapter draws on my prior publications, The Beauty Bias (New York: Oxford University Press, 2010), and The Injustice of Appearance, Stanford Law Review 61 (2009): 1033.
2. Shaun Dreisbach, How Women Feel Now, Glamour, April 2009, 254.
3. Nancy Etcoff, Foreword, The Real Truth about Beauty: A Global Report: Findings of the Global Study on Women, Beauty, and Well Being (2004).
4. Karen Dion, Ellen Berscheid, and Elaine Walster, What Is Beautiful Is Good, Journal Personality and Social Psychology 24 (1972): 285; Ellen Berscheid, An Overview of the Psychological Effects of Physical Attractiveness, in G. William Lucker et al., eds., Psychological Aspects of Facial Form 1 (Ann Arbor: Center for Human Growth and Development,1981): 9–10; Thomas F. Cash, The Psychology of Physical Appearance: Aesthetics, Attributes, and Images, in Thomas F. Cash and Thomas Pruzinsky, Body Images: Development, Deviance and Change (New York: Guilford Press, 1990), 51, 53
5. Steve Jeffes, Appearance Is Everything: The Hidden Truth Regarding Your Appearance and Appearance Discrimination (Pittsburgh, PA: Sterling House Publisher 1998), 56, 57; Judith H. Langlois et al., Maxims or Myths of Beauty? A Meta-Analytic and Theoretical Review, Psychological Bulletin 126 (2000): 390, 404–405.

6. M.Y. Quereshi and Janet P. Kay, Physical Attractiveness, Age, and Sex as Determinants of Reactions to Resumes, 14 Social Behavior and Personality 14 (1986): 103; David Landy and Harold Sigall, Beauty Is Talent: Task Evaluation as a Function of the Performer's Physical Attractiveness, Journal of Personality and Social Psychology 29 (1974): 299.

7. Sondra Solovay, Tipping the Scales of Justice: Fighting Weight-based Discrimination (New York: Prometheus 2000) 101–105; Janna Fikkan and Esther Rothblum, Weight Bias in Employment, in Kelly D. Brownell et al., Weight Bias: Nature, Consequences, and Remedies (New York: Guilford Press, 2005), 15, 16–18.

8. Daniel S. Hamermesh and Amy Parker, Beauty in the Classroom: Instructors' Pulchritude and Putative Pedagogical Productivity, Economics Education Review 24 (2005): 369; Vicki Ritts, Miles L. Patterson, and Mark E. Tubbs, Expectations, Impressions, and Judgments of Physically Attractive Students: A Review, Review of Education Research 62 (1992): 413.

9. Andrew Ross Sorkin, Never Mind the Resume: How Hot Is the C.E.O.?, New York Times, January 6, 2014.

10. Linda A. Jackson, Hohn F. Hunter, and Carole N. Hodge, Physical Attractiveness and Intellectual Competence: A Meta-Analytic Review, Social Psychology Quarterly 58 (1995): 108, 115.

11. Daniel S. Hamermesh, Beauty Pays (Princeton, NJ: Princeton University Press, 2011), 4; Megumi Hosoda, Eugene F. Stone-Romero, and Gwen Coats, The Effects of Physical Attractiveness on Job-Related Outcomes: A Meta-Analysis of Experimental Studies, Personnel Psychology 56 (2003): 431; Markus M. Mobius and Tanya S. Rosenblat, Why Beauty Matters, American Economic Review 96 (2006): 222, 233–234.

12. Jeff E. Biddle and Daniel S. Hamermesh, Beauty, Productivity, and Discrimination: Lawyers' Looks and Lucre, Journal Labor Economics 16 (1998): 172, Hamermesh, Beauty Pays, 79–80.

13. Solovay, Tipping the Scales of Justice, 103.

14. Eugene M. Caruso, Dobromir A. Raahnev, and Mahzarin R. Banaji, Using Conjoint Analysis to Detect Discrimination: Revealing Covert Preferences from Overt Choices, Social Cognition 27 (2009): 128.

15. Princeton Survey Research Associates, Possibilities and Perils: How Gender Issues Unite and Divide Women (Princeton, NJ: Princeton Survey Research Associates, 2001), 66; Nancy Friday, The Power of Beauty (New York: Arrow, 1996), 368.

16. Margo Maine, Body Wars: Making Peace with Women's Bodies (New York: Gurze, 2000), 19.

17. Nancy Etcoff, Survival of the Prettiest: The Science of Beauty (New York: Anchor, 1999); 85–87; Richard Layard, Happiness: Lessons from a New Science (New York: Penguin, 2005), 62–63.

18. Alex Kuczynski, Beauty Junkies: Inside Our $15 Billion Obsession with Cosmetic Surgery (New York: Doubleday, 2006), 7–8; Gina Kolata, Health and Money Issues Arise over Who Pays for Weight Loss, New York Times, September 30, 2004, A1.

19. Deborah L. Spar, Wonder Women: Sex, Power and the Quest for Perfection (New York: Faarrar, Straus and Giroux 2013), 98.

20. Francine Grodstein et al., Three-Year Follow-up of Participants in a Commercial Weight Loss Program: Can You Keep It Off?, Archives of Internal Medicine 156 (1996): 1302, 1306.

21. See FTC v. AVS Marketing, Inc., No. 04-C-6915 (N.D. Ill. June 13, 2005), http://www.ftc.gov/os/caselist/0423042/0423042.shtm (Himalayan Diet Breakthrough); FTC v. CHK Trading Corp., No. 04-CV-8686 (S.D.N.Y. June 8, 2005), http://www.ftc.gov/os/caselist/0423093/0423093.shtm (Hanmeilin Cellulite Cream); FTC v. Iworx, No. 2:04-CV-00,241-GZS (D. Me. May 24, 2005), http://www.ftc.gov/os/caselist/0423151/0423151.shtm (gel·ä·thin); FTC v. Femina, Inc., No. 04–61,467 (S.D. Fla.

May 17, 2005), http://www.ftc.gov/os/caselist/0423114/0423114.shtm (Siluette Patch, Fat Seltzer Reduce, and Xena RX).

22. Widespread Ignorance of Regulation and Labeling of Vitamins, Minerals, and Food Supplements, Health Care News, Harris Interactive (December 23, 2002), 1.

23. See Ian Ayres, FTC Lacks Muscle in Fighting Diet Scams, National Law Journal, January 20, 2014; Jodie Sopher, Weight Loss Advertising Too Good to Be True: Are Manufacturers or the Media to Blame?, Cardozo Arts and Entertainment Law Journal 22 (2005): 933; Michael Specter, Miracle in a Bottle: Dietary Supplements Are Unregulated, Some Are Unsafe—and Americans Can't Get Enough of Them, New Yorker, February 2, 2004, 64.

24. Mitchell Clute, European Union Regs Make Cosmetic Ingredients Safer, Natural Foods Merchandiser, March 2005, 20.

25. Russell Mokhiber, Toxic Beauty, Multinational Monitor, September–October 2007, 48.

26. For eating disorders, see Eating Disorders Coalition, Eating Disorder Statistics: 9 Million Americans, Thousands Dying Each Year (2007), http://www.eatingdisorderscoalition.org/documents/Statistics_000.pdf; see also Roberta Pollack Seid, Never Too Thin (New York: Prentice Hall, 1991), 21. For yo-yo dieting, see Paul Campos, The Obesity Myth: Why America's Obsession with Weight Is Hazardous to Your Health (New York: Gotham, 2004); Glenn A. Gaesser, Big Fat Lies: The Truth about Your Weight and Your Health (New York: Gurze, 2002), 35, 155–156. For cosmetic surgery, see Darlene Ghavimi, Cosmetic Surgery in the Doctor's Office: Is State Regulation Improving Patient Safety?, Widener Law Review 12 (2005): 249–255.

27. See studies discussed in Patricia R. Owen and Erika Laurel-Seller, Weight Shape and Ideals: Thin Is Dangerously In, 30 J. Applied Psychology 30 (2000): 979–980.

28. See Campos, The Obesity Myth; Laura Fraser, Losing It: America's Obsession with Weight and the Industry That Feeds on It 176 (New York: Dutton, 1997), 176; Tara Parker-Pope, Better to Be Fat and Fit Than Skinny and Unfit, New York Times, August 19, 2008, F5.

29. Thomas Pruzinsky, Psychopathology of Body Experience: Expanded Perspectives, in Body Images, 170, 181–182; Rebecca M. Puh and Kelly D. Brownell, Confronting and Coping with Weight Stigma: An Investigation of Overweight and Obese Adults, Obesity 14 (2006): 1802, 1812. For shame and anxiety linked to decisions to have cosmetic surgery, see Debra L. Gimlin, Body Work (Berkeley: University of California Press, 2002), 93–94.

30. Marc Linder, Smart Women, Stupid Shoes, and Cynical Employers: The Unlawfulness and Adverse Health Consequences of Sexually Discriminatory Workplace Footwear Requirements for Female Employees, Journal Corporate Law 22 (1997): 295; Alyssa B. Dufour et al., Foot Pain: Is Current or Past Shoe Wear a Factor?, Arthritis and Rheumatism 61 (2009): 1352.

31. Hillary Rodham Clinton, Living History (New York: Scribner, 2004), 491.

32. Alison Wolf, The XX Factor: How Working Women Are Creating a New Society (London: Profile Books, 2013), 227.

33. J. Eric Oliver, Fat Politics: The Real Story behind America's Obesity Epidemic (New York: Oxford University Press, 2006), 80, 102.

34. Campos, The Obesity Myth 65.

35. Gina Kolata, Rethinking Thin: The New Science of Weight Loss—and the Myths and Realities of Dieting (New York: Farrar, Straus and Giroux, 2007), 93, 116–125; National Institute of Health et al., The Practical Guide: Identification, Evaluation, and Treatment of Overweight and Obesity in Adults (2000), 5.

36. Kelly D. Brownell and Katherine Battle Horgen, Food Fight: The Inside Story of the Food Industry, America's Obesity Crisis, and What We Can Do About It (New York: McGraw Hill, 2004), 7–10; Elizabeth A. Baker et al., The Role of Race and Poverty in Access to Foods That Enable Individuals to Adhere to Dietary Guidelines, Preventing Chronic Disease 3 (2006): 1; Marsha Katz and Helen Lavan, Legality of Employer Control of Obesity, Journal of Workplace Rights 13 (2008): 59, 61.

37. Rebecca M. Puhl and Kelly D. Brownell, Confronting and Coping with Weight Stigma: An Investigation of Overweight and Obese Adults, Obesity 14 (2006): 1802, 1808.
38. EEOC v. Tex. Bus Lines, 923 F. Supp. 965, 967–968, 977–978 (S.D. Tex. 1996).
39. Elizabeth Fernandez, Teachers Says Fat, Fitness Can Mix, San Francisco Chronicle, February 24, 2002 (quoting Portnick).
40. Jennifer Friedlin, Gaining Weight Cost Me Job, Marie Claire, October 1, 2005; High Stakes Weight Discrimination, Good Morning America, ABC News Transcripts, May 3, 2005.
41. Paul Ernsberger, Does Social Class Explain the Connection Between Weight and Health?, in Esther Rothblum, Sondra Solovay, and Marilyn Wann, eds., The Fat Studies Reader (New York: New York University Press, 2009).
42. Elizabeth A. Baker et al., The Role of Race and Poverty in Access to Foods That Enable Individuals to Adhere to Dietary Guidelines, Preventing Chronic Disease 3 (2006): 1.
43. Jeffrey Kluger, How America's Children Packed on the Pounds, Time, June 23, 2008, 66, 69.
44. April Fallon, Culture in the Mirror: Sociocultural Determinants of Body Image, in Thomas F. Cash and Thomas Pruzinsky, eds., Body Images: Development, Deviance, and Change, 2nd ed. (New York: Guilford Press, 2012), 80, 92; Imani Perry, Buying White Beauty, Cardozo Journal of Law and Gender 12 (2006): 579, 590.
45. Cedric Herring, Skin Deep: Race and Complexion in the "Color Blind" Era, in Cedric Herring, Verna Keith, and Hayward Derrick Horton, eds., Skin Deep: How Race and Complexion Matter in the "Color Blind" Era (Chicago: University of Chicago Press, 2004), 9–10.
46. Robin Givhan, White Is the New White, Washington Post, September 30, 2007, M1.
47. April Fallon, Culture in the Mirror: Sociocultural Determinants of Body Image, in Cash and Pruzinsky, Body Images, 81.
48. Solovay, Tipping the Scales, 105; Janna Fikkan and Esther Rothblum, Weight Bias in Employment, in Brownell et al., Weight Bias, 15, 16–18; Kate Sablosky, Probative "Weight": Rethinking Evidentiary Standards in Title VII Sex Discrimination Cases, New York University Review of Law and Social Change 30 (2006): 325, 33–35.
49. American Society for Aesthetic Plastic Surgery, Statistics on Cosmetic Surgery, 3 http://www.surgery.org/download/2006stats.pdf.
50. Caryl Rivers, Mockery of Katherine Harris, WomenEnews.org, Nobember 29, 2000.
51. Peter Glick et al., Evaluations of Sexy Women in Low- and High-Status Jobs, Psychology of Women Quarterly 29 (2005): 389; Megumi Hosoda, Eugene F. Stone-Romero and Gwen Coats, The Effects of Physical Attractiveness on Job-Related Outcomes: A Meta-Analysis of Experimental Studies, Personnel Psychology 1.56 (2003): 431, 451–453.
52. Nelson v. Knight, 834 N.W. 2d 64 (Iowa, 2013) l.
53. Kate Brannen, Army PR Push: "Average–Looking Women," Politico, November 19, 2013, http://www.politico.com/story/2013/11/army-pr-push-average-looking-women-100,065.html.
54. American Psychological Association, Report of the APA Task Force on the Sexualization of Girls (2007), 32–33.
55. Fiona Morgan, No Way to Treat a Lady: Was the New York Times Profile of Condoleezza Rice Sexist, or Just Silly?, http://wwww.salon.com/politics/geature/2000/12/18/rice/index.html.
56. For the cartoon, see http//www.eagle.com/political/cartoons/pccartoons/archives/siers.asp?Action=GetImage, December 7, 2005.
57. Joe Garofoli, Obama Apologizes to California's Harris, San Francisco Chronicle, April 6, 2012.

58. Lisa O'Carroll, John Inverdale's Marion Bartoli Comments "Wrong," Says BBC News Chief, Guardian, July 9, 2013.

59. Deborah L. Rhode, Speaking of Sex (Cambridge, MA: Harvard University Press, 1997), 73; From the Women's Desk—Why Does Larry King Think Hillary Clinton's Hair, Legs, Smile and Figure are News, FAIR, June 14, 1999.

60. Jonathan Alter, Hillary Clinton: Woman of the World, Vanity Fair, June 2011, 201 (quoting Clinton).

61. Meghan Casserly, Yahoo's Marissa Mayer is the "Hottest CEO Ever"; And It's Great for Business, Forbes, July 17, 2012.

62. Michael Savage, comments during Savage Nation, April 9, 2010, http://mediamatters.org/video/2010/04/12/savage-kagan-looks-like-she-belongs-in-a-kosher/163043.

63. Jennifer Steinhauer, An Early Campaign Gaffe Makes a Non-Issue Big, New York Times, June 10, 2010.

64. Michael Luo, Top Salary in McCain Camp? Palin's Makeup Stylist, New York Times, October 24, 2008.

65. Name It, Change it, She Should Run, and Women's Media Center, An Examination of the Impact of Media Coverage of Women Candidates' Appearance (Chesapeake Beach Consulting, Lake Research Partners, 2013).

66. Janelle Brown, Baby, You Can Park My Car, New York Times, March 27, 2005, at E1 (valet parking service); Amy Roe, Some Coffee Stands Get Steamier, Seattle Times, January 22, 2007, at A1 (espresso bar); Waitresses Dressed as Naughty Nurses Rile RNs, MSNBC.com, December 8, 2006, http://www.msnbc.msn.com/ id/16112393/print/1/displaymode/1098/ (naughty nurse waitresses); Law360, Battling Weight Bias in the Workplace, Portfolio Media, February 10, 2011.

67. Jespersen v. Harrah's Operating Co., 444 F.3d 1104, 1107 (9th Cir. 2006) (en banc), aff'g 392 F.3d 1076 (9th Cir. 2005).

68. Jespersen v. Harrah's Operating Co., 1117 (Kozinski, J., dissenting)

69. Jespersen v. Harrah's Operating Co., 1116 (Pregerson, J., dissenting).

70. Rogers v. American Airlines, Inc., 527 F. Supp. 229, 231 (S.D.N.Y. 1981) (cornrows). For headscarves, see Anita L. Allen, Undressing Difference: The Hijab in the West, Berkeley Journal of Gender Law and Justice 23 (2008): 208, 211–216.

71. Rogers v. American Airlines, Inc., 231.

72. Ingrid Banks, Hair Matters: Beauty, Power, and Black Women's Consciousness (New York: New York University Press, 2000); Monica C. Bell, The Braiding Cases, Cultural Deference, and the Inadequate Protection of Black Women Consumers, Yale Journal of Law and Feminism 19 (2007): 125, 133.

73. Susan Brownmiller, Femininity (New York: Simon and Schuster, 1984), 23.

74. Brownmiller, Femininity, 60, 62.

75. Naomi Wolf, The Beauty Myth: How Images of Beauty Are Used Against Women (New York: Harper, 2002), 53.

76. Eve Ensler, The Good Body (New York: Villard, 2005), 5–6.

77. Thomas Pruzinsky and Milton T. Egerton, "Body Image: Change in Cosmetic Plastic Surgery," in Cash and Pruzinsky, Body Images, 217, 222–223. See also Kathy Davis, Reshaping the Female Body: The Dilemma of Cosmetic Surgery (New York: Routledge, 1995), 120–140, 156.

78. Kirsten Dellinger and Christine L. Williams, Makeup at Work: Negotiating Appearance Rules in the Workplace, Gender and Society 11 (1997): 151, 160, 165.

79. Laura T. Coffey, Do High Heels Empower or Oppress Women?, MSNBC, September 23, 2009.

80. Jan Breslauer, "Stacked like Me," Playboy, July 1997, 64, 66, 67.

81. Debra L. Gimlin, Body Work (Berkeley: University of California Press, 2002), 146.

82. Davis, Reshaping the Female Body, 71.

83. Davis, Reshaping the Female Body, 90, 98, 74.

84. Susan D. Powers, The Ugly-Girl Papers: Hints for the Toilet (New York: Harpers and Brown, 1874), 85, 95.

85. Articles from the women's magazines came from November 2006. The evangelical advice is recounted in Wolf, The Beauty Myth, 88. The skin advice comes from *More,* recounted in Sheila Gibbons, Women Need More from *More* Magazine, Women's enews, February 26, 2004.

86. Reberta Pollack Seid, Never Too Thin (New York: Prentice Hall, 1991), 261, 257.

87. Kirsten Dellinger and Christine L. Williams, Makeup at Work: Negotiating Appearance Rules in the Workplace, Gender and Society 11 (1997): 151, 156.

88. Davis, Reshaping the Female Body, 162.

89. Katherine Viner, The New Plastic Feminism, Guardian (London), July 21, 1997, T4 (quoting Angela Neustatter).

90. Breslauer, Stacked like Me, 66.

91. Randall Jarrell, Pictures at an Institution (London: Faber and Faber, 1954), 57.

92. Lisa de Morales, Greta Is That You? Analyst Moves from CNN to Fox, Washington Post, February 3, 2002, C1; Kim Ode, The Heart Has Reasons: It's Easy to Understand Why Van Susteren Chose the Eye Tuck: It May Even Be Tempting, Minneapolis Star Tribune, February 12, 2002, E12.

93. Maureen Dowd, Facing Up to a Botox Nation, Times Union, February 10, 2002, B5.

94. Jessica Valenti, Full Frontal Feminism (Berkeley, CA: Seal Press, 2007), 174.

95. NBC News/Wall Street Journal Poll, June, 2008, http://roperweb.ropercenter.uconn.edu.

96. Employment Law Alliance, National Poll Shows Public Opinion Sharply Divided on Regulating Appearance—From Weight to Tattoos—in the Workplace, March 22, 2005, http://www.employmentlawalliance.com/en/node/1321.

97. See Rhode, the Beauty Bias, 125–134 (discussing prohibitions in Michigan, Urbana, Illinois, the District of Columbia, San Francisco, Santa Cruz, California, and Madison, Wisconsin).

98. Gersh Kuntzman, Casino Gal's Fat Chance—Hotel's Weightress Rule: Gain Pounds, Lose a Job, New York Post, February 18, 2005, 3.

99. Yanowitz v. L'Oreal USA, Inc., 131 Cal Retr. 2d 575, 582, 588 (Ct. App. 2003); Steven Greenhouse, Going for the Look, but Risking Discrimination, New York Times, July 13, 2003, A12; Richard Ford, The Race Card (New York: Picador, 2009), 138–140.

100. Robert J. Barro, So You Want to Hire the Beautiful, Well, Why Not? Business Week, March 16, 1998, 18.

101. Southwest Airlines built an entire marketing campaign around its promise that "sexy" flight attendants would take passengers "skyward with love." Wilson v. Southwest Airlines Col, 517 F. Supp. 292 (N.D. 1981).

102. See Rhode, Beauty Bias, 99–101, 120–121.

103. Deborah L. Rhode, P.C. or Discrimination?, National Law Journal, January 22, 1996, A 19 (quoting Hooters spokesperson).

104. See Rhode, Beauty Bias, 108.

105. Jesprerson v. Harrah's Operating Co, 444 F. 3d 1104, 1106–1108.

106. Ford, The Race Card, 160–161.

107. Ford, The Race Card, 176.

108. Terry Poulton, No Fat Chicks (New York: Birch Lane Press, 1997), 136 (quoting Mario Cuomo).

109. Ford, The Race Card, 176; Peter Byrne, As a Matter of Fat, San Francisco Weekly, January 17, 2001; Margaret Carlson, And Now, Obesity Rights, Time, December 6, 1993, 96 (quoting Fred Siegal).

110. Rappaport v. Katz, 380 F. Supp. 808, 811–812 (S.D.N.Y. 1974).

111. For general discussion of in-group bias, see Marilynn B. Brewer and Rupert J. Brown, Intergroup Relations, in Daniel T. Gilbert et al., eds., The Handbook of Social Psychology, 4th ed. (Boston: McGraw Hill, 1998), 554; Susan T. Fiske, Stereotyping, Prejudice, and Discrimination, in Gilbert et al., Handbook of Social Psychology, 357.

112. 163 U.S. 537 (1896).
113. David M. Engel and Frank W. Munger, Rights of Inclusion: Law and Identity in the Life Stories of Americans with Disabilities (Chicago: University of Chicago Press, 2003), 241–245.
114. See poll data summarized in Rhode, Beauty Bias, 216, n 109.
115. Rhode, Beauty Bias, 113.
116. Pallavi Gogoi, An Ugly Truth about Cosmetics, Business Week online, November 30, 2004, http://www.businessweek.com (quoting Heather Hippsley).
117. Rhode, Beauty Bias, 141.
118. Rhode, Beauty Bias, 150.
119. Solovay, Tipping the Scales of Justice, 236.
120. World Briefing, Europe, Italy, Milan Bans Too Thin Models, New York Times, December 20, 2006, A6; Michael Gove, Fatten Up Models and You'll End Starvation Slavery, London Times, September 18, 2007, 7; Brenda Gazzar, Spain Sizes Up Fashion World Measuring Stick, Women's eNews, February 21, 2008, http://www.womensenews.org.
121. Richard Freeman and Joel Rogers, Worker Representation and Participation Survey, First Report of Findings (September 16, 2008) Appendix A.
122. Kelly D. Brownell and Katherine Battle Horgen, Food Fight: The Inside Story of the Food Industry, America's Obesity Crisis, and What We Can Do About It (New York: McGraw Hill, 2004), 103–104, 121, 196, 213–214; Zoltan J. Acs, Ann Cotten, and Kenneth R. Stanton, The Infrastructure of Obesity, in Zolten J. Acs and Alan Lyles, ed., Obesity, Business and Public Policy (Northampton, MA: Edward Elgar, 2007), 135, 147; Zoltan J. Acs et al., A Policy Framework for Confronting Obesity, in Acs and Lyle, Obesity, Business and Public Policy, 221, 245; Rogan Kersh and James A. Morone, Obesity Courts, and the New Politics of Public Health, Journal Health Politics, Policy and Law 30 (2005); 839, 843–844.
123. Kessler, The End of Overeating (New York: Rodale, 2009), 71.
124. Kessler, The End of Overeating, 131.
125. Michael Pollan, In Defense of Food (New York: Penguin, 2009), 39–41, 154.
126. Datamonitor, Profiting from Consumers' Desire for Healthy Indulgence (India: Bharat Book Bureau, 2005) http://www.bharatbook.com/detail.asp?id=8333; Kessler, The End of Overeating, 130.
127. Diane Barthel, Putting on Appearance; Gender and Advertising (Philadelphia: Temple University Press, 1988), 137 (quoting Baudrillard).

Chapter 8

1. Karen Middleton, Get Women Out of Binders and Into the Halls of Power, San Francisco Chronicle, October 22, 2012, A8.
2. Deborah L. Rhode, Perspectives on Professional Women, 40 Stanford Law Review (1988): 1163, 1173.
3. Gallup Poll, Atheists, Muslims See Most Bias as Presidential Candidates, June 21, 2012, http://www.gallup.com/poll/155285/atheists-muslims-bias-presidential-candidates.aspx.
4. Jennifer L. Lawless and Richard L. Fox, Men Rule: The Continued Under-Representation of Women in U.S. Politics (Washington, D.C.: Women and Politics Institute, 2012).
5. Christina Wolbrecht, Introduction: What Women Saw at the Revolution: Women in American Politics and Political Science, in Christina Wolbrecht, Karen Beckwith, and Lisa Baldez, Political Women and American Democracy (New York: Cambridge University Press, 2008), 7.
6. Center for American Women in Politics, Fact Sheet (2013), http://www.cawp.rutgers.edu/fast_facts/levels_of_office/documents/cong.pdf.
7. Jay Newton-Small, The Last Politicians, Time, October 28, 2013, 27: Donna Brazille, A Place at the Table, Ms., Winter/Spring 2014, 63.

8. Joan C. Williams, The End of Men? Gender Flux in the Face of Precarious Masculinity, Boston University Law Review 93 (2013); 699, 700.

9. Adam Nagourney, In Los Angeles, Women Yield Top Seats to Men When Politics Is Arena, New York Times, August 5, 2013, A1.

10. Sarah Mimms, Republicans Confront Lady Problems in Congress, National Journal. com, August 6, 2013.

11. Inter-Parliamentary Union, Women in Parliament (March–April, 2013), http://www. ipu.org/wmn-ecalssif.htm.

12. Kathleen Dolan, Women as Candidates in American Politics: The Continuing Impact of Sex and Gender, in Christina Wolbrecht, Karen Beckwith, and Lisa Baldez, Political Women and American Democracy (New York: Cambridge University Press, 2008), 110, 111; Lawless and Fox, Continued Underrepresentation, ii.

13. Molly Ball, A Woman's Edge, Atlantic, May 2013, 16–17.

14. For primary competition, see Jennifer L. Lawless and Kathryn Pearson, The Primary Reason for Women's Underrepresentation? Reevaluating the Conventional Wisdom, Journal of Politics 70 (2008): 67. For women's late start, see Kristin Rowe-Finkbeiner, The F Word: Feminism in Jeopardy: Women, Politics, and the Future, (Emeryville, CA: Seal Press, 2004), 222–223.

15. Lawless and Fox, Underrepresentation, ii.

16. Lawless and Fox, Underrepresentation, 7.

17. Elizabeth Kolbert, The Tyranny of High Expectations, in Susan Morrison, Thirty Ways of Looking at Hillary (New York: Harper Collins, 2008), 13.

18. Lawless and Fox, Underrepresentation, 9.

19. Lawless and Fox, Underrepresentation, 10.

20. Lawless and Fox, Underrepresentation, 11; Mimms, Republicans Confront Lady Problems.

21. Lawless and Fox, Underrepresentation, 12.

22. Lawless and Fox, Underrepresentation, 14.

23. Kohlbert, The Tyranny of High Expectations, 11–12.

24. Torben Iversen and Frances Rosenbluth, Women, Work, and Politics: The Political Economy of Gender Inequality (New Haven, CT: Yale University Press, 2010), xiv.

25. Iversen and Rosenbluth, 9, 135, 165; Lawless and Fox, Underrepresenation, 11.

26. Lawless and Pearson, The Primary Reason for Women's Underrepresentation, 75–78.

27. Krystal Ball on Sexy Photos Scandal: "It Was Devastating," Huffington Post, November 29, 2012, http://www.huffingtonpost.com/2012/11/29/krystal-ball-photos_n_ 2,212,963.html.

28. Manny Fernandez and Laurie Goodstein, Life Story Becomes Liability for Davis Campaign in Texas, New York Times, January 30, 2014, A1; Robert Draper, The Legend of Wendy Davis, New York Times Magazine, February 16, 2014, 46.

29. Newton-Small, The Last Politicians, 27.

30. Irin Carmon, Tim Gunn: Hillary Clinton Dresses Like She's Confused about Her Gender, Jezebel, July 27, 2011, http://jezebel.com/5825314/tim-gunn-hillary-clinton-dresses-like-shes-confused-about-her-gender.

31. Jessica Misener, Michele Bachmann Wears Tons of Makeup for CNN Debate, Huffington Post, November 23, 2011, http://www.huffingtonpost.com/2011/11/23/michele-bachmann-makeup_n_1,109,553.html.

32. Patrick Healy and Michael Luo, $150,000 Wardrobe for Palin May Alter Tailor-Made Image, New York Times, October 22, 2008, http://www.nytimes.com/2008/10/23/us/politics/23palin.html?_r=0.

33. Women's Media Center, Name It Change It: An Examination of Media Coverage of Women Candidates' Appearance, 2013, http://wmc.3cdn.net/63fa94f234fe3bb7eb_ g4m6ibsyr.pdf.

34. Karrin Anderson, Girls Gone Mad: The Wild-Eyed Lunacy of Bachmann, Palin, Pelosi, Clinton . . . Etc., Bagnews, July 16, 2011, http://www.bagnewsnotes.com/2011/07/the-wild-eyed-lunacy-of-bachmann-palin-pelosi-clinton-etc/; Maya, Bachmann Sexism Watch: "Crazy-Eyed Queen of Rage" Edition, Feministing, August 9, 2011, http://feministing.com/2011/08/09/bachmann-sexism-watch-crazy-eyed-queen-of-rage-edition/.

35. Jodi Kantor and Kate Taylor, In Quinn's Loss, Questions about Role of Gender and Sexuality, New York Times, September 12, 2013.

36. Leslie Bennetts, Women and the Leadership Gap, The Daily Beast, March 5, 2012, http://www.thedailybeast.com/newsweek/2012/03/04/the-stubborn-gender-gap.html.

37. Michele L. Swers, The Difference Women Make: The Policy Impact of Women in Congress (Chicago: University of Chicago Press, 2002), 1 (quoting Lincoln).

38. NBC News/Wall Street Journal Survey, April, 2013.

39. Beth Reingold, Representing Women: Sex, Gender, and Legislative Behavior in Arizona and California (Chapel Hill: University of North Carolina Press, 2000), 3.

40. Barbara Boxer, Susan Collins, Diane Feinstein, et al., Nine and Counting: The Women of the Senate (New York: Harper Perennial, 2001), 102 (quoting Boxer).

41. Reingold, Representing Women, 3, 219.

42. Beth Reingold, Women as Office Holders, in Wolbrecht, Beckwith, and Baldez, Political Women, 133.

43. Pamela Paxton and Melanie M. Hughes, Women, Politics and Power: A Global Perspective (Thousand Oaks, CA: 2007), 2, 193. For Congress, see Christina Wolbrecht, The Politics of Women's Rights: Parties, Positions and Change (Princeton, NJ: Princeton University Press, 2000); sources cited in Tracy L. Osborn, How Women Represent Women: Political Parties, Gender, and Representation in the State Legislatures (New York: Oxford University Press, 2012), 12. For state legislatures, see Michele Swers, The Difference Women Make: The Policy Impact of Women in Congress (Chicago: University of Chicago Press, 2002), 8, 72; Reingold, Representing Women, 243; Osborn, How Women Represent Women, 118.

44. Amy Caiazza, Does Women's Representation in Elected Office Lead to Women-Friendly Policy? Analysis of State-Level Data, Women and Politics, 26 (2004): 35.

45. Reingold, Representing Women (finding no evidence that Arizona women were better represented than California's, which had a lower proportion of women legislators); Kimberly Cowell-Meyers and Laura Langbein, Linking Women's Descriptive and Substantive Representation in the United States, Politics and Gender 5 (2009): 491, 512 (women's legislative representation predicted the presence of only five out of 34 women-friendly policies in the states and the non-adoption of three); Iversen and Rosenbluth, Women, Work, and Politics, xiii, 8 (the percentage of women in national legislatures has little relation to other measures of gender equality). See generally Beth Reingold, Women as Office Holders, 131.

46. Osborn, How Women Represent Women, 7; Swers, The Difference Women Make, 124; Julie Dolan, Support for Women's Interests in the 103rd Congress: The Distinct Impact of Congressional Women, Women and Politics 18 (1997): 81; Michele Swers and Amy Caiazza, Transforming the Political Agenda? Gender Differences in Bill Sponsorship on Women's Issues, Institute for Women's Policy Research, Research-in-Brief (October 2000); Susan Gluck Mezey, Increasing the Number of Women in Office: Does It Matter? In Elizabeth Adell Cook, Sue Thomas, and Clyde Wilcox, eds., The Year of the Woman: Myths and Realities (Boulder, CO: Westview Press, 1996), 255–270; Karen L. Tamerius, Sex, Gender, and Leadership in the Representation of Women, in Georgia Duerst-Lahti, and Rita Mae Kelly, eds., Gender Power, Leadership, and Governance (Ann Arbor: University of Michigan Press, 1996), 93, 107.

47. Madeleine M. Kunin, The New Feminist Agenda: Defining the Next Revolution for Women, Work, and Family (White River Junction, VT: Chelsea Green Publishing, 2012), 155–156 (quoting DeLauro).

48. Gail Collins, Twenty and Counting, New York Times, December 8, 2012, A21.
49. Kira Sanbonmatsu, Representation by Gender and Parties, in Wolbrecht, Beckwith, and Baldez, Political Women, 108; Beth Reingold, Women as Office Holders, 144.
50. Debra L. Dodson, The Impact of Women in Congress (New York: Oxford University Press, 2006), 255–256.
51. Katrin Bennhold, Feminism of the Future Relies on Men, New York Times, June 22, 2010.
52. S. Laurel Weldon, Beyond Bodies: Institutional Sources of Representation of Women in Democratic Policymaking, Journal of Politics 64 (2002): 1153, 1169.
53. Dara Z. Strolovitch, Do Interest Groups Represent the Disadvantaged? Advocacy at the Intersections of Race, Class, and Gender, Journal of Politics 68 (2006): 894.
54. Dara Z. Strolovitch, Affirmative Advocacy: Race, Class, and Gender in Interest Group Politics (Chicago: University of Chicago Press, 2007), 95.
55. Theda Skocpol, Protecting Soldiers and Mothers: The Political Origins of Social Policy in the United States (Cambridge, MA: Harvard University Press, 1992), 332 (quoting Dorr).
56. Jane Addams, The Modern City and the Municipal Franchise for Women, in Susan B. Anthony and Ida Husted Harper, eds., History of Woman Suffrage (Indianapolis, IN: Hallenback Press, 1902), iv, 178; Deborah L. Rhode, Justice and Gender: Sex Discrimination and the Law (Cambridge, MA: Harvard University Press, 1989),14.
57. Joe Freeman, We Will Be Heard: Women's Struggles for Political Power in the United States (Lanham, MD: Rowman and Littlefield, 2008), 115. More women than men also supported Eisenhower.
58. Dolan, Women as Candidates, 144.
59. Swers, The Difference Women Make, 5; Kristin A. Goss, The Paradox of Gender Equality: How American Women's Groups Gained and Lost their Public Voice (Ann Arbor: University of Michigan Press, 2013), 189.
60. Beth Baker, Fighting the War on Women, Ms., Spring–Summer 2012, 31 (quoting Maloney).
61. Aviva Shen, GOP Approves Most Conservative Platform in Modern History, Think Progress, August 22, 2012, http://thinkprogress.org/election/2012/08/22/723241/gop-approves-most-conservative-platform-in-modern-history/?mobile=nc.
62. Republican Platform 2012, http://www.gop.com/wp-content/uploads/2012/08/2012GOPPlatform.pdf
63. Kathleen Parker, What the *#@% is wrong with Republican Men?!,The Daily Beast, August 27, 2012, http://www.thedailybeast.com/newsweek/2012/08/26/what-s-wrong-with-the-republican-party.html (quoting Collins).
64. Katha Pollitt, Ladies, Don't Fall for Moderate Mitt!, The Nation, November 12, 2012, 10.
65. Ashley Parker and Trip Gabriel, Romney Taking Steps to Narrow His Gender Gap, New York Times, April 11, 2012.
66. John Cassidy, What's Up with White Women? They Voted for Romney, Too, New Yorker online, November 9, 2012.
67. Leonie Huddy, Erin Cassese, and Mary-Kate Liotte, Gender, Public Opinion, and Political Reasoning, in Wolbrecht, Beckwith, and Baldez, Political Women and American Democracy, 48.
68. Pew Research Center, The Gender Gap: Three Decades Old, as Wide as Ever, March 29, 2012, http://www.people-press.org/2012/03/29/the-gender-gap-three-decades-old-as-wide-as-ever/.
69. Andrew Dugan, Women in Swing States Have Gender-Specific Priorities, Gallup, October 17, 2012, http://www.gallup.com/poll/158069/women-swing-states-gender-specific-priorities.aspx
70. Barack Obama, State of the Union Address, February 11, 2013; Michael Scherer, 2012 Person of the Year: Barack Obama, the President, Time, December 31, 2012–January 7, 2013, 52.

71. Laurel Elder, Whither Republican Women, The Growing Partisan Gap among Women in Congress, The Forum 6 (2009): 13, 18.

72. Gail Collins, Twenty and Counting, New York Times, December 8, 2012, A21.

73. Center for Responsive Politics, Donor Demographics by Gender, http://www.opensecrets.org/pres12/donordemCID_compare.php?cycle=2012.

74. Fran Hawthorne, In Pursuit of the Female Philanthropists, New York Times, November 9, 1912, F10; Women's Philanthropy Institute at the Center on Philanthropy at Indiana University, Women Give 2010, Part 2: Causes Women Support, http://www.philanthropy.iupui.edu/womengive/

75. Deborah L. Rhode, Public Interest Law: The Movement at Midlife, Stanford Law Review 60 (2008): 2027, 2056 (quoting Shannon Wilbur).

76. Foundation Center, Highlights of Foundation Giving Trends (September, 2011), 3.

77. Rhode, Public Interest Law, 2056 (quoting heads of civil rights organizations); Hawthorne, In Pursuit of Female Philanthropists, F10 (noting that women donors want evidence of effectiveness). For the tendency of foundations to channel efforts away from fundamental social change, see Incite! Women of Color Against Violence, ed., The Revolution Will Not Be Funded: Beyond the Non-Profit Industrial Complex (Cambridge, MA: South End Press, 2007).

78. Diane Furchtgott-Roth and Christine Stolba, Women's Figures: An Illustrated Guide to the Economic Progress of Women in America (Washington, D.C.: American Enterprise Institute), 115.

79. Hawthorne, In Pursuit of Female Philanthropists, F10.

80. Audre Lorde, Sister Outsider (Berkeley, CA: Crossing Press, 1984), 122.

81. CBS Poll, February 11, 2009, http://www.cbsnews.com/2100-500,160_162-9,652,224.html.

82. Meghan Casserly, Arianna Huffington On Leaning In, Leaning Back and the Second Women's Movement, Forbes, March 21, 2013, http://www.forbes.com/sites/mechancasserly/2c.

INDEX